Bill Peoples, M.P.
Thursday 10/25/79

Thanks to Sri Rose Dawn and my Mayan Companions.

THE FIRST BOOK OF THE
ḤADĪQATU' L-ḤAQĪQAT

OR THE

ENCLOSED GARDEN OF THE TRUTH

OF THE

ḤAKĪM ABŪ' L-MAJD MAJDŪD SANĀ'Ī OF GHAZNA.

THE FIRST BOOK

OF THE

ḤADĪQATU' L-ḤAQĪQAT

OR THE

ENCLOSED GARDEN OF THE TRUTH

OF THE

ḤAKĪM ABŪ' L-MAJD MAJDŪD SANĀ'Ī OF GHAZNA.

EDITED AND TRANSLATED BY

MAJOR J. STEPHENSON,

Indian Medical Service; Member of the Royal Asiatic Society, and of the Asiatic Society of Bengal.

SAMUEL WEISER, INC.
New York

Reprinted 1968

Fourth Impression 1975

SAMUEL WEISER, INC.
734 Broadway
New York, N. Y. 10003

ISBN 0-87728-084-3

Printed in U.S.A. by
NOBLE OFFSET PRINTERS, INC.
New York, N.Y. 10003

PREFACE.

Several years ago, on looking up the literature pertaining to the earlier Sufi poets of Persia, I found that there was no European edition or translation, nor even any extended account of the contents of any of the works of Sanā'ī. Considering the reputation of this author, and the importance of his writings for the history of Sufiism, the omission was remarkable ; and I was encouraged by Dr. E. D. Ross, Principal of the Calcutta Madrasah, to do something towards filling up the blank. The present volume is an attempt at a presentation of a part of Sanā'ī's most famous work, which, it is hoped. may serve to give an idea of his manner of thought not only to Oriental scholars, but also to non-Orientalists who may be interested in the mysticism of Persia.

MSS. of Sanā'ī's *Ḥadīqa* are not rare in European libraries ; and a selection of those contained in the British Museum and India Office libraries furnished me with as many as I was able to collate during the time I could devote to this work on the occasion of a recent furlough. My selection of MSS. for collation was, I must confess, somewhat arbitrary ; *C* I took because it was the oldest of those to which I had access ; *H* because it also was of respectable age, and fairly well written ; *M* mainly on account of its being easily legible, this being a consideration, since my time in London was limited, and the British Museum does not allow MSS. to leave the building ; *I* I took because it was written in Iṣfahān and so might embody a Persian, as distinct from an Indian, tradition of the text; and *A* was selected because it was stated to be 'Abdu'l-Laṭīf's autograph of his revision of the text. I must here acknowledge my gratitude to the management of the India Office Library for the permission accorded me to take away these two valuable MSS. for collation in the country ; the materials upon which the present text is based would otherwise have been much poorer, and the result even more inconclusive than it is.

Though thus in some degree arbitrary, and restricted to only two collections, I do not think a limited choice of MSS. could have turned out much more fortunately. It has at least, I think, brought a considerable amount of light to bear on the history of the author's text, especially with regard to the labours of its editor 'Abdu'l-Laṭīf in the seventeenth century; though, as explained in the Introduction, I am very far from imagining that we have arrived at any close approximation to the author's original. I do not say that a reconstruction of Sanā'ī's original text is impossible; though judging merely from the MSS. I have examined, I am inclined to doubt the possibility. The text fell into confusion at a very early date, and it will perhaps only be by prolonged search or by a lucky chance that a future editor will obtain a copy which approximates in any close degree to the original; though a closer and more prolonged study of the copies we possess would, I have no doubt, give indications as to the place of many lines and passages which in the present edition are almost certainly wrongly placed or have been set apart as homeless. But at the present stage of Oriental studies it is unprofitable to devote to the preparation of a text the same prolonged research which we are accustomed to see in editions of the classical authors of Greece and Rome; and the labour of scholars in the province of Oriental letters is better expended on a first rough survey of the ground, so much of which remains as yet absolutely unknown; when a general knowledge of the whole has been obtained, it will be time to return for a thorough cultivation of each individual plot.

In the list of the variant readings I have found it quite impossible to indicate the different order of the lines and sections in the several MSS., nor have I as a rule given the variations in the titles of the sections. Otherwise the list is complete.

The translation is as literal as I have been able to make it. The notes are largely taken from the commentaries of 'Abdu'l-Laṭīf, published along with the text in the Lucknow lithograph (L), and of 'Alāu'd-Dīn, similarly given in the lithograph (B) which I obtained from Bombay. I have utilized all such portions of these commentaries as appeared to me to be helpful in arriving at an understanding of the text; matter taken from the commentary in the Lucknow lithograph I have distinguished by the letter L, also used in the list of variants to denote the readings of this lithograph; similarly the matter of 'Alāu'd-Dīn's commentary is distinguished in the notes by the letter B. Where the note presents a literal translation of the commentaries, I have indicated this by the use of inverted commas; where my note gives only the general sense of the commentary I have omitted the quotation marks, the source of the note being sufficiently indicated by the appropriate letter.

In the fuller explanation of the technicalities of Sufi philosophy I have drawn largely on the first volume of the late E. J. W. Gibb's "History of Ottoman Poetry," and especially on the second chapter of that work; where allusions to proper names, etc., are not explained by the commentators, I have often quoted from Hughes's "Dictionary of Islam." Quotations from the Qur'ān I have usually given in Palmer's translation. Finally, I am myself responsible for the notes in cases where no source is given; these are usually either in places where the meaning of the text is not easy to grasp, and where nevertheless the commentators, as not infrequently happens, pass over the line without explanation; or on the other hand such notes refer to matters of common knowledge to Persian scholars, which however may not be familiar to others; I have added a certain number of such in order, as stated already, to render the work of some use to non-Persianists who take an interest in the philosophies of the East.

Had I been able to devote myself continuously to the work, the number of references from one part of the text to another might have been considerably increased, and the author's meaning probably in many places thus rendered clearer; I think also, as I have already said, lines and passages that are here doubtless misplaced might have found, if not their original, still a more suitable home. But it has often happened that months, in one case as many as eleven, have elapsed between putting down the work and taking it up again; and thus all but the most general remembrance of the contents of the earlier parts of the text has in the meanwhile escaped me. I can only say that it seemed better to let the work go out as it is, than to keep it longer in the hope of obtaining a continuous period of leisure which may never come, for a more thorough revision and recasting of the whole.

GOVERNMENT COLLEGE,
LAHORE:
June 1908.

ABBREVIATIONS.

L (in the notes) refers to the commentary of 'Abdu'l-Laṭīf.

B (in the notes) refers to the commentary of 'Alāu'd-Dīn.

Gibb = A History of Ottoman Poetry, Vol. I, by E. J. W. Gibb, London, Luzac & Co., 1900.

Sale = Sale's Translation of the Qur'ān, with notes (several editions; a cheap one is published by Warne & Co.).

Stein. = Steingass's Persian-English Dictionary.

B.Q. = The *Burhān-i Qāti'* (a Persian Dictionary, in Persian).

The scheme of transliteration adopted is that at present sanctioned by the Asiatic Society of Bengal.

The references in the notes to other passages of the work are given according to the page and line of the Persian text (indicated also in the margin of the translation).

Quotations from the Arabic are indicated by printing in italics.

INTRODUCTION.

I.—Life of the Author.

Abū'l-Majd Majdūd b. Ādam Sanā'ī [1] was born at G͟hazna, and lived in the reign of Bahrāmshāh (A.H. 512-548, A.D. 1118-1152). Ouseley says of him that he "while yet young became one of the most learned, devout, and excellent men of the age which he adorned. His praise was on every tongue; for, in addition to his accomplishments in the Sūfī philosophy, he possessed a kind and benevolent heart, delightful manners, and a fine taste for poetry .... Sanāī in early life retired from the world and its enjoyments, and the reason for his doing so is supposed to have arisen from the following circumstance.

"He had frequented the courts of kings and princes, and celebrated their virtue and generous actions. When Sultan Ibrahim of Ghazni determined upon attacking the infidel idolaters of India, Hakim Sanāī composed a poem in his praise, and was hurrying to the court to present it before that monarch's departure. There was at that time in Ghazni a madman known as Lāi Khūr (the ox-eater), who often in his incoherent wanderings uttered sentiments and observations worthy of a sounder head-piece; he was addicted to drinking wine, and frequented the bath. It so happened that Sanāī, in passing a garden, heard the notes of a song, and stopped to listen. After some time the singer, who was Lāi Khūr, addressing the cup-bearer,

[1] For the facts contained in the following sketch I am indebted to Sir Gore Ouseley's "Biographical Notices of the Persian Poets," Lond., Or. Trans. Fund, 1846; Rieu's and Ethé's Catalogues; and Prof. Browne's "A Literary History of Persia," Vol. II.

said, ‘ Saki, fill a bumper, that I may drink to the blindness of our Sultan, Ibrahim.’ The Saki remonstrated and said it was wrong to wish that so just a king should become blind. The madman answered that he deserved blindness for his folly in leaving so fine a city as Ghazni, which required his presence and care, to go on a fool’s errand in such a severe winter. Lāi Khūr then ordered the Saki to fill another cup, that he might drink to the blindness of Hakim Sanaī. The cup-bearer still more strongly remonstrated against this, urging the universally esteemed character of the poet, whom everyone loved and respected. The madman contended that Sanāī merited the malediction even more than the king, for with all his science and learning, he yet appeared ignorant of the purposes for which the Almighty had created him ; and when he shortly came before his Maker, and was asked what he brought with him, he could only produce panegyrics on kings and princes,—mortals like himself. These words made so deep an impression on the sensitive mind of the pious philosopher, that he secluded himself from the world forthwith, and gave up all the luxuries and vanities of courts.

“ Sirājuddin Ali, in his ‘ Memoirs of the Poets,’ says, that in consequence of the sudden impression occasioned by Lāi Khūr’s remarks, Sanāī sought instruction from the celebrated Sheikh Yusef Hamdani, whose cell was called the ‘ Kaabah of Khorāsān.’

“ It was about this time that Behrām Shāh offered him his sister in marriage, which honour, however, he gratefully declined, and almost immediately set out on a pilgrimage to Mecca and Medinah. It is to the refusal of the royal bride that he alludes in his Hedīkeh, as an apology to the king, in the following lines :—‘ I am not a person desirous of gold or of a wife, or of exalted station ; by my God, I neither seek them nor wish them. If through thy grace and favour thou wouldest even offer me thy crown, I swear by thy head I should not accept it.’ ” The account of Sanā’ī’s conversion contained in the foregoing extract is probably, as Browne says, of little historical value.

Sanā’ī composed the present work after his return from the pilgrimage ; according to most copies he completed it in A.H. 525 (A.D. 1131), though some MSS. have A.H. 534 or 535 (A.D. 1139-1141).

Sanā’ī was attacked during his lifetime on account of his alleged unorthodoxy ; but a fatwa was published by the Khalīfa’s court at

Baghdād, vindicating his orthodoxy against his calumniators. His commentator 'Abdu'l-Laṭīf in his Preface (v. *post.*) mentions the suspicions of the various sects on the subject of the Ḥakīm's heresies.

Several dates are given for the Ḥakīm's death. His disciple Muḥammad b. 'Alī al-Raffā (Raqqām), in a preface to the work preserved in one of the Bodleian MSS., gives Sunday, the 11th Sha'bān A.H. 525 (A.D. 1131). This date, however, fell on a Thursday; the 11th Sha'bān of the year A.H. 545 (A.D. 1150), which is the date given by Taqī Kāshī and the *Ātashkada*, was, however, a Sunday. Daulatshāh and Ḥājī Khalfa give A.H. 576 (A.D. 1180, 1181). Since the poet completed his *Ṭarīqu't-Taḥqīq* in A.H. 528, the earliest of the three dates is impossible; the second would appear to be the most probable.

Besides the *Ḥadīqatu'l-Ḥaqīqat*, the first chapter of which is here presented, Sanā'ī wrote the *Ṭarīqu't-Taḥqīq* ("Path of Verification"), *Gharīb-nāma* ("Book of the Stranger"), *Sairu'l-'ibād ila'l-Ma'ād* ("Pilgrimage of [God's] servants to the Hereafter"), *Kār-nāma* ("Book of Deeds"), *'Ishq-nāma* ("Book of Love"), and *'Aql-nāma* ("Book of Reason"), as well as a *Dīwān*, or collection of shorter poems in various metres. All these works, with the exception of the *Ḥadīqa* and the *Dīwān*, are said by Prof. Browne, from whom the above list is taken, to be very rare.

II.—Manuscripts and Lithographs.

I have used the following manuscripts and lithographs in the preparation of the text:—

(1) Br. Mus. Add. 25329. Foll. 298, $7\frac{3}{4}'' \times 4\frac{3}{4}''$, 15 ll. $2\frac{3}{8}''$ long, in small Nestalik, with gold headings, dated Safar A.H. 890 (A.D. 1485) [Adam Clarke].

There are marginal additions by two other hands; f. 1 is on different paper, by a different and later hand. The letters ج چ ح خ are often not distinguished, چ never; ذ and پ are often not distinguished from د and ب; the small letters are often without dots; the scribe usually writes the modern undotted س with three dots below. There are large omissions as compared with later MSS. and the lithographs.

I denote this MS. by C.

(2) Br. Mus. Or. 358. Foll. 317, $6\frac{3}{4}'' \times 3\frac{3}{4}''$, 17 ll. 2″ long, in small Nestalik, in two gold-ruled columns, with two 'unvāns, apparently written in the 16th cent. [Geo. Wm. Hamilton].

There are many marginal additions, mostly by one, a later, hand; the MS. as a whole has been subjected to a great many erasures and corrections. The writing is good, the pointing of the letters fairly complete; the scribe usually writes ج and ب, the س rarely appears with three dots below. The MS. contains the prefaces of Raqqām and of Sanā'ī himself · but, like the preceding, shows omissions as compared with later MSS. and the lithographs.

I denote this MS. by H.

(3) Br. Mus. Add. 16777. Foll. 386, $10\frac{3}{4}'' \times 6\frac{1}{4}''$, 15 ll., $3\frac{1}{2}''$ long, in fair Nestalik, with gold-ruled margins, dated A.H. 1076 (A.D. 1665) [Wm. Yule].

This is a clearly written MS., the pointing of the letters usually full, چ and پ are frequently distinguished by their dots, and the pure س usually written with three dots below. Erasures are not frequent; the marginal corrections usually by the original hand. This MS. gives a very large number of divergent readings as compared with the others; its order is very different from that of the others; it is, as regards its extent, not so much defective as redundant, long passages appearing twice, and some passages not to be found in any of my other sources are also included. Some of these latter I have found in subsequent chapters of the *Ḥadīqa*, and it is possible that a more thorough search might have shown that they are all contained there.

This MS. is denoted by M.

(4) Ind. Off. 918. Ff. 395, 2 coll. each ll. 15; Nasta'līk; the last four pp. written by another hand; $9\frac{1}{2}'' \times 5\frac{1}{2}''$. Written at Iṣfahān A.H. 1027 (A.D. 1618); occasional short glosses on the margin.

A clearly written and well-preserved MS., closely related to the following. The letters پ and چ are frequently distinguished; the sign *madda* is usually omitted.

I denote this MS. by I.

(5) Ind. Off. 923. The description given in the Catalogue is as follows:—" Sharḥ-i-Ḥadîḳah. The revised and collated edition of Sanâ'î's Ḥadîḳah with a commentary and marginal glosses by 'Abdallaṭîf bin 'Abdallâh al-'Abbâsî, who is best known by his revised

and annotated edition of Jalâl-aldîn Rûmî's Mathnawî, his commentaries on the same poem, and a special glossary, Laṭâ'if-allughât (lithogr. Lucknow under title Farhang-i-Mathnawî 1877). He died 1048 or 1049 (A.D. 1638, 1639) in Shahjahân's reign. The present copy, which is the author's autograph, was finished by him 20th Jumâdâ alawwal A.H. 1044 (=Nov. 11th, 1634), and represents an abridgement from a larger commentary of his, the Laṭâ'if al Ḥadâ'iḳ, from which also the glosses are taken (marked لط). According to the dîbâca he began the larger work 1040 and completed it 1042 (1630-33) supported by his friend Mîr 'Imâd-aldîn Maḥmûd al Hamadânî, with the takhalluṣ Ilâhî, the author of the well-known tadhkirah of Persian poets the Khazîna-i-Ganj.''

The following is an account of the contents of this MS. First comes a short preface by 'Abdu'l-Laṭīf, introducing Sanā'ī's own preface, which is stated to have been written to the complete collection of his writings; it is frequently, states 'Abdu'l-Laṭif, not to be found in copies of his works. After Sanā'ī's preface comes another, called *Rāsta-i khiyābān*, by 'Abdu'l-Laṭīf, described as a short preface to this writer's commentary; this concludes with a reference to Ilāhī and his share in the work, and two *tārīkhs* by Ilāhī, giving A.H. 1040 as the date of its commencement, and 1042 as that of its completion. A few more lines by 'Abdu'l-Laṭīf introduce the work itself. The original numbering of the folia commences with the text; there is also a pencil numbering, in English characters, beginning with the first preface The poem closes with 59 verses, in the same metre, which form an address to Abū'l-Ḥasan 'Alī b. Nāṣir al-Ghaznawī, named Biryāngar, sent to him at Baghdād, because of the accusations of the traducers of the book. The date of completion of the text is given as A.H. 535; and, in a triangular enclosure of gold lines, it is stated that "this honoured copy was completed 20th Jumādā al-awwal, 1044 A.H." A few pages at the end, written by the same hand, give an account of how the book was sent to Biryāngar at Baghdād, on account of the accusations that were brought against it; how it was found to be orthodox, and a reply sent to Ghaznī.

This MS. I denote by A.

(6) The Lucknow lithograph published by the Newal Kishore Press, dated A.H. 1304 (A.D. 1886). This is an edition of the whole

work, including prefaces and 'Abdu'l-Laṭīf's commentary. It comprises 860 pp., of 15 verses to a page; the paper, as usual, is somewhat inferior; the text is on the whole easily legible, but the same cannot always be said for the commentary, written in the margins and in a much smaller hand. It contains first a list of the titles of all the sections of all the chapters, followed by some verses setting forth the subjects of the ten chapters each as a whole. The ornamental title-page follows, stating that the *Ḥadīqa* of Sanā'ī is here accompanied by the commentary *Laṭā'ifu'l-Ḥadā'iq* of 'Abdu'l-Laṭīf al-'Abbāsī. On p. 2 begins the 'First Preface', called *Mirātu'l-Ḥadā'iq*, by 'Abdu'l-Laṭīf, dated 1038 A. H.; this is not included in A; an abstract of it is given later (v. p. xxi). After this comes Sanā'ī's preface with 'Abdu'l-Laṭīf's introductory words, as in A; this is called the 'Second Preface'. The 'Third Preface', which is 'Abdu'l-Laṭīf's *Rāsta-i-khiyābān*, is here written in the margins of the 'Second Preface'. Then comes the text with marginal commentary, introduced as in A by a few more words from 'Abdu'l-Laṭīf. At the conclusion of the work is the address to Biryāngar; and finally some *qiṭ'as* on the dates of commencement and completion of the printing of the book.

I denote this lithograph by L.

(7) I obtained from Bombay, from the bookshop of Mirzā Muḥammad Shīrāzī, another lithograph, which comprises only the first chapter of the work accompanied by a copious marginal commentary. Pp. 15+4+31+188, 15 ll. to a page; published at Lūhārū (near Ḥiṣṣar, Punjab) 1290 A.H. (1873 A.D.). The title-page states that this is the commentary on Sanā'ī's Ḥadīqa by Nawāb Mirzā 'Alāu'd-Dīn Aḥmad, Khān Bahādur, chief (فرمان فرمای) of Lūhārū, called 'Alā'ī, the scribe being Maulavī Muḥammad Ruknu'd-Dīn of Ḥiṣṣār. Ruknu'd-Dīn states (p. 2) that he himself was doubtful of many words, and did not understand a number of the verses; he took his difficulties to 'Alā'ī, who explained all; and "Praise be to God, there never has been such a commentator of the Ḥadīqa, nor will be; or if there is, it will be an imitation or a theft from this king of commentators." This reads rather curiously when considered in connection with the fact, to be mentioned hereafter, that the authors have incorporated in their commentary the whole of that of 'Abdu'l-Laṭīf, and that their original contributions to the elucidation of the

text are of slight value. Ruknu'd-Dīn was asked one day by the printers (كار كنان مطبع) to bring them his copy (كاپي) of the *Ḥadīqa* on its completion, for printing and publication. Pp. 4—10 are occupied by an Arabic preface by Ruknu'd-Dīn, again in extravagant praise of 'Alā'ī and his accomplishments as a commentator. There follows (pp. 11—14) another title-page, and a short poem by 'Alā'ī; and then (p. 15) a *qiṭ'a*, giving the dates of commencement and completion of the work. Four pages of introduction (pp. 1—4) follow, and again with separate paging, 31 pp. of commentary on the first 28 pp. of the text, the reason apparently being that the whole of the commentary on these pages could not conveniently be written in the margins. The text comprises 186 pp., and includes (though I cannot find this stated anywhere) only the first book of the complete *Ḥadīqa*; the volume is concluded by some lines of 'Alā'ī in praise of Muḥammad, and a benediction. At the end of the marginal notes on every page is written "*'Alā'ī sallamahu,*" or "*Maulānā 'Alā'ī sallamahu Allāhu ta'āla.*"

III.—History of the Text.

Muḥammad b. 'Alī Raqqām informs us, in his preface to the *Ḥadīqa*, that while Sanā'ī was yet engaged in its composition, some portions were abstracted and divulged by certain ill-disposed persons. Further, 'Abdu'l-Laṭīf in his preface, the *Mirātu'l-Ḥadā'iq*, states that the disciples of Sanā'ī made many different arrangements of the text, each one arranging the matter for himself and making his own copy; and that thus there came into existence many and various arrangements, and two copies agreeing together could not be found.

The confusion into which the text thus fell is illustrated to some extent by the MSS. which I have examined for the purpose of this edition. C shows many omissions as compared with later MSS.; at the same time there is a lengthy passage, 38 verses, which is not found in any other; H, though also defective, is fuller than C but evidently belongs to the same family. M contains almost all the matter comprised in 'Abdu'l-Laṭīf's recension, much of it twice over, as has already been mentioned; and in addition about 300 verses, or altogether 10 folia, which apparently do not of right belong to this first chapter at all; the first chapter, too, is here divided into two chapters. The remaining MSS. and lithographs agree closely with each other and are evidently all nearly related.

The same story, of an early confusion of the text, is even more strikingly brought out if, instead of the omissions and varying extent of the text in the several MSS., we compare the order of the text. Here M startles us by giving us an order totally at variance with that of any other of our sources. There seems to be no reason for this; the arrangement of the subject is not, certainly, more logical; and it would appear that the confusion has simply been due to carelessness at some early stage of the history of the text; the repetitions, and the inclusions of later parts of the work, point to the same explanation. I need only mention the consequent labour and expenditure of time on the collation of this manuscript. C and H agree mostly between themselves in the order of the text, and broadly speaking the general order is the same as that of the later MSS.; the divergences would no doubt have appeared considerable, but that they are entirely overshadowed by the confusion exhibited by M. IALB agree closely with each other, as before.

The same confusion is again seen in the titles of the various sections as given in the several MSS. I am inclined to doubt how far any of the titles are to be considered as original; and it seems to me very possible that all are later additions, and that the original poem was written as one continuous whole, not divided up into short sections as we have it now. At any rate, the titles vary very much in the different MSS.; some, I should say, were obviously marginal glosses transferred to serve as headings; in other cases the title has reference only to the first few lines of the section, and is quite inapplicable to the subject-matter of the bulk of the section; in other cases again it is difficult to see any applicability whatever. It appears to have been the habit of the copyists to leave spaces for the titles, which were filled in later; in some cases this has never been done; in others, through some omission in the series, each one of a number of sections will be denoted by a title which corresponds to that of the next following section in other MSS.

It is then obvious that 'Abdu'l-Laṭīf is right in saying that in the centuries following Sanā'ī's death great confusion existed in the text of the *Ḥadīqa*. This text he claims to have purified and restored, as well as explained by means of his commentary; and it is his recension which is given in A, as well as in the Indian lithographs L and B. He says that he heard that the Nawāb Mirzā Muḥammad 'Azīz Kaukiltāsh, styled the Great K͟hān, had, while governor of Gujrāt in the year 1000 A.H., sent to the town of G͟haznīn a large sum of money in order to obtain from the tomb of Sanā'ī a correct copy of the *Ḥadīqa*, written in an ancient hand; this copy the Nawāb, on his departure on the pilgrimage, had bestowed on the Amīr 'Abdu'r-Razzāq Ma'mūrī, styled Muẓaffar K͟han, at that time viceroy of that country. 'Abdu'l-Laṭīf, however, being then occupied in journeys in various parts of India, could not for some time present himself before the Amīr; till in A.H. 1035 this chief came to Agra, where 'Abdu'l-Laṭīf presented himself before him and obtained the desire of so many years. This MS. of the *Ḥadīqa* had been written only 80 years after the original composition, but the text did not satisfy the editor, and it was besides deficient, both in verses here and there, and also as regards twenty leaves in the middle of the work.

In the year A.H. 1037 'Abdu'l-Laṭīf came to Lahore, where having some freedom from the counterfeit affairs of the world and the deceitful cares of this life, he entered again on the task of editing the text, with the help of numerous copies supplied to him by learned and critical friends. He adopted the order of the ancient MS. before-mentioned, and added thereto such other verses as he found in the later MSS. which appeared to be of common origin, and to harmonize in style and dignity and doctrine, with the text. As to what 'Abdu'l-Laṭīf attempted in his commentary, v. p. xxii *post.*

So far 'Abdu'l-Laṭīf's own account of his work. We can, however, supplement this by a number of conclusions derived from the MSS. themselves.

In the first place, it appears that A is not, as stated in the India Office Catalogue, 'Abdu'l-Laṭīf's autograph copy. The statement that it is so is apparently based on the fact of the occurrence of the words "*ḥarrarahu wa sawwadahu 'Abdu'l-Laṭīf b. 'Abdu'llāhi'l-'Abbāsī,*" at the end of the editor's few words of introduction to Sanā'ī's preface; and again of the occurrence of the words "*ḥarrarahu 'Abdu'l-Laṭīf . . . . ki s͟hāriḥ wa musaḥḥiḥ-i īn kitāb-i maimunat-niṣāb ast,*" at the end of the few lines of introduction immediately preceding the text. But both these sentences are found in the

Lucknow lithograph, and therefore must have been copied in all the intermediate MSS. from 'Abdu'l-Laṭīf's autograph downwards; the words in each case refer only to the paragraph to which they are appended, and were added solely to distinguish these from Sanā'ī's own writings.

I cannot find any other facts in favour of the statement that A is the editor's autograph; there are, however, many against it. Thus A is beautifully written, and is evidently the work of a skilled professional scribe, not of a man of affairs and a traveller, which 'Abdu'l-Laṭīf represents himself as having been. Again, there are occasional explanatory glosses to the commentary, in the original hand; these would have been unnecessary had the scribe been himself the author of the commentary. The handwriting is quite modern in character and the pointing is according to modern standards throughout; the late date of A is immediately brought out clearly by comparing it with I (of date 1027 A.H.) or M (of date 1076 A.H.); though the supposed date of A is 1044 A.H. it is obviously much later than either of the others. But perhaps the most curious bit of evidence is the following; at the top of fol. 11*b* of the text of A there is an erasure, in which is written او in place of an original reading را, and as it happens this line is one which has been commented on by the editor; in the margin is a note in a recent hand,—در اکثر نسخ بجای را او نوشته شده و شرحی که مولوی کرده اند بآن مربوط تر ست والله اعلم, which is true,—the commentary certainly presumes a reading او, but this MS. had originally را; the scribe could not therefore have been the commentator himself, i.e., 'Abdu'l-Laṭīf.

Further, not only is A not 'Abdu'l-Laṭīf's autograph, but it does not accurately reproduce that autograph. I refer to 34 short passages of Sanā'ī's text, which in A are found as additions in the margin; these, though obviously written in the same hand, I regard as subsequent additions from another source by the same scribe, not as careless omissions filled in afterwards on comparing the copy with the original. In the first place, the scribe was on the whole a careful writer; and the mistakes he has made in transcribing the commentary, apart from the text, are few. The omissions of words or passages of commentary, which have been filled in afterwards, are altogether 10; of these, two are of single words only; two are on the first page, when perhaps the copyist had not thoroughly settled down to his work; five are short passages, no doubt due to carelessness; and one is a longer passage, the whole of a comment on a certain verse,—an example of carelessness certainly, but explicable by supposing that the scribe had overlooked the reference number in the text indicating that the comment was to be introduced in relation to that particular verse. Roughly speaking, the commentary is of about equal bulk with the text; yet the omissions of portions of commentary by the copyist are thus many fewer in number and much less in their united extent than the omissions of the text,—supposing, that is, that the marginal additions to the text in A are merely the consequence of careless copying. The reverse would be expected, since owing to the manner of writing, it is easier to catch up the place where one has got to in a verse composition; it would seem therefore, as said above, that the comparatively numerous marginal additions to the text are rather additions introduced afterwards from another source than merely careless omissions in copying. In the second place, none of these 34 passages are annotated by 'Abdu'l-Laṭīf; in all likelihood, if they had formed part of his text, some one or more of the lines would have received a comment. The passages comprise, together, 63 verses; there is only one instance in the First chapter of the *Ḥadīqa* of a longer *consecutive* passage without annotation, and in general it is rare (eleven instances only) to find more than 30 consecutive verses without annotation; usually the editor's comments occur to the number of two, three or more on each page of 15 lines. I think, therefore, it must be admitted that the chances would be much against a number of casual omissions aggregating 63 lines falling out so as not to include a single comment of the editor. Thirdly, it is a remarkable fact that of these 34 passages the great majority are also omitted in both C and H, while they are present in both M and I; to particularize, C omits 30½, H omits 28, both C and H omit 25½, and either C or H or both omit every one of these 34 passages; while I and M each have all the 34 with one exception in each case; further, while many of these 34 marginally added passages in A correspond exactly to omissions in H, the corresponding omissions in C may be more extensive, i.e., may include more, in each case, of the neighbouring text.

We must therefore, I think, conclude that after completing the transcription of A the scribe obtained a copy of the *Ḥadīqa* of the type of I or M, and filled in certain additions therefrom ; and that 'Abdu'l-Laṭīf's edition did not originally contain these passages.

Let us turn to a consideration of I and its relation to 'Abdu'l-Laṭīf's edition. I is dated A.H. 1027 ; it is, therefore, earlier than 'Abdu'l-Laṭīf's edition of A.H. 1044. As we have seen, A is not 'Abdu'l-Laṭīf's autograph ; but we have, I think, no reason to doubt that it was either copied from that autograph, or at any rate stands in the direct line of descent ; so much seems to be attested by the occurrence of the words "*ḥarrarahu 'Abdu'l-Laṭīf* ...... ", and by the inscription at the end as to the completion of the book in A.H. 1044, the actual date of the completion of 'Abdu'l-Laṭīf's work. Regarding, then, A as presenting us (with the exception of the marginally added passages) with a practically faithful copy of 'Abdu'l-Laṭīf's own text, we notice a striking correspondence between this text and that of I. As to the general agreement of the readings of the two texts, a glance at the list of variants will be sufficient ; and it is not impossible to find whole pages without a single difference of any importance. The titles also, which as a rule vary so much in the different MSS., correspond closely throughout. The order of the sections is the same throughout ; and the order of the lines within each section, which is also very variable in the various MSS., corresponds in I and A with startling closeness. The actual spellings of individual words also, which vary even in the same MS., are frequently the same in I and A ; for example, at the bottom of p. ۲۱ of the present text the word کژ or کژی occurs three times within a few lines. The word may also be written کج, کجی ; thus while C and M have کژ کژی, H has first کج and then twice کژی ; I however has first کژ and then twice کجی, and this is exactly repeated in A. Another example occurs a few lines afterwards (p. ۲۲, l. ۶) ; the reading is مار شکنج, *mār-i shikanj*, *mār* being followed by the iẓāfat ; this I writes as ماری شکنج ; in A an erasure occurs between مار and شکنج, doubtless due to the removal of a ی originally written there as in I.

The above will serve to show the close relation between I and A, or between I and 'Abdu-l-Laṭīf's autograph, of which A is a copy or descendant. But, however close this relationship, 'Abdu'l-Laṭīf cannot actually have used I in the preparation of his revision of the text, or he would certainly have incorporated many of the 34 passages before alluded to, which are all, with one exception, contained in I. These, we have seen, were only added by the scribe of A, and by him only subsequently, from another source, after he had completed his transcription from 'Abdu'l-Laṭīf's autograph.

The facts, then, are these. There was in existence, before 'Abdu'l-Laṭīf's time, a tradition, probably Persian, of the order of the text, which he adopted even in detail. This is represented for us by I, written A.H. 1027 at Iṣfahān; but I itself is somewhat fuller than the copy of which 'Abdu'l-Laṭīf made such great use. This copy may be called P. Such use, indeed, did 'Abdu'l-Laṭīf make of P, that, so far as can be seen, it is only *necessary* that he should have had P before him, with one or two other copies from which he derived a certain number of variant readings, which he substituted here and there in his own edition for those of P.

We have now brought down the history of the text to A.H. 1044. Not much remains to be said; A, as we have seen, is quite possibly a direct copy of 'Abdu'l-Laṭīf's autograph, with, however, marginal additions from another source. This other source might be at once assumed to be I, but for the fact that only 33 out of the 34 marginally added passages occur in I; and it still seems to me at least possible that I was thus used. I, though written at Iṣfahān, was probably by this time in India, where A, the so-called "Tippu MS.," was certainly written; at least, that I did come to India may be assumed from its presence in the India Office Library. Again, though it is, I think, impossible that the whole of the 34 passages added marginally in A should have been careless omissions of the copyist, one or two might possibly be so, and it is possible that the single line now under discussion may be such an omission, filled in from the scribe's original, not from another source. Finally it is, of course, always possible that the additions were taken from two sources, not one only; *i.e.*, that while perhaps even 33 were filled in after comparison with I, the single remaining line may have been derived from elsewhere. Though absent in C, it is present in both H and M.

As to the lithographs, both are obviously descendants of A.

The above conclusions may be summarized in the following *stemma codicum*.

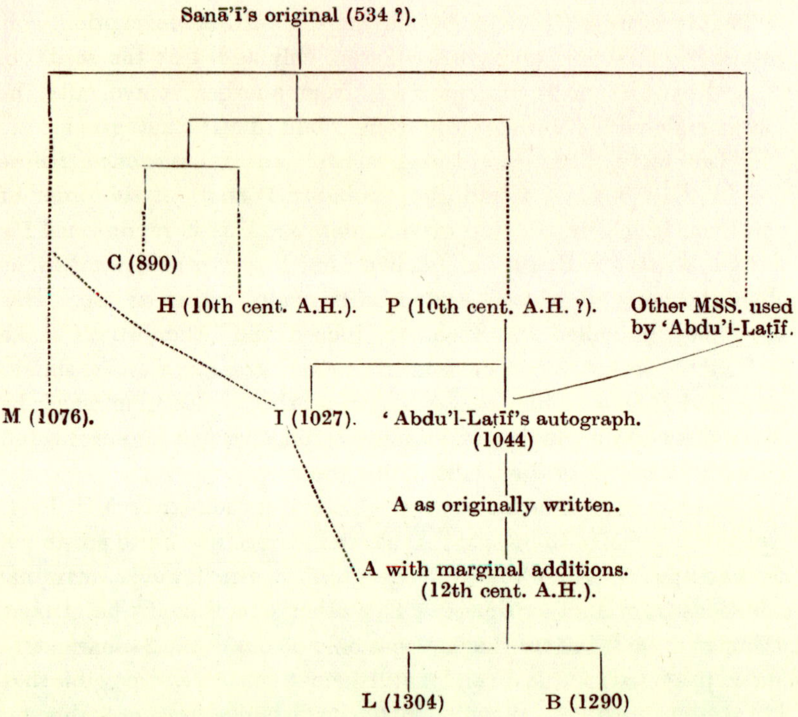

The present text is founded on that of the Lucknow lithograph L, with which have been collated the other texts mentioned above. L is practically a verbatim copy of A, the value of which has been discussed above. Though MSS. of the *Ḥadīqa* are not rare, at least in European libraries, I have not met with any in India ; and a considerable portion of the first draft of the translation and notes was done on the basis of L and B alone. The *Ḥadīqa* is not in any case an easy book, with the exception, perhaps, of a number of the anecdotes which are scattered through it ; and it was rendered far more difficult by the fact, which I did not recognize for some time, that a very great amount of confusion exists even in the text as it is published to-day, in the lithographs descended from 'Abdu'l-Laṭīf's recension. There appeared to be frequently no logical connection whatever between successive verses ; whole pages appeared to consist of detached sayings, the very meaning of which was frequently obscure ; a subject would be taken up only to be dropped immediately. I ultimately became convinced that the whole work had fallen into confusion, and that the only way of producing any result of value would be to rearrange it. This I had done, tentatively, for part of the work, before collating the British Museum and India Office MSS. cited above.

When I came to examine the MSS., the wide variations, not only in the general order of the sections to which allusion has already been made, but in the order of the verses within each section, showed me that probably no MS. at the present day, or at any rate none of those examined by me, retains the original order of the author; and I felt justified in proceeding as I had begun, altering the order of the lines, and even of the sections, if by so doing a meaning or a logical connection could be brought out. I need not say that the present edition has no claims to represent Sanā'ī's original; probably it does not represent it even approximately. In some cases there is, I think, no doubt that I have been able to restore the original order of the lines, and so to make sense where before it was wanting; in other cases this is possible, but I feel less confident; while in still others the reconstruction, preferable though I believe it to be to the order as found in any single MS., is nevertheless almost certainly a makeshift, and far from the original order. Lastly it will be seen that I have quite failed, in a number of instances, to find the context of short passages or single lines; it seemed impossible to allow them to stand in the places they occupied in any of the MSS., and I have, therefore, simply collected them together, or in the case of single lines given them in the notes.

IV.—The Commentators.

K͟hwāja 'Abdu'l-Laṭīf b. 'Abdullāh al-'Abbāsī, already so frequently mentioned, explains to us in his Preface, the *Mirātu'l-Ḥadā'iq*, what he has attempted in his commentary on the *Ḥadīqa*. He states that he was writing in A.H. 1038, in the second year of the reign of the Emperor S͟hahjahān, that he had already completed his work on Jalālu'd-Dīn Rūmī's Mathnawī, and that he had in A.H. 1037 settled down to work on the *Ḥadīqa*. What he professes to have done for the text of that work has been mentioned in the last section; the objects he has aimed at in the way of commentary and explanation are the following :—

Firstly, he has followed up the references to passages in the Qur'ān, has given these passages with their translations, and a statement of the sūra in which they are to be found. Secondly, the traditions referred to are also quoted. Thirdly, obscure passages have been annotated; and strange or curious Arabic and Persian words have been explained, after an investigation into their meanings in trustworthy books. Fourthly, certain signs have been used in transcribing the text, in order to fix the signification of various letters; thus the *yā'i khitābī* is denoted by خ subscript, the *yā'i majhūl* similarly by مج, the *yā'i ma'rūf* by مع, the Persian ک (گ) by ف, the Arabic ک by ع, and so on. Again the vocalization has been attended to in words which are often mispronounced; thus ignorant people often substitute *fatḥa* for *kasra* in such words as '*khizāna*', of which the *Qāmūs* says: "*Khizāna* is never pronounced with *fatḥa*"; '*Shamāl*', meaning the North wind, should be pronounced with *fatḥa*, not *kasra*, as is often done. The *iẓāfat*, *jazm*, and other orthographical signs have often been written in the text; and finally a glossary of the less known words has been added in the margin. Since it is inconvenient to have text and commentary separate, "in this copy the whole stability of the text has been dissolved, and the text bears the commentary along with it (این نسخه را حل کل قرار داده متن را حامل شرح نوشته شد), *i.e.*, text and commentary are intermingled, the commentary not being written in the margin, but each annotation immediately after the word or line to which it applies. These researches the author has also written out separately, and called them "*Laṭā'ifu'l-Ḥadā'iq min Nafā'isi'l-Daqā'iq.*" The date is again given as A.H. 1038.

It appears then that the original form of the commentary was not that of marginal notes, as it is presented in A and L; that it was completed in 1038 A.H., and, in its separate form, was called the *Laṭā'ifu'l-Ḥadā'iq*. That this is the name of the commentary we know and possess, seems to have been the opinion of the scholar who prepared the Lucknow lithograph, which is entitled "Sanā'ī's *Ḥadīqa*, with the commentary *Laṭā'ifu'l-Ḥadā'iq*."

Besides the preface just considered, there is also another, found in both A and L, called the *Rāsta-i Khiyābān*, written especially, it would seem, as an introduction to the commentary *Laṭā'ifu'l-Ḥadā'iq*. After dwelling on the unworthiness of the writer, 'Abdu'l-

Laṭīf states that the interpretations given by him are not mere expressions of private opinion, but are derived from the best Arabic and Persian books; the emendations of the text are all derived from authentic MSS., and are in accordance with the judgment of discerning men; everything has been weighed and discussed by the learned. He does not, however, say that these explanations are the only ones, nor that he has commented on every line that to some people would seem to require it. Though his work may seem poor now while he is alive, it may grow in the esteem of men after his death. The work has been done in the intervals of worldly business, while occupied with affairs of government. There follows a lengthy eulogy of his friend Mīr ʻImādu'd-Dīn Maḥmūd al-Hamadānī, called Ilāhī; two *tārīkhs* by whom close this preface. The first *tārīkh* says that the work having been begun in the year 1040, all the correction and revision was completed in 1042 (ابتدا دو هزار و چهل شده و بحسب تصحیح و مقابله و ملاحظه من جمیع الوجوه فراغ در هزار و چهل و دو حاصل آمده); the second simply gives the date 1040.

These dates evidently cannot refer to the edition and commentary as first written; since we have seen that the text and the *Laṭā'ifu'l-Ḥadā'iq* are referred to by ʻAbdu'l-Laṭīf in 1038 as having been completed. It would seem that the editor had either been at work on another, revised and improved edition; or, as is assumed in the India Office Catalogue (No. 923), on an abridgment of his earlier work. Lastly, we have the date 1044 for the completed work of which A is a copy (see description of contents of A, in Section II, p. xi); and this seems to represent the final form of the work, in which the annotations are written in the margin, not, as at first, intermingled in the text.

In the India Office Catalogue the series of events is interpreted somewhat differently. The commentary as it appears in A (and L, the only form, apparently, in which we possess it) is stated to be an abridgement from a larger commentary, the *Laṭā'ifu'l-Ḥadā'iq*; according to the preface (the Catalogue states) the larger work was begun in 1040 and completed in 1042. It is with diffidence that I venture to question this presentation of the facts; but A, in the description of which the above statements occur, does not contain the preface called *Mirātu'l-Ḥadā'iq*, and therefore presents no indication that the text and *Laṭā'ifu'l-Ḥadā'iq* had already been completed in

1038. That the work done between 1040 and 1042 consisted in the preparation of the original *Laṭā'ifu'l-Ḥadā'iq* is, from the statement of the *Mirātu'l-Ḥadā'iq*, impossible. We have seen, moreover, that the tradition in India is that the commentary as we have it, as it appears in A and L, is the *Laṭā'ifu'l-Ḥadā'iq* itself, and not an abridgement. I do not gather from the India Office Catalogue or elsewhere that two commentaries, a larger and a smaller, are actually in existence; there may be other evidences of their former existence of which I am ignorant, but so far merely as my own knowledge goes, I can see no reason for assuming two commentaries, and would look on the labours of 1040—1042 in the light of revision and rearrangement, a work which was perhaps only finally completed in 1044, the date given in A for the completion of the work.

Besides his work on the *Ḥadīqa*, 'Abdu'l-Laṭīf had previously, as has been mentioned, published a revised and annotated edition of Jalālu'd-Dīn Rūmī's Mathnawī, commentaries on the same poem, and a special glossary, the *Laṭā'ifu'l-Lughāt*, lithographed at Lucknow in A.D. 1877 under the title *Farhang-i Mathnawī*. He died in 1048 or 1049 A.H. (A.D. 1638, 1639).

A general description of the volume containing the other commentary which I have used in the preparation of the notes appended to the present translation, has already been given. Of the authors, or author and scribe, Mirzā 'Alāu'd-Dīn Aḥmad of Lūhārū, called 'Alā'i, and Maulavī Muḥammad Ruknu'd-Dīn of Hiṣṣar, I know no more than is to be gathered from their prefaces.

Their commentary is of slight value as compared with that of 'Abdu'l-Laṭīf; that is to say, that part of it which is original. The commentary is considerably more bulky than 'Abdu'l-Laṭīf's, perhaps between two and three times as extensive; but it includes, without one word of acknowledgment, the whole of 'Abdu'l-Laṭīf's work. This is, in the great majority of cases, reproduced verbatim; in some instances a paraphrase of 'Abdu'l-Laṭīf's commentary has been attempted, and in certain of these it is plain that the authors did not understand the sense of what they paraphrased. Of their own work, a certain amount is superfluous, the sense of the text being immediately obvious; a certain amount is mere paraphrase of Sanā'ī's words; and another portion consists in an attempt to read mystical meanings into the original in passages which, as it seems, were never intended by the author to bear them. Notwithstanding these facts, I have, as will be seen, quoted freely in my notes from their commentary ; for a certain portion of their work is helpful, and moreover, it seemed to me to be of interest to give in this way a specimen of present-day Indian thought and criticism in the field of Ṣūfīistic philosophy. I cannot, however, leave the subject of Sanā'ī's commentators without expressing my sorrow that scholars should have existed who were not only capable of such wholesale theft, but even lauded themselves on the results of it ; witness the extravagant praise of 'Alā'ī in Ruknu'd-Dīn's preface ; and again the words " Praise be to God ! There has never been such a commentator of the *Ḥadīqa*, nor will be ; or if there is, it will be an imitation or a theft from this king of commentators ! " There is also no indication that the volume comprises only one out of ten chapters of the *Ḥadīqa* ; it is everywhere implied that the complete *Ḥadīqa* is presented.

V.—The Ḥadīqatu'l-Ḥaqīqat.

The *Ḥadīqatu'l-Ḥaqīqat*, or the " Enclosed Garden of the Truth ", commonly called the *Ḥadīqa*, is a poem of about 11,500 lines ; each line consists of two hemistichs, each of ten or eleven syllables ; the bulk, therefore, is equal to about 23,000 lines of English ten-syllabled verse. It is composed in the metre بحر خفيف مسدس مشعث مقصور which may be represented thus :—

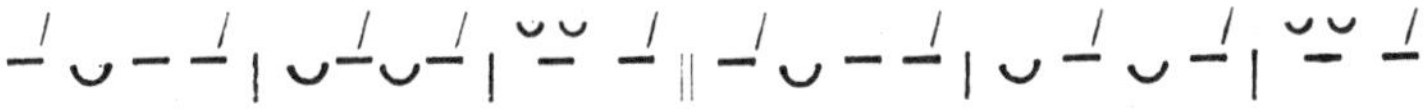

The two hemistichs of each verse rhyme ; and the effect may therefore roughly be compared to that of English rhymed couplets with the accent falling on the first (instead of the second) syllable of the line, and, occasionally, an additional short syllable introduced in the last foot.

The chapters of which the *Ḥadīqa* consists treat, according to a few lines of verse at the end of the table of contents in the Lucknow edition, of the following subjects ; the First, on the Praise of God, and especially on His Unity ; the Second, in praise of Muḥammad ; the Third, on the Understanding ; the Fourth, on Knowledge ; the Fifth, on Love, the Lover, and the Beloved ; the Sixth, on Heedlessness ; the Seventh, on Friends and Enemies ; the Eighth, on the Revolution of the Heavens ; the Ninth, in praise of the Emperor Shāhjahān ; the Tenth, on the characters or qualities of the whole work. This, however, is not the actual arrangement of the work as presented in the volume itself ; the first five chapters are as already given, but the Sixth concerns the Universal Soul ; the Seventh is on Heedlessness ; the Eighth on the Stars ; the Ninth on Friends and Enemies ; the Tenth on many matters, including the praise of the Emperor. Prof. Browne (Lit. Hist. Persia, vol. ii, p. 318) gives still another order, apparently that of an edition lithographed at Bombay in A.H. 1275 (A.D. 1859).

Sanā'ī's fame has always rested on his *Ḥadīqa* ; it is the best known and in the East by far the most esteemed of his works ; it is in virtue of this work that he forms one of the great trio of Ṣūfī teachers,—Sanā'ī, 'Aṭṭār, Jalālu'd-Dīn Rūmī. It will be of interest to compare some of the estimates that have been formed of him and of the present work in particular.

In time he was the first of the three, and perhaps the most cordial acknowledgment of his merits comes from his successor Jalālu'd-Dīn Rūmī. He says :—

"I left off boiling while still half cooked ;
Hear the full account from the Sage of Ghazna."

And again—

"'Aṭṭār was the Spirit, Sanā'ī the two eyes :
We walk in the wake of Sanā'i and 'Aṭṭār."

'Abdu'l-Laṭīf, in his preface called the *Mirātu'l-Ḥadā'iq*, enters into a somewhat lengthy comparison between Sanā'ī and Rūmī, in which he is hard put to it to avoid giving any preference to one or other. It is interesting to observe how he endeavours to keep the scales even. He begins by adverting to the greater length of the *Mathnawī* as compared with the *Ḥadīqa*, and compares the *Ḥadīqa* to an abridgement, the *Mathnawī* to a fully detailed account. Sanā'ī's work is the more compressed ; he expresses in two or three verses what the Maulavī expresses in twenty or thirty ; 'Abdu'l-Laṭīf therefore, as it would seem reluctantly, and merely on the ground of his greater prolixity, gives the palm for eloquence to Jalālu'd-Dīn.

There is the most perfect accord between Sanā'ī and Rūmī; the substance of their works, indeed, is in part identical. Shall it therefore be said that Rūmī stole from Sanā'ī? He asks pardon from God for expressing the thought; with regard to beggars in the spiritual world, who own a stock-in-trade of trifles, bankrupts of the road of virtue and accomplishments, this might be suspected; but to accuse the treasurers of the stores of wisdom and knowledge, the able natures of the kingdom of truth and allegory, of plagiarism and borrowing is the height of folly and unwisdom.

With regard to style, some suppose that the verse of the *Ḥadīqa* is more elevated and dignified than the elegantly ordered language of the *Mat͟hnawī*. The *Ḥadīqa* does indeed contain poetry of which one verse is a knapsack of a hundred *dīwāns*; nor, on account of its great height, can the hand of any intelligent being's ability reach the pinnacles of its rampart; and the saying—

"I have spoken a saying which is a whole work;
I have uttered a sentence which is a (complete) dīwān,"

is true of the *Ḥadīqa*. But if the sense and style of the Maulavī be considered, there is no room for discrimination and distinction; and, since "*Thou shalt not make a distinction between any of His prophets*," to distinguish between the positions of these two masters, who may unquestionably be called prophets of religion, has infidelity and error as its fruit. Who possesses the power of dividing and discriminating between milk and sugar intermingled in one vessel? 'Abdu'l-Laṭīf sums up thus; "in fine, thus much one may say, that in sobriety the Hakīm is pre-eminent, and in intoxication our lord the Maulavī is superior; and that sobriety is in truth the essence of intoxication, and this intoxication the essence of sobriety."

Prof. Browne, however, places the *Ḥadīqa* on a far lower level than the Eastern authors quoted above. He says[1]:—"The poem is written in a halting and unattractive metre, and is in my opinion one of the dullest books in Persian, seldom rising to the level of Martin Tupper's *Proverbial Philosophy*, filled with fatuous truisms and pointless anecdotes, and as far inferior to the *Mat͟hnawí* of Jalálu'd-Dín Rúmí as is Robert Montgomery's *Satan* to Milton's *Paradise Lost*."

---

[1] A Literary History of Persia, Vol. II., p. 319.

It is of course true that to us, at least, the interest of the *Ḥadīqa* is largely historical, as being one of the early Persian text-books of the Ṣūfī philosophy, and as having so largely influenced subsequent writers, especially, as we have seen, the Maulavī Jalālu'd-Dīn Rūmī. Yet I cannot but think that Prof. Browne's opinion, which is doubtless shared by other scholars, as well as the neglect to which the *Ḥadīqa* has been exposed in the West, is due not to the demerits of the original text so much as to the repellent and confused state into which the text has fallen; and I would venture to hope that the present attempt at a restoration of the form and meaning of a portion of the work, imperfect in the highest degree as I cannot but acknowledge it to be, may still be of some slight service to its author's reputation among European Orientalists.

The first Chapter or Book of the *Hadīqa*, which is here presented, comprises a little more than one-sixth of the entire work. The subjects of which it treats may be briefly resumed as follows:—

After an introductory section in praise of God the author speaks of the impotence of reason for the attaining a knowledge of God; of God's Unity, of God as First Cause and Creator; and delivers more than one attack against anthropomorphic conceptions of God (pp. 1—10). After speaking of the first steps of the ascent towards God, for which worldly wisdom is not a bad thing, with work and serenity (pp. 10—11), he devotes the next portion of the book to God as Provider, to His care for man through life, the uselessness of earthly possessions, and to God as guide on the road; but self must first be abandoned (pp. 11—16). A fine section on God's incomprehensibility to man might perhaps come more fittingly at an earlier stage instead of here (pp. 16—18). After overcoming self, God's special favour is granted to the traveller on the path; but we see crookedly, and He alone knows what is best for us; He has ordered all things well, and what seems evil is so only in appearance (pp. 18—25).

The greater part of the book is really concerned with the life and experiences of the Ṣūfī, and especially with continually repeated injunctions as to abandonment of the world and of self; to be dead to this world is to live in the other. Pp. 25—30 are thus concerned with poverty in this world, with loss of the self, humility, man's insignificance and God's omnipotence; pp. 30—34 with the necessity of continual remembrance of God, of never living apart from Him, and again of dying to the world ; death to the world leads to high position with God. There follows (pp. 34—41) a series of passages on the duty of thanksgiving for God's mercies ; His mercy however has its counterpart in His anger, and examples of His wrath are given ; then returning again to the subject of His mercies, the author speaks of God's omniscience, and His knowledge of the wants of His servants ; we must therefore trust in God for all the necessaries of life ; they will be given as long as life is destined to last. Two later pages (48—50), which are similarly devoted to the subject of trust in God, should probably come here. Pp. 41-48 deal with the Ṣūfī's desire for God, and his zeal in pursuing the path ; various directions for the road are given, especially as regards the abandonment of the world and of self, and fixing the desires on God only ; union with God is the goal. The abandonment of self is again the theme of pp. 50—51.

A portion of the book (pp. 51—56) is, curiously, here devoted to the interpretation of dreams ; after which the author treats of the incompatibility of the two worlds, again of the abandonment of earth and self, and of the attainment of the utmost degree of annihilation (pp. 56—58). There follows a passage on the treatment of schoolboys, a comparison with the learner on the Ṣūfī path, and an exhortation to strive in pursuing it (pp. 58—60). The next portion of the book (pp. 60—67) treats of charity and gifts as a form of renunciation, of relinquishing riches for God's sake ; prosperity is injurious to the soul, and the world must be abandoned ; possessions and friends are useless, and each must trust to himself ; each will find his deserts hereafter, and receive the reward of what he has worked for here.

Pp. 67—80 treat of prayer, the preparation for which consists in purity of heart, humility, and dependence upon God. Prayer must come from the heart ; the believer must be entirely absorbed in his devotions. Prayer must be humble ; the believer must come in poverty and perplexity, and only so can receive God's kindness. A number of addresses to God follow, prayers for help, and humble supplications to God on the part of the author. A few pages (80—82) treat of God's kindness in drawing men towards himself, though His ways may appear harsh at first. The progress of the believer is described in a strain of hyperbole (pp. 82—83); and this portion closes with a few sections (pp. 83—86) on God's majesty and omnipotence somewhat after the manner of those in the earlier part of the book.

In pp. 86—97 the author speaks of the Qur'ān, and its excellence and sweetness. The letter however is not the essential; its true meaning is not to be discovered by reason alone. The Qur'ān is often dishonoured, especially by theologians, and by professional readers, who read it carelessly and without understanding it. A short section (pp. 97—98) on humility and self-effacement follows, and the book is brought to a close by a description of the godlessness of the world before the advent of Muḥammad (pp. 98—100), which serves to introduce the subject of the Second Chapter.

Though it must be admitted that the author is occasionally obscure, sometimes dull, and not infrequently prosaic, some fine sections and a larger number of short passages of great beauty are contained in this chapter; I may perhaps be permitted especially to refer to the sections "In His Magnification," pp. 16—18, and "On Poverty and Perplexity," p. 74; while as characteristic and on the whole favourable passages may be mentioned "On His Omniscience, and His Knowledge of the Minds of Men," pp. 37—39; "On the Incompatibility of the Two Abodes," pp. 56—58; "On intimate Friendship and Attachment," pp. 62—63; and certain of the addresses to God contained in pp. 74—77.

VI.—Sanā'ī's Preface.

The author's Preface to the work, given in A and L, and occupying in the latter nearly thirteen closely printed pages, is here given in abstract. It was not, as will appear, written specially as an introduction to the *Ḥadīqa*, but to his collected works.

After an opening section in praise of God, the author introduces the tradition, "*When a son of Adam dies, his activity ceases, except in three things; a permanent bequest, and knowledge by which men are benefited, and pious sons who invoke blessings on him after his death.*" Considering these words one day, and reflecting that none of the three conditions was applicable to himself, he became sorrowful, and continued for some time in a state of grief and depression. One day while in this condition, he was visited by his friend Aḥmad b. Mas'ūd, who inquired the cause of his sorrow. The author told him that, not fulfilling any one of the above conditions, he was afraid to die; possessing not one of these three advocates at court, he would stand without possessions or adornment in the Presence of the Unity. His friend then began to comfort him, saying, "First let me tell you a story." Sanā'ī replied, "Do so."

Aḥmad b. Mas'ūd then related how one day a company of women wished to have audience with Fāṭima, Muḥammad's daughter. Muḥammad gave permission; but Fāṭima, weeping, said, "O Father, how long is it since I have had even a little shawl for my head? and that mantle that I had pieced together in so many places with date-leaves is in pledge with Simeon the Jew. How can I receive them?" But Muḥammad said, "There is no help; you must go." Fāṭima went ashamed to the interview, and came back in sorrow to her father; who was comforting her when the rustle of Gabriel's wings was heard. Gabriel looked at Fāṭima and asked, "What is this sorrow? Ask the women, then, what garments they had on, and what thou." Muḥammad sent a messenger to the women, who returned, and said, "It was so, at the time when the Mistress of Creation bestowed beauty on that assembly, that the onlookers were astounded; though clothed, they seemed to themselves naked; and among themselves they were asking 'Whence came this fine linen, and from which shop this embroidery? What skilful artificers, what nimble-fingered craftsmen!'" Fatima said, "O my father, why didst thou not tell me, that I might have been glad?" He answered, "O dear one, thy beauty consisted in that which was concealed inside thyself."

"By my life," continued Aḥmad, "such modesty was allowable in Fāṭima, brought up in seclusion; but here we have a strong and able man of happy fortune, one who is known as a pattern to others in both practice and theory! Though thou hast considered thyself naked, yet they have clothed thee in a robe from the wardrobe of Eternity. Is it proper for this robe to be concealed, instead of being displayed for the enlightenment of others?" And adverting to the saying, "*When a son of Adam dies, his work is cut short, except in three things*," he takes the three one by one. First, *a con-*

tinuing alms; but '*Every kindness is an alms; and it is a kindness that thou meet thy brother with a cheerful countenance, and that thou empty thy bucket into the pots of thy brother*;' that is, alms does not wholly consist in spreading food before a glutton, or giving some worthless thing to a pauper; it is a truer alms and a more imperishable hospitality to wear a cheerful countenance before one's friends; "and if others have the outward semblance of alms, thou hast its inward essence; and if they have set forth a table of food before men, thou hast set forth a table of life before their souls; so much for what thou sayest, 'I am excluded from a continuing alms!'"

Aḥmad b. Mas'ūd then takes up the second point, *knowledge that benefits*; and quotes, "*We take refuge with God from knowledge which does not benefit*" and "*Many a wise man is destroyed by his ignorance and his knowledge which does not advantage him.*" As examples of knowledge that does not benefit he takes the science of metaphysics, a science tied by the leg to desire and notoriety, lying under the opprobrium of "*He who learns the science of metaphysics is a heretic, and flys in circles in the air*;" as well as of the saying "*A science newly born, weak in its credentials,*"—"I have perfected it for the sake of heresy, and so peace." Then similarly the science of calculation, a veil which diverts attention from the Truth, a curtain in front of the subtilties of religion; and the science of the stars, a science of conjectures and the seed of irreligion, for "*Whoso credits a soothsayer has become an infidel.*" After a tirade against the ordinary type of learned man, he proceeds, "All their falsifyings and terrorizings and imaginings and conjecturings are limited by their own defects; that philosophy of the law is cherished which is notorious over all the quarters and regions of the world; there is your '*knowledge that men benefit by*'! From earth to Pleiades who is there sees any benefit in our doctors?" He then tells Sanā'ī that he is master of a more excellent wisdom; "*the poets are the chiefs of speech*;" "*the gift of the poets comes from the piety of the parents*;" "*verily from poetry comes wisdom*;" and will have none of such sayings as "*poetry is of the affairs of Satan.*"

As to the third part of the tradition, *and pious descendants to invoke blessings on him after his death*, Aḥmad says, "The sons which suffice are thy sons; what son born in the way of generation and begetting is dearer than thy sons, or more honoured? Who has ever seen children like thine, all safe from the vicissitudes of time? The sons of poets are the poets' words, as a former master has said—

> 'A learned man never desires son or wife:
> Should the offspring of both these fail, the scholar's offspring would not be cut off.'

A son according to the flesh may be a defilement to a family; but the son of intelligence and wisdom is an ornament to the household. These sons of yours you cannot disown."

He then asks Sanā'ī why he has thus become a recluse, and indolent and languid. This languidness is indeed preferable to a total heedlessness and forgetfulness of God, though Mutanabbī has said—

> "*I have not seen anything of the faults of men like the failure of those who are able to reach the end.*"

He asks Sanā'ī not to bring forward the saying, "*Laziness is sweeter than honey,*" but to bestir himself and collect and complete his poetical works.

Sanā'ī tells us that he submitted himself to the advice of his friend, but brought forward the difficulties of house and food, since the work could not be performed friendless and homeless. Aḥmad b. Mas'ūd thereupon built him a house, gave him an allowance for his maintenance for one year, and sent also a supply of clothing. He was therefore enabled to complete and arrange his writings free from all care and anxiety. The preface ends with the praise of his generous friend.

The First Book
of the Ḥadīqatu'-l-Ḥaqīqat of Sanā'ī.

IN THE NAME OF GOD, THE MERCIFUL, THE COMPASSIONATE. 1

O Thou who nurturest the mind, who adornest the body, O Thou who givest wisdom, who showest mercy on the foolish, Creator and Sustainer of earth and time, Guardian and Defender of dweller and dwelling; dwelling and dweller, all is of Thy creation; time and earth,
all is under Thy command; fire and wind, water and the firm ground, 5
all are under the control of Thy omnipotence, O Thou the Ineffable. From thy throne to earth, all is but a particle of what Thou hast created;[1] the living intelligence is Thy swift messenger.[2] Every tongue that moves within the mouth possesses life for the purpose of praising Thee; Thy great and sacred names are a proof of Thy bounty and beneficence and mercy. Each one of them is greater than heaven and earth and angel; they are a thousand and one, and they are
ninety-nine; each one of them is related to one of man's needs, but 10
those who are not in Thy secrets are excluded from them. O Lord, of thy grace and pity admit this heart and soul to a sight of Thy name!

---

[1] L refers to the saying of the Imām Ja'far (great-grandson of Ḥusain the son of 'Alī, considered by the Shī'as one of the twelve rightful imāms), "*This dome* (referring to the heavens) *is the dome of mankind; but God has many domes.*" The meaning then is, "Let no one think that God's whole creation is comprehended in this one; and though the living intelligence is one of His swift messengers between His court and this earth, yet He has many others."

[2] عقل با روح "the intelligence with the soul"; perhaps referring to the Intelligence and the Soul which belong, in Muslim philosophy, to each of the nine Spheres or Heavens: *cf.* Gibb, p. 44.

Infidelity and faith, both travelling on Thy road, exclaim, He is alone, He has no partner.[1] The Creator, the Bounteous, the Powerful is He ; the One, the Omnipotent,—not like unto us is He, the Living, the Eternal, the All-knowing, the Potent, the Feeder of creation, the Conqueror and the Pardoner. He causes movement, and causes rest ; He it is who is alone, and has no partner ; to whatever thing thou ascribest fundamental existence, that thou assertest to be His partner ; beware ![2]

Our weakness is a demonstration of His perfection ; His omnipotence is the deputy of His names. Both *No* and *He*[3] returned
2 from that mansion of felicity with pocket and purse empty. What is there above imagination, and reason, and perception, and thought, except the mind of him who knows God ? for to a knower of God, wherever he is, in whatever state, the throne of God is as a carpet under his shoe. The seeing soul knows praise is folly, if given to other than the Creator ; He who from earth can create the body, and make the wind[4] the register of speech, the Giver of reason, the Inspirer of hearts, who calls forth the soul, the Creator of causes ;—generation and corruption,[5] all is his work ; He is the source of all creation, and the place to which it returns ; all comes from Him and all returns to Him ; good and evil all proceeds to Him. He creates the freewill of the good and of the wicked ; He is the Author of the soul, the Originator of wisdom ; He from nothing created thee something ; thou wert of no account, and He exalted thee.

---

[1] B quotes a verse of a certain Ṣūfī, "I am astonished, for why is this enmity between faith and infidelity ? The Ka'ba and the idol-temple are both lighted by the same lamp."

[2] "True existence is God ; other existences exist only in an imagined existence. And whatever picture or conception of God's existence thou formest, if thou assert that He exists in that way, thou assertest that He has a partner. For God is different from that, nor can anyone understand or imagine at all the mode of existence of His essence." L.

[3] لا و هو the negation and affirmation of His existence. "The mansion of felicity is the plane of the absolute (مرتبۀ اطلاق) wherein is neither denial nor affirmation of belief." L.

[4] *i.e.*, the breath.

[5] كون و فساد the process of transmutation of the simple elements which is ever going on. *Cf.* Gibb, p. 47.

No mind can reach a comprehension of His mode of being; the reason and soul know not His perfection. The mind of Intelligence is dazzled by His majesty, the soul's eye is blinded before His perfection. The Primal Intelligence[1] is a product of His nature,—it He admitted to a knowledge of himself. Imagination lags before the glory of His essence; understanding moves confined before His nature's mode of being. His fire, which in haughtiness He made His carpet, burnt the wing of reason; the soul[2] is a serving-man in His pageant, reason a novitiate in His school. What is reason in this guest-house?[3] only a crooked writer of the script of God.

What of this intelligence, agitator of trifles? What of this changing inconstant nature? When He shows to intelligence the road to Himself, then only can intelligence fitly praise Him. Since Intelligence was the first of created things,[4] Intelligence is above all choicest things besides; yet Intelligence is but one word out of His record, the soul[5] one of the foot-soldiers at His door. Love He perfected through a reciprocal love; but intelligence He tethered even by intelligence.[6] Intelligence, like us, is bewildered on the road to His nature, like us confounded. He is intelligence of intelligence, 3
and soul of soul; and what is above that, that He is. How through the promptings of reason and soul and senses can one come to know God? But that God showed him the way, how could man ever have become acquainted with Divinity?

---

[1] عقل اول the Universal Intelligence or pure thought, the first emanation of the First Cause. *Cf.* Gibb, p. 42.

[2] نفس probably نفس اول or نفس کل, the Primal or Universal Soul, which flows from the Universal Intelligence.

[3] *i.e.*, the world.

[4] According to the tradition, *The first thing God created was Intelligence*, L. That is, in the Muslim philosophy, the Universal Intelligence.

[5] As above, the Universal Soul.

[6] "The love of the lover is not perfected till he receives the love of the beloved; then love attains perfection. But reason halts in the valley of sight and proof, and that same proof becomes a shackle for its feet. Hence the difference between love and reason; love is perfected by love itself, but reason is only bound by reason, and prevented from putting its foot beyond the things of reason, and has no power to perfect itself. *But God knows if this is right.*" L.

On the Knowledge of God.

Of himself no one can know Him ; His nature can only be known through Himself. Reason sought His truth,—it ran not well ; impotence hastened on His road, and knew Him.[1] His mercy said, Know me ; otherwise who, by reason and sense, could know Him ? How is it possible by the guidance of the senses ? How can a nut rest firmly on the summit of a dome ? Reason will guide thee, but only to the door ; His grace must carry thee to Himself.[2] Thou canst not journey there by reason's guidance ; perverse like others, commit not thou this folly. His grace leads us on the road ; His works are guide and witness to Him. O thou, who art incompetent to know thine own nature, how wilt thou ever know God ? Since thou art incapable of knowing thyself, how wilt thou become a knower of the Omnipotent ?[3] Since thou art unacquainted with the first steps towards a knowledge of Him, how thinkest thou to conceive of Him as He is ?[4]

In describing Him in argument, speech is a comparison,[5] and silence a dereliction of duty.[6] Reason's highest attainment on His road is amazement ;[7] the people's riches is their zeal for Him.[8]

---

1 " Impotence, acknowledging its inability, became the receptacle of divine mercy, and so succeeded in knowing Him ; according to the saying " *To be confounded in knowledge is knowledge.*" B.

2 Had this line stood alone, I should have liked, in view of the next line and the general tenour of the whole, to emend رهروِ لنگ (for رهبر و ایک), " reason travels but lamely to His door." See, however, l. 20 *inf.*, where also reason is styled ره نما.

3 L refers to the tradition من عرف نفسه فقد عرف ربه, " *he who knows himself knows his Lord.*"

4 Reading, with HI, سر ; others سزا, which makes the line tautological, or (adopting L's suggestion that ساختنش is equivalent to صنع او) brings in God's ' works ', which are not here under discussion.

5 *Sc.* of Him with something else, which is infidelity.

6 Hence the true believer is in a dilemma.

7 Referring to the words spoken, according to tradition, by Muḥammad, " *O Lord, increase my amazement at Thee.*" L.

8 " Till zeal becomes the stock-in-trade and capital of man's nature and character, he cannot claim to be a worshipper of the One, " L ; who also

Imagination falls short of His attributes ; understanding vainly boasts her powers ; the prophets are confounded at these sayings, the saints stupefied at these attributes. He is the desired and lord of reason and soul, the goal of disciple and devotee.[1] Reason is 20
as a guide to His existence ;[2] all other existences are under the foot of His existence. His acts are not bounded by 'inside' and 'outside' ; His essence is superior to 'how' and 'why.' Intelligence has not reached the comprehension of His essence ; the soul and heart of reason are dust upon this road ; reason, without 4
the collyrium of friendship with Him, has no knowledge of His divinity. Why dost thou instigate imagination to discuss Him ? How shall a raw youth speak of the Eternal ?

By reason and thought and sense no living thing can come to know God.[3] When the glory of His nature manifests itself to reason, it sweeps away both reason and soul. Let reason be invested with 5
dignity in the rank where stands the faithful Gabriel ; yet before all His majesty a Gabriel becomes less than a sparrow through awe ;[4]

---

says that غیرت may be referred to the Creator, and quotes '*Sa'd is jealous in honour, but I am more jealous in honour than Sa'd, and God than I*' ; غیور 'jealous in honour', being one of the names of God ; so, "but that God's jealousy for His own honour came to help the believer by removing false conceptions, who would keep his place or continue on the straight road, or be preserved from idolatry and infidelity ?"

1 Lit. 'traveller,' *sc.* on the road of God.

2 The meaning, perhaps, being that the function of reason is a subordinate one ; reason is a servant on the road, and can point the way. V. l. 9. *sup.* and note ; should the emendation of that line there suggested be adopted, this line would be brought into harmony by reading نا or نه for تا (which is at best doubtful, CHM having ما).

3 Both reading and translation are unsatisfactory, but perhaps less so than the alternative (v. crit. app.) 'by reason and thought and sense no one but God can know God' ; which L explains, "till reason and thought and sense become the instrument of God, and man the instrument of God's agency, he cannot by reason and thought and sense know God. Then, through God's agency, he comes to know God's nature by the means of reason and the rest."

4 The meaning perhaps being that the author will not refuse a certain degree of authority and dignity to reason ; but granting reason even archangel's rank, still that is as nothing before God's majesty.

reason arriving there bows down her head, the soul[1] flying there folds her wing. The raw youth discusses the Eternal only in the light of his shallow sense and wicked soul; shall thy nature, journeying towards the majesty and glory of His essence, attain to a knowledge of Him?

On the Assertion of the Unity.

He is One, and number has no place in Him;[2] He is Absolute, and dependence is far removed from Him; not that One which reason and understanding can know, not that Absolute which sense and imagination can recognise. He is not multitude, nor paucity;[3] one multiplied by one remains one.[4] In duality is only evil and error; in singleness is never any fault.

While multitude and confusion remain in thy heart, say thou 'One' or 'Two,'—what matter, for both are the same. Thou, the devil's pasture, know for certain what, and how much, and why, and how! Have a care! His greatness comes not from multitude; His essence is above number and quality; the weak searcher may

---

[1] مرغ 'the bird', for مرغ الاهي 'the bird of God', *i.e.*, 'the spirit, the reasonable soul.'

[2] "Not that God is numerically one, for numerical unity is circumscribed and finite, while he is free and pure of circumscription and finity. Aḥmad b. Yaḥyā was asked, Is *āḥād* the plural of *aḥad* (the word used for 'One' in the text, and generally as applied to God). He said, I take refuge with God! *aḥad* has no plural; and if it has, then it is *wāḥid* ('single'); *aḥad* is of its very nature single, to the degree that not even attributes can be discerned!" L.

[3] "Multiplicity has not befallen God on account of the multitudinous emanations that have proceeded from Him by way of manifestation of His essence and names and attributes, nor before the creation could fewness be affirmed. He is that One, which manifests itself as many by interfusion in created existence; yet multiplicity does not arise in His essence, for real existence is one only, and created existences all exist only in the mind. '*All things are vain but God!*' Absolute existence flows into and interfuses its own manifestations by emanation. '*There is no existence but God, no being but God; everything perishes except His face.*'" L.

[4] "The numerical one, in which multiplicity and paucity are (potentially) contained, multiplied however often by itself, gives one; how then can that Unity, which cannot be contained in the reason and understanding, manifesting itself so variously, be of the same nature?" B.

not ask '*Is it*' or '*Who*' concerning Him. No one has uttered the attributes of the Creator, HE,—quantity, quality, why, or what, who, and where. His hand is power, His face eternity; 'to come' is His wisdom, 'the descent' His gift;[1] His two feet are the majesty of vengeance and dignity, His two fingers are the effective power of His command and will.[2] All existences are subject to His omnipotence; all are present to Him, all seek Him; the motion of light is towards light—how can light be separated from the sun?[3]

In comparison with His existence eternity began but the day before yesterday; it came at dawn, but yet came late.[4] How can His working be bounded by eternity? Eternity without beginning is a houseborn slave of his; and think not nor imagine that eternity without end (is more), for eternity without end is like to eternity without beginning.

How shall He have a place, in size greater or smaller? for place itself has no place. How shall there be a place for the Creator of

---

[1] The references are to Qur. 48: 10, '*The hand of God is above their hands*;' Qur. 2:109, '*Wherever ye turn there is the face of God*;' Qur. 89: 23, '*And thy Lord comes with the angels, rank on rank*;' and to the tradition of Muḥammad '*Our Lord, who is blessed and exalted above all, descends to the lowest heaven every night, at the time when the last third of the night remains, and says, Whoso calls to me, I accept his prayer; who asks aught of me, I grant it; and who asks pardon, I pardon him; until the dawn breaks.*' L.

[2] The reference is to two traditions; '*The All-powerful places his feet in it, and it says, Enough, enough, enough,*' said of Hell, which never becomes full, nor ceases crying '*Is there any more?*' God's foot (قدم) here is explained to be either the number of the wicked whom God has doomed to Hell, (مقدم ساخته) as He has doomed believers to Paradise; or it may mean 'restraining' or 'subduing' (قمع - ردع); that is, God restrains Hell from asking for more; or perhaps subdues the boiling of Hell. *Cf.* 'to put one's foot on a thing,' وَضَعْتُهُ تَحْتَ قَدَمَيَّ. The second tradition is '*The heart of the believer is between two of the fingers of the Merciful, whether He wishes to confirm it in the faith, or whether He wishes to turn it to error*;' the two fingers being the two sets of God's attributes, those of awfulness and those of beauty. L.

[3] Other existences are compared to the rays of light of a lamp, which have no independent existence apart from the source of light.

[4] ازل eternity without beginning, opp. to ابد, eternity without end. "With reference to creation it came at dawn, *i.e.*, early, but with reference to God's existence late." L.

place, a heaven for the Maker of heaven himself? Place cannot attain to Him, nor time; narration can give no information of Him, nor observation. Not through columns is His state durable; His nature's being has its place in no habitation.

O thou, who art in bondage to form and delineation, bound by '*He sat upon the throne*';[1] form exists not apart from contingencies, and accords not with the majesty of the Eternal. Inasmuch as He was sculptor, He was not image; '*He sat*' was, not throne, nor earth. Continue calling '*He sat*' from thy inmost soul, but think not His essence is bound by dimensions; for '*He sat*' is a verse of the Qur'ān,[2] and to say '*He has no place*' is an article of faith. The throne is like a ring outside a door;[3] it knows not the attributes of Godhead. The word 'speech' is written in the Book;[4] but shape and voice and form are far from Him; '*God descends*' is written in tradition, but believe not thou that He comes and goes; the throne is mentioned in order to exalt it, the reference to the Ka'ba is to glorify it.[5] To say '*He has no place*' is the gist of religion;[6] shake thy head, for it is a fitting opportunity for praise.[7] They pursue Ḥusain with enmity because 'Alī spoke the word '*He has no place.*'[8]

---

[1] *i.e.*, 'relying on a verbal interpretation, imagining a statue,' B. Qur. 20:4, '*The Merciful sitteth on his throne*;' and 7:52, '*Verily your Lord is God, who created the heavens and earth in six days; and then ascended his throne.*' The author continues the subject in the chapter '*On the likening of God*,' p. 9, *q. v.*, and note thereon.

[2] *i.e.*, eternal as the Qur'ān is eternal. L.

[3] *i.e.*, a knocker in the form of a ring.

[4] *i.e.*, speech is attributed to God in the Qur'ān.

[5] *i.e.*, where God is spoken of as Lord of the Ka'ba the glorification of the Ka'ba is intended.

[6] I think the meaning is that a recognition and acceptance of the implications of the saying '*He has no place*' is the essence of the attitude of the truly spiritual believer. L explains the passage to mean that '*He has no place*' is the street (کوی with *kāf-i 'arabī*) of the produce of religion; this last being the good words and works which rise up to God, and are hence found in the street of '*He has no place.*'

[7] "Shake the head of praise at this saying, for it is impossible to utter a more excellent." B.

[8] L refers to 'Alī's saying '*Inquire of me concerning what is under the throne*,' but gives none which corresponds to the text, and confesses his inability to give a satisfactory explanation of the line.

He made an earth for His creation in this form ; behold how He 20
has made a nest for thee ! Yesterday the sky was not, to-day it is; again to-morrow it will not be,—yet He remains.[1] He will fold up the veil of smoke in front of Him ;—‘ *On a day we will fold up the heavens* ;[2] breathe thou forth a groan. When the knowers of God 6
live in Him, the Eternal, they cleave ‘ *behold* ’ and ‘ *He* ’ in two through the middle.[3]

On God as First Cause.[4]

The course of time is not the mould whence issues His eternal duration, nor temperament the cause of His beneficence ;[5] without His word, time and temperament exist not, as apart from His favour the soul enters not the body. This and that[6] both are wanting and 5
worthless ; that and this both are foolish and impotent. ‘ Old ’ and ‘ new ’ are words inapplicable to His essence ; He is, for He consists not of any existences except Himself. His kingdom cannot be known to its limits, His nature cannot be described even to its beginning ; His acts and His nature are beyond instrument and direction, for His Being is above ‘ *Be* ’ and ‘ *He* ’.[7]

Before thou wert in existence a greater than thou for thy sake brought together the causes that went to form thee ; in one place 10

---

1 L says نوز is for نوزا, and B that this again is for نوزاد. This seems highly improbable ; I think it stands for هنوز.

2 Qur. 21 : 103.

3 “ ‘ *Hā* ’ and ‘ *Hū* ’, words which are instruments of praise, and useful as such, for the specification and presentation of Him. But the true ‘*ārif* has an abode beyond these, which he cleaves in two and beyond which he passes.” L.

4 With the exception of H all MSS. and editions used by me have as title في التنزيه ‘ On Holiness,’ which is inapplicable. H has فصل في القدم in the red ink used for the headings, followed by و التنزيه , in black, by another hand. I have adopted في القدم, with قدم in the meaning of ‘ precedence, priority,’ here precedence in point of time and causation.

5 “ His beneficence is not due to His natural disposition, is not something as to which He has no choice ; it is His free choice, He being absolute master as regards His actions. ‘ *If He wills, He does it ; and if He wills, He leaves it undone.*’ ” L.

6 The revolution of time, and natural disposition, or human nature, as the authors of events.

7 ‘ *Be* ’ the creative word, God's instrument of creation.

under the heavens by the command and act of God were the four temperaments prepared;[1] their gathering together is a proof of His power; His power is the draughtsman of His wisdom. He who laid down the plan of thee without pen can also complete it without colours; within thee, not in yellow and white and red and black,[2] God has pourtrayed His work; and without thee He has designed the spheres; of what?—of wind and water and fire and earth. The heavens will not for ever leave to thee thy colours,—yellow and black and red and white;[3] the spheres take back again their gifts, but the print of God remains for ever;[4] He who without colours drew thy outlines will never take back from thee thy soul. By His creative power He brought thee under an obligation, for His grace has made thee an instrument of expression of Himself; He said, 'I was a hidden treasure; creation was created that thou mightest know me;[5] the eye like to a precious pearl through *kāf* and *nūn* He made a mouth filled with Yā Sīn.[6]

---

[1] The four temperaments which enter into man's nature, in accordance with the preponderance of one or other of which his natural disposition manifests itself.

[2] "But in the soul of man, which is incorporeal, not material," L. The colours represent the four humours, yellow bile, phlegm, blood, and black bile, B.

[3] V. *sup.*, *i.e.*, thy bodily life.

[4] *i.e.*, the incorporeal soul remains; *cf.* three lines back.

[5] 'Me,' مَن, lit. 'I': *cf.* p. 4, l. 22. 'He' nom. for accus. The reference is to the tradition according to which God said, '*I was a hidden treasure, and I desired to become known; and I created creation that I might be known.*'

[6] *Kāf* and *nūn* are the letters of the word '*kun*,' '*Be*,' by which God created all things: *yā* and *sīn* are the names of two letters, of unknown significance, which stand at the beginning of the 36th sūra of the Qur'ān, and give their name to the sūra; the sūra Yā Sīn is held in great honour as being, according to a tradition of Muḥammad, 'the heart of the Qur'ān.' The meaning of this line is not clear to the commentators, who (reading بدرّ) translate in various ways; (*a*) "made the eye a mouth full of Yāsīn," eye and mouth resembling each other, one being guarded by a row of teeth, the other by a row of eyelashes, both of which, moreover, resemble the letter sīn (س) in being a row of projections: (*b*) or, construing similarly, the meaning may be that when the mouth full of teeth is viewed by the eye, the latter by reflection of the precious pearl of the teeth becomes full of Yāsīn; (*c*) or "the mouth filled with Yāsīn was made, through its precious pearls, by the creative word *kun*, (a delight) to the beholding eye;" (*d*) or by the eye man may be meant, who

Sew no purse and tear not thy veil; lick no plate and buy not blandishment.[1] All things are contraries, but by the command of God all travel together on the same road; in the house of non-existence 7
the plan of all is laid down for all eternity by the command of the Eternal; four essences, through the exertion of the seven stars, become the means of bodying forth the plan.[2] Say, The world of evil and of good[3] proceeds not except from Him and to Him, nay, is Himself. All objects receive their outline and forms from Him, their material basis as well as their final shape.[4] Element and material substance, the form and colours clothing the four elements,—all things know as limited and finite, as but a ladder for thy ascent to God.

ON PURITY OF HEART.[5]

Then, since the object of desire exists not in any place, how canst thou purpose to journey towards Him on foot? The highroad by which thy spirit and prayers can travel towards God lies in the polishing of the mirror of the heart. The mirror of the heart becomes not free from the rust of infidelity and hypocrisy by opposition and hostility; the burnisher of the mirror is your steadfast faith; again, what is it? It is the unsullied purity of your religion. To him in

---

is the eye by which God is seen; as Rūmī says "Man is the eye which sees the eternal light." Among so many I may perhaps add another; reading with C چو در the meaning may be that through His creative power He made of the eye, in its purity and clearness like a precious pearl, a mouth full of the sūra Yāsīn, *i.e.*, of praise; the eye receives the manifestation of God as revealed in creation, and praises Him.

1 'Purse' stands for a lust after the arguments of philosophers and sages; 'veil' is belief and faith; the 'plate' is that of the defiled and polluted fragments, that is the sayings, of the so-called wise; and 'blandishment' represents the deceits and decoys of these. L.

2 The influence of the planets on the elements results in the formation of the three classes of natural objects, animal, vegetable and mineral. *Cf.* Gibb, p. 48.

3 Of darkness and of light, or the present world and that which is to come. L.

4 'Body' is compounded of matter, *hayūlē* (ἡ ὕλη), and form: the compound here is called *paikar*, the final shape. *Cf.* Gibb, p. 45.

5 Adopting an emendation of M's title, which is the only one which has any reference to the subject-matter.

whose heart is no confusion the mirror and the form imaged will not appear as the same thing; although in form thou art in the mirror, that which is in the mirror is not thou,—thou art one, as the mirror is another. The mirror knows nothing of thy form; it and thy form are very different things; the mirror receives the image by means of light, and light is not to be separated from the sun;—the fault, then, is in the mirror and the eye.[1]

Whoso remains for ever behind a veil, his likeness is as the owl and the sun. If the owl is incapacitated by the sun, it is because of its own weakness, not because of the sun; the light of the sun is spread throughout the world, the misfortune comes from the weakness of the bat's eye.

Thou seest not except by fancy and sense, for thou dost not even know the line, the surface and the point;[2] thou stumblest on this road of knowledge, and for months and years remainest tarrying in discussion; but in this matter he utters only folly who does not know the manifestation of God through his incarnation in man.

8 If thou wishest that the mirror should reflect the face, hold it not crooked and keep it bright; for the sun, though not niggardly of his light, seen in a mist looks only like glass, and a Yūsuf[3] more beautiful than an angel seems in a dagger to have a devil's face. Thy dagger will not distinguish truth from falsehood; it will not serve thee as a mirror. Thou canst better see thy image in the mirror of thy heart than in thy clay; break loose from the chain thou hast fettered thyself with,—for thou wilt be free when thou hast got clear from thy clay; since clay is dark and heart is bright, thy clay is a dustbin and thy heart a rose-garden. Whatever increases the brightness of thy heart brings nearer God's manifestation of Himself to thee; because Abū Bakr's purity of heart was greater than others', he was favoured by a special manifestation.[4]

---

[1] The fault which occasions this confusion between mirror and object imaged cannot be in the light, which, coming from the sun, is pure and faultless.

[2] "Thou knowest not the very elements of geometry and of common knowledge; how then canst thou attain to a knowledge of God, whom thought and sense cannot find out?" L.

[3] Yūsuf or Joseph is the type of beauty among Muslims.

[4] Referring to the following tradition; "Said the Prophet (may God

On the Blind Men and the Affair of the Elephant.[1]

There was a great city in the country of G͟hūr, in which all the people were blind. A certain king passed by that place, bringing his army and pitching his camp on the plain. He had a large and magnificent elephant to minister to his pomp and excite awe, and to attack in battle. A desire arose among the people to see this monstrous elephant, and a number of the blind, like fools, visited it, every one running in his haste to find out its shape and form. They came, and being without the sight of their eyes groped about it with their hands ; each of them by touching one member obtained a notion of some one part ; each one got a conception of an impossible object, and fully believed his fancy true. When they returned to the people of the city, the others gathered round them, all expectant, so misguided and deluded were they. They asked about the appearance
and shape of the elephant, and what they told all listened to. One 9
asked him whose hand had come upon its ear about the elephant ; he said, It is a huge and formidable object, broad and rough and spreading, like a carpet. And he whose hand had come upon its trunk said, I have found out about it ; it is straight and hollow in the middle like a pipe, a terrible thing and an instrument of destruction. And he who had felt the thick hard legs of the elephant said, As I have it in mind, its form is straight like a planed pillar. Every one had seen some one of its parts, and all had seen it wrongly. No mind knew the whole,—knowledge is never the companion of the blind ; all, like fools deceived, fancied absurdities.

Men know not the Divine essence ; into this subject the philosophers may not enter.

On the above Allegory.[2]

One talks of ' the foot ', the other of ' the hand ', pushing beyond all limits their foolish words ; that other speaks of ' fingers ' and ' change

---

pour blessings on him and his family and preserve him), O Abū Bakr, God has given thee his greatest blessing. He said, What is his greatest blessing ? He replied, Verily God manifests himself to everybody in general, but He manifests himself specially to thee.'' L.

[1] For a verse translation of this story, see Prof. Browne's ' A Literary History of Persia,' vol. ii., p. 319.

[2] H's title. That found, with variations, in other MSS., was probably

of place ' and ' descending ', and of His coming as an incarnation. Another considers in his science His ' settling himself ' and ' throne ' and ' couch ', and in his folly speaks of ' He sat ' and ' He reclined ', making of his foolish fancy a bell to tie round his neck. ' His face ' says one ; ' His feet ' another ; and no one says to him, ' Where is thy object ?' From all this talk there comes altercation, and there results what happened in the case of the blind men and the elephant.

Exalted be the name of Him who is exempt from ' what ' and ' how ' ! the livers of the prophets have become blood.[1] Reason

---

originally a pious annotation in the margin. In A it runs ' *On the Istiwā ; verily it is in accordance with reason, and its manner unknown ; and belief in it is commanded by authority.*' The chapter is an attack upon the anthropomorphists, whose arguments were drawn from the many allusions in the Qur'ān to God's bodily members, His face, hands, feet, etc. : and also especially from the word *istawā* (infin. *istiwā*), translated as ' He sat, settled himself ' on the throne, or ' He ascended ' the throne (v. *ant.* p. 5, l. 9, sqq.) These passages were a perpetual source of dispute in Islām ; see, on the early disputes of the orthodox with the Mu'tazilites on this subject, Macdonald's ' Development of Muslim Theology and Jurisprudence,' p. 145 ; and, for the way in which the *istiwā* was explained, *cf.* the creed composed by al-Ghazzālī, given in the same book, p. 301 ; ' He is seated firmly upon his throne, after the manner which He has said, and in the sense in which he willed a being seated firmly, which is far removed from contact and fixity of location and being established and being enveloped and being removed. The throne does not carry Him, but the throne and those that carry it are carried by the grace of his power, and mastered by his grasp. He is above the throne and the heavens, and above everything unto the limit of the Pleiades, with an aboveness which does not bring Him nearer to the throne and the heavens, just as it does not make Him further from the earth and the Pleiades.' For Malik b. Anas's dictum upon the *istiwā* v. op. cit., p. 186.

L furnishes us with an example of the means used in the interpretation of these passages, inasmuch as he translates *istiwā* as equivalent to *istīlā*, *i.e.*, ' the possession of absolute power ', and says that the reason why the throne is mentioned (in the passages of the Qur'ān where, according to the usual translation, we read that ' *God sat upon the throne* ') as being that over which God has absolute power, is that the throne is the greatest and mightiest thing of all creation. Sanā'ī himself, v. text, is content simply to say that the passages are allegories.

[1] *i.e.*, the prophets are in deep affliction, because even they have not attained to the heights of the knowledge of God. *Cf.* p. 3, l. 18.

hamstringed by this saying;[1] the sciences of the learned are folded up. All have come to acknowledge their weakness; woe to him who persists in his folly! Say, It is allegorical; depend not on it, and fly from foolish conceptions. The text of the Qur'ān—we believe it all; and the traditions—we admit the whole of them.[2]

Of those who Heed not. **10**

A discerning man questioned one of the indifferent, whom he saw to be very foolish and thoughtless, saying, Hast thou ever seen saffron, or hast thou only heard the name? He said, I have it by me, and have eaten a good deal of it, not once only, but a hundred times and more. Said the wise and discerning man to him, Bravo, wretch! Well done, my friend! Thou knowest not that there is a bulb as well! How long wilt thou wag thy beard in thy folly?[3]

He who knows not his own soul, how shall he know the soul of another? and he who only knows hand and foot, how shall he know the Godhead? The prophets are unequal to understanding this matter; why dost thou foolishly claim to do so? When thou hast brought forward a demonstration of this subject, then thou wilt know the pure essence of the faith;[4] otherwise what have faith and thou in common? thou hadst best be silent, and speak not folly. The learned talk nonsense all; for true religion is not woven about the feet of everyone.

On the Steps of Ascent.[5]

Make not thy soul's nest in hell, nor thy mind's lodging in deception; wander not in the neighbourhood of foolishness and

---

1 *i.e.*, the declaration of God as infinite and absolute.

2 *Sc.* 'though we reserve the right of interpreting them as allegories.'

3 Saffron is manufactured from the dried stigmas and part of the style of the saffron crocus, about 4,300 flowers being required to give an ounce of saffron. It has been used as a perfume, a dye, and a medicine, as well as in cookery, *e.g.*, mixed with rice, or in curries. The point seems to be that the man knew nothing of saffron except its condition after having been prepared for use.

4 Again insisting that to conceive of God aright is the foundation of religion.

5 M's title; the title, and the number and order of the lines differ considerably in the various MSS.

absurdities, nor by the door of the house of vain imagining. Abandon vain conceits, that thou mayest find admission to that court; for that mansion of eternity is for thee, and this abode of mortality is not thy place; for thee is that mansion of eternity prepared,—abandon to-day, and give up thy life for to-morrow's sake. This world's evil and good, its deceit and truth, are only for the ignoble among the sons of Adam.

To a high roof the steps are many,—why art thou contented with one step? The first step towards it is serenity, according to the attestation of the lord of knowledge;[1] and after it thou comest to the second step,—the wisdom of life, of form and matter.[2]

11 Know thou the truth,—that there is not in the world for the offspring of Adam a better staircase to mount the eternal heaven by, than wisdom and work. The wisdom of life makes strong the mind for both the upper and the lower abode; strive thou in this path, and although thou do not so in that,[3] yet thou shalt not do amiss. Whoso sows the seed of sloth, sloth will bring him impiety for fruit; whoso took unto himself folly and sloth, his legs lost their power and his work failed; I know nothing worse than sloth; it turns Rustams into cowards. Thou wert created for work, and a robe of honour is ready cut for thee; why are thou content with tatters? Why wilt thou not desire those striped garments of Arabia? Whence wilt thou get fortune and kingdom when thou art idle sixty days a month?[4] Idleness in the day, and ease at night,—thou wilt hardly

---

1 *i.e.*, Muḥammad. 'Serenity' is حلم, more commonly 'mildness', but v. *inf.*, p. 11, l. 14 sq. The tradition runs, 'Exalted be Thou, we praise Thee for thy serenity (or mildness), then for thy knowledge; exalted be Thou, we praise Thee for thy clemency, then for thy power.' B.

2 *i.e.*, as I think, 'the wisdom of this world'. I have ventured to read خردِ جان for خرد و جان, the reading of the MSS. and lithographs. *Cf.* حکمت جان three lines lower.

3 'This path,' the path of wisdom and work; 'that,' the higher spiritual life.

4 'Counting the nights as equal with the days; for to the traveller on this road a night is equal to a day,—nay, for the performance of acts of devotion and worship is brighter than the day,' L, who probably sees in the passage an exhortation to strenuous endeavour in the spiritual life, as B, who explains حکمت جان (l. 3) as 'spiritual wisdom', certainly does. I think, however,

reach the throne of the Sasanians. Know that handle of club and hilt of sword are crown and throne to kings who know not the moisture of weeping eyes;[1] but he who wanders about[2] after money and a meal cringes ignoble and vile before a clenched fist.

Possessing knowledge, possess also serenity[3] like the mountain; be not distressed at the disasters of fortune. Knowledge without serenity is an unlighted candle, both together are like the bee's honey; honey without wax typifies the noble, wax without honey is only for burning.[4]

Abandon this abode of generation and corruption;[5] leave the pit, and make for thy destined home; for on this dry heap of dust is a mirage, and fire appears as water. The man of pure heart unites the two worlds in one; the lover makes but one out of all three abodes.[6]

---

that the author intended a more earthly form of wisdom and work for so early a step in the ascent.

1 نم میغ کنایه از چشم گریان gloss in L.

2 گردون with gloss in L گردِن

3 Returning to the earlier division of the subject; 'serenity', حلم v. *sup.*

4 The intention apparently is to compare knowledge and serenity together to the honey-comb; and hence I read چو شهدِ زنبور for چو شهد و زنبور ('like honey and the bee'), in the MSS. and lithographed editions; which L explains by saying that 'the comparison of knowledge and serenity to honey and bee comes about through the close connection and dependence between honey and bee. Knowledge being the wax of the unlighted candle, serenity will be the honey, the wax's complement in the honey-comb; and this may be what is meant by saying that honey without wax رمز احرار است (L آزاد gloss on احرار), *i.e.*, typifies the noble-minded, who are above base cares, or free from low anxieties.

5 *Cf.* p. 2, l. 6.

6 The line here put at the end of the chapter is evidently out of place where it is found (after p. 11, l. 9) in the MSS. The two worlds are this and the next; the three abodes, according to B, are *nāsūt*, *malakūt*, and *jabarūt*, the worlds of mankind, of angels, and of might. The five worlds of the Ṣūfīs, also sometimes reckoned as three or two, are five different planes of existence, which loses in true Being as it descends. V. Gibb, pp. 54—56. L, however, supposes it possible, from the reduplication of دو, that by دودو عالم is meant the four worlds of *nāsūt*, *malakūt*, *jabarūt*, and *lāhūt* (Godhead);

20 ## On the Protection and Guardianship of God.

Whoso is fenced around by divine aid, a spider spreads its web before him ;[1] a lizard utters his praise, a serpent seeks to please him.[2]
12 His shoe treads the summit of the throne ; his ruby lip is the world's

---

and similarly by سه سه منزل the ten stages of repentance, thanksgiving and patience, fear and hope, poverty and piety, truth and sincerity, consideration and contemplation, reflection and deliberation, the acknowledging of the Unity and resignation, love and desire, and the remembering of death. The meaning of the line, he states, lies in the implication of the speed attributed to the traveller. It seems more probably to mean that all conditions whatever are alike to the saint and lover, who find heaven everywhere. 'Lover,' as usual, in its mystical sense.

[1] Referring to an incident in the flight of Muḥammad and Abū Bakr to Medina ; during the search they took refuge in a cave on the mountain of Abū Qubais near Mecca, in front of which a spider weaved its web. The searchers, supposing that the spider's web indicated that no one had entered the cave for some time, passed on without exploring it. L.

[2] L explains these allusions. The lizard is a reference to the story told in Mīr Jamālu'd-Dīn's *Rauẓatu'l-Aḥbāb*, on the authority of b. 'Abbās and 'Abdullāh b. 'Umar ; that an Arab hunter had caught a lizard, which he was taking home to kill and eat. Passing a number of people, he was told, on enquiring, "This is Muḥammad b. 'Abdullāh, who claims to be a prophet." He entered the crowd, and addressed Muḥammad, "O Muḥammad, I swear by Lāt and 'Uzza that I will not believe in thee till this lizard believes in thee;" and threw down the lizard before him. As it was running away, Muḥammad said, "O lizard, approach." The lizard turned, and in clear Arabic said, "*Labbaika wa sa'daika.*" Muḥammad asked, "Whom dost thou worship ?" It answered, "That God whose throne is in the heavens, whose power is in the earth, whose way is in the sea, whose mercy is in Paradise, and whose torment and punishment is in Hell." Muḥammad asked, "Who am I ?" The lizard answered, "The messenger of God and seal of the prophets ; all who believe in thee shall find felicity and salvation, and all who call thee liar shall perish." The hunter was astonished, and said, "I seek no other sign;" and acknowledged the one God and Muḥammad as his messenger.

The snake refers to the story told by traditionists and biographers, that as Muḥammad was returning with his army from Tabūk, a large and terrible snake came out into the road. The men were much frightened, and Muḥammad himself was careful to keep his camel away from it. The snake went off, and as it did so, raised its head, turned towards them, and lowered its head again. Muḥammad said, "This is one of the jinn who came to me and listened to the Qur'ān (referring to his journey back from Ṭā'if, after his fitting ornament ; in his mouth poison becomes sugar ;[1] in his hand a stone becomes a jewel.[2] Whoso lays his head on this threshold places his foot on the head of things temporal ; wise reason is powerless to explain these things, for all are powerless who come not to this door. I fear that through thy ignorance and folly thou wilt one day be left helpless on Ṣirāṭ ;[3] thy ignorance will deliver thee to the fire ; see how it is administering the soporific lettuce[4] and poppies to thee.

Thou hast seen how in the middle of a morsel of food that one eats there will appear a grain of wheat, which has survived the attack of locust, and bird, and beast, has seen the heat of heaven and the glow of the oven, and remained unchanged under thy millstone. Who preserved it ? God, God. He is a sufficient protector for thee,—for possessions and life and breath ; thou art of His creation, that is

---

rejection there) ; it came to greet me as we passed its dwelling ; now it greets you, return the salutation.'' They did so, and Muḥammad said, "Love the servants of God, whoever they are.''

1 Referring to the story of Muḥammad's being given poisoned meat by a Jewess of Khaibar. L also in this connection relates how in the wars of Abū Bakr's caliphate, when Khālid b. Walīd was besieging a certain fort, an aged man named 'Abdu'l-Masīḥ came to treat with him. Khālid seeing something in his hand asked what it was, and was told by 'Abdu'l-Masīḥ that it was poison; which he intended to take in case Khālid's answer was unsatisfactory, rather than be the bearer of bad news to his people. Khālid asked for it, and on obtaining it, swallowed it ; after remaining in a swoon for an hour, he recovered. L also relates how 'Umar, on receiving a phial of poison from the Roman Emperor, swallowed it in Muḥammad's presence without receiving any harm.

2 As in many instances in the lives of the saints. For example, Jalālu'd-Dīn Rūmī in an assembly of darwīshes took up a handful of earth, and threw it onto the drum of the darwīsh who was dancing in ecstasy, whereon his drum became full of gold. Says the author of the *Kashfu'l-Maḥjūb*, "I asked Imām Abū'l-Qāsim Qushairī concerning the commencement of his ecstatic experiences. He said, 'I one day wanted a stone for the window of my house, and every stone I picked up became a gem.' '' And such things are common in the experiences of the saints. L.

3 The bridge, finer than a hair and sharper than a sword, laid over the midst of hell, over which all must pass after the judgment, and from which the wicked, missing their footing, will slip down into hell.

4 کوک, a herb which induces prolonged sleep, in its medical properties cold and dry. L.

enough. If thou procurest dog and chain thou canst overcome the antelope of the desert, and in thy trust and sincere belief in this thou art free from anxiety as regards a maintenance and livelihood: I say to thee,—and with reason and judgment, so that thou mayst not shut the door of thine ear against my words,—Thy trust in dog and chain I see is greater than in the All-hearing and All-seeing; the light of thy faith, if standing on this foundation, is given over to destruction by a dog and a thing of iron.

The Parable of those who give Alms.

A certain wise and liberal man gave away so many bags of gold before his son's eyes that when he saw his father's munificence he broke forth into censure and remonstrance, saying, Father, where is my share of this? He said, O son, in the treasury of God; I have given to God thy portion, leaving no executor and none to divide it with thee, and He will give it thee again.

He is Himself our Provider and our Master; shall He not suffice us, both for faith and worldly goods? He is no other than the disposer of our lives; He will not oppress thee,—He is not of those. To everyone He gives back seventy-fold; and if He closes one door against thee, He opens ten.

On the Cause of our Maintenance.

Seest thou not that before the beginning of thy existence God the All-wise, the Ineffable, when He had created thee in the womb gave thee of blood thy sustenance for nine months? Thy mother nourished thee in her womb, then after nine months brought thee forth; that door of support He quickly closed on thee, and bestowed on thee two better doors, for He then acquainted thee with the breast,—two fountains running for thee day and night; He said, Drink of these both; *eat and welcome*, for it is not forbidden thee. When after two years she weaned thee, all became changed for thee; He gave thee thy sustenance by means of thy two hands and feet,—'Take it by means of these, and by those go where thou wilt!' If He closed the two doors against thee, it is but right, for instead of two, four doors have appeared,—'Take by means of these, by those go on to victory; go seek thy daily bread throughout the world!'

When suddenly there comes on thee thy appointed time, and the things of the world all pass away, and the two hands and feet fail in their office, to thee in thy helpless state He gives an exchange for these four. Hands and feet are shut up in the tomb, and eight heavens become thy fortune; eight doors are opened to thee, the virgins and youths of Paradise come before thee, that going joyfully to any door thou wilt thou mayest lose remembrance of this world.

O youth, hear this saying, and despair not of God's bounty. If God has given thee knowledge of Himself and put belief within thy heart, the robe of honour[1] which is to thee like thy wedding-garment He will not take from thee on the day of resurrection. If thou hast neither learning nor gold, yet hast this, thou wilt not be destitute. He will bring thee to glory,—thou shalt not be disgraced; He will set thee in honour,—thou shalt not be despised. Thy possessions,— **14** give not thy soul to their keeping; what He has given thee, hold thou fast to that. Thou layest up treasure,—thou shalt not see it again; if thou gavest it to Him, He would give it thee again. Thou puttest gold in the fire,—it burns up the dross; so He burns thy pure gold; when He has burnt out the bad, the good He gives to thee; fortune bends down her head to thee from the skies. The more enduring the benefit afforded by the fire, the kinder on that account is He who kindles the fire; thou knowest not what is good nor what bad; He is a better treasurer for thee than thou for thyself. A friend is a serpent; why seekest thou his door?[2] the serpent is thy friend; why fliest thou from it in terror?

O seeker of the shell of the pearl of '*Unless*', lay down clothing and life on the shore of '*Not*';[3] God's existence inclines only towards him who has ceased to exist; non-existence is the necessary provision for the journey. Till in annihilation thou lay aside thy cap[4] thou wilt not set thy face on the road to eternal life; when thou becomest nothing, thou runnest towards God; the path of mendicancy leads up

---

[1] *i.e.*, belief, religion (gloss in L).

[2] The line amplifies the preceding, "thou knowest not what is good nor what bad."

[3] '*Unless*' and '*Not*' to imply affirmation and negation; *i.e.*, 'first enter the world of annihilation, that so thou mayest find the jewel of eternal life.' B.

[4] On the metaphor of the cap *cf.* p. 57, l. 5 sqq.

to Him. If fortune crushes thee down, *the most excellent of Creators* will restore thee. Rise, and have done with false fables ; *forsake* thy ignoble passions, *and come hither.*[1]

Of the Right Guidance.[2]

Every indication of the road thou receivest, O darwīsh, count it a gift of God, not thine own doing ; He is the cause of the bestowal of benefits, He it is to whom the soul is guided,[3] and He its guide. Recognise that it is God's favour guides thee on the path of duty and religion and His ordinance, not thine own strength. He is the giver of the light of truth and instruction, both Guardian of the world and its Observer too. He is kinder than mother and father ; He it is who shall guide thee to Paradise.

Because of the unbelief of the people He made us our religion ; He made us see clearly in the darkness. See the favour of God the Guider ! for out of all creation He made man His chosen. His majesty needs not saint nor prophet for the enlightening of male or female ; for the guidance of the six princes He made a cat a prophet, a dog a saint.[4] Whoso comes to Him and lends his ear, comes not of

---

[1] A saying of Manṣūr Ḥallāj, who when asked by a certain person to show him the way to God, replied, '*Forsake thy passions, and come hither.*' L.

[2] The order of the text for a considerable number of pages is here obviously confused. I have tried to bring it somewhat nearer to a logical sequence ; but there are several short passages interspersed which appear to have no connection with this part of the book ; these I have grouped together later.

[3] مهدی according to L meaning مهدی الیه 'the thing to which one is guided', and not, as it literally should be, 'guided' ; 'unless it be so construed the meaning is not clear ; *but God knows best.*'

[4] L gives the following stories, here condensed, in illustration of this line. The six princes are six of the seven 'Companions of the Cave', the seventh being a shepherd's son who joined them under the following circumstances. Decianus was a tyrannical governor of Ephesus, who laid claim to Godhead ; these six princes, sons of rulers of Syria and Yaman, had been sent to do service in his court by their fathers, that they themselves might escape his tyranny. One day two cats fighting together on the roof fell down in front of him ; this so terrified him that he almost lost his senses. The young men, reasoning "How can he be a God who fears a cat ?" fled from the court, and meeting a shepherd, who joined them on hearing their story, were taken by him into a cave. The dog Qiṭmīr accompanied them, and was endowed with human speech. For their long sleep v. Qur. 18 ; and for the amplifications of the story

himself, but His grace leads him ; His grace will guide thee to the end, and then the heavens will be thy slave. Know that it is He who makes the soul prostrate itself, as even through the sun the clouds give bounteous rain.[1]

[On the Surrender of the Self.][2]

Dost thou desire thy collar of lace to be washed, then first give thy coat to the fuller.[3] Strip off thy coat, for on the road to the King's

---

in the commentators, *cf.* the notes in Sale. The cat, continues L, was a prophet in the sense of acting as a warning to the six, turning them towards the true God and strengthening their belief in Him ; and the dog of the text is the dog who was their companion in the cave.

Or, says he, the reference may be to the six guests of Shaikh Akhī Farj Zanjānī ; who had a cat, which on the arrival of vistors used to mew once for each person, and the servant used accordingly to put one cup for each mew. One day there was one person too many for the number of places set ; whereon the cat came in, smelt at each one, and made urine against one of them. On investigation this one was found to be an unbeliever. This same cat was present one day when a black snake fell into the cauldron where milk and rice were cooking ; the attendant took no notice of the cat's mewing and evident perturbation ; and finally the cat jumped into the cauldron and died. On emptying it, the snake was discovered.

The dog, he continues, may be the one of the following story. Shaikh Najmu'd-Dīn Kibrī of Naishāpūr was one day discussing with his disciples the story of the Cave and the dog of the sleepers. One of the circle, Shaikh Sa'du' d-Dīn Hamawī, chanced to wonder in himself, if in that company there were any one whose companionship could make an impression on a dog (as association with those seven pious men was supposed to have affected their dog). Knowing by his miraculous gifts what was passing in his mind, Shaikh Najmu'd-Dīn rose and went to the door of the cell ; a dog came up to him and wagged its tail. The Shaikh looked at it, whereon its nature became changed ; it became beside itself, left the city, went to the graveyard, and there rubbed its head on the ground. Wherever it went, subsequently, fifty or sixty dogs accompanied it in silence and great respect. It lived a long time thus, and finally died.

1 The comparison is with the clouds prostrating themselves on the earth as rain. جُود = 'abundant rain' ; جَود = 'liberality.' While the latter is the appropriate rhyme to the preceding hemistich, probably both senses were present in the author's mind.

2 There is no title in the original which fits this section, which appears as part of a long chapter entitled 'Also of the Right Guidance.'

3 زه, 'lace, border, hem or other ornament of gold or silk round the edge or collar of a garment,' (gloss in B گریبان). L and others read

gate there are many to tear it. At the first step that Adam took, the wolf of affliction tore his coat : when Cain became athirst to oppress, did not Abel give up his coat and die ? Was it not when Idrīs[1] threw off his coat that he saw the door of Paradise open to him ? When the Friend of God remorselessly tore their garments[2] from star and moon and sun, his night became bright as day, and the fire of Nimrod became a garden and a rose-bower. Look at Solomon, who in his justice gave the coat of his hope to the fuller ;[3] jinn and men, birds and ants and locusts, in the depth of the waters of the Red Sea, on the tips of the branches, all raised their face to him, all became subservient to his command ; when the lustre of his nature had been burnt in the fire of his soul,[4] the heavens laid his body on the back of the wind.[5]

When the venerable Moses, reared in sorrow, turned his face in grief and pain towards Midian, in bodily labour he tore off the coat from his anguished heart. For ten years he served Shu'aib,[6] till the door of the invisible was opened to his soul. His hand became

---

سمت for شستهٔ, misled perhaps by زه which also means 'bow-string'. پوستین is used here and in subsequent lines for the garment of borrowed existence and pride and self ; the section thus inculcates the giving up of the world and of self in order to obtain an enduring honour and distinction.

1 A prophet mentioned twice in the Qur'ān, and identified with Enoch.

2 Of borrowed existence ; and saw the heavenly bodies for what they were. The Friend of God is Abraham ; for the story of how he rebuked the idolatry of his people, and for so doing was thrown by Nimrod into a fire, which was powerless to harm him, see Qur. 6 : 74-82 ; 19 : 42-51 ; 21 : 52-75 and the commentators thereon *ap.* Sale ; and for the Jewish origin of the stories *cf.* Geiger's 'Judaism and Islam', Eng. tr., Madras, 1898, pp. 96, sqq.

This example does not seem to be quite on all fours with the preceding and succeeding ; since Abraham is here said to have torn their coats from sun, moon, and stars.

3 The act of renunciation here referred to may be Solomon's slaughter of a thousand mares, which he was inspecting one afternoon, and in doing so forgot the afternoon prayers. In his repentance he slew all the horses, and God thereupon gave him power over the wind, which travelled wheresoever he commanded it.

4 *i.e.* when he repented.

5 See, for Solomon, Qur. 21 : 81-82 ; 27 : 15-45 ; 38 : 29-39 ; 34 : 11-13.

6 So Jethro is called by the Muslims.

bright as his piercing eye ; he became the crown on the head of the men of Sinai.[1]

When the Spirit,[2] drawing breath from the spiritual ocean, had 20
received the grace of the Lord, he sent his coat to the cleanser of
hearts at the first stage of his journey. He gave brightness to his **16**
soul, He gave him kingship, even in childhood. By the Eternal
Power, through encouragement in secret and grace made manifest,
he lost the self ; the leprous body became dark again through
him as the shadow on the earth, the blind eye became bright as
the steps of the throne. Whoso like him seeks neither name nor
reputation, can produce ten kinds (of food) from one jar. A stone 5
with him became fragrant as musk ; the dead rose to living action
and spoke. By his grace life broke forth in the dead earth of the
heart ; by his power he animated the heart of the mire.[3]

When predestined fate had closed the shops, and the hand of
God's decree lay in the hollow of non-existence,[4] the world was full
of evil passions, the market full of ruffians and patrols. Then He
sent a vicegerent into this world to abolish oppression ; when he 10

---

1 L supposes the 'men of Sinai' to be a number of people whom Moses took up the mountain with him that they might observe what happened. This however would seem to be at variance with the Qur'ān and commentators, and I should prefer to refer the hemistich to Qur. 3 : 75 and the commentators thereon ; who say (*ap.* Sale *ad loc.*) that "the souls of all the prophets, even of those who were not then born, were present on Mount Sinai when God gave the law to Moses, and that they entered into the covenant here mentioned with him; " a story, Sale says, borrowed by Muḥammad from the talmudists. I find no reference to it in Geiger.

The 'white hand' of Moses in the previous hemistich is referred to in Qur. 7: 105. In the line which introduces this passage Moses is called 'Kalīm', that is, 'Kalīmu'llāh', 'the speaker with God', as often by the Muslims.

2 *i.e.*, of God, that is, Jesus.

3 The miracles of Jesus do not figure largely in the Qur'ān; v. 3 : 43—46 and 5 : 112—115. The last hemistich refers to 3 : 43. "*I will create for you out of clay as though it were the form of a bird, and I will blow thereon and it shall become a bird by God's permission.*" The commentators state that the bird was a bat. For the circumstances v. Sale note *ad loc.*; Hughes, Dict. of Islam, s. v. Jesus Christ, III, The miracles of Jesus ; as also for the raising of the dead. For the miracle of the provision of various kinds of food and the table sent down from heaven, Hughes, l.c., and Sale, note on Qur. 5 : 112.

4 Referring to the 'fitrat', or interval between Jesus and Muḥammad. L.

appeared from mid-heaven,[1] fervid[2] in soul and pure in body, he wore no coat on the religious path; then what could he give to the fullers of the land?[3] When he passed from this mortal state to eternal life he became the ornament and glory of this perishable world.

In His Magnification.

When He shows His Nature to His creation, into what mirror shall He enter?[4] The burden of proclaiming the Unity not everyone bears; the desire of proclaiming the Unity not everyone tastes. In every dwelling is God adored; but the Adored cannot be circumscribed by any dwelling. The earthly man, accompanied by unbelief and anthropomorphism, wanders from the road; on the road of truth thou must abandon thy passions;—rise, and forsake this vile sensual nature; when thou hast come forth from Abode and Life, then, through God, thou wilt see God.[5]

How shall this sluggish body worship Him, or how can Life and Soul know Him? A ruby of the mine is but a pebble there; the soul's wisdom talks but folly there. Speechlessness is praise,—enough of thy speech; babbling will be but sorrow and harm to thee,—have done!

17 His Nature, to one who knows Him and is truly learned, is above '*How*' and '*What*' and '*Is it not*' and '*Why.*' His creative power is manifest, the justice of His wisdom; His wrath is

---

[1] دلِ آسمان is 'mid-heaven, a star, the earth.' I have taken آسمان دل in the same sense, reading it without the iẓāfat, the ن being fully pronounced and followed by the nīm-fatḥa.

[2] lit. 'drunk', *i.e.*, with the love of God.

[3] The elders of his family and tribe, B. The meaning is that he never possessed any 'self' of which the tribulations he experienced at the hands of his tribe could deprive him.

[4] *i.e.*, how can He manifest Himself so as to be comprehensible?

[5] The texts insert before the last line a line which runs, "Abode and Life both are Thy servants, Thy stewards and attendants;" which I take to be a gloss, perhaps of Indian origin, because of the address to God in the second person, and the use of the foreign word كوتوال. 'Attendants' is نفس شمار, *i.e.*, those who are in such close attendance that they count their master's breaths, awaiting his orders.

secret, the artifice of His majesty.[1] A form of water and earth is dazzled by His love, the eye and heart are blinded by His Nature. Reason in her uncleanness, wishing to see Him, says, like Moses, '*Show me*'; when the messenger[2] comes forth from that glory, she says in its ear, '*I turn repentant unto thee.*'[3] Discover then the nature of His Being through thy understanding ![4] recite his thousand and one pure names. It is not fitting that His Nature should be covered by our knowledge; whatever thou hast heard, that is not He. 'Point' and 'line' and 'surface' in relation to His Nature are as if one should talk of His 'substance' and 'distance' and 'six surfaces'; the Author of those three is beyond place; the Creator of these three is not contained in time.[5] No philosopher knows of imperfection in Him, while He knows the secrets of the invisible world; He is acquainted with the recesses of the mind, and the secrets of which as yet there has been formed no sketch upon thy heart.

Kāf and *nūn* are only letters that we write, but what is *kun*? the hurrying of the agent of the divine decree. If He delays, or acts quickly, it depends not on His weakness; whether He is angry or placable depends not on His hate. His causation is known to neither infidelity nor faith, and neither is acquainted

---

1 His creative power, the origin and source of created things, is a result of the justice of His wisdom, and is apparent; and His wrath is the artifice of His majesty and glory, and is hidden; outwardly it appears as glory, and in reality it is wrath. So L, but in this case His majesty should be called the artifice of His wrath and not *vice versâ*.

2 پیک *i.e.*, پیک غیبی B, the invisible messenger, Reason.

3 'In its ear' = in the ear of that glory. "For the words which Reason says to that glory will necessarily be said in the ear and in secret," L. The reference is to Qur. 7 : 138 sq. "*And when Moses came to our appointment, and his Lord spake unto him, he said, O my Lord, show me, that I may look on thee. He said, Thou canst not see me; but look upon the mountain, and if it remain steady in its place, thou shalt see me; but when his Lord appeared unto the mountain He made it dust, and Moses fell down in a swoon. And when he came to himself, he said, Celebrated be thy praise; I turn repentant unto thee, and am the first of those who are resigned.*"

4 Said ironically; v. next line.

5 The texts all have درون, but برون seems obviously required.

with His Nature. He is pure of those attributes the foolish speak of, purer than the wise can tell.

Reason is made up of confusion and conjecture, both limping over the earth's face. Conjecture and cogitation are no good guides; wherever conjecture and cogitation are, He is not. Conjecture and cogitation are of His creation;[1] man and reason are His newly-ripening plants. Since any affirmation about His Nature is beyond man's province, it is like a statement about his mother by a blind man;[2] the blind man knows he has a mother, but what she is like he cannot imagine; his imagination is without any conception of what things are like, of ugliness and beauty, of inside and outside.

In a world of double aspect such as this, it would be wrong that
18 thou shouldst be He, and He thou.[3] If thou assert Him not, it is not well; if thou assert Him, it is thyself thou assertest, not He. If thou know not (that He is) thou art without religion, and if thou assert Him thou art of those who liken Him. Since He is beyond 'where' and 'when', how can He become a corner of thy thought? When the wayfarers travel towards Him, they vainly exclaim, 'Behold, Behold!'[4] Men of hawk-like boldness are as

---

[1] And so must fall immeasurably short of Him.

[2] According to B بر نیست is equivalent to نزدیک فاني, *i.e.*, 'an affirmation about God's nature by a mortal.' But the introductory زانکه is a difficulty which he does not explain. Hence I have retained رنگ, for which some texts have هست through assimilation to نیست, and have divided the words as برنی ست (برنی = foreign, external).

[3] The full meaning of this and the following lines L explains thus:—"in this world of unreality, with two faces and necessary duality, it would be wrong, with your borrowed existence and without discarding self, to claim unity of existence with God and knowledge of Him. If you assert not His necessary Existence and affirm not His Being in its oneness, it is not well, and you are an unbeliever; whereas if you do this, and assert His Existence, whatever you assert is yourself and not He, for He is above and free from anything you imagine and think. And if you know not that there exists a God, and take reason for guide, you are without religion; while if you assert it you are an anthropomorphist; for He cannot be designated or described by any description, and however you describe Him you fall into the error of 'likening' Him."

[4] Vainly, because He is not there.

ringdoves in the street, a collar on their necks, uttering 'Where, Where ?'[1]

If thou wilt, take hope, or if thou wilt, then fear; the All-wise has created nothing in vain. He knows all that has been done or will be done; thou knowest not,—yet know that He will assuage thy pain.[2] In the knowledge of Him is naught better than submission, that so thou mayest learn His wisdom and His clemency. Of His wisdom He has given resources to His creatures, the greater to him who has the greater need; to all He has given fitting resources, for acquiring profit and warding off injury. What has gone, what comes, and what exists in the world, in such wise it was necessary; bring not folly into thy conversation; look thou with acceptance on His decrees.

On the Earnest Striving.

When thou hast passed from Self to being naught, gird up the loins of thy soul and set forth on the road; when thou standest up with loins girt thou hast placed a crown on thy soul's head. Set then the crown of the advance on the head of thy soul; let the foot that would retreat be the companion of the mire;[3] though the thoughtless man laughs at this act, yet the wise chooses no other course.

Whoso turns not his face towards God, all his knowledge and possessions deem thou an idol. Who turns away his face from God's presence, in truth I call not him a man; a dog is better than a worthless man who turns away his face, for a dog finds not its prey without a search. A dog that lives in ease,[4] though it gets fat, is not therefore more useful than a greyhound.

---

1 کو کو 'Coo, coo,' the sound of the doves, as well as meaning 'Where, where ?'

2 L refers to the reading کرد کند, and suggests کرد as equivalent to کرداد; he says the rhyme is defective if it be not adopted; but the rhyme is defective in any case (کُند and کَند).

3 L gloss (under گل) تن, *i.e.*, the mire is the body, opposed to the soul in the preceding hemistich.

4 کَهْدان is a place where straw is put for dogs, etc.

19 He will not take hypocrisy and deceit and lying,[1] but looks to a man's belief in the Unity and his sincerity. The eye that is fixed on wisdom chooses the Truth ; the pleasure-regarding eye sees not the Truth. False is what delights the eye ; the Truth enters not among earthy thoughts.[2] Infidelity and faith both have their origin in thy hypocritical[3] heart ; the path is long because thy foot delays : were it not so, the road to Him is but one step,—be a slave, and thou becomest a king with Him. Know that the different names of the colours are illusory, that thy sustenance is to be sought in the river of the Absolute. Leave off thy talk, and come to the pavilion ; loose thy heavy bonds from off thyself. Perhaps thou hast not tasted the true faith, hast not seen the face of truth and sincerity ; so that thou thoughtest the mystery was plain to be seen, and things thou sawest plainly have been mysteries to thee. I see in thee no rightness of belief ; if there were I would be the true dawn of religion to thee ;—I would have made the path of the true faith plain to thee hadst thou not been a fool and a madman.

[Of the Traveller on the Path.][4]

A man should be like Abraham, that, through God, his shadow may become a shady place ;[5] in fear of him[6] and by his teaching the universe dares to breathe ; Pharaoh is destroyed by the mighty aid of a Moses whom God assists.

To the wayfarer towards God on the path of love His cheek is the dawn of morning ; (who but He can tear away the veil by day,

---

1 مخرقه - the commentators seem to have mistaken the meaning here, giving as the equivalent دِرّة, which means 'an instrument of hitting and striking ; a wooden sword' (B.Q.).

2 'The Truth' in these lines (حق) may equally be rendered 'God', or 'reality'.

3 Lit. 'of two colours'.

4 This chapter can scarcely claim to be more than a series of short passages and single lines, at variance with the context in which they stood, and collected here as having somewhat in common with each other.

5 Perhaps referring to Abraham's being unharmed in Nimrod's fire ; these first three lines speak of the powers given by God to those who seek Him.

6 *i.e.*, the seeker after God.

or hang the veil by night ?) [1] His mind is snatched away from bonds of earth ; the spiritual rule of the world is made manifest to him. He treads the Throne under his feet like a carpet ; he is an owl, but bears with him a phœnix.[2] He becomes lord of this abode and that,[3] the loyal slave of God ; the pure Intelligence reveals its face to man, and beautifies his body with its own light. The bounty of God throws its shade over his heart ; then he says, '*How He prolongs the shadow.*' [4] When his soul feels the touch of God, '*We make the sun*' reveals its face to him.[5] The dumb all find tongues when they receive the perfume of life from his soul.

In His path the lovers recite to their souls the verse '*Every creature on the earth is subject to decay* ;' [6] the heavens, and the natural world and its varied colours seem vile to his perception. Whoso is turned away from this wine, for him all its fragrance and colour is destroyed ; so that when with new ear thou shalt hear the shouts of '*He is One, He has no partner*,' thou shalt no longer in madness desire the varied colours, even though thy Jesus be the dyer.[7] Thou shalt take what thou wilt of the colours, put them into one jar, and bring them out again ;—listen truly, and not in folly ; this saying is not for fools ;—all these deceitful colours the jar of the Unity makes one colour. Then being now of one colour, all has become Him ; the rope becomes slender when reduced to a single strand.[8]

---

[1] The meaning may be that God is the light of the way, and the last line is possibly a parenthesis, the thought of which was prompted by the preceding.

[2] The owl is a bird of ill-omen ; the phœnix (هما) is a bird of happy omen, prognosticating a crown to every head it shades.

[3] *i.e.*, 'of both worlds.'

[4] Qur. 25 : 47. "*Hast thou not looked to thy Lord, how he prolongs the shadow?*"

[5] Qur. 25 : 48. "*Then we make the sun a guide thereto ; then we contract it towards us with an easy contraction.*" This and the last quotation are part of a passage descriptive of God's benefits to man.

[6] Qur. 55 : 26.

[7] عیسیٔ تو 'thy Jesus', paraphrased by B as سنگ دل تو 'thy stony heart'.

[8] I suppose the meaning to refer to the simplification of phenomena,—that they are more easily grasped when reduced to unity.

[On being Silent.]

The path of religion is neither in works nor words; there are no buildings thereon, but only desolation. Whoso becomes silent to pursue the path, his speech is life and sweetness; if he speaks, it will not be out of ignorance, and if he is silent, it will not be from sloth; when silent, he is not devising frivolity; when speaking, he scatters abroad no trifling talk.

15 Those fools, the thieves and pickpockets, keep their knowledge to use in highway robbery.[1] Thou seest, O Master, thou of many words, that thou hadst better have light in thy heart than words; when thou becomest silent, thou art most eloquent, but if thou speakest, thou art like a captain of war.[2] '*Kun*' consists of two letters, both voiceless; '*Hū*' consists of two letters, both silent.[3] Doubt not concerning these words of mine; open thine eyes, pay heed for a little.

20 There exists the dog,[4] and the stone; the stove of the bath, and
21 the slave; but thou art excellent, like a jewel inside a casket.[5] The king uses his silver for his daily needs, but his ruby he keeps for his treasure-house; silver is evil in its own ill-starred nature, the ruby is joyous because it is full of blood within.[6]

The family of Barmak[7] became great through their liberality; they were, so to say, close companions of generosity. Though fate

---

1 The 'fools' are the learned and the philosophers.

2 بطریق 'a commander of ten thousand.' L and B interpret in this sense, meaning, perhaps, 'blustering inconsequentially' (B هرزه سرای). Or بطریق = 'a patriarch'; B.Q. gives مجتهد ترسایان 'a theologian of the Christians,' and so, from the Muslim point of view, a vain babbler.

3 '*Kun*' is 'Be', the word used at the creation; '*Hū*' is 'He', God. هوا is 'wind, sound, voice, tone'; so بی هوا 'silent.' The commentators give no real help on this line; it seems to imply that the mightiest existences and actions do not require speech.

4 The following fragments do not appear to have their place in any of the chapters near which they are found in the texts.

5 "Dog and stone are of His creation, the stone being created for driving off the dog; and so the stove of the bath and the slave are of His creation, the slave to light the fire of the stove; but thou, who art of the most excellent of the marvels of God, art like only to a ruby, deposited with care in casket." B.

6 The commentators give no help as to the meaning of the passage.

7 The Barmecides, who attained to great power in the reign of Hārūnu'r-Rashīd.

pronounced their destruction, their name endures, indestructible as the spirit. The people of this generation, though amiable, are impudent as flies and wanton; in word they are all sweet as sugar, but when it comes to generosity, they tear men's hearts and burn their souls.[1]

When He had adorned thy soul within thee, He held up before thee the mirror of the light; till pride made thee quick to anger, and thou lookedst upon thyself with the evil eye.[2]

He has balanced day and night by the ruler of his justice, not by chance or at random.[3]

While Reason digs for the secret, thou hast reached thy goal on the plain of Love.[4]

The heart and soul of the seeker after God are concealed, but his tongue proclaims in truth, '*I am God.*'[5]

The Parable of those who heed not.[6]

A fool saw a camel grazing, and said, Why is thy form all crooked? Said the camel, In disputing thus thou censurest the sculptor;

---

[1] This passage occurs shortly after the chapter 'Of the Right Guidance,' and I think is very probably spurious. It seems to be connected with the word جود in the last line of that chapter, p. 15, l. 4, and possibly represents the pious reflections of some reader, noted down by him in the margin of the original or of an early copy, and thence taken up into the text by subsequent copyists.

[2] "The Incomparable Creator, after adorning thee inwardly, that is, designing thy inward being as He had done thy outward parts, held up before thee a mirror of light, that is, understanding and clear comprehension, by means of which thou mightest come to know good and evil. Then, till pride and self-conceit became natural to thee, He kept thee from lust and anger; and, until He gave to thee the eye of vanity, He kept thee from being acceptable in thine own eyes," B; but in adding '*And God knows the truth of the matter,*' he does not appear to be very sure of his explanation. In the absence of the proper context interpretation is perhaps impossible; the lines occur in the texts in 'Again the Parable of the Companions of Indifference,' p. 23.

[3] In the middle of the passage which I have called 'On being Silent,' p. 20.

[4] In the passage which I have called 'Of the Traveller on the Path,' p. 19. The third person is used in the lines amongst which it occurs; otherwise it is written in the same sense.

[5] At the end of the above passage.

[6] A similar title has been used before, p. 10.

beware! Look not on my crookedness in disparagement, and kindly take the straight road away from me. My form is thus because it is best so, as from a bow's being bent comes its excellence. Begone hence with thy impertinent interference; an ass's ear goes well with an ass's head.[1]

22 The arch of the eyebrow, though it displease thee, is yet a fitting cupola over the eye; by reason of the eyebrow, the eye is able to look at the sun, and in virtue of the bloom of its strength becomes an adornment to the face. Evil and good, in the estimation of the wise, are both exceeding good; from Him there comes no evil; whatever thou seest to come from Him, though evil, it were well thou look on it all as good. To the body there comes its portion of ease and of pain; to the soul ease is as a treasure secured; but a twisted snake is over it, the hand and foot of Wisdom are at its side.[2]

The Parable of the Eye of the Squint-eyed.

A squint-eyed son asked his father, O thou whose words are as a key to the things that are locked up, why saidst thou that a squinter sees double? I see no more things than there are; if a squint-eyed person counted things crookedly, the two moons that are in the heavens would seem four.

But he who spoke thus spoke in error; for if a squinter looks at a dome, it is doubled.[3]

I fear that on the high-road of the faith thou art like the crooked-seeing squinter, or like the fool who senselessly quarrelled with the camel because of God's handiwork. His flawless creation is the

---

1 سر خر in a secondary sense, which is also applicable here, means 'a shameless fellow, one who intrudes himself into a place where he has no business; a blundering intermeddler.' So also Ar. راس حمار, *cf.* Browne, "A Year amongst the Persians," p. 224.

2 On the 'twisted snake' AB have gloss نفس; as B in a note explains نفس سهمناک, a terrible spirit, *i.e.*, to guard it. The 'hand and foot of Wisdom' is simply Wisdom, 'a sound, guiding, prudent understanding,' B. The meaning of the last two lines would thus be, that though misfortunes may happen to the body, a serene wisdom will preserve the soul's peace in every condition.

3 *i.e.*, such a large and obvious thing as a dome.

qibla of our understanding; His changeless nature is the *ka'ba* of our desire. He has exalted the soul in giving it wisdom; He has nourished His pardoning mercy on our faults. God well knows your turning to Him; His wisdom it is which prevents His answering your prayers. Though the physician hears his patient when he begs, he does not give earth to an earth-eater; and though his soul desire it, how shall He give earth through all his life to him who digs the earth? How shall His act be without a reason, or His decrees in accordance with thy weak understanding?[1]

There are exceeding many who have drunk the cup of pure poison and have not died of it; nay, it is life's food to him who from the violence of his disease is wasted to a reed. In His wisdom and justice He has given to all more than all that is requisite; if the gnat 23
bites the elephant's hide, tell him to flap his ears,—he has a gnat dispeller in them; if there is a louse, thou hast a finger-nail; punish the flea, when it jumps on thee; though the mountains were full of snakes, fear not,—there are stones and an antidote on the mountain too; and if thou art apprehensive of the scorpion, thou hast slipper and shoe for it. If pain abounds in the world, everyone has a thousand remedies.

In accordance with his scheme He has suspended together the sphere of intense cold and the globe of fire.[2] The motions of the

---

[1] The texts have نمودۀ تو. I have however adopted what was apparently the original reading of 'Abdu'l-Laṭīf's edition; since the commentary runs آنچه نموده یعنی کرده و بوده اعنی مقدر حقست.

[2] اثیر according to B is "the globe of fire, an element, the highest of the four, called sometimes the *charkh-i-athīr*;" so far agreeing with Gibb, p. 46, who discussing Muslim philosophy says:—"The first manifestation of specific form is in the 'Four Elements', Fire, Air, Water and Earth. The arrangement of the elemental world is, like that of the ethereal, a series of concentric, spherical layers. As Fire is the lightest and subtlest of the four, its region is the highest, lying within and touching the concave surface of the Sphere of the Moon. In its pure state Fire is colourless and transparent, consequently the Sphere of Fire is invisible."

B proceeds, "*Zamharīr* = 'intense cold', and the globe o intense cold is the limiting stratum of the air." The sphere of air is the next inside that of fire; it "is subdivided into three strata (*tabaqāt*). The Sphere of Fire and the highest stratum of the Sphere of Air, though by their own nature stationary, are carried round by the Sphere of the Moon in its revolution." Gibb. op. cit.

body are rendered equable, the coolness of the brain and the warmth of the heart are both moderated ; the liver and heart, by means of the stomach and arteries, send forth water [1] and air to the body, that through breath and blood the heart by its movement, and the liver by its quiescence, may give the body life.[2]

There is a spiritual kingdom in the universe, and also a temporal power ; above the throne light, and below darkness ; both these principles He bestowed at the creation, when He spread His shadow over His handiwork. The temporal world He has given of His bounty to the body, the spiritual world as a glory to the soul ; that so both inner and outer man may receive food, the body from the lord of this world, the soul from the Lord of the spirit-world ; for through all His creation God keeps a benign grace for the benefit of the noble soul.

The acute thinker knows that what He does is well ; it is thou who namest some things evil and some good, otherwise [3] all that comes from Him is pure kindness. Evil comes not into existence from Him ; how can evil subsist with Godhead ? Only the foolish and ignorant do evil ; the Doer of good Himself does no evil. If He gives poison, deem it sweet ; if He shows wrath, deem it mercy. Good is the cupping-glass our mothers apply to us, and good too the dates they give.

Again the Parable of those who heed not.

Dost thou not see how the nurse in the earliest days of its childhood sometimes ties the little one in its cradle, and at times is ever laying it on her bosom ; sometimes strikes it hard and sometimes soothes it ; sometimes puts it away from her and repels it, sometimes kindly kisses its cheek and again caresses it and bears its grief ? A stranger is angry with the nurse when he sees this, and sighs ; he says to it, The nurse is not kind, the child is of little account with

---

1 *i.e.*, blood, according to the old pathology.

2 The arteries being found empty after death, the heart was supposed to be the means for pumping air over the body The liver was thought to be the storehouse of the blood.

3 *i.e.*, were it not for the name.

her. How shouldst thou know that the nurse is right? Such is always the condition of her work.

God too, according to his compact, performs his whole duty towards his slave; He gives the daily food that is required, sometimes disappointment, sometimes victory; sometimes He sets a jewelled crown upon his head, sometimes He leaves him needy with only a copper.

Be thou contented with God's ordinance; or if not, then cry aloud and complain before the Qāẓī, that he may release thee from His decree! A fool is he who thinks thus! Whatever it is,—whether misfortune or prosperity,—it is an unmixed blessing, and the evil only transitory. He who brings the world into being with '*Be, and it was*,'—how, how shall He do evil to the creatures of the world? Good and evil exist not in the world of the Word;[1] the names 'good' and 'evil' belong to thee and to me. When God created the regions of the earth He created no absolute evil; death is destruction for this one, but wealth for that; poison is food to this, and death to that.

If the face of the mirror were black like its back, no one would look at it; the usefulness belongs to the face of the mirror, even though its back be stuffed with jewels. The bright-faced sun is good, be its[2] back black or white; if the peacock's foot were like its feathers, it would shine splendid both by night and day.[3]

In Praise of His Omnipotence.

He is the Pourtrayer of the outward forms of our earthly bodies; He is the Discerner of the images of our inmost hearts. He is the Creator of existent and non-existent, the Maker of the hand and what it holds. He made a wheel of pure emerald, and on the wheel

---

[1] سخن — جهان سخن apparently in a technical sense; I cannot say to which, if to any, of the various planes the جهان سخن corresponds. Perhaps سخن is the word *kun*. *Cf. infra*, p. 25, l. 12.

[2] *i.e.*, the sun's.

[3] Meaning, I think, that it would be altogether too gorgeous. The preceding short paragraph is to the effect that things are made for use and benefit, and that God knows best what is required.

he bound silver jars ;[1] He caused a candle and candlestick to revolve in the heavens in the path of the ignoble.[2] Before His creation was non-existence ; eternal being belongs to His Essence alone. He made Intelligence proclaimer of His power ; He made matter capable of receiving form. To Intelligence He gave the path of vigilance ; what thinkest thou of Intelligence ?

How can the artist of the pen [3] picture forth in man the image of the Eternal ? Fire and wind and water and earth and sky, and Reason and Spirit above the sky, and the angels in the middle place, wisdom and life and abstract form ,—know, that all come into being by command, and the command is God's.

He is the origin and root of material things,[4] the Creator of beneficence, and thanks, and the thankful man. In the high-road from this life to the next He has associated action and power with this world of generation and corruption. In the world of the Word [5] His Omnipotence made power pregnant with action, made its place for whatever comes into action, created its product for whatever possesses power.

On the Proverbs and Admonitions 'Poverty is Blackness of the Face' (the Recital of Proverbs is the best of Discourses) and 'The World is a House of Departure and Changing Affairs and Migration.'[6]

Keep thy blackness, thou canst not do without it ; for blackness admits no change of colour. With blackness of face there goes happiness ; a blushing face seldom causes joy. The scorched

---

[1] The stars in the heavens are compared to the vessels on the wheel used for raising water from the well,—the common 'Persian wheel' of the East.

[2] So that the wicked may see. The sun and moon are the candle, the sky the candlestick, which revolves in هوا , 'the space between heaven and earth.'

[3] Perhaps the Primal Intelligence, L.

[4] پرکار in B.Q. = اشیای عالم.

[5] Perhaps the word *kun*, 'Be'; and so the world, or plane, where God's commands issue, and hence possibly equivalent to the '*ālam-i-jabarūt*, 'the plane of power.' *Cf.* p. 24, l. 13.

[6] The title is perhaps made up of glosses. It differs in the various MSS.

In the technical language of the Ṣūfīs, says L, poverty, فقر , means annihilation in God, the union of a drop with the ocean, the last stage of the perfected ones. '*Poverty is blackness of the face in both worlds*' means that the traveller

pursuer is black of face before the flame of his heart's desire ;[1] though 20
in tribulation, the ugly Ethiopian finds gladness in his blackness of
face ; his gladness comes not from his beauty, his happiness comes
from his sweet odour.[2] Brighter than the splendour of the new moon
is the display of the moon of Bilāl's shoe ;[3] if thou dost not wish thy
heart's secret known, keep thy blackness of face in both worlds, since 26
for him who seeks his desire, day tears the veil and night spreads it.

Withhold thy hand from these vain lusts ; know, desire is poison,
and the belly as a snake ; the serpent of desire, if it bite thee, will soon
despatch thee from the world.[4] For in this path in evil there is good ;
the water of life is in the midst of darkness. What sorrow has the 5
heart from blackness ? For night is pregnant with day, and the men
who are now imprisoned without food or drink in this old ruin throw
aside all instruction[5] when they march proudly in the garden of God.

Everything except God, all that is of earth, is aside from the path of the true faith. Loss of self is the hidden goal of all ; the refuge of the pure soul is with the Word.[6]

---

becomes entirely annihilated in God, so that—externally, internally, in this world, in the next—he has no existence, and returns to his essential and original non-existence. This is true ' poverty ' ; hence it is said ' *When poverty is absolute, that is God.*' And till the traveller experiences perfect non-existence, or absolute annihilation, he cannot experience absolute existence, which is eternal life with God. And death from self is the essence of life to God, and absolute life is seen to consist in absolute death. To this degree nothing can attain but the perfect man, who is thus the most perfect of all created things, the object of the creation of the world.

1 Perhaps a reference to the moth and the candle. All texts give تپش or تبش which would require a preposition. A hint of what I take to be the original reading is given in M.

2 Lit. ' odour of musk ' ; but the appropriateness of the hemistich depends on a second meaning of مشک, *viz.*, ' blackness, ink.'

3 Bilāl was the negro mu'adhdhin of Muḥammad. The reference is to a saying of Muḥammad's, " When I went on my night journey to heaven, I heard the sound of the feet of Bilāl," B.

4 Lit. ' will not cook with thee these colours long.'

5 تلقین, with gloss in B, قیل و قال و تقلید, ' controversy and imitation.

6 To be transformed from self and personal existence to non-being and annihilation is the hidden goal of all wayfarers ; and the place to which the pure soul returns is the Word, which we may take to be the word *kun* ; or the confession

O thou, who hast rolled up the carpet of time, who hast passed beyond the four and the nine,[1] pass at one step beyond life and reason, that so thou mayst arrive at God's command. Thou canst not see, forasmuch as thou art blind at night; and in the day too hast but one eye, like the wisdom of fools. I do not speak to thee with wink and nod,[2] but in God's way, with mystical significations and allegories.

Till thou pass beyond the false, God is not there;[3] the perfect truth belongs not to this half-display. Know, that as provision for the journey to the eternal world, *lā khair* is your strength and *lā shai* your gold;[4] *lā khair* is the strength of the rich, as *lā shai* is the wisdom of the wine-drinkers.

On the Need of God, and Independence of all beside Him.[5]

He is wholly independent of me and thee in his plans;[6] what matters infidelity or faith to His Independence? What matters that or this to His Perfection? Know that God exists in real existence; in pursuance of His decree and just designs, the Independent seeks thy favours, the Guardian gives thee thanks.[7]

---

of the Unity (*tauḥīd*); or the confession of the Muslim faith (*kalima*); or lastly we may take the Word to be a characterization of the authority of God. L.

1 The four elements, and the nine spheres or heavens.

2 That is, perhaps, by common signs understood among men; though غمز and رمز, here put in opposition, have much the same primary meaning.

3 Refers to the saying 'All things, except God, are false.'

4 '*Lā khair*,' "there is no good," '*lā shai*,' "there is nothing," *sc.* except God.

5 The chapter seems to have been mistakenly named; its theme is rather God's independence of all things.

6 Lit. "of me and thee for His plans, perfection is (an attribute) to His independence." The commentators quote the Quranic verse "*Verily God is independent of the worlds*;" and a quatrain whose source is not given:—

"The affluent skirt of perfect Love is clear
From taint of need of me, of dust the peer;
Since He Himself is sight and object both,
If thou and I enter not there, what fear?"

7 Or 'praises'; *i.e.*, for accepting His guardianship, B.

The wolf and Yūsuf appear to thee to be small and great;[1] but with Him, Yūsuf and wolf are the same. What, to His Mercy, 27
matters opposition or help? What, to His Wrath, are Moses and Pharaoh?[2]

Thy service or thy rebellion are an honour or a shame to thee, but with Him the colour of both is the same. What honour has He from Reason, or from the lightning, what greatness from the soul, or the sky? The soul and the heavens are His creatures. Happy the man who is chosen of Him.

The heavens and He who causes them to revolve are as the millstone and the miller; the supreme Disposer and the obedient Reason are as the carver's self and the matter he shapes. The motion of the restless heavens and of the earth is as it were an ant in the mouth of a dragon; the dragon does not swallow the ant, and the revolution of the unconscious heavens sweeps on. He has imposed its task upon the mill-wheel of misfortune, itself unmindful and closed round by annihilation.[3] Think of thy life as an atom in His time,[4] His banquet as accompanied by His affliction.[5]

---

1 *i.e.*, appear different in size and degree. The wolf was supposed to have torn Joseph to pieces.

2 "What help can Moses give, what does the might of a Pharaoh matter when His Wrath goes forth?" B.

3 Lit. 'within the fœtal membranes of *Not*.' 'The dragon' is the same as 'annihilation', *cf.* Jāmī, نهنگ لا برارد سر "The dragon does not swallow the ant because of its excessive insignificance; and the revolution of the heavens goes on while they are unconscious of their position. As the ant passes into the dragon's mouth, and knows not of its passage into non-existence and destruction, so the revolution of the heavens and the earth they contain passes along, they themselves not knowing that they are in the mouth of the dragon of annihilation. And on the heavens, the millstone of calamity [so called since their revolutions are the cause of terrestrial events], God has imposed their labours, while they, enclosed in the membranes of *Lā*, know not what is being effected by themselves." So L, who adds, as an alternative, that the subject in the last line of the text may be چرخ understood. B gives a different explanation again.

4 Or, carrying on the metaphor of the ant in the dragon's mouth, perhaps, 'Think of thy life as a grain of corn in His mouth.'

5 *i.e.*, life as inevitably attended by death.

Thou knowest that thy goblet[1] has four feet[2] for movement; yet though thou be persevering in His service thou wilt not reach His path but by His grace. When will the slave who wishes to attain to God reach Him by means of reason, or by hand and foot?[3] When will he attain to God, who in his own body attains (only to the recognition of) his hands and feet?[4]

On Self-abasement and Humility.

Lowliness befits thee, violence suits thee not; a naked man frantic in a bee-house is out of place.[5] Leave aside thy strength, betake thyself to lowliness, that so thou mayest trample the heights of heaven beneath thy feet; for God knows that, rightly seen, thy strength is a lie, and thy lowliness truth. If thou layest claim to strength and wealth, thou hast a blind eye and a deaf ear. Thy face and thy gold are red,[6] thy coat is of many colours,—then look to find thy honour disgrace, thy peace strife. Come not to God's door in the dust of thy strength, for in this road it is through lowliness that thou becomest a hero. This comes not of discharging thy debt, but from bartering thy indigence.[7] Look not on His Omni-

---

1 The goblet holding the wine of life, the body.

2 *i.e.*, hands and feet; also a metaphor indicating great perplexity, B.

3 *i.e.*, external actions (gloss in B).

4 In accordance with B. "Thou who in the knowledge of thine own self canst not arrive at truth, to know fundamentally what thou art, except that thou recognisest thine own hands and feet, how canst thou with this weak power of knowledge know God?" L in addition to the above suggests "He who arrives at the knowledge of his own nature only by struggles with all his limbs and by excessive labour, how can he, etc....?" The texts, except I, insert as the last line of the chapter "Since even in self-knowledge thou art weak, how then canst thou become a knower of God?" which has appeared before, in the chapter 'On the knowledge of God'; where perhaps this last short paragraph as a whole might suitably be placed.

5 The world compared to a bee-house. شور, gloss in B شورنده.

6 *i.e.*, thou art honoured (سرخ رو) and prosperous.

7 'This' refers perhaps to advancement in the path, which is not merely a matter of conventional rectitude, but is obtained by means of abasement and loss of self. L gives several explanations of the line; referring 'this' to lowliness, he supposes that the debt is the obligatory services, prayer, fasting, alms, pilgrimage; humility is not attained thus, but by bartering, and thus turning

potence with thy impotent eye; O my master, commit not such an outrage.[1]

So long as thou art thy own support, clothe thyself, and eat; but if thou art upheld by Him, thou shalt neither sew nor tear.[2] All that exists, O friend, exists through Him; thine own existence is as a pretence,—speak not folly. If thou lose thyself, thy dust becomes a mosque; if thou hold to thyself, a fire-temple:[3] if thou hold to thyself, thy heart is hell; if thou lose thyself, heaven. If thou lose thyself, all things are accomplished; thy selffulness[4] is an untrained colt. Thou art thou,—hence spring love and hate; thou art thou,—hence spring infidelity and faith.[5] Remain a slave, without lot or portion; for an angel is neither hungry nor full. Fear and hope have driven away fortune from thee; when thy self has gone, hope and fear are no more.[6]

The owl that frequents the palace of the king is a bird of ill-omen, ill-fated and guilty; when it is contented in its solitude, its

---

to profit, our poverty. Again in the second hemistich نیازی فروختن may be in amplification of, and not in opposition to, فام توختن in the first, "This comes not of discharging thy debt, which is a selling of thy poverty, *i.e.*, of thyself." The possibility that the line belongs elsewhere is of course always present where the connection appears difficult or defective.

1 Reading with H, contrary to the rest, as خواجه cannot have the *iżāfat*. To accord with the sense of the comments of L and B, we should read آزاد (as most do), and assuming the *iżāfat*, trans. 'Make not thus of thyself a lord, with powers of manumission.' "Imagine not that His absolute Omnipotence can be comprehended or perceived by thy feeble eye; for that is as if one were to imagine the impossible within his power, as if a slave were to pretend to be a lord, with the power of manumission, and were to expatiate on his power and state," L.

2 "When thou hast hastened to the abode of *eternity with God* and art united to Him, thou wilt neither gaze with (lit. sew, *i.e.*, fasten upon anything) the eye of desire, nor tear the collar of indigence (*sc.* in despair)." B.

3 *i.e.*, a worshipping place of the infidel Zoroastrians. Or 'a Jews' Synagogue,' or 'a pigsty.'

4 باتو used as an abstract noun. I would suggest 'selffulness' as the opposite of 'selflessness.'

5 *Cf.* p. 1, l. 12 and note; and for a similar thought p. 29, l. 15, *inf.*

6 "When thou passest from thyself into resignation towards God, hope and fear are no more; the grace of God has been bestowed on thee," B.

feathers are finer than the splendour of the phœnix. Musk is spoilt by water and by fire ; but to the musk-bladder what matters wet or dry ?[1] What matters, at His door, a Muslim or a fire-worshipper ? What, before him, a fire-temple or a monk's cell ?[2] Fire-worshipper and Christian, virtuous and guilty, all are seekers, and He the sought.

God's essence is independent of cause ; why seekest thou now a place for cause ? The sun of religion comes not forth by instruction ; the moon goes down when the light of the truth shines out.[3] If the holy man is good, it is well for him ; if the king is bad, what is that to us ? To be saved, do thou thyself persevere in good ; why contendest thou with God's decree and predestination ?

In this halt of but a week, to be is not to be, to come is to go.[4] Recite the word '*hastening on*' ;[5] for in the resurrection the believer calls "*Make way !*" Muṣṭafā[6] exclaimed 'How excellent !' ; through this the hand of Moses became a moon, the Friend of God grew pitiful ;[7] the *wāw* of *awwah* gave him the sincerity of his faith, the

---

[1] So long as it remains in its native place, that is, it is not liable to harm. The passage is apparently directed against the assumption of a claim to honour with God.

[2] *i.e.*, a peculiarly Christian institution.

[3] Nor has the theological disputant any honour with God. "The sun of the faith, which is the light of the knowledge and truth of God, shines not forth by disputes and discussion, that is, by exoteric learning; and when the light of the truth appears, the moon, that is the science of externals, disappears." B.

[4] That is, this life is so fleeting, that things that happen are as if they happened not, and our coming is synchronous with our going.

[5] Or, "running on," يسعى ; referring to Qur. 57 : 12. "*On the day when thou shalt see believers, men and women, with their light running on before them and on their right hand,—' Glad tidings for you today : gardens beneath which rivers flow, to dwell therein for aye ; that is the grand bliss !'* " Their light is their belief in the Unity of God, which goes in front of them so that they pass easily over the bridge Ṣirāṭ, and on their right hands to guide them into Paradise. L.

[6] lit. 'the chosen', *i.e.*, Muḥammad.

[7] "Muṣṭafā said 'Well done !' in praise of that light ; through the light Moses' hand became a moon, and the Friend received the honour of '*Verily Abraham was pitiful and clement.*'" Qur. 9 : 116; 11 : 78, L. The 'light' however is not mentioned in the text. According to the Muslim theologians the 'white hand of Moses' was not due to leprosy.

majesty and beauty of his belief,[1]— then when the *wāw* goes out of *awwah* there remains but *āh*, a sigh,— how wonderful ![2] *Āh* 29
remains, a memorial of Him ; His religion remains as a manifestation of Him.[3]

Before the trumpet sounds kill thou thyself with the sword of indigence ; if they accept it,[4] thou art at rest ; if not, think of what has happened as if it had not been. If thou come small or great to the door of the Absolute,[5] or if thou come not at all, what is that to Him ? Shall the day subsist for the sake of the cock ? it will appear at its own time.[6] What is thy existence, what thy non-existence to Him ? Many like thee come to His door.

When the fountain of light[7] starts forth, it has no need of any to scourge it on ; yet all this magnificence is but water and earth,— the pure life and soul are there.[8] What can the '*Make way !*' of a

---

[1] The middle letter و of اوّاه (Ar. 'he was pitiful'), is the first of وفا, 'sincerity.'

[2] This is a kind of word-play the author is rather fond of. B carries it on thus :—"When *wāw* disappears from *awwah*, the pitiful, *i.e.*, Abraham, remains as a sigh only. We may say that this sigh, آه, is of the essence of the affirmation of the light, *i.e.*, his doctrine and belief. For when thou viewest the word آه with the eye of truth, thou seest it is composed of a single *alif*, which denotes one, without companion, and *ha*, which denotes *Hūwa*, He ; *i.e.*, there is none but He. And this is the essence of the affirmation (of belief)."

[3] V. note on previous line, the affirmation of the Unity being the essence of His religion.

[4] Gloss in B نیاز را 'thy indigence' ; or perhaps understand rather 'thy sacrifice of thyself.' 'They,' an indefinite plu., here, as often, =' the higher powers' ; or as we might say 'if heaven accepts it.'

[5] بینیازی, 'absence of dependence on anything else' ; *cf.* p. 26, ll. 18, 19, 21.

[6] That is, shall God exist for the sake of, or in dependence on, any of His creatures ? The line occurs eight lines lower in the MSS., but it evidently belongs to this argument and not to the later one.

[7] *i.e.*, the sun ; in giving as a gloss 'the light of the Essence of the One,' B seems, as often, to read mystical meanings into the text where they are not intended.

[8] There,—with God and not in material things : for ورنه in a purely adversative sense *cf.*, *inter alia*, p. 26, l. 22 ; p. 27, l. 2.

handful of straw effect? His own light alone cries '*Make way!*'[1] That lamp of thine is thy trust in thyself; the sun[2] comes forth of himself in brightness, and this flame the cold wind cannot extinguish, while half a sneeze wrests from that its life.

So then your road lies not in this street; if there be a road, it is the road of your sighs. You are all far from the road of devotion, you are like asses straying for months and years deluded with vain hopes. Since thou art sometimes virtuous, sometimes wicked, thou fearest for thyself, hast hope in thyself; but when thy face of wisdom and of shame[3] grows white,[4]—go, know thou that fear and hope are one.

On the Justice of the Prince and the Security of his Subjects.

'Umar one day saw a group of boys on a certain road all engaged in play and everyone boasting of himself; everyone was in haste to wrestle, having duly bared his head in Arab fashion.[5] When 'Umar looked towards the boys, fear of him tore the curtain of their gladness; they all fled from him in haste, except 'Abdu'l-lāh b. Zubair. 'Umar said to him, "Why didst thou not fly from before me?" He said, "Why should I fly from before thee, O beneficent one? Thou art not a tyrant, nor I guilty."

If a prince is pious and just, his people are glad in his justice; but if his inclination is towards tyranny, he plunges his country in ruin. When thou hast provisioned thyself with justice, thy steed has passed beyond both halting-places.[6]

---

1 *Cf. sup.*, p. 28, l. 19. "When the pure light of God, the Glorious, the Exalted (may my soul and my children and my life be His sacrifice!), shines, no cry of '*Make way!*' rises from us, who are a handful of base straw; it is His light that cries '*Make way!*'". B.

2 The light of His essence, B.

3 Thy face, which at present displays both these by turns.

4 سپیدرو is the equivalent of روشن رو , سرخ‌رو , نیک بخت (B.Q.); so = 'when thou findest fortune.'

5 برای خط ادب = 'in accordance with the code of propriety'? Perhaps corrupt.

6 *i.e.*, this world and the next.

What matters acceptance or rejection, good or evil, to him who knows his own virtue? Be virtuous,—thou wilt escape an aching head; if thou be bad, thou breakest the whole compact. So stand in wonder at His justice that thou losest memory of all else but of Him.[1]

On celebrating the Praise of God.[2]

To call on the name of friends, and the unhappy ones[3] of this world, how thinkest thou of it? It is like calling on old women. Oppression, if He ordain it, is all justice; a life without thought of Him is all wind. He laughs who is brought to tears through Him; but that heart is an anvil that thinks not on Him. Thou art secure when thou pronouncest His name,—thou keepest a firm footing on thy path; make thou thy tongue moist, like earth, with remembrance of Him, that He may fill thy mouth, like the rose, with gold.[4] He fills with life the soul of the wise man; the heart of the lover of self He leaves thirsty.[5] That thy purpose and judgment may be true, leave not His door at all; to pay heed to those about us[6] is the act of a thoughtless fool.

Concerning the Pious Disciple and the Great Master.

Thaurī, by way of obsequiousness and in anxiety to acquire a good reputation, asked an excellent question of Bāyazīd Bisṭāmī; weeping, he said, "O Master, tell me, who is unjust?" His master,

---

1 The lines following on the story proper seem to form two 'morals', one drawn from 'Umar's justice, and one from the boy's fearlessness, and I have rearranged them accordingly.

2 Two words signifying "to repeat *Ṣubhāna'l-lāh*, '*praise be to God*,'" and "to repeat *lā ilāha illā'l-lāh*, '*there is no God but God.*'"

3 کم سخن = 'unable to speak from emotion or grief, unhappy, unfortunate;' that is, they can do nothing to help you.

4 Referring to the yellow stamens of the wild rose.

5 B takes in an opposite sense;—"The learned worshippers of outward form and the brainless philosophers (*the mercy of God be not on them*) He has filled with thoughts of self; but the heart of the lover who seeks Him he makes thirsty" (*i.e.*, for Himself). If the second hemistich stood by itself, the rendering would be allowable; but there is an obvious antithesis, and it seems to be training the sense to take جان as 'thoughts of self,' and بپرورد in a bad sense.

6 B explains rather as 'those of lofty station.'

giving him a draught out of the law, answered him and said, "Unjust is that ill-fated one who for one moment of the day and night in
31 negligence forgets Him: he is not His submissive slave." If thou forget Him for one breath, there is none so shamelessly unjust as thou; but if thou be present[1] and commemorate His name, thy being is lost in the fulfilment of His commands.[2] So think upon Him that in thy heart and soul thou lapse not into forgetfulness even for an instant. Keep in mind this saying of that ever-watchful traveller on this road, the impetuous lion, '*And worship thou the Lord in prayer as if thou sawest Him;*'[3] and if thou do not thus, thou wilt be forced to cry '*Help, help!*' So worship Him in both worlds, as if thou sawest Him with thine outward eye; though thine eye sees Him not, thy Creator sees thee.

The commemoration of God exists only in the path of conflict; it exists not in the assembly of the contemplation:[4] though remembrance of Him be thy guide at first, in the end remembrance is naught.[5]

Inasmuch as the diver seeks pearls in the seas, it is the water too that kills his cry;[6] in absence the dove calls 'where?'—if present,

---

1 With the presence of the heart (gloss in B).

2 Thou art submerged in acquiescence in His ordinance (gloss in B).

3 حیدر کرّار, "the lion of repeated attack," is 'Alī, the fourth caliph. The saying attributed to him, which is here referred to, is, "*And worship thou thy Lord as if thou sawest Him* (کانّک تراه); *and if thou see Him not, verily He seeth thee.*" L quotes also a similar tradition of Muḥammad. The translation of the line in the text is not strictly accurate ('*and thou shalt see Him*'); since however the line is only an adaptation to metre of the tradition referred to, I have kept the original sense.

4 *i.e.*, the contemplation (in the sense of viewing, witnessing) of the divine Essence. "The calling to mind and glorifying of God exists in asceticism and struggles; it no longer exists when the advance has been made to presence and contemplation," B.

5 lit. 'wind'. "Though progress in this path is by means of memory nd glorification, yet when thou arrivest at the abode of contemplation (vision, مشاهده), memory no longer exists," B.

6 There is a play on the word آب, which is used for both 'pearls' and 'water', hence the 'too'. Thus the meaning is that the thing he seeks (آب) is the same as that (آب) which puts an end to his cries when he drowns;

why recite 'He'?[1] Those in His presence are rich in His majesty; weep thou, if absence is thy portion.

Listen to the ringdove's plaint of yearning,—two grains of barley changes it into joy; but he who seeks the only true contentment, seeks the light of the Unity in the grave.[2] To him the tomb is the garden of Paradise; heaven[3] is unlovely in his eyes. Then wilt thou be present, when in the abode of peace thou art present in soul, not in body; whilst thou art in this land of fruitless search, thou art either all back or all front;[4] but when the soul of the seeker has gone forward a few paces out of this land, love seizes the bridle.[5] Unbelief is death, religion life,—this is the pith of all that men have said.

Whoso for one moment takes delight in himself, he is imprisoned in hell and anguish for years. Who then shall have this honour and high dignity conferred upon him? Only he who possesses the princi- 32
ple of Islām; in loving, and in striving towards that world, one must not talk about one's life; those who travel on this road know nothing of grief for life and sorrow of soul. When thou hast passed out of this world of fruitless search, then seek thou in that the fountain of life.

Concerning the House of Deception.

Death[6] comes as the key of the house of the Secret; without death the door of true religion opens not. While this world stays, that is not; while thou existest, God is not thine. Know, thy soul is

---

so the seeker crying out after God, is ultimately silenced by what he seeks for,—*i.e.*, when he arrives at the contemplation of the Essence.

[1] کو *Kū*, (= 'where ?') also represents the sound made by the dove. The implication is as before; religious exercises have no meaning in the presence and vision of God.

[2] 'The dove's plaint of love, which is a matter of mimicry, is like the discussions of the philosophers, and not worth two grains of barley; but the plaint of the perfect knower of God is the utterance of the saying "*Die ye before your death*," B.

[3] *i.e.*, the heaven of common opinion.

[4] *i.e.*, the bodily presence is never complete; thou canst not show more than one side, be present with more than one side of thyself, to anyone at one time.

[5] *i.e.*, takes possession of and guides it.

[6] *i.e.*, the annihilation of one's self, not death as commonly spoken of, L.

a sealed casket; the love-pearl within is the light of thy faith.[1] The Past sealed the writing, and delivered it for thee to the Future; as long as thou shalt depend for thy life upon the revolutions of Time, thou shalt not know what is inside. Only the hand of death shall unloose the binding of the book[2] of God, the Exalted, the Glorious. So long as the breath of man flies not from thee, the morning of thy true faith will not dawn in thy soul's East.

Thou wilt not reach the door of the King's pavilion without experiencing the heat and cold of the world: at present thou knowest naught of the invisible world, canst not distinguish faults from virtues; the things of that world are not those of sense, are not like the other things of wont. The soul reaches His presence, and is at rest; and what is crooked then is seen to be straight.

When thou arrivest in the presence of the decree[3] the soul sets forth, and like a bird leaves its cage for the garden; the horse of religion becomes familiar with the verdant meadow.[4] Whilst thou livest true religion appears not; the night of thy death brings forth its day. On this subject a man of wisdom, whose words are as a mufti's decision,[5] said, "Through desire and transgression men have gone to sleep; when death shows his face, they awake." All the people of this world are asleep, all are living in a vicious world: the desire that goes beyond this[6] is use and custom, and not religion;

---

1 مُهرَهٔ 'a small shell or pearl used as a philtre by women.'

2 The *iẓāfat* required here by the sense and inserted in several MSS. must be omitted in scansion.

3 The decree of death; the commentators refer to Qur. 89, 28 sq. "*O thou comforted soul! return unto thy Lord, well pleased and well pleased with. And enter amongst my servants and enter my Paradise.*"

4 Reversing in the translation the order of the hemistichs.

5 The reference is to 'Alī, one of whose reputed sayings, "*Men are asleep, and when they die, they awake,*" is copied from a tradition of Muḥammad, L.

6 *i.e.*, perhaps, 'the desire to find more in this world than a vicious place'; but the next line begins with ورنه 'but, on the other hand,' *cf.* p. 26, l. 22; p. 27, l. 2; the sense however is parallel and allows of no adversative meaning. A change in the position of the negative particle (رسم و عادت نه بود دین باشد or رسم و عادت نبُوَد که دین باشد) would give the adversative sense:—"the desire that goes beyond this (present world) is not (mere) custom and use,—it is true religion; but the religion which is only of this life . . . ."

for the religion which is only of this life is not religion, but empty 33
trifling.

To knock at the door of non-existence is religion and fortune ; knocking little comes of being little.[1] He who esteems of small account the substance of this world, say to him, " Look thou on Muṣṭafā and Adam" ;[2] and he who seeks for increase, say to him, " Look thou on 'Ād and on Qārūn ;[3] the foot of the one clave to his stirrup, the other lived pierced through with terror ; the Eternal destroyed the foot of the one ;[4] remorse turned the hand of the other into a reed ; the dire blast falls on 'Ād, the dust of execration is the abode of Qārūn.

What harm is it, if from fear of misfortune thou sacrifice thyself like wild rue for the sake of virtue ?[5] Inflame not thy cheek before[6] the men of the Path ; burn thyself, like wild rue ; thou hast the wisdom and religion of a fool if thou pretendest to eminence before God. Let not man weave a net about himself ; rather the lion will break his cage.[7]

---

1 *i.e.*, being weak and worthless, B.

2 *i.e.*, " thou shalt see the essential perfections of Muḥammad and Adam ; for the former constitutes the ultimate stage in the knowledge of the secrets of God, and the latter was the first receptacle of prophecy and the divine light and mysteries, and was the reason for the creation of the phenomenal world ; and both were elected to honour from their holding of small account the substance of the world." So B, who does not seem very sure of his exegetical effort, as he adds " *And God knows best.*" There is a play upon words, کم زدن being both ' to knock little,' and ' to esteem of small account.'

3 According to B the reference is to Shaddād, son of 'Ād ; who " ordered the construction of a terrestrial paradise in the desert of 'Adan (Aden), ostensibly to rival the celestial one, and to be called Iram after his great grandfather. On going to take possession of it, he and all his people were struck dead by a noise from heaven, and the paradise disappeared " (Hughes, Dict. of Islam s.v. Iram). Qārūn is the Korah of the Bible, who was swallowed up in the earth ; to Muslims he is the type of a rich man ; Sanā'i seems to refer to some further tradition about him.

4 By hamstringing (gloss in B).

5 سپند — wild rue, of which, and of its seeds, a fumigation against malignant eyes is prepared (Stein.). گزند — misfortune, and, specially, a fatal misfortune in consequence of witchcraft (*ib.*).

6 *i.e.*, associate not with nor pretend to equality with, B.

7 The ' lion ' is the ' man of the Path ' (gloss in B).

O thou, who art sated with thyself,[1]—that is hunger ; and thou, who bendest double in penitence,—that is prayer.[2] When thou art freed from thine own body and soul, then thou findest isolation[3] and eminence. Display not at all thy city-inflaming countenance ; when thou hast done so, go, burn wild rue.[4] What is that beauty of thine ?[5] it is thy lust ; and what is thy wild rue ? it is thine own being. When thy lip touches the threshold of true religion, Jesus, son of Mary, becomes thy sleeve.[6] In this quest do thou melt thyself ; adventure thy life and soul in the path of fidelity ; strive thou, that so through non-existence thou mayest pass to existence ;[7] that thou mayest be drunk with the wine of God. The ball and stick[8] of the universe are in the hand of him whom true religion makes to live ;[9]

---

1 *i.e.*, to leave oneself, turn away from oneself, B. ; and so to hunger for God. It would perhaps be equally permissible to take سیر in its primary meaning of 'full.' "O thou, who art full of self,—that is hunger," *i.e.*, really emptiness. *Cf.* p. 30, l. 15.

2 رکوع the inclinations of the body performed in the recital of prayers.

3 *i.e.*, distinction (gloss in L).

4 *Cf.* note, l. 8, *ant.*

5 *i.e.*, what do I mean by thy face which rouses the city to enthusiasm ? "Thy city-inflaming countenance is the sum-total of bodily existence (حقیقت جامعهٔ انسانی) ; or it may be actual beauty (جمال حال)," L. B however having paraphrased L's note (substituting 'external beauty and grace' حسن و لطافت ظاهری for جمال حال) proceeds, "And what is that world-adorning beauty ? it is thy desire towards God. And what is that wild rue ? it is the annihilation of thy own existence." In thus explaining مستی, 'lust,' by 'desire towards God,' he is, as it seems to me, at variance both with the more evident sense of the passage, and also with L's note which he had before him ; being led thereto perhaps by the occurrence of مست a few lines lower in a mystical sense ('intoxicated with the wine of God'). If the meaning of مستی as 'the bewilderment of the Ṣūfī in the contemplation of God' be adopted, the sense would then be "Make not a parade of thy ecstasies, of thy esoteric knowledge."

6 *i.e.*, subsidiary in position to thee.

7 "When thou hast passed through the stage of annihilation in God, thou existest externally in the Absolute Essence, which is not liable to destruction," B.

8 The implements of a game resembling polo.

9 On the plain of Love the ball and stick of the universe, that is all powers in their perfection, fall into his hand whose existence is in the Absolute Essence." B.

when thy soul becomes drunk with this draught, thou hast reached the summit; from being naught thou comest into existence.

Every freed man of that place is a slave, bound by the foot, with a ring in his ear;[1] but those bonds are better than the steed of fortune; but that ring is better than the striped garments of Arabia and a throne. The bonds that He imposes, account a crown; and if He 34
gives thee sackcloth, reckon it brocade;[2] for He bestows benefits, and He gives beauty; He is kind, and He is bounteous.

Seeing that thou art needy, what dost thou with Gladness, and what with Cleverness, both bought with a price?[3] Be glad in Him, and clever in His religion, that thou mayest find acceptance and honour with Him. That man is wise whom He lifts up; joyful is he whom He abandons not; and fortunate, who is His slave, approved by Him in all his works. When thou hast cast these branches,[4] and hast grappled with death, thou wilt no longer turn away from death, and shalt come to know the world of Life. When thy hand reaches the branch of death,[5] thy foot treads the palace of power;[6] the foot which is far from the dome of right guidance is not a foot,—it is a drunken brain.[7]

On Giving Thanks.

Ingratitude's only seat is the door of sorrow; thankfulness arrives with certainty at the treasure.[8] Utter thy thanks for the sake of increase, of the hidden world, and of the sight of God; then when

---

1 "He who is a freed man of the court of Glory is bound by command and prohibition in the world of acquiescence and resignation, which is the highest degree attainable by His chosen servants," B.

2 دواج 'a bed-quilt, sheet'; but B, "a doubled sheet of brocade."

3 "Thou who art given in pledge to poverty and indigence,—what art thou doing with <u>Sh</u>ādī, and what with *Zīrak*; for these two are slaves bought with thy money. Slaves are often called <u>Sh</u>ādī and *Zīrak*," B. (*Zīrak*, lit. 'clever,' not 'cleverness.')

4 The concerns that attach us to this world, B.

5 *i.e.*, annihilation (gloss in B).

6 *i.e.*, eternal life (gloss in B).

7 *i.e.*, feeble and powerless (gloss in L).

8 Referring to Qur. 14 : 7. "*When your Lord proclaimed, 'If ye give thanks I will surely give you increase; but if ye misbelieve, verily, my torment is severe.'*" L.

thou hast become patient of His decree He will name thee 'giver of thanks'; whoso presses forwards towards God, speaks not without uttering his thanks to God.[1] Who can tell the sweetness of giving thanks to Him ?[2] Who can pierce the pearl of the celebration of His name ? He bestows, and He gives the reward; He speaks, and He imparts the answer.[3] Whatsoever He took away from thee of kindness or show of love, the same or more than that He gives back to thee.[4] If every hair became a tongue, and each an interpreter at thanksgiving's door to swell thereby His thanks, they could not utter due thanks for the divine grace of the power to give thanks.

Then let men seek to give thanks for His mercies; if they utter them, it is even through Him they do so,—body and soul drunk with His decree, the heart singing "*O Lord, thanks!*" And if not, then as far as regards the path of knowledge and prudence, woman and man, young and old, are blind of eye in the world of lust, are naked of body like ants and flies.

On His Wrath and His Kindness.

The pious are those who give thanks for His kindness and mercy, the unbelievers those who complain of His wrath and jealousy. When

---

[1] The MSS. here insert two lines:—

اوست بی شکل و جسم و هفت وچهار   ایزد فرد و خالق جبّار

شکل و جسم و طبائع و تبدیل   آدمي راست سال و ماه عدیل

"He is without form or body, is not dependent on the seven (planets) and the four (elements), the one God, the all-powerful Creator; form, body, the humours, their changes, all balancing each other for months and years, belong but to man." The lines are, apparently, part of a passage on God's absoluteness, and have wrongly found a place here.

[2] Most MSS. have که داند رُفت, which is obviously wrong. M alone has که داند کفت; Dr. Ross has very kindly informed me that this is also the reading of the Calcutta Madrasah MS., and has thus removed the very considerable doubt which would have attached to the reading if adopted on M's authority alone.

[3] *i.e.*, as B explains, He by His grace bestows the power of giving thanks, and then rewards thee for giving thanks; He speaks that which thou utterest, that is, causes thee to speak, and Himself answers.

[4] Referring to Qur. 2 : 100. "*Whatever verse we may annul or cause thee to forget, we will bring a better one than it, or one like it.*"

God becomes angry, thou seest in the eyes what is rightly in the spring.[1] His wrath and His kindness, appearing in the newly-formed world, are the cause of the error of the Guebre and the doubt of the Magian.[2] His kindness and His wrath are imprinted on the pulpit and the gallows ; the rendering of thanks to Him is the mansion of honour, and forgetfulness[3] of Him, of disgrace. His kindness is comfort for men's lives, His wrath a fire for their souls ; His kindness rejoices the slave ; His wrath makes man its mock. When the *lām* of His kindness shows itself, the *dāl* of fortune gains the victory ;[4] if the *qāf* of His wrath[5] rushes forth, it melts Mount Qāf like silver. The whole world dreads His anger and His subtlety ; the virtuous and the ungodly are alike in their terror. When His kindness mixes the draught of exhilaration, the shoe of the Ṣūfī mounts to ecstasy ; when His wrath comes forth again, ecstasy draws in its head like a tortoise. His wrath melts even His beloved ; His kindness cherishes the beggar. He it is who nourishes thy soul in unbelief or in the faith, He who gives thy soul the power of choice. Thy life's soul lives through His kindness ; for by His kindness thy life endures.

By His disposing wrath and kindness He brings to life the dead, to death the living ; His wisdom cares for the slave, His favour accomplishes our undertakings. When His wrath came forth in conflict, it killed the country's king by means of an impotent gnat.[6] Then

---

1 *i.e.*, water. The periphrasis is in order to play upon the words ; " thou seest in the *chashm* what is rightly in the *chashma*."

2 The purpose of this line is to refute the error of the Guebre and the doubt of the Magian, the false opinion of which two erring sects is that good comes from God (Yazdān) and evil from Ahrimān. But God's attributes of wrath and kindness, appearing in the newly-formed world, will account for the origin of good and evil ; and Guebre and Magian forget that the world is the theatre of all the names and attributes of God, the origin of good being in the name " the Kind " and of evil in " the Avenging." L.

3 سکر بمعنی غفلت B.

4 *Lām*, the initial letter of *luṭf*, 'kindness' ; *dāl*, the initial letter of *daulat*, 'fortune.'

5 *Qāf*, the initial letter of *qahr*, 'wrath.'

6 *Lit.* 'a lame, maimed gnat.' The reference is to Nimrod ; when Nimrod waged war against Abraham, God "plagued those who adhered to him by swarms of gnats, which destroyed almost all of them ; and one of these gnats having entered into the nostril, or ear, of Nimrod, penetrated to one of the membranes of

when He saddled the horse of kindness, he caused the food of worms to gather locusts ; through God he abode in wisdom and right counsel,—
36 the worms were silver, the locusts gold ;[1] and as in the midst of God's favour he suffered a proving trial, when again in favour he laughed at his misfortunes. When His wrath spreads the snare, He turns the form of Bil'ām into a dog ;[2] when His kindness worked, He brought the dog of the Companions of the Cave into the cavern.[3] The magicians through His kindness exclaimed "*No harm*" ;[4] His wrath caused 'Azāzīl to say, "*I am better.*"[5]

With God no good and no evil has power ;[6] with whom[7] can it be said that there exists no one else in the world ? No matter whether small or great, His wrath and His kindness reach everyone

---

his brain, where growing bigger every day, it gave him such intolerable pain that he was obliged to cause his head to be beaten with a mallet, in order to procure some ease ; which torture he suffered four hundred years ; God being willing to punish by one of the smallest of his creatures him who insolently boasted himself to be lord of all." (Hughes, Dict. of Islām, s.v. Nimrod.)

1 Referring to Job, who was reduced to poverty and on whose body worms fed. At last he was restored to health, riches were given him beyond what he possessed before, the barley and wheat in his granaries became gold and silver, golden locusts rained upon his house ; the worms which fell out of his body became silkworms, and the flies which had settled on him became honey-bees. L.

2 Qur. 7 : 174-5. "*Read to them the declaration of him to whom we brought our signs, and who stepped away therefrom, and Satan followed him, and he was of those who were beguiled. Had we pleased we would have exalted him thereby, but he crouched upon the earth and followed his lust, and his likeness was as the likeness of a dog, whom if thou shouldst attack he hangs out his tongue, or if thou shouldst leave him, hangs out his tongue, too.*" The verses are referred to others besides Balaam.

3 And endowed it with human characters; v. Qur. 18, and for the Christian tradition, Gibbon's Decline and Fall, chap. xxxiii.

4 Qur. 26 : 49-50. Pharaoh's magicians repented on seeing Moses' miracles, whereupon Pharoah said, "*I will surely cut off your hands and your feet from opposite sides, and I will crucify you all together !*" *They said,* "*No harm ; verily unto our Lord do we return !*"

5 Qur. 38 : 77. When the angels were commanded to adore the newly created man, Iblīs refused, and on being asked the reason, *Said he,* "*I am better than he ; Thou hast created me from fire, and him thou hast created from clay.*"

6 Gloss in B. (on بس), بسنده و کافی, 'effective, effectual' ; *i.e.*, God is uninfluenced by the good or harm that men do.

7 *i.e.*, except Him.

alike. Emperors humble themselves[1] on His path, heroes bow down their heads at His door; kings are as dust before His door, Pharaohs fly in terror from before Him. By means of a Turkish demon, a slave just bought, He overthrew a hundred thousand standards of war;[2] while yet he had no more than a couple of retainers, he folded up the carpet of a hungry band.[3]

If He says to the dead, Come forth, the dead comes forth, dragging his winding-sheet behind him; and if He says to the living, Die, he dies on the spot, though he be a prince. The people are proud of heart through His kindness; because of the respite He gives them they fear not at all; but whoso manifests presumption in His kingdom has broken away from the straight road. His poison shall be the sufficient food of the champions, His wrath an adequate bridle for the haughty; He has broken the necks of heroes by His wrath; to the weak He has given a double share of His kindness. The quickness of His forgiveness obliterates the marks of our pleading from the path of speech; He gives shelter to him who repents of his sin, and cleanses his pages of the crime; His forgiveness outruns the fault,—"*My mercy outstrips*" is a wonderful saying.[4] He is

---

[1] کله بازان with gloss in B خاشع. *Lit.* 'lose their tiaras at play.'

[2] Referring to Amīr Naṣīru'd-Dīn Sabuktagīn, whom Naṣr Ḥajī, the merchant, brought to Bukhārā from Turkistān, and who was bought by Alptagīn the chamberlain and slave of Aḥmad b. Ismā'īl Sāmānī. After Alptagīn's death the people of Ghaznī made him their governor in A.H. 365. He conquered Bust (Qandahār) in 367; and having seized Qaṣdār he died on the road to Balkh in 375; Mahmud of Ghaznī was his son.

[3] Neither reading nor meaning is clear. L, reading زان یکی دوتا, says, "At a time when his servants had not increased from one to two, he alone rolled up the carpet of a hungry multitude, *i.e.*, folded up the carpet of poverty of a hungry band, and brought them to wealth and fortune; which is a result of the kindness of God." B interprets "folded up the carpet of a hungry band" as "turned a world upside down"; but مشتی, *lit.* 'handful,' implies fewness.

In B's text there occurs here a line, not in the others,—

از پی لطف و غایت کرمش   کرده بر اوج آیت کرمش

"Of His kindness and exceeding mercy He has placed in the zenith the sign of His clemency."

[4] Referring to the tradition "*As he has said, my mercy outstrips my anger.*" B.

the giver of the soul; not, as we are, a creature to whom a soul is given; He holds up the veil, He does not tear it as we do.[1] He is thy shepherd, and thou choosest the wolf; He invites thee, and thou remainest in want; He is thy guardian, and thou thyself carest not;
37 O well done, thou senseless sinning fool! He reforms our nature within us; kinder than ourselves is He to us; mothers have not for their children such love as He bestows. The worthless He makes worthy by His kindness; from His servants He accepts thankfulness and patience as sufficient.[2] His beneficence has shut the door of sense against the eye of wisdom and uprightness, and opened to it the path of the spirit.[3]

Since His clemency has established thee [4] thou art secure against the plunderers; [5] the mountain-dweller ever escapes in the plain the affliction of the north-east wind.[6] Though invisible to us, He knows our faults; [7] His pardon can wash them away. His knowledge has concealed our imperfection; the secret thou hast not yet spoken,

---

1 Referring to the name of God *as-Sattār*, 'the Veiler (of sin).' B.

2 "As recompense for His kindness He only requires thankfulness for benefits and patience in affliction." B.

3 "Human reason cannot comprehend the perfection of the essential beneficence of the Bountiful; and because the door of the senses is closed against the eye of knowledge and uprightness, it cannot thus acquire the comprehension of His beneficence; but to that eye the path of the spirit is opened, *i.e.*, the inward mode of existence is placed within the reach of the reasonable soul; which mode of existence is obtained only by him who is single of eye and of heart, who exists every moment in contemplation of the world of thanksgiving; and to exist thus is the perfection of the spirit of the knowers and the saints and the prophets." B.

4 *i.e.*, made firm thy foot in the path of acquiescence and resignation. B.

5 *i.e.*, carnal desires, the wiles of the devil, and the things of the world of sense. B.

6 نکبا 'an oblique wind, harsh and rough, which rises from the north-east.' B.; who also names the other oblique winds, S.W., S.E., N.W. Stein. (Dict.) however gives نکبا as a general name for a wind blowing obliquely, and names the N.E. الصّابیه. B, reading مرد کوئی, 'the townsman,' adds, "When a man comes out of the street and market into the open plain he escapes the torment of the whirlwind and the *nakbā*:" though to our ideas it would seem that he was more fully exposed to both.

7 *lit.* 'His absence, or invisibility, knows our faults.'

He has heard. The sons of men, ever unjust and ignorant,[1] talk in folly of God's kindness ; He works good, and ye work evil : He knows the hidden things, and ye are full of fault. Behold, after thy so many doubts, this care of the Knower of the hidden for a wicked world ; had it not been pure favour on His part, how could a handful of earth have come to wear a crown ?

The alighting-place of His pardon is on the plain of sin, the army of His kindness comes out to meet our sighs ; when the sigh of the knower of God raises the veil,[2] hell seizes its shield from fear of Him. His forgiveness grants itself to our sins ; His mercy descends to bestow benefits.[3] Thou hast committed the iniquity, yet He keeps faith with thee ; He is more true to thee than thou art to thyself. His bounty brought thee into activity ; otherwise how could this market have been set up on earth ?[4] Whoso becomes non-existent, to him is given existence ; whoso slips receives a helping hand. He it is who takes the hand of the friendless, and chooses weeds like us.[5] Forasmuch as He is pure, He desires the pure ; the Knower of the hidden desires the dust.[6]

On His Omniscience, and His Knowledge of the Minds of Men.[7]

He knows the draught of each of His creatures ; He has given it, and He can give its opposite. He is the Creator of thy wisdom ; **38**

---

[1] B compares Qur. 33 : 72. " *Verily he* (man) *is ever unjust and ignorant.*"

[2] *i.e.*, perhaps, ' causes God to come forth and manifest Himself in power.'

[3] Or perhaps, more literally, " His forgiveness possesses the faculty of favourable reception on account of our sins ; His mercy possesses the faculty of descending in order that it may bestow benefits.'

[4] The ' market ' is the human body. " Brought thee into activity," *i.e.*, caused thee to exist.

[5] B reading, as most do, a negative, —" those who are vile like us He chooses not "—says, " He does not choose dogs like us, who derive their power as individuals from the sensual savours of this house of deception ; but He chooses him whose individuality has no other friend but God's essence, and who in his friendless state desires no one else." The tenor of the passage, however, is in the opposite sense, and the positive is supported by H and M.

[6] " Since a substance becomes not pure till it has been burnt and turned to ashes, He the pure, who will only have the pure, seeks only the dust." B.

[7] The order of the verses of this chapter varies in the various MSS. ; none, however, gives a logical sequence, and I have not been able to adopt the order of any single MS.

but His wisdom is untainted by the passage of thought.[1] He knows concerning thee what is in thy heart, for He is the Creator both of thy heart and of thy clay. Dost thou think that He knows as thou knowest ? then is the ass of thy nature stuck fast in thy clay.[2] He sees what is best for His creatures before the desire is formed ; He knows the mind before the secret thought exists. He knows what is in thy heart ; before thou speakest He performs the work. God brings joy and takes away sorrow ; God knows our secrets, and He keeps them safe.

Silence before Him is the gift of tongues ;[3] thy life's food thou receivest from a table bare of bread ; man's desire cannot wish for such things as He has prepared for him.[4] He knows the condition of His creatures ; He sees it, and can give accordingly ; He has prepared for thee thy place in Paradise, that to-morrow thou mayest enter into joy.[5] It is enough that He speaks,—be thou dumb and speak not ; it is enough that He seeks, remain thou a cripple, and run not to and fro.[6] In presence of the power and omniscience of God, feebleness and ignorance are best ; feebleness makes thee wise, weakness confers eminence on thee.

---

1 "His wisdom does not, like ours, depend on what occurs in the mind ; for mind has its place in the system of the elements and of matter, not in the essence of the Ineffable and Inscrutable ; for cogitation has no place with Him." B.

2 "If thou hast this idea thou wilt never get onto the road." B.

3 The implication being, apparently, that there is no need of prayer for material blessings.

4 L refers to the tradition of Muḥammad, "*Eye hath not seen, nor ear heard, nor hath it entered the heart of man.*"

5 An alternative reading might be rendered, "See to it that thou hast joined tomorrow with to-day ;" *i.e.*, prepare to-day for the judgment day (tomorrow).

6 "Since He, who speaks to thee, is all-knowing, thou needest not to speak to Him of thy desire. And since He in mercy seeks to forgive and spare thee, and the services He has commanded He has commanded only that thou mayest justify His mercy to thee ; and since it is certain that thou canst arrive nowhere without His generosity, do not let thy search for the things of the external world enter in between thee and thy union with thy desire ; but rely thou on His desire and love for thee. When thou abandonest the search for externalities, and enterest the stage of resignation, and givest thyself up to Him, He will be sufficient as a searcher." L.

Whoso can make existence non-existent, can also change non-existence into existence. He in His mercy arrests the rhythmical forces in the wombs for the due constituting and establishing of the offspring ;[1] and forasmuch as His inscrutability pourtrayed thy form, knowest thou not that thou canst not remain hidden ?[2] He knows thy case better than thyself ; why frequentest thou the neighbourhood of folly and deceit ? Speak not of thy heart's sorrow, for He is speaking ; seek thou not for Him, for He is seeking.[3]

He perceives the touch of an ant's foot, though in night and darkness the ant move on a rock ;[4] if a stone moves in the dark night in the depth of the water, His knowledge sees it ; if there be a worm in the heart of a rock, whose body is smaller than an atom, God by His knowledge knows its cry of praise, and its hidden secret. To thee He has given guidance in the path ; to the worm He has given its
sustenance in the rock. No soul has ever rested in patience apart 39
from Him ; no understanding deceived Him by its subtlety. He is ever aware of the minds of men,—ponder thou this, and thy duty is fulfilled.

---

[1] مُتَقاضی is "a dun, a person who exacts a debt ; importunate." Here the idea is that of recurrence, a recurrent force. L wanders into medical details ; but errs, I think, in taking قائم کردن as 'establish' ; for the establishment of a regularly recurring force would not tend to the formation and constituting of the developing organism ; on the contrary, the suspension of active movements in the womb is what is required,—a period of rest for the undisturbed development of the offspring. The arrest, during pregnancy, of the expulsive action of the womb as regards menstruation, was probably present in Sanā'ī's mind.

[2] L prefers a different interpretation : "inasmuch as His inscrutability has pourtrayed thy form, knowest thou not that thou canst not contain Inscrutability in the compass of thy comprehension ? For the picture can by no means know the nature of the artist, nor can what it comprehends contain the artist." In view of the next line, however, the translation given seems the better.

[3] *Cf. sup.* l. 11.

[4] "So small a thing as an ant, on an unimpressible mass like a rock," B. "A denial of the doctrine of the philosophers, who say that God knows the parts by the way of the whole, not particularly ; the truth, however, is that He knows the parts as parts,—"*nor does the weight of an atom escape thy Lord in earth or in heaven; nor is there less than that nor greater, but it is in the perspicuous Book*" (Qur. 10 : 63). L.

If thou turn thy face from evil usage,[1] thy mind shall preserve the true religion of Islām; but since thou choosest to hold false ideas of His clemency, thou shalt have no light, but hell-fire in thy heart; for since thou wilt not take account of His knowledge, O man, cherish no hope of clemency from Him.[2] His omniscience kindles the lamp of the understanding; but His clemency teaches nature to sin;[3] were not His clemency a perpetual refuge, how could a servant dare to sin?[4]

If then thou committest a sin, that sin falls under one of two cases; if thou thinkest that God knows not, I say to thee, Well done,[5] O thorough-going infidel! and if thou thinkest that God knows, and still thou committest it,—Bravo, impudent one, and vile! Myself I acknowledge that no man knows thy secrets; God knows,—God is not less than man;[6] and I take it that if He hides this forgiveness from thee, is it not that His omniscience knows that it is thus with thee? Then turn from this vile conduct of thine; otherwise on the day of thy resurrection thou wilt forthwith see thyself drowning in the sea of thy shame.

Concerning His Beneficence,—and verily He is the Provider of Provisions.

When He lays the table of its food before the creature, He provides a fare more ample than the eater's needs; life and days and daily food come to all from Him; happiness and fortune are from Him. He supplies the daily bread of each, nor seals the door of the

---

1 آئین here of mode of belief.

2 "To take account of His knowledge is to hold Him in truth the knower of all secrets; and if one does so, one may hope for His mercy. For to hold Him omniscient is to fear Him, and to fear Him makes thee the recipient of His mercy." B.

3 Apparently—"His omniscience, if reflected on, will kindle . ."; so B, "when thou fully understandest His omniscience, the lamp of the understanding becomes bright; but if thou hast no knowledge of His omniscience, and reliest on His clemency, and hast abandoned thy fear of God, thou becomest persistent in sin (ابرام بگناه رفت) and hast lost thy place."

4 "This confidence in His clemency springs from the servants not understanding His omniscience and not fearing Him." B.

5 Ironically; gloss in B. اینست *i.e.*, "this is a thorough-going..."

6 *i.e.*, is greater, and therefore knows.

storehouse ; infidel and true believer, wretched and prosperous,—to all their daily food and life renewed. While the *Ḥā* of necessity [1] is still in their throat, the *Jīm* of His munificence [2] has given His creatures their sustenance. Except by bread we cannot live, and appetite is our only relish ; He shuns not His servants when they turn to Him,—He has given the relish, He will give the bread too.

Thy bread and life are in the treasury of God ; thou dost not hold, according to His word, that it is He.[3] If thy daily bread be in China, thy horse of acquisition is ready saddled to bear thee speedily to it, or to bring it to thee whilst thou art sleeping.[4] Has He not said to thee, I am thy Sustainer, the Knower of what is hidden and the Knower of what is manifest ; I gave life, I give the means of livelihood ; whatsoever thou askest, I give forthwith ? Know that, like the day, the matter of thy daily bread is well assured, for thy daily bread is a present which the day brings with it; forasmuch as the kindness of God is on thee, thou holdest thy life as a pledge for thy food. Take thought for thy life, and thou hast done the same for thy bread ; loaf succeeds loaf as far as the edge of the grave. Hold firmly to this pledge, and eat thy bread ;[5] and when the pledge passes from thee, still shalt thou eat the food of Life.[6] Life without bread God gave to none, for life endures through bread ; and when life quits the body, know for a certainty that now indeed sustenance has reached thee.[7]

The ignoble fear for their daily bread ; the generous man does not eat his food warmed up a second time. The lion eats not his prey

---

1 حاجت *ḥājat*, 'necessity, need'; of which *ḥā* is the initial letter. This being a guttural, pronounced (unlike the soft aspirate) deep in the throat, the hemistich has, as B notes, a peculiar aptness.

2 جود *jūd*, 'munificence'; of which *jīm* is the initial letter.

3 *i.e.*, bread and life are given to thee from God's treasury ; yet wilt thou not believe, as His word says, that He is the giver.

4 *i.e.*, God creates means by which thou mayest obtain thy daily food, wherever it may be. B.

5 *Cf.* l. 7, *sup.*

6 *i.e.*, in the upper world.

7 *i.e.*, thy true spiritual food (gloss in B), *cf.* l. 9, *sup.* Life is always maintained by food, whether the life in the body or out of it.

alone ; when he is satisfied, he abandons the rest.[1] It is for women to hoard up the old ; to men new sustenance with the new day.[2] Thy daily bread is a charge on the All-knowing and All-powerful,—be not angry against prince or minister ; it comes from God's door, and not by teeth or throat or pipe.[3]

The lordship of a house is a lordship with sorrow, especially for him who has no wealth or treasure ; the lordship of a house is all sorrow and desire,—leave aside the *house*, and *God* is sufficient for thee.[4] Let thy trust at all times be on God, rather than on mill and sack; for if the clouds give thee no water for a year, I foresee that thy affairs will be altogether ruined.[5]

A Story.

An old man put forth his head, and seeing his field dried up
41 spoke thus :—" O Lord of both new and old,[6] our food is in Thy
hands, do what thou wilt. The sustenance Thou givest to fair
and foul depends not on tears of cloud nor smiles of field; I well know
Thou art the Uncaused Sustainer ;[7] my life and my food, all comes
from Thee. Thy one is better than thousands of thousands, for Thy
little is not a little."

---

1 *Sc.* to others, and does not save it up ; the lion being a type of nobility.

2 *Lit.* " to women the old, fold on fold." " The men of the Path, who are the men of wisdom (the Knowers), every day make new progress in acquisitions and struggles and austerity, which are their daily food ; while it is for women to gather up and watch over fragments." So B (illustrating his tendency to read mystical meanings where they are not intended).

3 " Not from our teeth that (showing them) we should importune others ; or throat, that we should cry out at men's doors ; nor in anyone's face that we should fall to lamentation (به نای و نالۀ در افتیم) " B. It would seem, however, that ' teeth ' is used rather in reference to the teeth of wild animals, by which they seize their food ; ' throat,' as B, to calling aloud on others ; and ' pipe ' is perhaps the pipe of the dervishes, and so means beggary.

4 *Kadkhudā'ī*, ' the lordship of a house,' splits up, according to its derivation, into *kad*, ' house,' and *Khudāy*, ' a lord, God.'

5 *i.e.*, in case thou dependest on mills and sacks.

6 آن بمعنی مالک gloss in B. That is, ' Lord of all.'

7 Rain, etc., is not the ultimate cause of our sustenance ; the ultimate cause is Thou, who art uncaused.

A flame from Him, and a hundred thousand stars appear; a drop from Him, and a hundred thousand palm-trees spring up.[1] He who is in fear about his daily food is not a man,—truly he is less than a woman.

A STORY.

Hast thou not heard how in a rainless time some birds received their food from a Magian's door? Many Muslims spoke to him, and among them one clever and eloquent—"Though the little birds take your corn, yet this generosity of yours will not find acceptance." Said the Magian, "If He does not choose me, still He sees my toil; since He himself is kind and generous, He does not think the same of niggardliness as of liberality."

Ja'far[2] sacrificed his arm in His Path; instead of arms God gave him wings. None shall discover thy work but God; truly nothing can happen to thee from men. Pay no heed to the doing and bustling of men; fasten thy mind on Him, and thou hast escaped from sorrow and bondage. So far as thou canst, take thou no friend but Him; take men not into thy account at all. Your bread is laid up in God's eternity; His friendship He gives you,—it is your life; know that both of these are represented in the world of love and search by the Persian *water* and the Arabic *father*.[3]

---

[1] اخضر *lit.*, 'green.' B supposes it to refer to rivers.

[2] Ja'far was Muḥammad's cousin, the son of Abu Ṭālib and brother of 'Alī. On the death of Zaid during the battle of Mūta A.H. 8 he took command of the force, and hamstringing his horse fought till he too fell. Muhammad is reported to have said, "I saw Ja'far as an angel with two wings, covered with blood, his limbs stained therewith." Hence Ja'far is known as 'the winged martyr.' *Cf.* Muir, Life of Mahomet, 3rd ed., p. 383.

[3] The line is obscure to me, nor can I derive much illumination from the commentators. 'Water' in Pers. is *āb*, and 'father' in Ar. is *ab*, words which differ only in the quantity of the *alif*. B says, "Although they differ in meaning, yet in nature and pronunciation (? they are the same, and) by any means of arrangement to take away *alif* from the words referred to is impossible; so there is also a relation between the *alif* of *ālā* (favours, l. 17) and your life (*jān*), which is indissoluble and indestructible; while life lasts God gives His favours." Similarly L, whom B has imitated and expanded; both mention the possibility of *āb* referring to the semen (*cf.* Qur. 86: 5 sqq.).

[On the Desire for God.[1]]

So long as thou art a stranger to the light of Moses,[2] thou art blind to the day, like the bird of Jesus;[3] since thou hast no knowledge of the path of poverty, thou art in hiding, like the inside of an onion.[4] First, for the sake of His comforting love, do thou make thy head thy foot,
42 like the reed,[5] and continue seeking Him; that by thy perfect search thou mayest reach that place, where thou knowest thou needest seek no more.

Did not an indolent one, when he heard murmurs of sloth on his heart's tongue, ask 'Alī, "Say, O Prince, illuminer of the soul, is the dark night better, or the day?"[6] Murtaẓā[7] said, "Hear, O questioner; yield not to this backsliding; for to the lovers in this soul-inflaming path the fire of the secret is better than the splendour of the day."[8] He whose soul the path has fired stays not behind on foot at the halting-place;[9] in that world where love tells the secret, *thou* no longer art, thy reason no longer endures.

On Affection and Isolation.[10]

The lovers are drunk in His Presence, their reason in their sleeve

---

[1] There is no indication of the beginning of a fresh chapter here in any of the MSS. The subject of the following verses, however, is different, and we seem here to begin a fresh section of the book.

[2] The desire to see God which burned in Moses, B.

[3] The bat; *cf.* Qur. 3 : 43. One of Jesus's miracles was the creation of a living bird out of clay; which the learned suppose to have been a bat, as the most perfect of birds in make: v. Sale's Qur'ān, n. *ad loc.* and Hughes, Dict. of Islam, s.v. Jesus (III. Miracles).

[4] *i.e.*, in layers of husk.

[5] *i.e.*, bend thy head to thy feet in humility.

[6] Hoping, I suppose, to be able to put off his religious exercises.

[7] *Lit.* 'the chosen'; usually applied to Muḥammad, here to 'Alī.

[8] "What matters day or night? for when the Secret comes it is well, whether it come by day or night," L. "The soul-consuming yearning for the Secret is what is necessary, not the question of night or day; for in the rule of the search there is no captivity to time or season or day or night," B.

[9] "For the searchers halt not night or day." B.

[10] The word 'affection' is not the same as that translated 'love'; it is used also of friendship. 'Isolation' is the separation or detachment from entanglements of the world and of sense, thus almost 'renunciation.'

and their soul in their hand.[1] Lo, when they urge the Burāq[2] of their heart on towards Him, they cast all away under his feet;[3] they throw down life and heart in His path, and make themselves of His company. In the face of his belief in the Unity, there exists for him no old or new; all is naught, naught ; He alone is. What worth have reason and life in his eyes ? the heart and the true faith pursue the road together.[4] The veil of the lovers is very transparent; the tracings on these veils are very delicate.[5] Love's conqueror is he who is conquered by love;[6] '*love*' inverted will itself explain this to thee.[7]

---

1 *i.e.*, they are amazed and confounded, reason and soul escaping from within them.

2 The name of the animal which bore Muḥammad on his night-journey to Heaven.

3 ركاب *lit.* 'stirrup,' *i.e.* of the Burāq of their heart.

4 "According to certain Ṣūfīs the heart (mind, *dil*) is superior to the spirit (soul, *rūḥ*), and religion (*dīn*) to life (soul, *jān*); for there are unbelieving souls, and these, according to the Qur'ān, will die. The *jān* ought therefore to possess religion (*dīn*) and faith (*īmān*)." L.

5 " The veil is the mystery (رمز) of the lovers of God, so subtle that its corporeal existence (كيفيت جسمي) cannot be discerned; and the characters on that veil are the secret matters that are far removed from explanation and comment and interpretation." B.

6 Or, "by God"; the pronoun used might refer either to love or to God. "Love ('*ishq*) has been interpreted as the essence of God; that is, as the might of love in the lover increases, the more utterly conquered does he become." L. "The strong men of love thou thinkest powerful; it is not so, for love has conquered them and they are overcome by his hand, and none can conquer love." B.

7 '*Ishq*, 'love,' inverted becomes قشع ; the verbal noun *qash*' being 'to disperse, dispel, as the wind disperses clouds'; and *qashi*' being 'an inconstant or frivolous fool.' B, I think rightly, having regard to the allusion to the clouds in the next line, supposes the interpretation to lie in the first meaning (*qash*', dispelling, as equivalent to conquering and overcoming). L, however, refers to the derivation of *qashi*', 'a fool from whom reason has been taken away (dispelled),' and observes that "since the loss of reason is essential in love, it is certain that love's conqueror will be conquered." As L further observes, 'love' is again expressed here only by a pronoun; which may not refer to love at all, but to the preceding hemistich as a whole, *i.e.* "the converse of this (statement) will itself. . ." The converse of course would be "He who is conquered by love is love's conqueror."

When the clouds fall away from the Sun, the world of love is filled with light.[1] The cloud is dark and murky as a Magian, but water may be useful as well as harmful;—a little of it is man's life, but his life is destroyed by too much of it; so he who believes in the Unity is the beloved of His Presence, though affection, too, is a veil over His glory.[2]

He is not in evil plight to whom He addresses His instruction. What then is evil ?—to be the friend who toils.[3] Look at the letters

---

[1] 'The clouds' are this visible and phenomenal existence, which hides the sun of Truth or Reality.

[2] "Though the cloud of (mundane) existence, which hides the sun of Reality, be dark and murky, still water, the end for which it exists, is beneficial, though also at times noxious. So with the Unitarian, who is the friend of His Presence. For though on the one hand affection (محبت) is the origin of love (عشق) just as learning (علم) is the beginning of the knowledge (معرفت) of God's essence;—still on the other hand, since it is a matter of relation, and involves the duality of lover and beloved, affection is a veil (which separates us from Him)." L.

[3] Apparently following up the idea of the inferiority of *mahabbat* and by consequence of the *muhibb* (friendship and the friend). The distinction in this line the commentators would make to lie between the active and the passive states; of which the passive is the more blest, and the *muhaddath* superior to the *muhibb*. L, pointing مُحَدَّث. defines it as "one whom God most High, purely by His compassionating mercy, has chosen out and made the receiver of His holy communion." Then, taking in contrast the act. part. مُحَدِّث as "one who by struggling and endeavour and by traversing the stages of the journey wishes to attain the lofty dignity of converse with God," he draws a parallel between these, and the pair مُخْلَص and مُخْلِص; of whom it is said in the Qur'ān

إِلَّا عِبَادَكَ مِنْهُمُ الْمُخْلَصِين and إِنَّ الْمُخْلِصِين علي خطرٍ عظيمٍ

The whole of his lengthy argument, especially the definition of the act. part. مُحَدِّث, seems to me to be somewhat far-fetched. Is it not possible, especially in view of the next line, that there may be no depreciation of the *muhibb*, as such, intended ? Might not محب محنت بين, *lit.* 'the friend who sees toil (labour, pain, trouble),' be 'the friend who regards toil,' *i.e.*, considers it, takes it into consideration, instead of looking on it as nothing, or as a pleasure ? And so, "Evil is the friend who calculates his trouble; for the very characters of the words 'friendship' and 'trouble' are the same," friendship being equivalent to toil and trouble undertaken for one's friend.

of *maḥabbat* (friendship); the very word *miḥnat* (labour) is shown in its characters.[1] O thou who lovest[2] the Beauty of the Presence of the Invisible, till thou seek for the meeting with His face thou wilt never 43
drink the draught of communion with Him, nor taste the sweetness of inward converse with Him.[3] Since thou knowest the One, and assertest the One, why search after the two, and three, and four? Together with *alif* go *be* and *te*,—count *be* and *te* an idol, and *alif* God.[4]

Continue to ply hand and foot in search; when thou reachest the sea, talk not of the rill.[5] Since glory and shame have made of thee a slave, O youth, what hast thou to do with the Eternal?[6] Thou art but newly come into existence,—talk not of the Eternal,[7] thou who dost not know thy head from thy foot. There are a hundred

---

1 The words differ only as the dot of the third letter is above or below.

2 Again *muḥibb*, 'friend'; in view of the meaning (v. next note) it is necessary to express an active sense, though 'lover' must be considered as appropriated to *'āshiq*.

3 "To manifest an affection for His Beauty is to manifest an affection for one of His attributes only, not for His Essence; and is in opposition to the seeking for union with His Essence. For there should be no distinction between Beauty and Majesty (*i.e.*, the groups of attributes called by these names, the merciful and the terrible), and the sight should be fixed on their origin only." L.

4 *Alif*, *be* and *te* being the first three letters of the Arabic alphabet, *be* and *te* accompany *alif*, the initial letter of Allah, as His attributes accompany His Essence. *Be* and *te* form the word '*but*,' 'an idol,' and so His attributes are to be regarded, if looked on and worshipped to the exclusion of His Essence. As L puts it, "The two, three and four are His attributes, of which His Beauty is one; in the contemplation of Essence *plus* attributes, howsoever in truth the attributes are not disjoined from the essence, the imagination of number remains; but communion with the face of the Invisible is communion with the pure Essence disjoined from contemplation of the attributes whether of Beauty or of Majesty." And the traveller in search of God is to count the attributes as idols and the Essence alone as God. Again, since thou believest and proclaimest God to be in truth One, think Him not to be One numerically, for that is bounded and circumscribed; He is one without number; but to conceive Him as numerically one is to assert number of His Essence."

5 جوي, which also means 'search,' as well as 'rivulet, stream.'

6 *i.e.*, since thou art still anxious about such things as disgrace and renown, honour and dishonour, and art occupied with them.

7 قدم, as previously, 'existing from eternity without beginning.'

thousand obstructions in thy path; thy courage fails, and falls short; thy talk is trickery still, still thou remainest in the snare. Betake thyself at once to the ocean of righteousness and true religion, thy body naked like wheat-grains,[1] or like Adam; that so He may approve thy complete renunciation; then see that thou meddle not again with these useless encumbrances. Thou art as yet a follower of Satan; how canst thou become a man without repenting?

When He admits thee in His court, ask from Him no object of desire,—ask Himself; when thy Lord has chosen thee for friendship, thy unabashed eye has seen all there is to see. The world of love suffers not duality,—what talk is this of Me and Thee?[2]

When thy Thee-ness leaves thee, fortune will uplift thy state and seat; in a compact of intimacy it is not well to claim to be a friend, and then—still *Me* and *Thee*! How shall he that is free become a slave?[3] How canst thou fill a vessel already full? Go thou, all of thee, to His door; for whoso in the world shall present himself there in part only, is wholly naught.[4] When thou hast reached to the kiss and love-glance of the Friend, count poison honey from Him, and the thorn a flower.[5]

For the rust on the mirror of the free, *No* is the nail-parer, —with it cut off existence.[6] Be not filled with thy incapacity time

---

1 *i.e.*, divested of husk.

2 This Me-ness and Thee-ness is separation, not union. B.

3 "How shall he, who deems himself a free man, become a slave, or perform God's service? For a vessel already full cannot be filled. The object of servitude is freedom; but when a slave deems himself free he is necessarily excluded from freedom, which is the outcome of servitude." L.

4 "Go all, that is, in every way be of Him, and in all ways give up thyself to Him; for whoso goes to His court except in his completeness, that is, being partly of Him and partly of other than Him, is in every way naught (کم)." L.

5 The flower خیری is the ox-eye, a yellow flower black in the middle, also called همیشه بهار, L.

6 For آئینهٔ دل *cf.* p. 7, l. 10, and for scansion of آئینهٔ also p. 7, l. 11, and five following lines. ناخن بُر or ناخن بُرا or ناخن برای is an implement for paring or cutting nails, knife or scissors. The line presents difficulties. L, taking هستي بر as an adjective to ناخن برا, "To remove the rust from the mirror (*i.e.*, a mirror of polished steel) of the heart of the free man (for the 'free man' *cf.* l. 17 and note),—the rust being هستي, this imaginary existence,

after time, as a boat is filled;[1] dost thou not read in God's book that those who die are not dead but living?[2]

Receive alike good and evil, fair and foul; whatever God sends 44
thee, take it to thy soul. Did not 'Azāzīl,[3] receiving from God both His mercy and His curse, deem them both alike? Whatsoever he obtained from God, good or evil, he held both equal. But the likeness of him who waits at the door of princes is as a sail in unskilled hands.[4]

On Renunciation and Strenuous Endeavour.[5] 5

Whoso desires to be lord of his isolation and whoso seeks to guard his seclusion,[6] must take no ease within, nor adorn himself without;

—*No*, that is the denial of all else than God, is the nail-cutter which cuts off existence. If the nail-cutter be scissors, the resemblance in shape to لا *Lā* ('No') is evident. Otherwise [*i.e.*, if a knife ?], placing on one side the cutter, on the other what is cut from the nail, we have the same form لا; in any case the comparison of لا *Lā* with the nail-cutter is very good.''

To which it may be said that a nail-cutter is not a suitable implement for cleaning away rust; the finger-nail would be more suitable, with which to scratch it off. Accordingly B, ''*Lā* is a nail with which to cut (ناخنیست بُرنده),''—but this is not what the text says.

1 '' With regard to thy impotence in polishing the mirror of the heart, be not like the boat, filled again and again with people crossing the river. Admit not the thought (of thy impotence) to thy mind; for so thou wilt give up striving, and necessarily become a fatalist (*jabarī*).'' L.

2 Qur. 3 : 164. ''*Count not those who are killed in the way of God as dead, but living with their Lord.*''

3 *i.e.*, even 'Azāzīl, the devil. The story of the devil, there called Iblīs, of his expulsion from heaven and of the respite he received, is told in Qur. 7 : 10 sqq. I find no special point to which the text could refer, nor do the commentators mention any.

4 Perhaps meaning that the man who works for earthly rewards keeps no fixed course, has no firm and steadfast character. The last few lines seem doubtfully in place here.

5 تجرد 'renunciation,' from the same root as and with similar meaning to تجرید in the title of the last chapter. تجرید is used again in the first line of the present chapter.

6 L distinguishes between تجرید and تفرید, both in ordinary use having the meaning of 'solitude' or 'loneliness'; تجرید is the cutting off of connections with externals (*i.e.*, things of the world), and تفرید the rejection of things pertaining to the inner man, the mind (*i.e.*, false knowledge).''

that praise which is bestowed on outward seeming imports the abandonment of true praise and adornment.[1] The beggar asks bread at the door of the king; so the lover begs food for his soul. On the path, naked[2] and fearless, he has cast water and fire and earth to the winds.[3] Standing on the plain of the sign-posts of time,[4] what matter fools to him, what the philosopher of the age? O brother, hold thy liver as roast meat in the fire of renunciation, not a broth.[5] The mean-spirited dog seeks a bone; the lion's whelp seeks the marrow of life. The lovers have sacrificed soul and heart, and day and night have made His memory their food.

---

[1] L and B both interpret differently. L gives no paraphrase, but notes that او in the first hemistich refers to God, in the second to the seeker. He thus reads an iẓāfat before او in each case; B following him paraphrases, "Till thou abandon thy attachment to things both inward and outward, which are the praise and the adornment of the unspiritual, thou wilt not obtain the sight of God (از نمایش حق قرین نگردي — نمایش for ستایش ?) whose commendation is the root of all praises." It is hardly probable that او would have a different reference in the two hemistichs, as supposed by the commentators; nor is the interpretation of the first hemistich satisfactory. Accordingly B next proposes to refer او in both cases to God; "till thou ceasest to care for adornment or commendation by God, thou art not fit for the sight and praise of God; that is, in travelling along the stages of knowledge, cherish no anxiety about thy reception or its manner, and pursue not thy labours with a view to praise and adornment; so that thou mayest obtain a true vision of God (نمایش اصلي), and true praise." Here, too, besides the improbability of the rendering, the paraphrase is not a fair interpretation of any possible meaning of the first hemistich. I can see no objection to reading the line without the iẓāfat after ستایش and نمایش, and the sense then connects immediately with the last words of the preceding line.

[2] مُجَرَّد, 'stripped'; or 'alone'; being the pass. part. corresponding to تجرید l. 6, *sup.*

[3] *i.e.*, has cast away all mundane attachments.

[4] Gloss in B مشاهیر, *i.e.*, eminent men.

[5] The line reads curiously to us. For تجرید, 'isolation,' *cf.* p. 42, l. 8 and l. 6 *sup.* and notes. کباب "in Persian by a metaphor somewhat strange to European taste, frequently used as emblem of a bosom burning with love or grief" (Stein.). ثرید is "crumbled, grated or sliced bread for putting into milk or broth, bread-soup." "You obtain nothing from eating *t͟harīd* and abandoning delights (*t͟harīd* being, I suppose, a tasteless sort of dish), unless you make your liver a *kabāb* in the fire of the love and remembrance of God." B.

The man of high resolves seeks not bondage ;[1] a dog[2] is a dog, made happy by a bite.

If revelation become a restraint on thee,[3] make of it a shoe and beat thy head with it ;[4] talk fewer superfluities, and keep thy weakness before thee ; leave the bone to the dogs. In virtue of thy essential nature thou hast obtained a high station ; then why be mean in spirit like a dog ? On the man of high endeavour both worlds are bestowed ;[5] but whoso is mean-spirited like a dog, like a dog runs about after a meal.

If thou desirest to possess thy soul free from the body,[6] *Lā* is as a gallows,[7]—keep company with it. How can pure Divinity admit thee till thy humanity has been uplifted on the gallows ?—for on the path to divinity thy soul [8] will suffer many crucifixions. Put an end to all imitation and speculation,[9] that thy heart may become the house of God. As long as thy existence is with thee in thy soul, the ka'ba is a tavern, though thou serve Him ; but if thy soul has parted from thy existence, through thee an idol temple becomes the Inhabited House.[10]

---

1 *i.e.*, to be kept back on his journey. "Be not content with any one stage on thy path ; desist not from labouring in thy search, like a dog that stands at the door for a morsel of food." B.

2 *i.e.*, a dog of a man.

3 Holding thee back from pursuing the path, L. Revelation, كشف, *lit.*, 'uncovering, manifestation.' *Cf.* Gibb, p. 59 : "But such experience, which is technically termed 'unveilment' (keshf), in allusion to the veil interposed by sensual perception, is not the aim of the true Sūfī ; it comes, so to speak, fortuitously. His real goal is absorption in the Deity." *Cf.* also especially pp. 57, 58.

4 A common Oriental mode of punishment.

5 "What then does he desire from revelation ? For that too he has received." B.

6 *i.e.*, "to escape from the obscuring gloom of this water and earth (the material body)". B.

7 Which frees the soul from the body. B supposes also that a comparison in actual shape is intended between the form of لا and a gallows.

8 *Lit.* 'thy Jesus.'

9 *Lit.* 'road (*i.e.*, the road of others) and opinion,'—worldly discussions and disputes on things of sense. B.

10 The heavenly prototype of the Ka'ba, in the first or lowest heaven (Gibb), or the fourth (B) or seventh heaven (Hughes, Dict. of Islam). For an account of it v. Sale, note on Qur. 52 : 4, and Introd., Chap. IV with notes ; and especially Gibb, *op. cit.*, pp. 37-38.

O seeker of taverns, full of wretchedness, thou art but an ass's son, and asses are thy fathers! [1] Thy understanding is muddied with thy Self and thy Existence; thy reason's sight is dark before that other world. Thine own soul it is that distinguishes unbelief and true religion; of necessity it colours thy vision.[2] Selflessness is happy, selffulness most unhappy; cast away the cat from under thy arm.[3] In the Eternal, unbeliefs and religions are not; such things exist not if the nature be pure.

On Following the Path of the Hereafter.

All this knowledge is but a trifling matter; the knowledge of the journey on God's road is otherwise, and belongs to the man of acuter vision. What, for the man of wisdom and true religion, whose bread and speech are alike of wheat, distinguishes that path and points it out? Inquire its mark from the Speaker and the Friend.[4]

And if, O brother, thou also ask of me, I answer plainly and with no uncertainty, 'To turn thy face towards the world of life, to set thy foot upon outward prosperity, to put out of mind rank and reputation, to bend one's back double in His service, to purify ourselves from evil, to strengthen the soul in wisdom.'

What is the provision for such a journey, O heedless one? By looking on the Truth[5] to cut oneself off from the false;[6] to leave the abode of those who strive with words, and to sit before the silent; to journey from the works of God to His attributes, and from His attributes to the mansion of the knowledge of Him;[7] then from know-

---

1 A play on words in the original.

2 "When thy self and thy opinion leave thee, thine eye sees no colour but the colour of pure light; and when the man of single eye looks away from the dust, the distinction disappears. When thou recognizest the full reality, thou wilt recognize that the distinction does not exist." B.

3 Meaning 'to cast away the impurities of the soul,' B.

4 The Speaker with God, and the Friend of God, Moses and Abraham. "For the one was submerged in the rays of the light of the Eternal, and the other absorbed in the secrets of His conversation," B.

5 *Haqq*, that is, God.

6 *i.e.*, the things of this world.

7 Though B paraphrases صفت in the singular by صفات in the plural, with the meaning 'attributes', I do not think this is quite accurate.

ledge to the world of the secret, then to reach the threshold of poverty; then when thou art become the friend of poverty, thy Soul 46
destroys thy impure Self; [1] thy Self becomes Soul inside thee; it becomes ashamed of all its doings, and casting aside all its possessions is melted on its path of trial; then when thy Self has been melted in thy body, thy Soul has step by step accomplished its work; then God takes away its poverty from it,—when poverty is no more, God remains.

Not in folly nor ignorance spoke Bāyazīd, if he said '*Glory to me*;' [2] so too the tongue that spoke the supreme secret moved truly when it said, '*I am God*.' [3] When he proclaimed to the back the secret he had learned from the face, [4] it became his executioner and killed him; his secret's day-time became as night, [5] but God's word was what he spoke; [6] when in the midst of the rabble he suddenly

---

For صفت 'nature,' *cf.* p. 2, l. 12, p. 45, l. 9; and so perhaps, 'the description of His nature by His attributes, His nature as set forth in His attributes' is what is meant; معرفت, *i.e.*, معرفت ذات, the knowledge of His essential nature, comes afterwards.

1 Soul, دل; Self, نفس,—here as well as in the following lines and p. 45, l. 18 *sup.* L considers it equivalent to نفس امارة, 'animal passions'; but though the meaning inclines towards this, it would not quite suit نفوس in p. 45, l. 18; 'lower nature' would perhaps be nearly right, دل being then 'higher nature.'

2 B recounts the story as follows:—"Bāyazīd Basṭāmī was preaching one day, when the light of the beams of knowledge fell on him. He went from himself, and being beside himself uttered the cry of union, "*Glory to me, how magnificent is my state!*" When he recovered consciousness his friends informed him of what he had said. He said, 'If I say it a second time, kill me.' Another day during his religious exercises the same thing happened. His friends used their knives on his head and breast; but however hard they struck, his insensible body received no mark at all. When he recovered they found that the wounds they had inflicted, they had inflicted on themselves, their own bodies showing the marks of the blows." The expression used by Bāyazid is of course only applicable to God.

3 The celebrated saying of Manṣūr al-Ḥallāj, who was executed on that account in 309 A.H.

4 The face is the face of God, the back God's creation. L.

5 "In reality it was truth, though it appeared false." L.

6 "In the technical language of the Ṣūfīs, this is the stage of قرب فرائض 'propinquity to the divine laws', God the agent and Manṣūr the tool." L.

disclosed, unauthorized, the secret, his outward form was given to the gallows, his inward being was taken by the Friend; when his life's soul could speak no longer, his heart's blood divulged the secret.[1]

He spoke well who said in his ecstacy, *Leave thyself, O son, and come hither*. From thee to the Friend is not long; thyself art the road, —then set thy feet on it,[2] that with the eye of Godhead thou mayest see the handwriting[3] of the Lord of power and the land of spirits.

When shall we be separated from our Selves,—*I* and *thou* departed and God remaining? the heart arrived at God's threshold, the Soul[4] saying, Here am I, enter thou. When by the doorway of renunciation heart and soul have reached the dome of a true belief in the Unity, the soul locks itself in the embrace of the Houris, the heart walks proudly in the sight of the Friend.[5]

O thou who knowest not the life that comes of the juice of the grape, how long then wilt thou be drunk with the grape's outward form? Why boastest thou falsely that thou art drunk? So that they say, 'The fellow has drunk butter-milk!' If thou drink wine, say naught; the drinker of butter-milk too will guard his secret.[6]
47 Why seekest thou? Deem it not like thy soul; drink it as thou dost thy faith.[7] Thou knowest not what *mās* is in Persian; when thou

---

1 It is related that his blood, as it fell on the ground, formed itself into the letters '*Anā'l haqq*', thus again publishing the secret. L.

2 *i.e.*, it is self that thou hast to bring under thy foot.

3 Or 'pathway', B.

4 Probably the Universal Soul, روح مجرد و حقیقی - روح آمیغی. B.

5 The distinction between جان - دل - روان - روح spirit, life, heart, soul, appears to be seldom accurately definable, and in passages like the above it seems impossible to say in what the distinction consists.

6 As the buttermilk-drinker, who feigns his intoxication, keeps secret the fact that he has been drinking only buttermilk, so refrain thou also from disclosing thy secret, if thou hast drunk wine. If it is the wine of reality, it is not well to proclaim the secret; and if earthly wine, to tell it will cause thee to be blamed and disgraced.'' L.

7 L interprets differently. ''He thus addresses the traveller on the path of the hereafter,—Why seekest thou the path of God, like the soul, whose nature can never be comprehended by anyone? (مانند جان که کنه او مدرک کسی نمیشود راه حق را جست و جو چه میکنی). It is not necessary that thou shouldst know the true nature of this path at first, before thou settest foot on it. Rather drink it like the faith, which at first is a matter of conformity (تقلید),

hast eaten it, thou recognizest the taste.[1] When in this ruined hall thou drinkest a cup of wine, I counsel thee put not thy foot outside the house of thy drunkenness, lay down thy head where thou hast drunk the wine ; till thou hast drunk it, hold it an unlawful thing, and when thou hast drunk it, rub a clod of earth on thy lips.[2] When with a hundred pains thou hast twice drunk the dregs,[3] I will say, Look at the man's courage !

---

and afterwards comes to be really present with one (به مرتبهٔ شهود میرسد), *i.e.*, deeming it good and wholesome, put thy foot on the road of striving and austerity...... *And God knows best if this is right.*'' This is unsatisfactory; there is no hint of the search being for a path, the context before and after being about wine; L has to talk, and makes the text talk of 'drinking' a path ; the search for one's own soul has not before been alluded to ; and to suppose a break at the end of the first hemistich (instead of taking چون جان تو with the second) leaves تو مدان awkwardly by itself without object.

Again B :—" If thou wishest to be successful in the search for thy desire, which is Reality, as in the search for thy soul, it will not be obtained at the first stage. As it is difficult to find the soul in the body, so also it is difficult to find Reality at the first stage. Thus first thou must set out on thy quest without knowing His Reality. As at first the faith is accepted in a conventional manner...." etc., as L. This is open to similar objections, and is rather further from the text.

Taking the text as it stands, the search must be for wine ; and چون جان تو must go with تو مدان. Hence the translation I have given, the meaning being the exact opposite of B's interpretation. "Why seekest thou further? The wine is at hand, not hard to get at like thy soul." The line is unsatisfactory, and I can see no reason for introducing جان in this connection. A possible emendation would be توم دان for تو مدان --- توم being plural of Arabic تومة "a pearl" ; so, "Why seekest thou (for anything better)? Know that it (the wine) is pearls, (as precious) as thy soul..."

1 "If thou dost not know that the Persian for *mās* is *jughrāt*, thou wilt know from the taste, on eating it, that it is *jughrāt*. So also, if now thou knowest not this path, when thou treadest it and attainest thy high desire and reachest thy wished-for goal, thou wilt know that it was right and true." L. What dialect *mās* or *māsī* may be I do not know ; 'sour, coagulated milk' is in Persian *māst*, and *jughrāt* is used in the dialect of Samarqand for the same (Stein., B.Q.). With regard to the 'path' in L's explanation, v. previous note.

2 *i.e.*, keep silence about it, B. The lines refer primarily to earthly wine, with a hint at the spiritual wine in the last hemistich ; "wine being unlawful for the orthodox Muslim, hold it so—till thou drink it ; and then tell nobody."

3 I think the emphasis is on the 'twice' ; *i.e.*, if, knowing what it is, thou get drunk a second time, thou art indeed a brave man.

More numerous than asses without head-stalls are all the carrion-hearted wine-drinkers ; wine has eaten up and the grape has carried off both their understanding and their soul. In this company of youths, in their cowardice no longer men, if thou speak not, thou remainest true ; but if thou speak, thou blasphemest.[1]

How canst thou go forward ? there is no place for thee ; and how then wilt thou leap ? thou hast no foot ; he feeds on sorrow for whom there is no place, and he is destitute who has no foot. Those who, freed from being, stand at the door of the true Existence, did not to-day for the first time gird up their loins at His door ; from Eternity the sons of the serving-men, giving up wealth and power, have stood before Love as numerous as ants.

Strive that when death shall come with speed he may find thy soul already in his street. Leave this house of vagabonds : if thou art at His door, remain there ; if not, repair thither : for those who are His servants are contented in His Godhead,[2] ever their loins of servitude girt up, the lord of the seven heavens even as a slave.

Of the Learned Man and the Fool.[3]

The shaikh of Jurjān[4] said to his son, "Thou must have a house in this street for thy private pursuits ; and it will be well if the lock be a cunning one."[5]

---

[1] *i.e.*, 'cast not your pearls before swine'. The preceding paragraphs, which begin in praise of the heavenly wine, pass into a condemnation of the earthly wine and wine-drinkers.

[2] Referring to Qur. 39 : 36. "*Is not God sufficient for His servants ?*"

[3] This 'story' seems to be only two lines in length, and to bear on the necessity, for one who engages to follow the Path, of retirement from and abandonment of the world. The subject of the Path is immediately resumed.

[4] Abū 'Alī Jurjānī, B.

[5] "Thou needest a house in the street of the true religion, and it will be well if, to conceal thyself and destroy thy tracks, thou make the lock (turn) to the left (كليدان بچپ كني, *i.e.*, in the direction opposite to the usual one ?), that is, reverse the horse's shoes (نعل واژگونه كني to mislead as to the direction taken). كليدان is a wooden lock, common everywhere, especially in Ghaznī." L. Merely to have a lock turning in the opposite direction would perhaps not be of much use ; چپ may imply 'stratagem, deceit'; and in this sense I have translated it : *cf.* p. 10, l. 19.

Contrive thy finery in the path of renunciation with its head[1] of the Law, and its secret parts of the Unity ; and enter this lodging of trouble and distress like a traveller, and quickly pass on from it. At the door of the garden of *Except God* strip off and make away with thy coat and cap : become naught, that He himself, engaging thee to answer, may with justice call to thee, "*To whom belongs the kingdom?*"[2] 48

A Story.[3]

The saint Shiblī said in private converse, after a period of inward communion with God, If, for that I am not far from Him, He give me leave to speak, and with just purpose ask, *To whom belongs the kingdom?* then in sincerity I will answer Him and say, To-day the kingdom belongs to him who from yesterday and the day before has administered it ; to-day and to-morrow Thy kingdom, O Mighty over us, is for him whose yesterday and the day before it was. The sword of Thy wrath cuts off the head of the valiant, and then gives back to the head its life.[4]

Know that traffic[5] is good for gain, and the lance of the sun healthful for the sunflower.

When[6] thou shalt be offended with all but God, Gabriel will appear to thee as naught. No one knows how long the way may be

---

1 *i.e.*, what is visible of it, B.

2 Implying "it belongs to thee." Or, as B takes it, 'engaging himself' to answer ; "so become naught, that thou endure in Him till at the last day thou hear from Him himself the call of "*To whom belongs the kingdom?*" And no one will say it but He ; nor will anyone else speak the answer ; for in the spiritual annihilation is the essence of union ; who except Himself shall answer Him?". That is, God and the seeker being one, the answer also will come from God. *Cf.* p. 48, ll. 8, 9. *inf.*

3 Here is inserted, as a parenthesis, an anecdote in reference to the words immediately preceding.

4 "The valiant (سرفرازان) are the lovers of God, not (as it might be translated) the haughty and proud ; for the first step of the lovers in the path of God is intrepidity. And the wrath is not the wrath of this world (نه قهر مجازي), but a wrath which is in truth the essence of kindness. Qur. 3: 163, '*Count not those who are killed in the way of God as dead, but living with their Lord.*'" L.

5 *i.e.*, the labour and inconvenience which trade involves ; the line emphasizes the previous one by means of these comparisons.

6 Continuation of the former chapter, on the Path.

from the word *Not* to God ;[1] for while thou holdest to thy Self thou wilt wander day and night, right and left, for thousands of years ; then when after laying long toil upon thyself at last thou openest thine eyes, thou seest Self, because of its essential nature and its limitation to conjecture, wandering round about itself, like the ox in a mill. But if, freed from thyself, thou begin at all to labour, thou wilt find admission at this door within two minutes ; the two hands of the understanding, holding but *this* distance, are empty ;[2] but what *that* distance is, God knows.

O Sikandar, on this path of troubles and in this darkness, do thou, like the prophet Khiẓr, bring under foot thy jewel of the mine,
49 that so thou mayest obtain the water of life.[3] God will not be thine whilst thou retainest soul and life ; both can not be thine,—this and that.[4] Bruise thy Self through months and years, then deem it dead and leave it where it lies ; when thou hast finished with thy vile Self, thou hast reached eternal life and joy and Paradise.

---

[1] '*Not*,' لا ; *i.e.*, the negation of aught else than God ; and 'God' is the existence in Him for ever of the seeker.

[2] *i.e.*, it is too small to be estimated.

[3] 'Jewel of the mine' = 'soul, life,' روح حيواني L. 'Sikandar' is the Persian form of 'Alexander' (the Great), here equivalent to 'man of courage, hero.' Khiẓr is a mysterious figure in Muḥammadan theology. "Some say he lived in the time of Abraham, and that he is still alive in the flesh, and most of the religious and Ṣūfī mystics are agreed upon this point, and some have declared that they have seen him ; and they say he is still to be seen in sacred places, such as Mecca or Jerusalem. Some few traditionists deny his existence. Others say he is of the family of Noah, and the son of a king. His name does not occur in the Qur'ān, but....nearly all the commentators believe that al-Khiẓr is the mysterious individual referred to in..........Sūrah 18 : 59-81.......... In some Muslim books he seems to be confounded with Elias, and in others with St. George, the patron saint of England. In the above quotation [of the Qur'ān] he is represented as the companion of Moses, and the commentator Ḥusain says he was a general in the army of Dhū'l-Qarnain (Alexander the Great)." Hughes, Dict. of Islām, *sub voce*. He is supposed to have discovered and drunk of the water of life, and so to have become immortal.

'In this darkness'—the water of life being always referred to as found in darkness.

[4] *i.e.*, God and self.

Remain unmoved by hope and fear; why contendest thou with Mālik and Riẓwān?[1] To non-existence, mosque and fire-temple are one; to a shadow, hell and heaven are the same:[2] for him whose guide Love is, infidelity and faith are equally a veil before His door; his own being is the veil before the friend's eyes, hiding the court of God's essence.[3]

On Trust in God.

Set not thy foot in His court with hypocrisy. The men of the Path walk in trust; if thou hast a constant trust in Him, why not also in His feeding thee?[4] Bring then thy belongings to the street of trust in God; then fortune will come out to meet thee. Listen to a story concerning trust in God, so that thou remain not a pledge in the hand of the devil; and learn the law of the Path from a woman besides whom a braggart man shows but contemptibly.[5]

On the Trust in God shown by Old Women.

When Ḥātim set out for the sanctuary,[6]—he whom thou callest

---

1 "The one quality belongs peculiarly to the characteristics of Mālik, the guardian of Hell, and the other to those of Riẓwān, the doorkeeper of Paradise." B.

2 A shadow is a thing having no separate or substantial existence; so, 'when thou hast ceased to exist, such things as heaven and hell, mosque and fire-temple, have no meaning for thee; therefore destroy self, and find eternal life.' *Cf.* p. 49, l. 6.

3 اوی *Ū'ī*, *lit.*, He-ness, as previously منی and توی "Me-ness and thee-ness"; that is, 'the intimate essence of Himself.' To take *dūst* in both cases as referring to the traveller on the Path gives a meaning more in harmony with the context. L points out that the first *dūst* may refer to God and the second to the seeker; or that both may refer to God. If the first refers to God, the هستی دوست would appear to be some mode of existence interposed before, and concealing, His pure Essence; as B puts it (among other interpretations), "the being (هستی) of God, even in the sight of the perfect Knower, is a veil before His pure Essence, or His He-ness."

4 اوست is apparently taken by the commentators to be a particle of emphasis merely.

5 The reference is to the following story.

6 *Ḥaram*, 'sacred territory, a sanctuary'; usually of Mecca and the land immediately around it.

Aṣamm,[1]—when he set out for the Ḥijāz[2] and the Sacred House,[3] making towards the tomb of the Prophet (*on whom be peace!*),[4] there remained behind a colt[5] of his household, with no supplies whatever and owning nothing; he left his wife alone in the house, with no means of support, and set forth on the road; alone and in trouble he
20 left her, her life or death the same to him.[6] Her womanhood was a fellow-traveller with him towards trust in God, for she knew her Provider; she had a friend behind the curtain, being a sharer in God's secret.

The men of the quarter assembled, and all went cheerily to the
50 woman; when they saw her alone and in trouble, they all began at once to ask her her affairs, and by way of advice and counsel, in sympathy said, "When thy husband set out for 'Arafāt[7] did he leave thee any means of support?" She said, "He did: I am
5 quite contented,—my maintenance is what it was before." Again they said, "How much is thy maintenance? for thy heart is contented and happy." She said, "However long my life lasts, He has given into my hands all the support I need." The other said, "Thou knowest not aught thyself, and what does he know, about thy life?"[8]

She said, "The Giver of my daily bread knows; while life lasts, He will not take away my sustenance." They answered, "He does not give it apart from means;[9] He never gives dates from the willow-
10 tree; thou hast no sort of earthly possessions, and He will not send

---

1 *Lit.* 'deaf'; a celebrated Muḥammadan saint, disciple of Shaqīq of Balkh, who in turn was a disciple of Ibrāhīm Adham. L.

2 That part of Arabia bordering the Red Sea which contains the two sacred cities Mecca and Medina.

3 The temple at Mecca.

4 The tomb is at Medina, not, as might seem to be implied, at Mecca.

5 B points گُرِه *i.e.*, 'a company, a number'; but we are immediately told that his wife was left quite alone.

6 Said not, of course, in blame, but as showing his independence of all besides God, and his trust in God to accomplish His own purposes.

7 A hill near Mecca, the scene of certain of the ceremonies of the Hajj.

8 She referring to God, her interlocutor to her husband.

9 *i.e.*, He works through causes, and all things obey natural laws.

thee a wallet from heaven.'' She said, ''O ye of clouded minds! How long will ye utter folly and perversity? He needs to use a wallet who owns no piece of land; but His are heaven and earth entirely; what He wills He does; His is the authority. He brings it to pass as He desires; sometimes He gives increase, sometimes He takes away.''

How long wilt thou talk of trust in God? Thou bearest the name of a man, but art less than a woman. Since on thy journey thou comportest thyself not as men do, go learn how to journey from the women. Thou hast chosen sloth, O body of woman! Alas for the man who is less than a woman!

Look[1] to thy soul, and abandon thy lower nature,[2] for this is as a hawk, and that a heron;[3] that in that place, where it comes to comprehend '*We*' and '*Thou*'[4], when it has been wholly burnt, '*He*' and '*He*' shall remain.[5] Reason, that, living in this world, cannot like soul attain to aught, arrives but as far as itself and reaches not to Him.

The ears of the head are two, the ear of love one; this is for religion, those for doubt;[6] though the ear of the head listens to innu- 51
merable things, the ear of love listens only to the story of the One. Those two ears are set on each side of thy head like waterspouts; why dost thou still cry and howl? Thou art but a child;—go, turn thine eyes away from the devil, lest he put ears on the sides of thy head.[7]

---

1 Resuming here once more the former theme, left at p. 49, l. 7.

2 Or 'self', نفس *cf.* p. 46, l. 1 and note.

3 *i.e.*, unless thou look to it, thy lower nature will devour thy higher. The heron, بوتیمار, is a bird "which lives on the banks of water, and though it be thirsty, yet does not drink, lest the water should become less; .... the eating of its flesh induces wakefulness, and strengthens the memory and sharpens the intellect,'' B.Q.

4 *i.e.*, to comprehend that they are nothing, B.

5 *i.e.*, in place of '*We*' and '*Thou.*' 'It' refers in both places to دل 'the soul, the higher nature.'

6 The doubt and obscurities of the world, B.

7 "As they frighten children by saying that 'unless thou stop doing such or such a thing, they will put thy head between two ears,' so thou too art a child who knowest nothing of love; till thou become perfect, there are dangers for thee in this path,'' B. Was the wearing of large ears a punishment for children, somewhat of the nature of the dunce-cap?

[On the Kalima.][1]

As the inhabited world[2] is computed at twenty-four thousand leagues, so, if thou add the hours of night to those of day, there are twenty-four of those torturers of mankind also. Exchange them, if thou art dexterous and versed in transformations, for the twenty-four letters;[3] the *qāf*[4] of the affirmation of the two testimonies, if these be uttered without deceit or hypocrisy or disputation[5] or contention, will take thee completely out of thy world,[6] bringing thee, not to any instrument, but to *kāf* and *nūn*:[7] on this road and

---

[1] This section is placed, in all the copies, after the first two lines of the Chapter 'On Trust in God', with which it very evidently has no connection. I have added the above title.

[2] *Rub'-i-maskūn*, 'the inhabited quarter.' "The geographers divide the surface of the terrestrial globe into two parts, land and water. The land part they subdivide into halves by the equator. That to the south is reckoned uninhabitable through the greatness of the heat. That to the north alone is peopled and cultivated. This is called the 'Habitable Quarter' and is divided into seven zones by as many imaginary lines drawn parallel to the equator, the space between the seventh and the north pole being reckoned uninhabitable through the greatness of the cold. The seven zones are famous as the 'Seven Climates,' and the countries and cities situated in each are carefully noted; but it is enough for us to know that the First Climate is that next to the equator, and the seventh that farthest from it." Gibb, *op. cit.*, p. 47, n. 1.

[3] *i.e.*, the letters of the *kalima*, v. *inf.* L has no notes on the whole of this passage; B gives a long paraphrase of the whole, which is however useless, since it evades the difficulties and gives no help towards the real meaning and connection of the passage. I have transposed ll. 5 and 6, as otherwise the line about the hours is left unconnected and meaningless; I suppose the meaning to be, "Barter both space and time, and all contained in them, for the true religion, whose expression is the confession of the faith."

[4] 'Affirmation' is '*qaul*', whose initial letter is *qāf*. The 'two testimonies' are the two parts of the Muḥammadan confession of faith, "*There is no God but God*" and "*Muḥammad is the prophet of God.*" The reference is presumably more especially to the first of these, and for the sense in which it is understood *cf.* l. 9 *inf.* and note.

[5] کیف *lit.* 'how?'

[6] *i.e.*, thy being, self, B.

[7] The two letters forming the word *kun*, 'be,' the word by which God created the universe; hence 'not to any intermediary agent, but to the creative power of God himself.'

in this street, beyond where wisdom[1] is, this is thy sufficient task, to repeat, '*None is God but He.*'[2]

The confession of the faith when reckoned up gives twenty-four as the number of its letters, half of them twelve jewel-caskets from the ocean of life, the other half the twelve zodiacal constellations of the heavens of the faith;[3] the caskets are full of the pearls of hope, the zodiac filled by the moon and sun:—not the pearls of any sea of this world, not the moon and sun of these heavens; but the pearls of the ocean of the world of Power,[4] the moon and sun of the heaven of peace.[5]

ON THE INTERPRETATION OF THE DREAM.

In the phantoms of sleep He has ordained for men of understanding both fear and hope.[6] When a man has laid down his head in sleep, his tent-ropes are severed.[7] As long as men are in the world

---

[1] Perhaps meaning خرد نخستين, the first or primal Intelligence.

[2] لاهو الّا هو, *hū* (he) being constantly used for God, this is simply the first part of the *kalima*, here understood as equivalent to 'the negation of the existence of aught besides God, and the affirmation of the existence of His essence.' B.

[3] The twenty-four letters of the *kalima*,—the number being that of the hours of the day and of the thousands of leagues supposed to measure the earth,—are divided into two halves, of twelve each for each of the two propositions it contains.

[4] '*Ālam-i-jabarūt*, the second in order of the 'Five planes of Existence,' the 'World of the Intelligences and the Souls,' *v.* Gibb, p. 55. The expression does not appear to be used here in its strict sense, but rather as generally equivalent to the invisible world as a whole.

[5] Also in a general sense and not with any definite limitation of application.

[6] The history of this line is curious. It occurs, in all the copies, after p. 38, l. 6, where it has been a source of great difficulty to the commentators. L in a long and sometimes somewhat obscure note, advancing several possible meanings, confesses himself uncertain; B simply follows him, in one place apparently without understanding him. No suggested meaning, however, brings it into place there, while the natural and unstrained meaning of the words permits it to fall easily into place here, as the head of the section on Dreams.

[7] This line also appears to be seriously misplaced in all copies, occurring towards the end of the section, "On Charity and Gifts," *post.* B annotates there:—"But notwithstanding his actual existence and his continuance in his present state without change of body or of earthly soul, there comes to him

of causes, they are all in a boat, and all asleep; waiting for what their soul shall see in sleep, of what awaits them of reward and punishment.[1]

A fierce fire means the heat of anger; a spring of water is a beloved child.[2]

To weep in a dream is a provision of happiness afterwards; slavery
52 means immunity from disgrace. Playing at draughts or chess in sleep brings war and conquest and misery.

Water in a dream, if it be pure and sweet and clean and wholesome, is daily bread lawfully earned; but if it be muddy, know that it means an unhappy life;—though it be water, deem it fire itself. Earth in a dream brings food; to the farmer it indicates prosperity. A wind, if it be either hot or cold, is equally a store of grief and pain; but if it be temperate to the skin it is grief to an enemy and joy to a friend.

To give anything to the dead in a dream is loss of wealth and property. Laughter is anxiety and dangers; silence is affection for one's wealth. To drink water and have one's thirst increased is knowledge, for one is never satiated with it. And he who is naked in his dream falls into disgrace, like the drunken libertine. A drum in a dream,—the secret leaks out; a trumpet in a dream results in a

---

in sleep a condition which cannot be understood or made an object of the senses (مفهوم ومحسوس), the condition which comes upon the tent from the cutting of the tent-ropes; which is also the state which occurs through strivings and asceticisms.'' On dreams and their significance, cf. Gibb *op. cit.*, p. 57 and note; ''it is only at rare intervals when the body is asleep and all the avenues of the senses are closed, that such a soul can for a brief space, in a vision or a dream, look into its own world.'' On the similarity of this state with that of '*kashf*' ('unveilment'), referred to by B above, consult Gibb, pp. 58, 59.

1 L quotes the saying attributed to 'Ali (*cf.* p. 32, l. 20), ''*Men are asleep, and when they die, they awake*;'' and proceeds:—''He likens the world to sleep, the good and bad acts of men to dreams, and the rewards and punishments that follow to the interpretation of the dreams; the good acts having rewards as their interpretation, the bad punishments. While men are in this world, they are like people in a boat, or men asleep; for he who is seated in a boat knows not where he will arrive, and a sleeper knows not beforehand what he will see in his dream, or what the result of it will be. So men know not in this world (their sleep) what good or bad acts (what dreams) they will see, or what rewards and punishments (what interpretations) will follow them.''

2 *Lit.* 'light of the eye.'

quarrel. Bonds and fetters are a repentance of Naṣūḥ;[1] to see a garden is food for the soul. Fruit in a dream is a stipend from the king,—not at once, but at some future time; when the time comes for him to obtain it, the man who saw the dream will attain thereby to affluence.

When a man sees his own hand outstretched, he will be of singular generosity and munificence; but if his hands be withdrawn, he will surround himself with an army by his stinginess. The hands are brother and sister, the left the girl, the right the boy; the fingers represent sons; the teeth refer to father and mother; daughters are represented by the breast and nipple. Hidden wealth and riches are shown as the belly; in a dream, the liver and heart are a store of wealth. The leg and knee are weariness and trouble. The brain is hidden wealth; the side a woman, for veil the skin drawn round her body.[2] The organ of generation is a son,—good or bad, ugly or fair, wretched or fortunate.[3]

To wash the hands is despair in regard to the matter in hand; to 53
dance is impudence and deceit. Bathing drawers[4] and can[5] and implements of bathing all point to servants; and he who in his dream plays upon the lute will certainly marry in haste.[6] To wrestle with another is to conquer and to harass; and he who takes medicine in his dream escapes from pain and sorrow and torment.

Perfume in a dream is of two kinds, one meaning pleasure, the other nothing but affliction; the kind that is rubbed on brings pleasure, that which they scatter about, trouble. Since by smoke is meant an

---

1 "Naṣūḥ was a man who dressed himself in women's garments and sat with the women. One day a necklace having been lost they wished to search the women for it. Being unwilling that this should happen to him, he vowed to God that he would not continue this practice of his. The Veiler of secrets guarded him, and the lost article was found before the search reached him. He held to his vow and mixed no more with the women." B.

2 B differently; "a woman's side, and the brain, and the skin like a covering drawn over one, are signs of a hidden treasure." But پهلو has in no copy the ی of the iẓāfat.

3 *i.e.*, without distinction as to qualities.

4 صيزر; B explains that this in Hindustani is لنگي حمامي.

5 سطل, 'a vessel with one handle used in baths to pour water upon the bathers' (Stein.).

6 *lit.* 'heat.'

increase of trouble, such an one's comfort will be small compared with his distress. A sick man, and perfume, and a new coat, is bad,—the bad that I represent to thee as good.[1] To dance in a boat in a dream means danger from drowning, and brings wretchedness; but for one who is in prison, to dance is of good omen.

Whoever sees blood running from his body will find that happiness is denied him; permitted him, however, if he does not see a wound; but otherwise, if a wound be there,[2] his affairs will cause him heavy trouble; he will be captive in sorrow's hands. And if a woman dreams of menstruating, she will give birth to a dead child. If a sick man seeing meat in a dream, eats of it, hope not for his recovery. To dream of drunkenness and madness from drinking wine, if it be Arabian wine, is bad; if Persian,[3] deem it a livelihood, honour, and good-fortune. Milk in a dream is profit from one's possessions, an ample and lawful subsistence.

On Dreams of Vessels and Garments.[4]

An old garment is grief and sorrow; a new garment is great wealth; best of all is a garment that is closely woven,[5] so my master
54 told me. For women, a garment of many colours is a cause of joy and happiness and honour. A red garment brings gladness and the unrestricted enjoyment of a lasting good-fortune. The garment of fear is black; if yellow, it is pain and trouble and sighing; blue clothes are grief, a sorrow heavier than a mountain on the heart. Mantle and cloak are beauty; purse and moneybag are a source of riches.

A ladder will result in a journey, but one full of danger for the man.[6] A millstone is a trusty man, the chosen one of a house. A snare in a dream is a block in the business in hand.[7] A mirror is a

---

1 *i.e.*, death, B.

2 این apparently refers to حلال, not to the whole phrase از حلال برون; *v.* next line.

3 Arabian wine is made from dates, Persian from grapes, B.

4 آواني, 'vessels,' here apparently used of a variety of implements.

5 هنگفت, 'of plain, hard, closely woven cloth.'

6 Gloss in B, 'that is, a journey to the next world.'

7 بستن کار in the sense of 'closing up, obstructing.' Or alternatively, to set to work, to apply oneself.'

woman ; be well on thy guard. Captivity is plainly shown thee by a lock ; so by a key thou obtainest thy release.

On Dreams of Handicraftsmen.

A cook means great riches, just as a butcher means that one's affairs are ruined. A physician is pain and sickness, especially to one who is wretched and needy. The tailor is the man in virtue of whom troubles and affliction are all changed to good-fortune. A bootmaker and shoemaker and cobbler are among the heritages of one who will possess a secret. A draper, a goldsmith, and a druggist mean a successful undertaking and great wealth. A vintner, a musician, and a dancer bring joy and gladness; a horse-doctor and horse-breaker and oculist point like a finger-post to ruin. To see a hunter in a dream brings trickery and deceit into one's path. A maker of swords indicates affliction ; so too an arrow-maker, preparing arrows. A water-carrier, a potter, and a porter, all three are to be considered as indicating wealth.

On Dreams of Beasts.

An ass is a servant, but a lazy one, who refuses to work. A horse, O thou of unparalleled wisdom ! is a woman; both are suitable possessions for a man. A mule is bad for him whose wife is pregnant; a child will not be born to him. A journey comes to thee in a dream as a camel,—a terrible journey, grievous and painful. A cow points to a year of plenty ; the owl grows arrogant before the king.[1]

On Dreams of Wild Animals.

A lion is a powerful and haughty adversary whose actions show no regard for humanity. An elephant is a king,—but a terrible one, whose rage is feared by all. Fortune and wealth come before thee as a sheep; a year of plenty demands the same sign. A goat signifies men mean and base by nature, clamorous, full of wickedness in their actions. A bustard is in every way advantageous ;—this is no more than my master's words. The deer, O aged in wisdom ! rather receives its interpretation from the women's apartments. The leopard, of evil deeds, represents an enemy perfidious in his dealings; the tiger also is considered to be an enemy,—so they relate in the book. The

---

[1] Meaning, I suppose, that the masses become presumptuous in consequence of prosperity.

bear is a treacherous adversary, and a robber; no one will come by any good from seeing him. A hunting-leopard and hyena and wolf and fox are enemies, evil-disposed every one of them. And although the fox is a worker of wiles, yet it is still worse if thou see one dead. Every snake is a rancorous enemy ; but again it is worse for thee if it makes towards thee. A scorpion and tarantula and other creeping things all and each denote calamities. Though in waking life a dog is a shepherd, in a dream it means war.

On Dreams of Lights and Stars.

To see the sun in a dream is said in every case to mean a king.
56 The moon is as a counsellor ; another has said, No, it is a woman. The globe of Mars or Saturn in a dream brings trial and grief and torment; Mercury represents a writer; Jupiter comes as a treasurer and minister of state ; Venus is the origin of joy, of pleasure, of desire and of ease. And the other stars deem thou brothers ; when thou interpretest them pronounce them such, for thus Ya'qūb, who established this method of interpretation, disclosed the secrets of this science to his son ; the sun and moon were his father and mother, the stars represented his brothers.[1]

Has anyone seen the sorrowing ones perplexed like we have ? Now we will leave the dreams of those who wake ; to awaken a sleeper is easy, but the heedless is like one dead. Make an end of divination and augury and interpretation: pass hence,—thou hast finished thy recital.

On the Incompatibility of the Two Abodes.[3]

The sun and earth produce the day and night; when thou hast passed beyond, neither the one nor the other will exist for thee.[4]

---

[1] *Cf.* Genesis 37 : 9 sqq.

[2] Perplexed, that is, from inability to interpret their dream ; hence an apology for devoting so much space to this subject.

[3] دارين —*i.e.*, the two worlds. In the following section the texts differ much as to the order of the lines ; M is especially confused. I have followed no single text strictly, though keeping closest to CH. These omit several lines found in the others, which are possibly glosses ; I have rejected some of these, but perhaps not enough.

[4] Neither cause nor effect but Unity only. "When thou hast passed beyond this house of deception, there will be for thee no distinction of light and

O thou in whose imagination desire and desirer are two, know that the duality belongs to thy understanding, and belongs not to the Unity. Since in the Presence of One such as He all things are one, if thou wilt listen to my words, then seek not thou duality; know that in duality is pain and opposition,[1] in Unity Rustam and a catamite are alike.

Till on the battlefield of purity and in the court of the soul, standing above thy life and treading on thy earthly body, thou cast away thy sword, thou wilt not become a shield;[2] till thou lay aside the crown thou wilt not become a leader. So long as thy soul is a slave to the crown, thy acts will ever be wrong; when thou no longer heedest crown and zone, then art thou chief over the chiefs of the age. To abandon the world is to mount the horse of God's favour; its repudiation is the establishment of pure truth.[3] The death of the soul is the destruction of life; the death of the life is salvation for the

---

darkness, nor any difference between seeker and sought. For this comes from thy ignorance, or rather is a result of thy earthly knowledge, which sees double, not single.'' B.

1 تمييز —*lit.* ' discrimination, distinction, separation ' ; *i.e.*, according to B, '' the discord and contradiction which afflict the people of this world through lack of contentment and trust in God, and through their not having familiarized themselves with resignation and acquiescence.''

2 B paraphrases, '' Till thou throw aside the sword, *i.e.*, leave the tumult of the flesh and beauties of the world, thou wilt not become, like the shield, an instrument of safety and of trust in the high place of patience and contentment.'' If, however, I thought that افگندن could mean ' to wield,' I would translate in accordance with B's second suggestion, '' till thou wield thy sword against thy life and the head of thy earthly body ''; or, as he paraphrases, '' till thou cut off thy head and give up thy life, thou wilt not stand in the place of safety.'' But the last sentence can hardly be a fair rendering of سپر نشوی, the interpretation of which remains in any case a difficulty. I cannot twist the original into any agreement with a third suggestion of B's. The upshot, however, as he says, is '' that humility and destruction of self and lowliness in this world is chieftainship and a protection in the world of true religion, and that is enough.''

3 As B points out, the line may be interpreted differently if the iẓāfat is placed after the first word of each hemistich. '' The abandonment of the ordered arrangement of the beauties of this world is the saddling of the Divine favour in one's search, and preparedness in the path of God and religion; and so too the renunciation of the external order, the aforesaid beauty, is the essence of reality.''

soul.[1] By no means stand still on this path; become non-existent,—non-existent too as regards becoming non-existent;[2] when thou hast abandoned both individuality and understanding, then for thee this world changes to that one.

57 Every desire[3] that springs up in thee, strike that moment at its head, as thou dost with the lamp, the candle, and pen;[4] for every head that comes in sight is on this Path meet to be cut off. To be headless[5] before heroes is due respect; for ever a chief seeks a cap of honour.[6] To lose thy head brings thee a head again for its fruit;[7] by reason of its headlessness the pomegranate is a casket full of pearls.[8]

Though a crown is a protection to a bald head, with such a head it is wrong to wear a crown.[9] Thou hast corruption under thy cap,

---

1 "The death of the soul through alloy with worldly affairs and with the delights of the flesh is destruction to life,—the life that is filled with the secrets of God and belongs to the world of light and knowledge. But the death of the life, that is, the annihilation of the traveller on this path and the giving up of the earthly life of externals, is, as it were, the life of the soul." B.

2 "This points to an annihilation within annihilation; become non-existent, and even as regards the knowledge of thy becoming non-existent, which in reality is a form of existence, become non-existent, that is, without knowledge," L. Amplifying the above, B says:—"Hasten on the road, till thou becomest naught and art annihilated; and this is the high place of the Knowers. But even this is not the place on reaching which thou mayest be content; for the culmination of the search is this, that even in annihilation thou shouldst be annihilated, and shouldst cast into the place of non-existence the knowledge thou hast acquired in becoming non-existent; that is, that thou shouldst exist as nothing that can come within the comprehension of anyone, nothing that thou canst estimate thyself as being."

3 سر, — also 'head'; so through the next few lines the word is the same for 'head' and 'desire.' "Destroy every thought of self and selffulness even at the moment of its passing through the mind," B.

4 "For till they are trimmed, the light is bad, and the writing imperfect," B.

5 *i.e.*, humble.

6 *i.e.*, only chiefs are entitled to be anything else than humble.

7 Or 'to be without desire brings thee power'; cf. l. 1. n.

8 "The pomegranate, hanging on the tree like one with head bowed down, may be said to have no head; hence it is like a casket full of pearls, to which its seeds are here compared." B.

9 The baldness referred to is the common form of baldness in the East, due to disease of the scalp, in which scabs form and the hair-roots are destroyed; Eng.

—then canst thou not possibly pass the bridge of fire.[1] Better for a man than earthly fortune is a well;[2] a bald man becomes arrogant when he receives a crown;[3] so is it well that while on this night-journey,[4] when thou puttest thy hand to thy head, thou shouldest find no crown thereon; for while the baldheaded man desires a crown to cover his defect, the man of the Path seeks for the invisible. If the crown hurts thee, no less too inverted it destroys thy life;[5] the head that is a slave to the crown is a prisoner, like Bīzhan, in a well.[6] Then own neither head[7] nor crown on the Path; if thou dost, thou wilt have thy heart aflame like wax;[8] and if thou must needs have a crown, take one of fire, like the candle; for he who in

---

'scald-head.' "The crown prevents exposure of the defect, and protects the head so afflicted against injury; but this is wrong, for such a head ruins the crown. The idea is this, that the polluted people of this world, who in the assembly of the religious are like unto men with bald and diseased heads, consider that the ornaments of this world give ease and comfort, which they do not; on the contrary, these decorations are in the path of religion worse than a thousand inelegancies." So B, but I do not think this is the meaning, which is simply that the diseased head is unworthy of honour

1 The bridge as-Sirāṭ, leading to heaven, and passing over the flames of hell, finer than a hair and sharper than a sword, over which mankind must pass after the last judgment. The righteous will pass safely over, but the condemned will fall down into hell.

2 *i.e.*, to fall into a well. The words (*jāh* and *chāh*) are doubtless chosen partly on account of the assonance.

3 Referring to the evil effect of earthly riches on their possessors.

4 معراج, Muḥammad's night-journey to heaven; *lit.* 'ascent.'

5 *i.e.*, "if because of the hurt thou invert it." 'Crown', کلاه (or, as previously, 'cap', when for 'inverted' understand 'turned with lining outwards') here as elsewhere stands for worldly goods, honour, and eminence. The appositeness of the last hemistich consists in the fact that هلاک, 'destruction', is almost کلاه, 'crown', spelt in the reverse way (*halāk*, *kulāh*).

6 Bīzhan was the son of Gīv and nephew of Rustam, who having fallen in love with the daughter of Afrāsiyāb and his secret being discovered, was ordered to be confined in a well.

7 *Cf.* p. 57, l. 1 n.

8 "As long as the wax has a wick," *i.e.*, a head or crown, "men continue to burn it; when the wick falls away, the fire falls away too, and the wax no longer burns and melts." B.

his love is the light of the Path, like a candle has a crown of fire.[1]

If thou demandest Yūsuf's place and power, invert thyself before God, like a well;[2] guard like Sulaimān the perfectness of the Path;[3] like Yūsuf look upon the well as beautiful; till thy bodily form becomes a dweller in the well, thy hidden figure will not be of God.

Arise, and leave this ignoble world to find the ineffable God; abandon body and life and reason and religion;[4] and in His path get for thyself a soul. Know, that whatso is of the true essence of learning and knowledge is all mere falsehood to him who is learned in attributes.[5] Form, and attribute, and essence,—the first is like the womb; the next the membranes, the last the child;[6] thy outward form covers in thy attributes, thy attributes again are a rampart around
58 thy inmost essence; that, like a lamp, is bright in itself, while the other two are as a glass and a niche in the wall.[7]

---

1 "For he who, in the love of God, becomes the light and candle of the Path, *i.e.*, becomes by his light a guide, has ever a cap of fire; for it is by means of this radiance, and his illumination of the road, that he has attained the position of guide. In fine, till thou settest fire to thy head and givest thyself and thy head over to destruction, no one will follow thee, nor wilt thou be fit for the task of showing the way; and this is necessary for the Knowers, that their soul should inevitably, and not from self-interest or desire for show, wish to guide others and show them the way," B.

2 Reminding one of the story, of which the idea at all events is similar, of a foolish Arab solving the wonder of the building of a tall minaret by suggesting that it had first been dug as a well and then inverted upwards. But the reading is probably corrupt.

3 The Quranic accounts of Solomon may be found in Suras 21, 27, 34, 38.

4 "This arid religion, discussion and dispute and argument about externals," B.

5 "For the latter is on a stage below the knower of pure essence," L; and so cannot comprehend it.

6 "The womb lies outside and covers the fœtal membranes, and similarly the membranes the embryo; so with form and properties and essence or the real object." L.

7 'The other two' are the attributes and outward form; which like the glass and the niche in the wall "are abundantly bright and shining because of the beams of the essence, but of themselves have no light," L. Cf. Qur. 24: 35. "*God is the light of the heavens and the earth: His light is as a niche in which is a lamp, and the lamp is in a glass, the glass is as though it were a glittering star.*"

Till on that road thou hast endured distress,[1] thou hast two souls, though thy effigy[2] is single. O thou, who art related to phenomenal existence but as soul is to body, whose soul is related to thy individuality but as a man to his name,[3] exertion originates in the body, attraction in the soul; but the search begins in leaving both of these. Contingent existence is for ever an infant before the Eternal;[4] but he who has been purified is free from these dregs.[5]

---

1 نگشتي تنگ with a hint also at the narrowness of the road.

2 *Lit.* 'doll, puppet,' referring to the human body. The two souls are the animal and the human (حيواني و انساني), L.

3 " He speaks generally to men or specially to the Lover :—' O thou, who art as pure and separate from the world of phenomena as soul from body,—since the soul, in spite of being bound and connected in arrangement and use, is pure and free from the body, and has not been entirely brought away from its blessed home into the impure world,—thou also, notwithstanding that thou existest in the phenomenal creation, art free from the pollution of matter, and thy soul also from thy individual self (وحدت), —that is, from the power of expressing the individual (يعني غلبهٔ وصف وحدت) ; just as a man and his name are separate, and notwithstanding that the name points to the man's exterior, his actual existence has no admixture or inward connection with his external name. Thy soul has the same relation to its numerous connections with external things, through the power it has of expressing the individual (بواسطهٔ غلبهٔ صفت وحدت) as the man to his name.' The above address, in the form of praise of the one addressed, whether a definite individual (*i.e.*, the Lover) or not, is very fitting. And if it be spoken blamingly, by way of instigation to the traveller on his journey, the meaning will be :—' O thou, entangled in the strait place of phenomena, or earthly pollution, like the soul in the narrow habitation of the body, and whose soul has as little connection with the Unity (وحدت , here of the Unity of God) as the real man with his name,—for there are many men bearing the names of Hājī, Ghāzī, Fāẕil, 'Ālim, who have no lot in the qualities thus denoted;—exertion springs from the body, and attraction from the soul; but neither exertion nor attraction are of use till search is joined to them; and the search, the sincere seeking, rises from abandonment of body and soul.' *And God knows best which is right.*" L.

4 'Contingent existence', حدث ; 'Eternal', قدم, as before, the Eternal *from* everlasting.

5 " *Ṣāfī* is the perfect man, pure from the impurity of the body, as contrasted with the imperfect man who because of the grossness of the body sits in the dregs of contingent existence (ممكنات)," L. "In the court of the Eternal, the place where shine the rays of the divine essence, contingent existence is a

So long as the race of man endures, there are two mansions prepared for him; this, for pain and want, that one, for blessing and delight. While earth is the habitation of the sons of men, the tent of their daily supplies is erected over them; esteem then this earth a guest-house, but count man the master of a family;[1] though till he has suffered pain on this dust-heap he will not reach the treasure of that mansion.

I ask thee, since thou art heir to the knowledge of philosophy and law, their principles and deductions,[2] (religion ever flees from form, that she may constrain men from evil),[3]—give me an answer truly, if thou art not dead, nor art asleep: Since thou hast been constituted with a soul, is not the soul a sufficient reward for thee in exchange for thyself ?[4]

THE PARABLE OF THE SCHOOLBOYS.[5]

Thou knowest not the difference between the hidden world and this,—canst not distinguish between welfare and affliction. In truth,

---

thing of recent birth, like a young infant; and he who becomes free from the weight of existence (reading ثقل for نقل) becomes eternal, and is united with the Eternal; for if the perishable one becomes not free from contingency (حدث) he becomes not eternal,'' B.

1 مهمان سرای not here an inn, or caravansarai, but 'a place where food is regularly given to the poor and helpless; such as places of pilgrimage, shrines, and such like,' B.Q. The 'master of a family' on the other hand is a person of some consequence, who is 'looked up to with reverence and respect' (Stein.). The world, therefore, is not fit for the dignity of man.

2 باصل و بفرع *lit.*, '' in their root and branch.'

3 Form, صورت , *i.e*, bodily or material form.

4 This passage I take to be addressed to the scholastic theologian, who, the author implies, (l. 13), is dead or asleep; while l. 12, which I have enclosed in a parenthesis, is a warning that in outward knowledge, such as the ordinary theologian is concerned with, no true religion is to be found. The last line is also obscure; the commentators labour the first hemistich with نهاد as equivalent to بنیاد, *i.e.*, 'foundation'; L proceeds, '' So cleanse thy soul by austerity and striving and inward purification,........for though phenomenal existence is perishable, the pure soul which mounts to him will remain and endure immortally; and this is the reward of thy phenomenal existence. *But God knows best what is right.*''

5 Following M in title and arrangement of this section.

thou art not a man travelling on this Path; thou art a child of the Path, knowest not the Path; thou art but a boy,—go about thy play, go back to thy pride and independence. The airs and graces of thy mistress are enough for thee,—what, O son, hast thou to do with God? What concern hast thou with Paradise and eternal delight, who hast rejected the life to come for this present world? He knows thy baseness; how shall He invite thy thee-ness to Himself? He offers thee the virgins and palaces of Paradise, but thou art beguiled by this
present world and its beauties. O unfruitful one![1] be not feebler than 59
a boy to follow the path of God.

If a boy is unequal to learning his task, hear at once what it is that he wants; be kind to him and treat him tenderly; make him not to grieve in helpless expectation;[2] at such a time give him sweetmeats[3] in his lap to comfort him, and do not treat him harshly. But if he will not read, at once send for the strap; take hold of his ears and rub them hard;[4] threaten him with the schoolmaster, say that he will have strict orders to punish him, that he will shut him up in a rat-house, and the head rat will strangle him.

In the path that leads to the life to come be not thou less apt than a boy to receive admonition; eternity is thy sweetmeat,—haste thou then, and at the price of two rak'ahs obtain Paradise. Otherwise the rat-house will for thee be Hell,—will be thy tomb[5] which meets thee on thy way to that other mansion. Go to the writing-school of the prophets for a time; choose not for thyself this folly, this affliction. Read but one tablet of the religion of the prophets; since thou knowest nothing thereof, go, read and learn, that haply thou mayest become their friend, mayest haply escape from this stupidity;—in this corrupt

---

1 ای کم از یک و یک which L explains as "less than the product of one and one when multiplied, which is nothing (*i.e.*, no increase), and only what we had before (هیچست و تحصیل حاصل)." B suggests "who art now an individual but wert formerly less," *i.e.*, non-existent (یک هستی امّا کم از یک بودهٔ).

2 Sc. of kindness. مگدازش *lit.*, 'melt him not.'

3 کاکا = تنقل L; نقل . نقلیات B, 'dried fruits.'

4 The common form of punishment for school-children.

5 برزخ = قبر B, *lit.* 'the interval,' usually of the interval between a man's death and the resurrection.

and baleful world deem not thou that there is aught worse than stupidity.

[ON STRIVING IN GOD'S PATH.][1]

If thou wouldst possess the pearl, O man, leave the barren waste and wander by the sea; and if thou obtainest not from the sea its pellucid pearl, at least thou shalt find that thou hast not failed to reach the water.[2] Strive in God's path, O soldier; if thou hast no ambition, thou shalt have no honour; saddle and get ready thy horse for the journey to the Court of the Blest. The man who disowns in shame the dust and water of his being rides on the air like fire; crown not thy head with the heavens,[3] so mayest thou receive the diadem from Gabriel; thine shall be the angels' crown, while the crown of the firmament shall be cast down.

The true believer ever labours; for merely to hint at labour is a sick man's prayer.[4] What knowest thou of contempt of life, having no will to show thyself a warrior?[5] When thou hast laid low the

---

[1] The present section occurs as the last part of that entitled 'On the Participation of the Heart in Prayer,' where it seems out of place. I have added the present title.

[2] "Thou must not stop short of the water; thou wilt have used thy best endeavours," B.

[3] *i.e.*, I think, "be not satisfied with the heavens for a crown."

[4] "The believer is always occupied in good works thoroughly performed, for a work which is only hinted at, *i.e.*, incomplete (عمل بایما که ناقص است), is the prayer of a sick man (who cannot perform the various prostrations and risings); and a true believer is not satisfied while any defect remains in his actions," L; who then notes the reading ایمان...... بیم آر, which he explains "for religion is the bringer of prayers of fear," adding, "how then shall the religious man not be continually active, as befits his duty?" With نماز بیم *cf.* the technical term صلوة الخوف, 'prayers of fear,'—"said in time of war. They are two rak'ahs recited first by one regiment or company and then by the other" (Hughes, *op. cit.* s.v. Prayer).

B, among several other explanations gives, "The believer is always occupied in prayer, even if sick, praying by sign, and never sitting down without occupation." The translation of the line would then be inverted,—"for even a sick man prays, if only by signs."

[5] سر انداز *lit.*, 'a scatterer of heads.'

head of pride [1] then hast thou prostrated thyself before the door of the search; the heart's ka'ba has become God's dwelling-place. But the dog's ambition extends only to its bone.[2]

On Charity and Gifts. 5

Whatsoever thou hast, relinquish it for the sake of God; for charity is the greater marvel when it comes from beggars. Bestow thy life and soul, for the endeavour of the poor is the best gift of mortal clay; the prince and chief of the family of the cloak was honoured by the Sūra "*Does there not come*,"—such regard he found with God from those three poor barley-cakes.[3]

---

1 وصف جود, 'the attribute of the long-necked,' is equal to درازگردني 'long-neckedness,' B; and so 'pride.'

2 The texts, except CH which omit the line, and M which is very corrupt, have کعبهٔ دل ز حق شده مقصور همت سگ بر استخوان و قصور; for which I have ventured to read معمور .. مقصور. This seems manifestly right as regards the second hemistich. There is no reason why both should not end in the same word مقصور; I cannot find, however, that مقصور is used in any sense which would admit it in the first hemistich (though مقصورة is 'an innermost chamber, a sanctuary').

3 'The prince and chief' is 'Alī, and 'the family of the cloak' refers (B) to the story told by the commentators on Qur. 33 : 34, that one day Muḥammad drew Fāṭima and 'Alī and their two sons under his cloak, reciting the 'verse of purification,' "*Verily God wills to take away uncleanness* (*abomination*, Sale; *the horror*, Palmer) *from you the people of the house and to purify you thoroughly.*" The Sura '*Does there not come*' is the 76th, of which the opening words are "*Does there not come on man a portion of time when he is nothing worth mentioning* (*i.e.*, in the womb)"? The reference is more especially to v. 8. "*And who give food for His love to the poor and the orphan and the captive*" (Palmer's trans.); which is supposed to refer to 'Alī and his household. For the story about the giving away of barley-cakes, told in connection with this verse by the commentators, v. Sale n. *ad loc.* L is inclined to take '*for His love*,' عَلَى حُبِّهِ, in the above verse (Qur. 76 : 8) as 'though needing the food themselves, and desiring it'

Of the Story of Qais ibn ʻĀṣim.[1]

When the command of ʻ *Who is there that will lend* ʼ[2] came down from God to the Prophet, everyone brought before the Prince[3] what he could lay hands on, not disobeying,—gems and gold, cattle and slaves and goods, whatever they possessed at the time. Qais b. ʻĀṣim was a poor man, for he sought no worldly gain. He went into his house, and spoke with his family, concealing nothing of what he had heard :—Such a verse has been revealed to-day; rise, and do not make me burn in waiting; bring whatever is to be had in the house, that I may present it before the Prince. His wife said, There is nothing in the house,—you are not a stranger here.[4] Said he, Seek at least for something; whatever you find, bring it to me quickly.

She went and long searched the house, to see if by chance something would turn up; and found in the house a measure of dates, bad ones, and dried up, not fit for food, which she straightway brought
61 to Qais, saying, We have nothing more than this. Qais put the dates in his sleeve, and brought them joyfully before the Prophet. When, not meaning a jest, but in all seriousness, he entered the mosque, one of the Hypocrites[5] said to him, Bring it in; come, present quickly what thou hast brought: are they jewels, or gold, or silver, these valuables that thou art entrusting to the Prince? At this speech Qais suddenly became ashamed.

Look now what was the outcome. He went into a corner and sat down sorrowing, folding his hands together in shame. Gabriel

---

[1] This story is a parenthesis within the last section, which is afterwards resumed.

[2] Qur. 2: 246. " *Who is there that will lend to God a good loan? He will redouble it many a double: God closes his hand and holds it out, and unto Him shall ye return.* "

[3] *i.e.*, Muḥammad.

[4] *i.e.*, You know our circumstances.

[5] The third of the parties at Medina. Besides the Refugees, who had come from Mecca about the time of Muḥammad's own flight, and the Helpers, at whose invitation Muḥammad had come, and upon whom he could thoroughly depend, there were a number who outwardly acknowledged him as prophet and ruler, though in their hearts they were at best lukewarm, or actually disaffected.

the trusty came from the sidra-tree [1] and said,[2] O lord of time and earth, do not keep the man waiting, and deem not contemptible what he has brought. He acquainted Muṣṭafā with the matter, and '*Those who defame the willing ones*' was thereupon revealed.[3] The angel world came and looked on,—how they watched the man! An earthquake fell upon the angel world,—no place of rest, no place of peace. God Most High thus speaks, and in His kindness

---

1 Referred to in Qur. 53 : 14, '*the sidra-tree of the extremity*,' and ib. v. 16. "This tree, say the commentators, stands in the seventh heaven, on the right hand of the throne of God; and is the utmost bounds beyond which the angels themselves must not pass; or, as some rather imagine, beyond which no creature's knowledge can extend" (Sale *ad. loc.*).

2 *i.e.*, to Muḥammad.

3 Qur. 9: 80. "*Those who defame such of the believers as willingly give their alms, and such as can find nothing to give but their exertions, and who mock at them —God will mock at them, and for them is grievous woe.*" Though I cannot find that the verse from the second sūra, referred to in the first line of the present section, is supposed to have a special relation to any particular occasion, the verse here quoted from the ninth sūra, like much of the sūra from which it comes, was revealed in relation to,—before, during or after (Nöldeke, Gesch. d. Qorans, p. 167)—the expedition of Rajab A.H. 9 to Tabūq. Sale *ad loc.* supposes that the collection was made to defray the charge of the expedition, and says:— "Al Beidāwi relates that Mohammed exhorting his followers to voluntary alms, amongst others Abda'lrahman Ebn Auf gave four thousands dirhems, which was one-half of what he had; Asem Ebn Adda gave a hundred beasts' loads of dates; and Abu Okail a saá [the word translated 'measure' in the text; a quantity equal to $5\frac{1}{3}$ pints, dry measure (Stein.)] which is no more than a sixtieth part of a load, of the same fruit, but was the half of what he had earned by a night's hard work. This Mohammed accepted; whereupon the hypocrites said that Abda'lrahman and Asem gave what they did out of ostentation, and that God and his apostle might well have excused Abu Okail's mite; which occasioned this passage." Nöldeke, however (*op. cit.* n. p. 167), "Wir nehmen hier keine Rücksicht auf die vielen Fabeln, welche die Kommentare zu den einzelnen Versen anfuhren; z. B. von den Nachstellungen der Heuchler u.s.w. Hiervon findet sich nichts bei Hisham. Dennoch bleibt es merkwürdig, dass sich an diesen Zug, wie ein paar andere, so viele Fabeln knüpfen, während einige andere Feldzüge des Propheten ganz geschichtlich treu erzählt werden." And Muir (Life of Mahomet, 3rd ed., p. 431 note), "But a great number of the stories belonging to this campaign may be suspected (on the analogy of similar traditions regarding other texts) to have been fabricated for the purpose of illustrating the text of the Coran."

seeks out Qais's heart: O exalted, and O chosen as my Prophet, accept forthwith this much from Qais, for before me these poor dates show better than the others' gold and gems. I have accepted this small merchandise from him, because he has no date-palm. Of all the choicest things the endeavour of the poor is most approved.

Hence it was that Qais's act triumphed over the deed of that evil-spoken hypocrite. The hypocrite was straightway humiliated, and Qais's work thus completed; that thou mayest know that whoso comes forward, even in the state he is, does well. He who acts the hypocrite towards God is shamed by all his works. Sincerity is better than all else,—thou wilt at least have read so much.

An alms of a single diram from the hand of a darwīsh is more than
62 a thousand dirams of the wealthy; forasmuch as the darwīsh's heart is sore, the alms he gives from his sore heart is greater than the other's. See the rich man, how his soul is dark and clouded, like his clay; the darwīsh's clay is for ever pure,[1] his soul is imperishable essence of gold.[2] Hear what God's bounty has said; but to whom shall I tell it, for no one bears me company?—to the king of kings and lord of '*But for thee*'[3] He said "*Nor let thine eyes be turned from them.*"[4]

On Intimate Friendship and Attachment.[5]

There is no injury in the world for thee like thy prosperity; there is no such enduring imprisonment as thy existence; '*the light has*

---

1 صفوت the choicest, best part of anything.

2 كيميا 'alchemy; the philosopher's stone; an elixir'; or, as here, 'the basis of gold and silver,' B; who refers to Muḥammad's saying, "*Poverty is my glory* (الفقر فخري)."

3 That is, 'But for thee the world would not have been called out of non-existence,' referring to Muḥammad; according to the tradition quoted in B, "*But for thee I had not created the heavens.*"

4 Qur. 18: 26. "*And keep thyself patient with those who call upon their Lord morning and evening, desiring His face; nor let thine eyes be turned from them, desiring the adornment of the life of this world.*" God here commands the prophet to incline towards the darwishes, thus honouring and exalting them. L.

5 The title, as often, is somewhat astray from the contents of the following section, and is probably spurious. The subject is still the abandonment of the world.

appeared' it is that bestows favours, '*the lie has failed*' is both life and body. Wishest thou the Invisible? take Self out of the path; what has imperfection to do with the mansion of Invisibility? Thou art full of fault, yet intendest the invisible world;—it is above all impossible in incredulity and doubt. The chains of thy selfhood will not fall from the two feet of thy nature under the compulsion of thy folly; when thy being appears to thee as a veil, thy understanding will have fallen under thy anger.

Abandon talk, and bid farewell to thy lower self; if thou canst not, then turn thy two eyes into rivers, day and night in thy separation from God grieve over thy understanding,[1] no longer employ it to meditate evil; free it from this tether,[2]—then has thy task become easy for thee. When thou findest thy sustenance in the Soul,[3] thou wilt look out on the land from the window of the angel world.

How long wilt thou say, "What is the arriving? In the path of religion what is it to be chosen?" Lay bonds upon thyself,—then wilt thou be chosen; plant thy foot upon thy head,—then wilt thou have arrived.[4] As long as thou art a biter, thou art not chosen;[5] whilst thou inclinest to this world, thou hast not arrived.[6]

---

1 B points دَر فراقِ عقل, *i.e.*, 'in the absence of thy understanding'; which does not seem good, as the implication is that thy understanding is only too much with thee.

2 عقیله which B points عُقَیله, and explains as the diminutive of عُقله, the tethering of a camel's foot, here fo" "the affairs of the world."

3 Not in the understanding.

4 "Then wilt thou be chosen, when by abandoning sensual passion and envy and covetousness thou puttest the restraints of endeavour and austerity on the hand and foot of thy nature; and wilt have arrived and wilt be perfected when thou plantest thy foot on thy head and Me-ness; or bringing one end to the other, completest the circle of thy journey [for the Ṣūfī's journey as a circle, ending in the embrace of the First Intelligence whence it set forth, v. Gibb, *op. cit.*, pp. 52-53]; and wilt arrive at the shadow of that Name which is the origin of particularization [تعیُّن cf. Gibb, pp. 60-61]. *Al Junaid was asked concerning the end, and he said, It is the return to the beginning.*" L.

5 A play on the words گزنده and گزیده.

6 "As long as, through the vileness of thy soul, thou livest in this world like a biting dog, thou wilt not be chosen and approved in the Court of God; and

20 How shall a true son of Adam[1] be such a biter as thou, or how shall devil or wild beast rend as thou dost ? Thou art ever heedless and arrogant, a beast of prey and a devil, far removed from man's estate ; like a tiger ever malevolent,—the people of the world in distress
63 through thy evil disposition. Upon this high road of debasement thou wilt attain to Self,—thou wilt not attain to Him.[2]

The Kufan has given forth but one verse about the Ṣūfī ; but what has Love to do with the decision of Quraishite or Kufan ;[3]

---

as long as thou art a lover of this world (تا بدین عالم رسندهٔ) and cherishest an inclination for it, thou wilt not have arrived in the Court of the Glorious.'' B ; whose second explanation (''till thou understandest this mystery in its entirety,'' تا برین رمز نرسیدهٔ بکمال) would require in the text a negative with رسندهٔ.

[1] آدمي ''for we in truth are degenerate sons of Adam,'' B.

[2] L, reading نرسي در خود و درو برسي, comments, ''When thou enterest the street of nothingness and humility thou hast naught further to do with the arriving at Self, *i.e.*, I and Self are far away from thee ; and since this is so, thou wilt reach the Court of God and gain access to Him.'' He mentions also a reading برسي...برسي (''thou wilt arrive at Self, and wilt arrive at Him'') ; which he explains thus :—''When by much striving and austerity thou attainest the essence of thy soul (or self, حقيقت نفس) which is nothingness, and arrivest at the secret of this, thou wilt arrive at God and wilt discover the truth of ''*Who knows himself knows his Lord.*'' B, reading نرسي ... نرسي, says ''Abandonment of self is a road to which thou wilt not come by means of Self, and since thou canst not get onto the beginning of the road, thou wilt not arrive at God :'' but I do not understand how he arrives at this paraphrase.

The weight of evidence is for نرسي at the end of the line, and therefore, probably, by opposition, for برسي at the beginning of the second hemistich. And I think the confusion has arisen from a wrong conception of the meaning of *hīchkasī*, which is not here used, as the commentators assume, in the technical sense of 'nothingness,' 'abandonment of self,' or 'humility,' but in the more ordinary sense of 'baseness, vileness.'

[3] From the lengthy notes of the commentators on this line I extract the following, premising that 'the Kufan' refers to Abū Hanīfah an-Nu'mān, the founder of the Hanīfī sect of Sunnī Muslims, and 'the Quraishite' to ash-Shāfi'ī, the founder of the Shāfi'ī sect, called also al-Muṭṭalibī from his descent from Muḥammad's grandfather.

''What the Kufan imām has said of the mysteries and secrets of religion is only one sign out of all those that serve to describe the Ṣūfī state, and is no more or the Ṣūfī and his love with ‘ Further, it is in the tradition,’ with negation and affirmation, and ‘ *It is lawful* ’ and ‘ *It is not lawful* ’ ? The Ṣūfīs have lifted up their hands,[1] and for ‘ *Yes* ’ have substituted ‘ *No.*’[2]

---

than a mark of his recondite knowledge. Hence it is not necessary that he should have been ignorant of all the Ṣūfī secrets, but that he should have declared a little, a verse, of the Ṣūfī secrets that were known to him, in order to veil those secrets from the vulgar. For those meanings and mysteries come not into the enclosure of recital, and cannot be further indicated,'' L; who also considers that the words آيتى and كوفي may incidentally have a reference to the ‘ Kufan āyat,’ ‘ āyat ’ being technically the mark put at the end of each of the verses of the Qur'ān. The Kufan āyat is a cipher with the letters لب (*i.e.* ليس آية البصري, ‘‘ *This is not the end of the verse according to the school of Baṣra* ’’). The school of Kūfa counts 6,239 verses, that of Baṣra 6,204 ; the Kufan divisions are the ones generally followed (on the manner of marking verse-divisions, and the prevalence of the Kufan readings, *cf.* Nöldeke, *op. cit.*, pp. 324, 355).

‘‘ This road, the science of the knowledge of God, on which thou wishest to travel, perhaps thou imaginest it to be possible by the science of argument of external things. God forbid ! there is an absolute separation between the road of Love and that of outward knowledge, and between the usages of the men of each of these....The Kufan may perhaps have looked on the Ṣūfī and the Ṣūfī path as something analogous to the marks in the Qur'ān, the signs placed there on account of differences among the readers. God forbid that anything should result, as regards Love, from this discussing and disputing ! For the differences of the marks are matters of human decision and intention ; Kufan and Quraishite have no place in Love, and words and calling to mind and being lawful and not being lawful and negation and affirmation as to the external questions of the law have no connection with it. Still they (*i.e.*, the Kufan and the Quraishite) were not without a knowledge of the mysteries......it is only thou whose thought regarding the Qur'ān, is that the Kufan āyat is so-and-so, and that the Quraishite has said so-and-so, and that the rival schools permit such and such things. Know, however, that they entered this valley and breathed of the mysteries,'' B.

Would it not, however, be possible to translate the first hemistich ‘‘ A text of the Qur'ān will make a Kufan doctor of a Ṣūfī,'' *i.e.*, a too rigid adherence to the literal text, or discussing and disputing about it, is fatal to the Ṣūfī, and turns him into a formal theologian ? Note in this connection H's reading, الفي كرد, which can only be ‘‘ an *alif* turned a Ṣūfī into a Kufan (theologian).''

1 In prayer or supplication.

2 *i.e.*, make no distinctions of affirmation and negation in these external matters.

The earth-scatterers in the bridal-chamber of His affection, and those who sit by the road which leads to the cell of His sanctity, all are moon-bright signs on the curtain of jealousy, immersed in tears from foot to head;[1] all are recipients of His clemency, all captive to the knowledge of Him. Lay down thy burden of Self, that so thou mayest become the beloved of every street. The pure eye sees the purity of religion;[2] when the eye is pure, it sees purely. Those who are not steadfast in Him are covered with dust;[3] those who wear His crown are kings indeed. Take off thy head this many-coloured cloak;[4] hold to a garment of one colour, like 'Isā,[5] that like him thou mayest walk upon the water, and make of sun and moon thy fellow-travellers. Take all of self away from thyself, and then with that same breath speak the story of Adam.[6] Till thy Self becomes small as an atom to thee, thou canst not possibly reach that place; that desire will never harmonize with Self; rise, and without thy Self pursue thy path.

He who is indifferent to the World finds a Kingdom that shall not wane.[7]

There was an old ascetic in Baṣra, none in that age so devout as he. He said, I rise every morning determined to fly from this vile

---

[1] I am not certain of the interpretation; nor does the following from B give much help. "Those of honeyed palate in the bridal-chamber of God's affection, who are the scatterers of earth in the court of Truth, and those who know the holy secrets, who are the sitters by the road of the court of Majesty, are like a sign, bright as the full moon and shining, but concealed and hidden behind the curtain of envy, burnt and drowned, but immersed in a flood of tears."

[2] *i.e.*, the heart or kernel of religion, the knowledge of God, the essence of the Truth, B.

[3] بادسار —، خاکسارند بادسارانش is given by B as meaning 'proud, haughty; a chief, chieftain.' B.Q. and Stein., however give 'light, trifling, volatile, swift; and as the words in the second hemistich are of homologous import (in fact identical), it seems probable that those in the first have both a contemptuous significance. Otherwise, "His chieftains are the humble."

[4] *Lit.*, 'seven-coloured', expressive of deceit.

[5] *i.e.*, Jesus.

[6] *i.e.*, tell the story of Adam, and how he was honoured by God's saying, "*I will place upon the earth a deputy*" (Qur. 2 : 28). B.

[7] Qur. 20: 118. "*But the devil whispered to him. Said he, O Adam, shall I guide thee to the tree of immortality, and a kingdom that shall not wane?*"

Self. My Self says to me, Come, old man, what wilt thou eat this morning? Make some preparation, come, tell me what I am to eat. I tell him, Death; and leave the subject. Then my Self says to me, What shall I put on? I say, The winding-sheet. Then he questions me, and makes most absurd requests, such as, O thou of blind 64
heart, where dost thou wish to go? I say to him, Silence! to the grave-side; so that perhaps while in rebellion against my Self I may draw a breath in freedom from the fear of the night-watchman.[1]

Honour to him who contemns Self, and does not permit it to stand before him.[2]

On the Asceticism of the Ascetic.

An ascetic fled from amongst his people, and went to the top of a mountain, where he built a cell. One day by chance a sage, a learned man, wise and able, passed by and saw the ascetic, so holy and devout. Said he, Poor wretch! why hast thou made thy dwelling and habitation and home upon this height? The ascetic said, The people of this world have been clean destroyed in their pursuit of it: the hawk of the world is on the wing, calling aloud in every country; he speaks with eloquent tongue, seeking his prey throughout the world, ever calling on its people afflicted and parted from their lord, "Woe to him who fears me not, who shows no anxiety to seek me! Let it not happen as in Fusṭāṭ,—few birds and hawks in plenty![3]

On the Love of the World and the Manner of the People of it.[4]

There is a great city within the borders of Rūm, where a large number of hawks have made their home. Fusṭāṭ is the name of that

---

1 *i.e.*, the devil. "Every answer that I give my Self shall be displeasing to him, that perhaps I may so draw a single breath out of the reach of the dangers of the devil." B.

2 'Self' throughout the above is نفس, *i.e.*, as previously, 'the lower self'; often 'sensuality.'

3 *i.e.*, "See that I have enough to eat." Fusṭāṭ is ancient Cairo. "The world practises its deceptions with alluring voice, making the ignoble its prey. The seekers of the world are the world's prey, and the birds of Fusṭāṭ, which are few in number, are the religious." B.

4 The next five lines, to which alone this title applies, are a digression in the course of the ascetic's speech.

city of renown; it extends to the borders of Dimyāṭ.[1] Within it no house-sparrows fly, for the hawks hunt them through the air and leave no birds inside that city, for they devour them within an hour. The times are now become like Fusṭāṭ; the wise are like the birds, despised and helpless.

I have hidden myself[2] upon this height to be at peace from the evil of the world. The sage said, Who lives here with thee? How farest thou on this hill-top? Said the ascetic, My Self[3] is in this house with me by day and night. The sage said, Then hast thou accomplished nothing; cease, O fool, to follow the path of asceticism. The ascetic said, They have fixed my Self within me, and sold me into his hands; I cannot separate myself from him—what means of escape could I contrive? Said that worthy philosopher to the ascetic, Thy Self instructs thee in evil deeds. The ascetic said, I have come to know my Self, and so I am able to get on with him; he is a sick man, and I am as it were his physician; day and night I look after him and am busy treating him, for he keeps saying he is indisposed. Sometimes I determine to bleed him, and open the vein before his eyes;[4] as the blood spouts out, he subsides,[5] and the bleeding calms him. Sometimes I give him a purge to clear out his distempers; and his love of the world, and hatred, and rancour, and envy, and treachery, and deceit are expelled from his body; on taking it he thrusts aside his natural inclinations and shuts the door of desire against himself. Sometimes I forbid him to indulge his appetites, that haply he may relinquish pleasure; I feed him on two beans, and make the room like a tomb upon him. Sometimes I put my Self to sleep, and then in

---

[1] *i.e.*, Damietta.

[2] The ascetic's speech is here resumed.

[3] نفس v. note *ant.*, p. 64, l. 3.

[4] اکحل 'the middle vein of the arm,' probably the median basilic, on which the operation of bleeding is usually performed. B explains it as 'the vein of seven members (رگ هفت اندام) called the river of the body (نهر البدن).' There are in fact numerous veins on the front of the forearm which join about the elbow to form two large trunks. The meaning of از دیدگانش might perhaps be "when he is not looking."

[5] Gloss in B نشیند (under بارد).

haste make one or two obeisances;[1] but even before he awakes from his sleep he clings to me like a sick man; and when I have got through one or two obeisances without him, then my Self wakes up.

On hearing these words the sage tore his garments one by one upon his body and said, How excellent art thou, O ascetic! May God bless thy life, thou pious man! Such words are granted but to thee; thy wealth is not less than the kingdom of Jam. That which thou possessest today is adornment, and what thou mayest have to-morrow,[2] impurity.

He is not stained who leaves his sins, from whom in sorrow a sigh **66**
of 'Alas' arises; a woman nimbly adorns her eyebrows and her ringlets for a feast.[3]

In three prisons, deceit and hatred and envy, thou hast made thy understanding captive to thy body. The five senses, having their origin in the four elements, are the five tale-bearers of these three prisons. The soul is a stranger here, and a fool, so long as it is in bondage to the four elements; how can the soul that is admitted to the treasury of the secret pay honour to spies and informers? But here[4] wisdom empties the quiver,[5] for persistence in one's purpose is useless at the Ka'ba.[6] Haply a fool at the Ka'ba will hear much philosophy about the direction of the qibla; but at the Ka'ba whoso should strive even till he died would but take fresh cuminseed to Kirmān.[7]

---

1 رَکعت, an obeisance made in prayer.

2 *i.e.*, any further worldly riches thou mayest acquire.

3 B explains the connection, which is not very apparent, thus:—"As a woman does this, so a man should adorn himself with contrition and shame in order to attain perfection." But perhaps the line is misplaced, or one has dropped out. The main theme is now again resumed, after the insertion of the above two illustrative stories.

4 *i.e.*, the other place, in opposition to the 'here' preceding.

5 *i.e.*, throws away her arrows.

6 *i.e.*, the pilgrimage is accomplished. "At the Ka'ba the object sought is in front of the eyes of him who prays there; then why should he persist further? For in these circumstances wisdom has no butt to aim at, since to shoot the arrows of forethought when the object is before one is useless; nor is it the business of wisdom to discover this target." B.

7 *i.e.*, would carry coals to Newcastle, and lose his pains.

His tongue the tongueless speak;[1] some mark of Him those seek who have no mark.[2] Cast in the fire all else besides the Friend, then raise thy head from out the water of Love. On the journey from this life to the next the slave has no ally in what he does of right or infamy;[3] surrender not thy heart and thy desire to the companionship of men; cut thyself off from them, lest they cut thy throat.[4] At the last day thou shalt weary of men, but thou art far off now, and it will take thee long to come;[5] then wilt thou discover the onion's value, when thou art denied admittance to the straight road.[6] Those who are not friends, yet whom thou deemest such, thou wilt see that they all break their faith with thee. The rose-tree of the garden of those who cherish Self is become as a boil, a malignant pimple. Understand well, the state of men will be no whit different at the resurrection; whatsoever he chooses, that will be set before him, and what he takes from here he will see there. When the second command of God has uttered four *takbīrs* upon thy three pillars, the cloth-weavers of the eternal world will recite thine own words and poems to thee.[7]

---

1 Tongueless, *i.e.*, silent, not vainly disputing.

2 The undistinguished, *i.e.*, humble, poor, and insignificant; 'those of burnt hearts,' B. بی نشان in a different sense is applied to God in Sa'dī's lines,

گر کسی وصف او ز من پرسد   بی دل از بی نشان چه گوید باز

3 Meaning, I think, no one to take the consequences of his acts; hence the uselessness of human friendships.

4 *i.e.*, destroy thee spiritually.

5 To this attitude, when thou art weary of men and desirest only God.

6 "The value of the onion, *i.e.*, thine own stinking existence, thou wilt then discover, when thou art refused admission to the straight road on account of thy stink. Or 'the onion' may suitably refer to the companionship of the world spoken of in the preceding line; thou wilt find what its value is when, like an eater of onions, thou art refused admission because of the effects it leaves." L.

7 The *takbīr* is the recital of the words *Allāhu akbar*, 'God is most great': the four *takbīrs* signify the funeral prayer, B.

L conceives that these two lines may be taken in the sense of praise, or the reverse; if in the sense of praise, the second sentence of death is the natural death, the first death having taken place in the sense of the abandonment of the life of this world (نشاء مجاز) in accordance with the command "*Die before your death*," and the words of Jesus, "*He who is not twice born shall not enter the kingdom of heaven*;" in this case the angels will bring before thee the pious desires and the good words that have risen from thee to God. If on the

The things[1] the worthy shopkeeper sends to his house from the market, whatever they may be, his family bring before him at home 67
in the evening; so whatever thou takest away from here is kept, and the very same is brought before thee at the resurrection. There is no change or substitution there; by no possibility can an evil become a good. Nothing will be given free to anyone there; what is due is given, and nothing besides.[2] Rise and read, if thou knowest it not, the explanation of this in the Divine Word; 'thou shalt not find any change in the ordinance of God, thou shalt not find any alteration in His religion.'[3] No alteration comes over His inexorable sentence, no change upon His all-embracing decree. Rise, and put away thy uncleanness, or thou wilt not receive thy pardon in that world; if now thou piercest thy Self with an arrow thou wilt throw into the fire thy sorrow and thy pain.[4]

---

contrary the lines are to be read as a condemnation, there is a reference to Qur. 40: 11. "*They shall say, O Lord, Thou hast killed us twice, and Thou hast quickened us twice; and we do confess our sins; is there then a way for getting out?*" The first death is at the end of one's appointed time, the first quickening is in the tomb (*i.e.*, in order to be examined); the second death follows in the tomb, and the second quickening at the resurrection; thus when the second sentence of death is passed on thee in the tomb, the embroidery workers of the eternal world will recite to thee the words and verses thou sangest in the world in passion and lust; and then the true nature of thy acts will be brought before thee.

As to the second death, in addition to the explanation given by L, v. the notes in Palmer and Sale *ad loc.* The first death may be interpreted as the first creation of man, in a state of death or void of life and sensation; the first birth is then the natural birth, the second death the natural death, and the second birth the resurrection.

1 A title, as of a fresh section, is inserted before this line in all copies; in L it runs "*God Most High was at rest from the Creation, and their Qualities, and Food and Doom*"; which has nothing to do with the text, the sense of which is continued on without a break.

2 وان دگر همه باد, "and the rest is all wind."

3 For ملتش B notes an alternative reading سنتش, so bringing the passage more closely into line with Qur. 35: 43. "*For thou shalt not find any change in the ordinance of God; and thou shalt not find any alteration in the ordinance of God.*" The line as it stands in the text is mixed Arabic and Persian, and incapable of being construed.

4 زحیر *lit.*, 'dysentery.'

Of Addresses to God, and Self-abasement, and Humility.[1]

Prayer will not draw back the veil of Majesty till the servant comes forth from his defilement;[2] as thy purity opens the door of prayer, so know that thy corruption locks it against thee. When wilt thou plant thy foot upon the heavens' roof,[3] when drink wine from the angels' cup? How can God in His kindness take thee to Himself, or freely accept thy prayers, while like an ass within this rotting mansion thy belly is full of food and thy loins of water?[4] How wilt thou ever see

---

[1] The title of this section, as given in most copies, is somewhat as follows (from B), with variations in each of the several MSS., etc. "*On the Obligations of the Five daily Prayers, of Addresses to God, Self-abasement, and Humility, and Modesty, and calling upon God. God Most High has said, 'Those who believe in what is hidden, and are steadfast in Prayer'; and the Prophet (on whom be Peace) said when near his Death, 'And what your right hands possess'; and he said (Peace be upon him), 'Whoso of set purpose abandons Prayer is an Unbeliever, and the Distinction between Islām and Unbelief is the Abandoning of Prayer'; and he said also, 'Three things are dearer to me than this World of yours; Perfume, and Women, and my chief Delight is in Prayer.'*" With regard to Muḥammad's speech '*And what your right hands possess*' (*i.e.*, your slaves, *cf.* Qur. 4 : 3, 28, 29, 40; 23 : 5; 24 : 33; 33 : 49), this probably refers to a passage in Muḥammad's address to the people on the occasion of his 'Farewell pilgrimage,' *cf.* Muir *op. cit.*, p. 458. I have not been able to find this particular passage in b. Hishām or Ṭabarī, though the passages which in Muir precede and succeed it are given in both these authorities. This particular sentence stands, as it were, for the farewell speech as a whole; and the connection with prayer, the subject of the present section, then appears when it is remembered that Muḥammad at this time declared the ordinances of Islām fixed for all future time; and of these ordinances prayer, of course, is one (*cf.* Muir, *loc. sup. cit.*, the last sentences of the speech); at least I cannot understand its inclusion in the title otherwise.

'*My chief delight*' is lit. '*the coolness of my eye*'; for a similar saying *cf.* Muir, *op. cit.*, p. 476. This last tradition does not form part of the title in L.

I do not suppose that the original title comprised more than a few words,— if indeed any of the sectional titles are original. The rest of the title, as found today in the MSS. and lithographs, has evidently been made up by the incorporation of sentences *apropos* of prayer written by pious readers in the margins of early copies.

[2] Or "comes forth out of contingent existence."

[3] B refers to the saying, "*Prayer is the ladder of the believer.*"

[4] Seminal fluid, *i.e.*, pride, B.

the Lord of the divine Law, thy lower parts sunk in the water and thy nose in heaven ?[1]

Thy beggar's food and cloak must both be pure, or thou wilt come to thy destruction in the dust; if food and raiment be not pure how is thy prayer better than a handful of dust? Keep pure for the glory of God's service thy habitation and thy raiment and thy soul; the dog sweeps his lair with his tail, but thou sweepest not with sighs thy place of prayer.

Though all thou hast be spotless, yet is all polluted before God. He who seeks Him makes use first of a bath, for God accepts not the prayers of the unclean; and how canst thou perform thy neglected 68
ablution so long as thy heart holds enmity and hatred? Thy envy, anger, avarice, desire, and covetousness,—I marvel indeed if these will admit of thy coming to prayer! Till thou banishest envy from thy heart, thou wilt never be free from its evil workings. If thou hast not washed thyself free from blame, the mighty Lord will not receive thy prayer; but when thy heart draws thee out from thyself, then true prayer rises up from thy destitution. The whole of prayer lies in ablution and purification;[2] recovery from a grievous sickness depends on the use of remedies.[3]

Until thou sweep the path with the broom of *Not*, how canst thou enter the abode of *Except God*?[4] So long as thou art under the dominion of the four, the five and the six,[5] thou shalt not taste of wine save from the jar of lust. Burn and destroy all else but God; cleanse thyself from everything but the true faith. The soul's qibla is the threshold of the Most High; the heart's Uḥud is the sanc-

---

[1] "In thy pride of self thy gait upon this earth is as a man who walks with his nose in heaven and feet sunk in the ground." B.

[2] وضو the ceremonial ablution before prayer, performed in a certain specified manner.

[3] The two hemistichs of this line have no very evident connection; I take it that the sickness is man's natural state, and purification the remedy to be applied.

[4] Referring to the sentence *Lā shaia illā-l-lāh*, '*There is naught except God.*' That is, until thou washest thyself pure from Self, and thy Self passes away and becomes non-existent, thou canst not attain unto the true religion, which sees nothing but God, nor recognises aught besides Him.

[5] The four elements, five senses, and six surfaces (of a cube), B.

tuary of the One ;[1] at Uḥud devote thy life like Hamza, that so thou mayest taste the sweetness of the call to prayer.

Come not in thy pride to prayer ; take shame to thyself and stand in awe of God ; him God receives in prayer who has no commanding dignity in his own eyes.[2] Helpless, thou wilt be received with kindness ; wanting for nothing, thy prayer will not be accepted. Wanting for nothing, if thou give thyself the trouble of prayer, thou shalt consume thy liver fried in the pan with onions.[3] But if along with prayer goes helplessness, the hand of kindness shall raise the veil of the secret ; then, speeding into the Court of God's kindness, he renders what is due, he obtains what he sought ;[4] and if it be not so,[5] Iblīs will hear thee when thou art at prayer, and drag thee forth again.

Thou camest abject, thy prayer is honoured ; thou camest as a raw youth, thy prayer is as one of venerable age. Know, that the seventeen rak'ahs of prayer given forth from the soul's heart are a kingdom of eighteen thousand worlds ;[6] a kingdom of eighteen thousand worlds belongs to him who performs the seventeen rak'ahs ; and say not that this reckoning is too small,[7] for seventeen is not far from eighteen.[8]

---

1 Uḥud is the name of the site of one of the early battles of Islām, where Muḥammad and his forces were repulsed with great slaughter by the Meccans A.H. 3. Hamza, Muḥammad's uncle, was one of the slain. 'The heart's Uḥud' thus means the place where the self is to be sacrificed.

2 سوی خود هرکه نیست بار خدای   دهدش در نماز بار خدای

بار in the first hemistich = شوکت, B : خدای in the sense of 'lord, master.'

3 'To eat one's liver' is 'to grieve, to be sorrowful.'

4 'What is due,' *i.e.*, fit and acceptable prayers ; 'what he sought,' God's bounty and graciousness, B.

5 ورنه 'otherwise,' *i.e.*, if thou prayest not in helplessness, referring to l. 16.

6 Seventeen is the number of rak'ahs or sections comprised in the obligatory prayers of one day, as follows :—two at morning prayers, four at the noon, four at the afternoon three at the sunset, and four at the night prayers. The 'eighteen thousand worlds' refers to the tradition, "*Verily God hath created eighteen thousand worlds, and verily your world is one of them.*"

7 *i.e.*, as I understand it, that this number of prayers is too small to bring such a glorious reward.

8 "Know that the soul's heart is *alif* [i.e. *one* in reckoning by *abjad* ; *alif* is also the Arabic word for a thousand]. When thou addest that, the symbol for

Thy self-esteem[1] utters no prayer, for it sees no profit for thee in religion; while thy self-esteem guides the reins I doubt indeed if it will ever come where Gabriel is. Thy prayer will not admit thee to God if thou hast not purified thyself in indigence; thy purification lies in lowliness and selflessness, thy atonement in the slaughter of thy Self; and when thou hast slain thy Self upon the path, God's favour will quickly manifest itself. Come in thy poverty if thou wouldst find admission; and if thou do not so, then thou wilt quickly find thyself trebly divorced;[2] for the prayer that is received into His presence has no concern with the pollution of worldly glory.[3] 69

When death drags forth thy life, then from thy indigence there springs true prayer; when thy body has gone to the dust and spirit to the skies, then mayst thou see thy soul engaged, as angels are, in prayer.

On the Participation of the Heart in Prayer.

At the battle of Uḥud ʿAlī the Prince, the impetuous Lion, received a grievous wound. The head of the arrow remained in his foot, and he knew that it was necessary to take it out, this being the only cure for him. As soon as the surgeon saw it, he said, "We must cut it open with a knife; to find the arrow-head, a key must be applied to the closed wound."[4] But ʿAlī had no strength to bear the inser-

---

the idea of one, to seventeen, eighteen results, and thus thou obtainest the eighteen thousand worlds," B. I cannot follow B in his further elucidation of the a thor's meaning, though I may perhaps be permitted to doubt if the author meant to imply all that seems there to be attributed to him.

[1] قيمت, *lit.*, 'worth, value'; *i.e.*, whilst thou thyself retainest any worth, thou canst utter no true prayer; for thy self-importance will not let thee see that there is any advantage in religion, the first step in which is the laying aside of self and becoming poor.

[2] *i.e.*, irrevocably divorced. A husband may take his wife back again after having divorced her once, or twice. "*But if he divorce her a third time, she shall not be lawful unto him after that, until she marry another husband*" (Ḳur 2 : 230).

[3] Or, "The shame or the pride and honour of the world;" gloss in L (خجالت يا رعونت و آبروي دنيا). But B, with تري in a different meaning. "In it there appears nothing fresh or blooming, splendid or shining." In either case the iẓāfat, or some other particle, is suppressed *metri gratia.*

[4] بسته 'clotted, congealed (matter).' the blood in and about the wound.

tion of the forceps;[1] "Let it alone," said he, "till the time of prayer." So when he was engaged in prayer his surgeon gently took out the arrow-head from his limb,[2] bringing it clear away while 'Alī was unconscious of any suffering or pain.

When 'Alī ceased from prayer (he whom God called Friend), he said, "My pain is less,—how is that? And why is there all this blood where I have been praying?" Ḥusain,[3] the glory of the world, splendid above all the children of Muṣṭafā, answered him, "When thou enteredst into prayer, thou wentest up to God, and the surgeon took out the arrow-head before thou hadst finished thy prayer." Said the Lion, "By the most great Creator, I knew nothing of the pain of it."

O thou, who art well known for thy prayers, who art commended before men for thy piety, pray in this wise and discern the interpretation of the story; or else rise, and cease vainly to wag thy beard.

When thou enterest into prayer in sincerity, thou wilt come forth from prayer with all thy desire obtained; but if without sincerity thou offer a hundred salutations,[4] thou art still a bungler, thy work a

---

1 دم کاز, دم in the sense of 'point,' and کاز 'a two-bladed instrument, such as shears, scissors, or forceps' (Stein.). The preliminary incision had apparently been made at this time, and it was the subsequent extraction of the arrow-head with forceps that 'Alī could not bear.

2 The texts all read لطیف اندامش, omitting از; evidently understanding بریدن here, as above, as 'to cut'; "he cut into that graceful body of his." But v. l. 16 *sup.*, where دم کاز can hardly be anything else than the point of the forceps, *i.e.*, the cutting had already been done; and t was this that had so exhausted 'Alī that he could not bear any more pain at the time. Moreover, reading لطیف اندامش there is an hiatus between the two words, which (though allowable) is awkward, and has evidently been felt so, since M reads مبارک for لطیف, thus avoiding it. It seems justifiable therefore to retain the sense of the passage, and improve the form of the line by reading ببرید with از in the sense of 'sever, remove.' But the readings in ll. 14, 15 and 18 vary considerably, and it is difficult to frame an exact picture of the steps of the operation.

3 His son, the martyr of Karbalā. As a matter of fact, Ḥusain was born the year after Uḥud.

4 سلام, the technical name for the last of the prescribed sentences to be uttered on each occasion of prayer. Thus here 'a hundred salutations' is the equivalent of 'a hundred prayers.'

failure. One salutation is the same as two hundred ;[1] one prostration in sincerity is worth thy standing erect [2] a hundred times, for the prayer that is mere matter of custom is dust that is scattered by the wind. The prayers that reach God's court are those that the soul prays ; the mere mimic is ever a mendicant, praying unworthily, without intelligence, since he chooses the path of folly. For on this Path prayer of the spirit is of more account than barren mimicry.

When thou callest on God, bring supplication meet for Him, that His good pleasure may receive thee. From time to time, divided from the real and bound up in the phenomenal, thou comest to pray the obligatory prayers ;[3] calling not on God, without self-abasement, without humility, thou carelessly performest a rak'ah or two. Thou deemest it prayer,—I marvel if thou art listened to at all ! Thou comest before God in thy pride,—how shall God hear thee when thou callest ? Let thy prayer be free from Self, and He will accept it as pure ; if it be smirched with Self He will not receive it. The message that the tongue of anguish utters is an envoy from this world of men to Him ; when it is thy helplessness that sends the messenger, thy cry is '*O Lord*', and His is '*Here am I.*'[4]

As a proud lord marches to the arms of his servants and slaves
so thou layest the load of obligation on Him ;—"*I* am *Thy* friend,"
sayest thou, "honour be mine !" Thou deemest thyself a friend,
not a slave ; is this the manner of a man of wisdom ? Better were 71
it, O son, that thou offer not such service to Him ; go, strive not
with Him. Without right guidance man is less than a beast ; whoso
is without guidance labours in vain.

---

1 *i.e.*, one salutation performed in sincerity is worth two hundred that are merely conventional. Or one salutation is just as good as two hundred, if both are without sincerity.

2 قیام the act of assuming the standing position at the prescribed places in the daily prayers.

3 فرض '*farẓ*', those rak'ahs, or forms of prayer said to be enjoined by God. There are also the '*sunnah*', those founded on the practice of Muḥammad ; '*nafl*', the voluntary performance of two rak'ahs or more, which may be omitted without sin ; '*witr*', an odd number of rak'ahs, either one, three, five, or seven, said after the night prayer. (Cf. Hughes, Dict. of Islam, s.v. Prayer).

4 یارب, 'O Lord', *i.e.*, a lamentation, a cry of sorrow. God answers with the ejaculation لبیک, '*labbaik*,' of the pilgrims on the hajj.

Have done with this service, thou fool! Never again call thyself a slave! If thou wert mighty in the world thou wouldst say what Pharaoh did, every word![1] who in his surpassing fatuity, and his supreme insolence and folly, averse from service and submission, drew aside the veil from before his deeds,[2] saying, "I am greater than the kings, I am above the princes of the world." All have this insolence and pride; Pharaoh's words are instinct in everyone; but daring not through fear to utter their secret, they hide it away even from themselves.

On Failure to Pray Aright.

Bū Shu'aib al-Ubayy was a leader in religion whom everyone used to praise; one who rose in the night[3] and fasted continually, one who was distinguished in that age for his asceticism. He betook himself from the city to a cell on the mountain, and made his escape from pain and sorrow.[4]

It chanced that a certain woman had an affection for him; she said, "O Shaikh,[5] would it be fitting for thee to have a wife? If thou wilt, I place myself at thy disposal, and will willingly become thy wife; my soul will cheerfully be satisfied with little, and I shall never think of my former ease." He answered, "Excellent; it is very fitting; I approve. If thou art satisfied, I am content."

She was a modest woman called Jauhara, and had a full share of beauty and grace; chaste, refined,[6] of sweet disposition, an incarnation of good deeds;[7] content with the decree of the revolving heavens, she left the city for the hermit's cell, and there seeing a piece of matting lying on the floor, she straightway took it up. The

---

1 "I am your most High Lord"; words said to have been spoken by Pharaoh, L.

2 *i.e.*, shamed himself, made himself an object of reprobation.

3 *sc.* for devotional purposes.

4 The pain and sorrow of the world, which oppressed him while he lived in the city.

5 Primarily 'an old man, one over 50,' and generally 'a doctor, learned man, spiritual guide.'

6 کفاف B interprets by سلیقه, 'good taste.'

7 آیت إحسان, *lit.*, 'a mark or sign of charity, good-nature, or kindliness.

devout Bū Shu'aib said to her, "O thou, now my cherished wife, why hast thou taken up the carpet? For the black earth is only the 72
place for our shoes."[1] She said, "I did it because it was best so; for I have heard you say that any act of devotion is best performed when no screen interposes; and the mat was an obstacle between my forehead and the actual earth.[2]

Every night Bū Shu'aib's daily meal consisted of two round cakes for his querulous belly;[3] with these two barley-cakes that pious man broke his fast and was always content. But he fell ill from the risings that so afflicted his nights;[4] and so, being helpless,[5] the good man, because of the weakness brought on by fasting, said the *farz* and *sunnah* prayers[6] that night sitting. His wife laid one cake before him, and gave him a drop of vinegar,—nothing more. Said the Shaikh, "O wife, my allowance is more than this! Why is it so little, wife! She said, "Because the worshipper who says his prayers sitting receives only half the full reward; and if thou sittest to say thy prayers, thou eatest the half of thy usual allowance. Ask no more from me, O Shaikh, than half thy dole; I have warned thee. For the portion that belongs to prayers said sitting is the half of the reward given for those said standing; why expect the reward of the whole when thou performest but half thy devotions? Perform the whole, and then ask for the whole reward; otherwise such worship is absolutely wrong."

O thou, in the path of sincerity thou art feebler than a woman, laggest far behind such of thy fellow-creatures as she. By such prayer as comes not from the heart thou canst not anywise obtain thy soul's release.[7] No one regards as of any worth the service whose life-

---

1 *sc.*, when we pray,—not the place where we ourselves should kneel. The matting was that which Bū Shu'aib used as a prayer-carpet.

2 *i.e.*, at those places in the recital of the prayers where the worshipper bends down so that his forehead touches the ground.

3 ة: وظيفة *lit.*, 'the place where his allowance went.'

4 ز قيام شب رنجور *i.e.*, as B says قيامیکه شب رنجور کند. قائم را

5 معذور. or 'excusable' *sc.*, from saying his prayers.

6 V. note on p. 70, l. 13 *ant.*

7 نیست جان الدی بگرد صل *lit.*, 'digging out of the soul,' usually of the agonies of death; here the freeing of the soul from the world and the things of the world, and the entanglements of phenomenal existence.

principle comes not from the heart;[1] for a bone is of itself no delicacy on one's plate without the marrow. Know that at the resurrection no prayer that is imperfect will be taken into account; the marrow of prayer consists in lowliness, and if there be not lowliness it will not be
73 received. A man must come to prayer as one wounded, sorrowing, and in poverty; and if there be not lowliness and trust the devil derides him.[2]

Whoso is wholly taken up with fasting and prayer,[3] poverty ever locks the door of his soul;[4] in this world of deceit and desire, in this hundred-thousand-years-enduring cage, the cap of thy degree is the compliment thou offerest it;[5] but thy head is greater than the cap.

Whoso enters into prayer with fitting preparation, the reward of his prostration is the cave of the West.[6]

Go then, perform thy prayers without breath of desire, for the dew of desire utterly corrupts them; the baseness of thy prayers and thy fasting is such that the slipper of thy foot is the only present in thy hand.[7]

---

1 طاعتی کان ز دل ندارد روح   کس ندارد وجود آن بفتوح ; فتوح is explained by B as کشایش but this, and his paraphrase, leave the meaning, to me, still obscure. I take it to be, literally, "no one considers the acquisition (finding, وجود) of such to be a gain (فتوح, 'income received gratuitously; gains, pickings,' Stein.)."

2 *Lit.* 'sports with his whiskers.'

3 *i.e.*, the repetition of his prayers, the forms of religion, without attending to its spirit.

4 *i.e.*, as I take it, poverty, by reason of his not embracing it in its true sense, is a bar to his soul's progress. But B paraphrases "the path of indigence and lowliness remains shut against him."

5 دست موزه a conciliatory or complimentary present. Thy religious position, whatever it may be, is a mere trifle, which perhaps pleases and conciliates the world, but is quite unnecessary to thee.

6 غار مغرب; I do not know the origin of this expression or what allusion it contains. B explains as 'the furthest horizon of the earth's globe.' Perhaps the implication is that he is enabled to leave all earthly things far behind him when he prays. B reads سرای سجده, 'the place of his prostration.'

7 دست موزه cf. l. 5, *sup.* The slipper is drawn off the foot with the hand at the time of prayer, B.

Speak in pleasant tones on coming to the mountain ; why offer it the braying of an ass ?[1] Thou hast raised up a hundred thousand ruffians in the path of prayer, who drown thy cries.[2] It must needs be that the words of thy prayer come back in their entirety,[3] like an echo, from the mountain of the world.

On Laud and Praise.

In every mouth the tongue that utters speech becomes fragrant as musk in praising Thee. In Thy decree and will, as Thou art far or near, lies for the heart and soul eternal happiness or ruinous disaster, an imperishable kingdom or everlasting beguilement ; Thy servants wander to and fro by day and night, all seeking Thyself from Thee. Fortune, and empire, and the glory of both worlds he knows who understands things manifest and hidden, yet longs not for them ; for all is nothing without Thee,—nothing. Destruction and creation are alike easy to Thee ; all that Thou hast willed, takes place. The cunning man, though mightier he be, is yet the feebler in Thy praise ; or in this court Zāl-i-zar, though full of fury, is powerless as an old woman ;[4] in face of Thy decree of ‘ *Be, and it was,* ’ no one dares to question, ‘ What is this ? How comes that ?’

---

[1] The mountain will echo back in whatever way it is spoken to. And so “ if thy deeds in this world be good, thou wilt have their reward, and contrariwise ; as the Maulavī Rūmī says :—This world is a mountain, our deeds are a voice ; the echo of our voices comes back to us, ” B.

[2] عون cf. p. 16, l. 8. “ Roughs who, when they set about making a disturbance, shout out ‘ Get off, get away, seize it, take it ! ’ Anger, desire, passion, lust, the evil thoughts in thy mind are like such bullies in the market, intent on making a disturbance ; and just as their clamour deprives others of the power of making themselves heard (صوت رباست), so the evil passions and thoughts of thy mind prevent thee from calling on God,” B.

[3] هم برمّت. *lit.*, ‘ even with the halter ’ ; said of one who has given a thing away completely, “ *He has given it with its halter* (اعطاه برمّته) ”, (L, quoting from the Qāmūs). B mistranscribes the above from L, and apparently misunderstands it ; paraphrasing the text, “ That apparently fresh and sweet prayer of thine which goes up, falls down again like a broken rope upon thy head ” (رمّت being also ‘ an old, rotten rope ’).

[4] A pun ; Zāl (Zāl-i-zar) being the father of Rustam, besides meaning ‘ an old woman.’

He hears the heart's low voice of supplication. He knows when the heart's secret rises up to Him ; when supplication [1] opens the door of the heart, its desire comes forward to meet it ; the '*Here am I*' of the Friend goes out to welcome the heart's cry of '*O Lord*' as it ascends from the high road of acquiescence. One cry of '*O Lord*' from thee,—from Him two hundred times comes '*Here am I*' ; one '*Peace*' from thee,—a thousand times He answers '*And on thee*' ;[2] let men do good or ill, His mercy and His bounty still proceed.

Poverty is an ornament in His court,—thou bringest thy worldly stock-in-trade and its profits as a present ;[3] but thy long grief is what He will accept, His abundance will receive thy neediness. Bilāl [4] whose body's skin was black as a sweetheart's locks, was a friend in His court ; his outward garment [5] became as a black mole of amorous allurement upon the face of the maidens of Paradise.[6]

---

1 نیاز ; or 'poverty', cf. p. 73, l. 3.

2 'O Lord', '*Yā rabb*', typifies a cry of distress ; *labbaik*, 'here am I (present in thy service)', is an ejaculation used by the pilgrims on the road to Mecca. 'Peace', '*salām*' (*salām 'alaika*, 'peace be on thee'), is of course the common salutation of Musalmāns ; to which the answer is '*wa 'alaika as-salām*.' 'and upon thee peace.'

3 نیاز here 'a present, gift.' B reads آر without iẓāfat ; it might then be translated, "Then bring thou poverty ; it is capital and interest too."

4 A negro, one of Muḥammad's first converts, the mu'a<u>dh</u><u>dh</u>īn of his mosque at Medina.

5 *i.e.*, his black skin.

6 A mole, of course, being a mark of beauty. In all copies there follows here a line, "He changes the skin of both enemy and friend in their future state, to make it new again." This is evidently a reference to Qur. 4 : 59 "*Verily, those who disbelieve in our signs, we will broil them with fire*; *whenever their skins are well done, then we will change them for other skins, that they may taste the torment.*" The commentators add, "In the original it refers only to the unbelievers ; here (in the text) however it means that the skins of God's enemies shall be changed so that they may be further tormented, and those of His friends that God may show them further mercy," L ("to give them a new beauty," B). But the tenor of the line is in direct contradiction to the preceding one, which speaks of Bilāl's skin in Paradise as a *mole* on the face of the houris ; and it is exactly the sort of comment which would suggest itself to a pious and

O Thou who marshallest the company of darwīshes, O Thou who watchest the sorrow of the sore at heart, heal him who is now like unto a quince,[1] make him like the bowstring who is now bent as the bow.[2] I am utterly helpless in the grasp of poverty; O Thou, who rulest the affairs of men, rule mine. I am solitary in the land of the angels, lonely in the glory of the world of might;[3] the verse of my knowledge has not even a beginning, but the excess of my yearning has no end.

On Being Glad in God Most High, and Humbling oneself before Him.

O Life of all the contented, who grantest the desires of the desirous: the acts in me that are right, Thou makest so,—Thou, kinder to me than I am to myself. No bounds are set to Thy mercy, no interruption appears in Thy bounty. Whatever Thou givest, give thy slave piety; accept of him and set him near Thyself. Gladden my heart with the thought of the holiness of religion; make fire of my human body of dust and wind.[4] It is Thine to show mercy and to forgive, mine to stumble and to fall. I am not wise,—receive me, though drunk; I have slipped, take Thou my hand. I know full well that Thou hidest me; Thy screening of me has made me proud. I know not what has been from all eternity condemned to rejection; I know not who will be called at the last. I have no power to anger or to reconcile Thee, nor does my adulation advantage Thee. My straying heart now seeks return to Thee; my uncleanness is drenched by the pupil of my eye.

---

not too careful reader. I think, therefore. that the line in question was originally a marginal note in an early copy, which has been transferred to the text.

A second line also is inserted here; "It avails nothing to come forth for the purpose of protecting faith and country." This has evidently no connection with the context, and has probably been introduced from elsewhere by mistake; though I cannot say where it may have come from. B explains "since His is the sole authority in this matter He gives to no head (or chief) any guarantee on account of having protected either religion or state."

[1] "Of yellow countenance, like a quince," B. There is a pun on the words 'quince' and 'heal.' 'Him' refers to the writer.

[2] *i.e.*, 'make him straight again who is now bent with grief.'

[3] جبروت. ملكوت two of the five worlds or five planes of existence of the Ṣūfīs; cf. Gibb. *op. cit.*, pp. 55, 56.

[4] *i.e.*, "destroy it, burn it in the fire of love," B.

Show my straying heart a path, open a door before the pupil of my eye, that it [1] may not be proud before Thy works, that it [2] may have no fear before Thy might.[3] O Thou who shepherdest this flock with Thy mercy,—but what speech is all this? they are all Thee.[4] ....Show Thou mercy on my soul and on my clay, that my soul's sorrow may be assuaged within me.[5] Do Thou cherish me, for others are hard; [6] do Thou receive me, for others themselves are rent asunder.

How can I be intimate with other than Thee? They are dead,—Thou art my sufficient Friend. What is to me the bounty of Theeness and doubleness, so long as I believe that I am I, and Thou art Thou?[7] What to me is all this smoke, in face of Thy fire? Since Thou

---

1 *i.e.*, the straying heart.

2 *i.e.*, the pupil of the eye.

3 And so may not falter in the search, B.

4 *i.e.*, "What is all this I have been saying about shepherd and sheep? All that is, is Thee, shepherd and sheep both," B. I am unable to translate the next line.

5 Or, reading نگاهد for بکاهد ('may not be assuaged'), the meaning will be, 'Bestow on me the grace of the search, that I may ever have in me anxiety of heart, and never let go out of my heart the thought of perfect excellence," B.

6 Reading زَفت اند with B, to rhyme with کَفت اند; L, reading زُفت, explains as بخیل و ممسک

7 'The bounty of Thee-ness and doubleness,' *i.e.*, the blessings of this phenomenal existence, of this existence apart from union with God, of this present world. "As long as I deem that aught remains of my phenomenal being, which necessitates this 'Thee-ness' and doubleness and disunion, and have not arrived at the stage of annihilation and union and essenceship (عینیّت), what have I to do with the bounty of Thee-ness and doubleness? Every favour which comes under the form of duality (اثنینیّت) and want of concordance (which is a necessity of phenomenal existence), and which comes before the stage of annihilation is reached, whether it be of this world or the next, is to me a favour of Theeness and doubleness. And he who seeks essenceship and union, what shall he do with it?" L, (*i.e.*, he is pressing on to something better). If there were any evidence for it I would however read که من منم و توئی "What are the bounties of a separate existence to me, when I know that I am I and Thou art me also," *i.e.*, when my union with God is complete.

art, let the existence of all else cease ;[1] the world's existence consists in the wind of Thy favour, O Thou, injury from whom is better than the world's gain.

I know not what sort of man he is, who in his folly can ever have sufficiency of Thee. Can a man remain alive without Thy succour, or exist apart from Thy favour ? How can he grieve who possesses Thee ; or how can he prosper who is without Thee ? That of which Thou saidst, Eat not, I have eaten ; and what Thou forbadest, that have I done ; yet if I possess Thee, I am a coin of pure gold,[2] and without Thee, I am a mill-wheel's groaning.[3] I am in an agony[4] for fear of death; be Thou my life, that I die not.[5] Why sendest Thou Thy word and sword to me ? Alas for me, who am I apart from Thee ?

If Thou receive me, O Thou dependent on no cause,[6] what matters 76
the good or ill of a handful of dust ? This is the dust's high honour, that its speech should be in praise of Thee ;[7] Thy glory has taken away the dust's dishonour, has exalted its head even to the Throne. Hadst Thou not given the word of permission, who, for that he is so far from Thee, could utter Thy name ? Mankind would not have dared to praise Thee in their imperfect speech.[8] What is to be found in our

---

1 "Since Thou, who art the permanent root, art, let everyone else, whose existence is contingent, perish ; for the perishing of the branch harms not the root," L.

2 درست شش دانگم , — درست being the gold coin commonly called an ashrafī ; دانگ , the sixth part of anything. Hence 'a coin of six sixths,' *i.e.*, of pure gold.

3 *i.e.*, nothing.

4 زحير , the pains of colic or dysentery.

5 B refers to Qur. 10 : 64. "*Are not, verily, the friends of God those on whom there is no fear, neither shall they be grieved ?*"

6 ای ز علّت پاک , cf. p. 28, l. 14 نیست علت پذیر ذات خدای , 'God's essence is independent of cause.'

7 B apparently would take this as a rhetorical question with a negative implication, "Shall the dust then have the honour of speaking Thy praise ?"

8 C's variant (يان بودي) shows how the first hemistich is to be scanned. مجاز is the metaphoric, allegorical, symbolic, as opposed to the real and true ; as in the saying '*The symbolic is a bridge to the Truth.*' Hence مجاز is used of this world as opposed to the world of reality and truth.

reason or our drunkenness ?[1] for we are not, nor have we an existence.

Though we be full of self, purify us from our sins ; by some way of deliverance save me from destruction. In presence of Thy decree, though I be wisdom's self, yet who am I that I should count as either good or evil ? My evil becomes good when Thou acceptest it ; my good, evil when Thou refusest it.[2]

Thou art all, O Lord, both my good and ill ;[3] and, wonderful to say, no ill comes from Thee ![4] Only an evil-doer commits evil ; Thou canst only be described as altogether good ; Thou willest good for Thy servants continually, but the servants themselves know naught of Thee. Within this veil of passion and desire[5] our ignorance can only ask for pardon at the hands of Thy Omniscience. If we have behaved like dogs in our duty, Thou hast found no tigerishness in us,—then pass over our offence.[6] As we stand, awaiting the fulfilment of Thy promised kindness at the bountiful door of the Court of Thy generosity, on Thy side all is abundance ; the falling short is in our works.

On His Kindness and Bounty.

O Lord, the Enduring, the Holy, whose kingdom is not of touch or sense ; by Thee we conquer, without Thee we fail ; in Thee we are content, apart from Thee unsatisfied. Though none amongst us is of any avail, is not Thy kindness a sufficient messenger of promise ? Thou hast given us our religion, give us a sure belief in it ; though we have the faith, give us yet more. Checkmated on the chessboard of

---

1 *i.e.*, whether we praise Him with our understanding or whether with our want of it, we are unable to do so fittingly, B.

2 Reading نگرفتي for بگروفي, as B suggests to be possible. Cf. the reading in CH.

3 نیک و بد, an expression meaning simply ' all,' as سیاه و سفید. قلیل و کثیر etc., L.

4 *i.e.*, as L explains it, " the epithet of evil does not apply to Thee ; as when a painter pourtrays good and evil in his pictures, the good and the evil are in the painting, not properties of the painter."

5 *i e.*, being, as we are, in this imperfect world.

6 Tigers being slain and destroyed outright, but dogs more mildly punished, B.

our passions as we are,[1] we thirst for the heavenly valley; none of us can tell the good from ill,—give us what Thou knowest to be good. O Thou, desire of the desirous,[2] O Thou, the hope of those who hope, O Thou who seest what is manifest, who knowest what is hidden, Thou surely accomplishest my hope; all my hope is in Thy mercy,—life and daily bread, all is of Thy bounty. From the river[3] of the true religion give to my thirsty heart a draught full of the light of the Truth. **77**

Not by wisdom and not by skill can I obtain other intercessor with Thee than Thyself. All that Thy decree has written for me is well; it is not ill. I can dispense with everything,—all that is; but Thou art indispensable to me; receive me Thou! In the rose-tree of the search the nightingale of love trills its song of "Thou art all!" The falcon of my glory[4] flies up from the path of lowliness higher than the sidra-tree. He rules empires who presses on towards Thee; but whoso makes not for this door, wretched is he.

Who shall give me speech[5] but Thou? Who shall save me from myself but Thou? Thou buyest not[6] perfume and paint and deceit; save me from all this, O Thou who art all! Thou buyest weakness and helplessness and feebleness, but not indolence and stupidity and uncleanness. Pain becomes ease at Thy court, silence[7] is perfect eloquence. Kill everything[8] and, for it all, to be received by Thee will be sufficient blood-money. To turn the reins of hope away from Thee,—what is that but the sign and mark of a fall?[9] Thy vengeance

---

1 *i.e.*, in the theatre or battlefield where we wage war with our lower selves we are helpless and overthrown.

2 اهل نگاران, those who draw, paint, picture their desire; "who have the figure of their desires in their heart," B.

3 کوثر, *lit.*, abundance. Qur. 108: 1. "*Verily we have given thee abundance*" (*al-kauthar*). The name also of a river in Paradise; v. Hughes, Dict. of Islām; and Sale *ad loc.*

4 بازِ بازِ من, "the incorporeal soul; or love, strong desire," B.

5 سخن, which B interprets of the نفس ناطقه, the reasonable soul.

6 *i.e.* acceptest not, hast no use for.

7 بی زبانی, *i.e.*, resignation and acquiescence, B.

8 All our desires and passions and follies and impurities, B.

9 زلل according to B is used especially for the falling and slipping of saints and prophets.

takes shape in the soul of whoso seeks aught but to be beloved of Thy presence ; O Guardian of the mysteries, save our inward nature from the impress which marks the wicked !

20 On Turning to God.

O Creator of the world, who preservest the soul in beauty ; O Thou who guidest the understanding to the path of true devotion ; in the Paradise of the skies they are all raw youths ; in Thy Paradise are
78 those who drink of Hell.[1] What are good and ill to me at Thy door ?[2] What is Heaven to me when Thou art there ? Who can show forth in this deceptive mirror[3] the import of the words "All-knowing" and "All-powerful" ?[4]

When the heart's blood bores the liver, what is Hell, what a baker's live coal ?[5] Hell would become Heaven through fear of
5 Him ; how can clay become a brick without a mould ?[6] Those who

---

1 B explains the Paradise of the skies as the Paradise of the temporal delights described by the theologians. "'Thy Paradise' is God Himself and His radiant face, *i.e.*, His approval of and kindness towards His servants, the bestowal of blessings which cannot be imagined. This Paradise is what those seek who drink of Hell ; *i.e.*, those who give their heads in the wādī of knowledge and search, who in their search experience a hell of hardship, whose souls are as a thousand fire-temples with the flame and blaze of love of the True Beauty ; to them the other Paradise is nothing."

2 "What have I to do with distinction of good and ill ? The Court of Glory is not concerned with that ; there is naught else there but Thee," B.

3 *i.e.*, the world, full of deceits. B.

4 عرض نکتهٔ علیم و قدیر, "the explanation of the attributes of God by means of earthly teaching, and the suitable particularization of the meanings of His names according to the special signification of each. Hence, because of this impossibility, the variations and differences, both verbal and of meaning, which have arisen as to the interpretations of the names of God......But such contradictions will disappear hereafter when we are united to Thee, for there where Thou art none of these words (نکتهٔ) exist, nor does the question of their meanings sully that place," B.

5 *i.e.*, what difference is there between Hell and a baker's live coal ? "To those whose livers are burnt, who are bored through by love, Hell with all its fire and flame is no more than a spark that is extinguished," B.

6 "So too the life of the Knower becomes not perfect without the disposing power of the Master," B. The connection with the preceding hemistich is not, however, very clear.

love Thee weep in their laughter because of Thee ; those who know Thee laugh in their weeping because of Thee.[1] They rest in Paradise who are in Thy fire ;[2] but the most are contented apart from Thee with the maidens of the eyes.[3] If Thou send me from Thy door to Hell, I will not go on foot but on my head ;[4] but whoso opposes Thy decree, his soul shall hold up a mirror to him, because of his recklessness.[5]

His standing and his occupation Thou givest to everyone ; a friend is a snake,—a snake a friend if sent by Thee. Though threatened with " *None will think himself secure,*" I cannot have enough of Thee ; nor do I become bold because of " *Be not in despair.*"[6] If Thou givest poison to my soul, I cannot mention anything bitterer than sugar.[7] He only is secure from Thy craft who is mean and

---

1 The first expression meaning ' to weep from joy,' the second ' to laugh at bitterness ' ; " they being patient under trial are sad at heart though outwardly smiling. Or they weep sore at their own true state, and laugh with joy at being accepted by God," B.

2 جحیم, also a name for Hell. " Those who are in the fire of trial and seeking are, as it were, reposing in Paradise ; for that fire is their souls' peace and rest," B.

3 The maids with modest glances, with bright and large eyes, of Qur. 55. That is, they are contented with the ' Paradise of the skies ' and its delights as described in sensual language.

4 *i.e.*, with absolute submission. " If Thou send me from Thy door to Hell,—if Thou so approve,—I will make my head my foot and go ; for that Hell will not be Hell......Thy decree will give me such delight that Hell will become Heaven," B.

5 دل خود از غفلتش غلاف آرد ; *i.e.*, " the delight of being accepted by God shall be reversed in his experience (as the image in a glass is reversed) ; that is, his state shall become Hell, and naught but Hell shall be the outcome," B. Or taking غلاف in the more usual meaning we might interpret " his soul makes his recklessness a cover for him," to harden him still further and make him more refractory.

6 The references are to Qur. 7 : 96. " *But none will think himself secure from the craft of God except the people who perish ;* " and Qur. 39 : 54. " *Be not in despair of the mercy of God ; verily, God forgives sins, all of them.*"

7 *i.e.*, the poison is so sweet that sugar, by comparison, is the bitterest thing possible. Or, " I can say nothing bitterer, no bitterer word, than 'sugar,' *i.e.*, ' it is sugar,' " L.

lowly ; Thy peace and Thy craft appear alike,[1] but at Thy craft the wise man trembles. We must not think ourselves secure against Thy craft, for neither obedience nor sin is of avail ;[2] he only thinks himself secure, who knows not Thy craft in dealing with wickedness.

He who trusts in his Submission suffers a Manifest Hurt.

An old fox said to another, " O master of wisdom and counsel and knowledge, make haste, take two hundred dirams, and convey our letter to these dogs." He said, " The pay is better than a headache, but it is a heavy and perilous task ; when my life has been spent in this venture, what use will your dirams be then ?"

A feeling of security against Thy decree, O God, is, rightly understood, the essence of error ; it made both 'Azāzīl and Bal'ām infamous.[3]

---

1 " Thy peace and Thy craft are to outward appearance alike ; the craft consists in following up Thy servant with benefits and then seizing him in a way of which he is unaware........He is the wise man who can distinguish between Thy peace and Thy craft," L.

2 " For often sin, inasmuch as it is a cause of repentance and turning to God, is by His mercy esteemed as equal to obedience ; and obedience, because of the pride to which it gives rise, by His wrath as on the same level as sin; and so, since even sin is not without its advantage, both sin and obedience are here mentioned together," L.

3 The fox would not have escaped injury, though obedient ; obedience is no guarantee against suffering. Or as B says :—" A confidence which arises from trusting in one's obedience is, in the matter of God's decrees, sinful ; for the divine decree is not restrained by obedience, nor permitted by the commission of a fault. Hence 'Azāzīl with all his submission, and Bal'ām with all his piety and dignity of priesthood, were rejected at the Court of Majesty." I cannot say in what the appositeness of these references consists ; 'Azāzīl, as before, is probably Iblīs, who was expelled from heaven for refusing to worship Adam ; Balaam is not mentioned in the Qur'ān, but the Jalālain (v. Hughes *s.v.* Balaam) say " that he was a learned man among the Israelites, who was requested by the Canaanites to curse Moses at the time when he was about to attack the Jabbārūn or 'giants,' a tribe of Canaanites. Balaam at first refused to do so, but at last yielded, when valuable presents were made to him."

Say, "Grind sleep under the foot of the horsemen of thy thought:" for this is of Thy Court.[1] When Thou strikest off the head of him in whom Self no long dwells, he rejoices in Thee, like a candle.[2] If I have Thee, what care I for intellect, and honour, and gold? Thou art both world and faith; what care I for aught else? Do Thou give me a heart, and then see Thou my valour; call me to be Thy fox, and see how like a tiger I shall be.[3] If I fill my quiver with Thy arrows, I grip Mount Qāf by loins and armpits.[4] Thou art his Friend who is not knowledgeless;[5] Thou belongest to him who belongs not to Self. No one who regards Self can see God; he who looks at Self is not one of the faith; if thou art a man of the Path, and of the true religion, cease for a time to contemplate thyself.

O God, Omnipotent, Forgiving, drive not Thy servant from Thy door; make me Thy captive; take away my indifference;[6] make me athirst for Thee,—give me not water![7] Why should I seek my soul in this or that? my pain itself leads me to Thee, my goal.

---

1 'This,' *i.e.*, the thought. 'Sleep' is the sleep of indifference in the house of sorrows (دار المحن, *i.e.*, the world). The 'thought' is the thought of Reality. (خيال حقيقي), referring to those delights of thought which the Knowers of God experience in thinking of His Essence, B.

2 As a candle burns more brightly (here compared to rejoicing, *lit.*, laughing), when its head is struck off, *i.e.*, when snuffed.

3 The fox being a weak animal; so "if I am one of Thy weak ones, I shall be brave enough."

4 Mount Qāf being the mountain that in the popular view encircles the world. It consists of eight circular mountain-chains, which "alternate with the seven seas, the innermost Qāf being within the innermost of the seas, which bears the name of the 'Encircling Ocean' (Baḥr-i-muḥīṭ). The breadth of each Qāf and of each sea is a five hundred years' journey (Gibb, *op. cit.*, p. 38). For a reference to the Baḥr-i-muḥīṭ v. *inf.* p. 80, l. 3. The metaphor in the text is mixed; 'if I fill my quiver with Thy arrows' is equivalent to 'if I draw my strength from Thee.'

5 "Who knows Thee, who has the knowledge of the Knowers, the Ṣūfīs, the Saints,—not the knowledge of externals or the knowledge of the philosophers," B.

6 *lit.* 'sleep.'

7 "Give me a desire for Thee, and increase that desire,—do not quench it. Or 'water' may signify worldly honour and rank," B.

Like an ass without headstall before its greens,[1] thou now beginnest to employ thy worthless life. Thou idly wanderest from city to city; seek thy ass on that road where thou hast lost it.[2] If they have stolen thy ass from thee in 'Irāq, why art thou to be seen in Yazd and Rai?

Till thou becomest perfect, there is a bridge for thee; when thou hast become perfect, what matters sea or bridge to thee?[3] Let thy burden on this road be thine own right-doing and knowledge,[4] and

---

1 *i.e.*, idly ranging at large, not in strenuous fashion.

2 L states that the word 'ass' is a sort of peg (مناط سخن). often used in examples in grammar, in the same way as 'Zaid' and 'Bakr' (words used independently of their meaning, and standing for whatever may be required). He proceeds, "Here it is equivalent to 'the strayed animal of the believer,' for "*Wisdom is the strayed animal of the believer*"; and this wisdom is the faith given to the prophets, the righteous, and the faithful. This faith he lost in that other state of existence (or as B paraphrases L here, that first state of existence, نشأة الأولى, the world of incorporeal beings, عالم مجردات, *i.e.*, the angel world) and seeks in this. And the conventional believer (مقلد) or the unbeliever who has not lost the faith, seeks for nothing; and if, in imitation, he does seek, since he does not know what it is like, he will not recognise it when he finds it. Hence the meaning of the text:—Why dost thou wander in folly from city to city? What thou hast lost in that state of existence comes not to thee in this world of plurality, except, having abandoned the plurality and appurtenances of this transient existence, in perfect strenuousness thou turn thy face towards that other state of existence, thy lost goal; so mayest thou find the object that thou seekest. And as is said in the next line, if thou hast lost thy religion in that state of existence, what seekest thou here? Return thither. *And God knows best what is right.*"

On this passage cf. Gibb, *op. cit.* p. 56 sq. "The human soul is a spirit, and therefore by virtue of its own nature, in reality a citizen of the Spirit World. Its true home is there; and thence, for a certain season, it descends into the Physical Plane, where, to enable it to act upon its surroundings, it is clothed in a physical body. So long as it is thus swathed in corporeity the soul ever, consciously or unconsciously, seeks to regain its proper world......etc."

3 "Till thou become altogether of God, attainest to the degree of completeness in God, when all contingent existences become parts or members of thee, there is a bridge for thee, for thou hast many obstructions and hindrances in the path of thy journey. But when thou art complete, bridge and ocean are the same to thee, and the obstructions, great or small, that stood in the way of thy arriving, can no longer hinder thy union with God," L.

4 "The products of thy religion," B.

trouble not thyself about any bridge. Make not for the boat, for it is not safe; he who goes by boat knows nothing of the sea; it would be a strange sight to see a duck, however young and inexperienced, seeking for a boat.[1] Though a duckling be born but yesterday, it goes up to its breast in the water. Be thou as a duck,—religion the stream; fear not the fordless sea's abyss; the duckling swims in the midst of the sea of 'Umān, whence the ignorant boatman turns back. O Lord, for the honour of Adam,[2] **80**
confound these fools of the world!

If thou maintain thy foot in the path of the Eternal, thou wilt hold the sea in thy hand; the surface of the outer encircling ocean[3] is a bridge to the foot that speaks with the Eternal.[4]

[Of His Mercy.][5]

Malice and rancour are far removed from His attributes; for hate belongs to him who is under command. It is not permissible

---

1 "Though the journeyer be young and new in his surroundings, he must be like a duck in swimming in the spiritual ocean · and a duck that sought for a boat, *i.e.*, in this case, a traveller who on the path was in bondage to the customs and habits of this world, would be a strange sight. So the wayfarer must abandon these, and swim on the sea of Truth without the help of the things of this world," L.

2 With reference to whom it was said (in the Qur'ān) "*Verily I will place upon the earth a vicegerent*," B.

3 V. note on p. 79, l. 6 *sup.*

4 كه با قدم بقل ست,—قل imper. of Ar. قال 'he spoke', here for سخن 'speech.' "The foot can cross unhindered over that sea without any bridge; or possibly 'the ocean' may be used of the sea of Truth. Or سطح محيط may mean the highest heaven, which encloses all (*i.e.*, the ninth sphere, enclosing all the others, v. Gibb *op. cit.*, pp. 43, 44); to the foot which speaks with God the encircling extent of the high throne of God (عرش, —but I cannot find that the فلك الافلاک was identified with the عرش) is as a bridge beneath it, because of the foot's dignity and high honour," L.

5 The texts entitle this Chapter '*Of blameworthy Qualities; verily they are not among the Attributes of God Most High*,' or something closely resembling this. But such a title is quite inapplicable to any but the first few lines, and I have felt obliged to omit it.

to speak of anger in respect of God, for God has no quality of anger;[1] anger and hatred are both due to constraint by superior force, and both qualities are far distant from God. Anger and passion and reconciliation and hatred and malice are not among the attributes of the one sole God; from God the Creator all is mercy; He is the Veiler[2] of His slaves; of His mercy He gives thee counsel; He draws thee to Himself by the kindness of the noose.[3] If thou comest not, He calls thee towards Himself; He offers thee Paradise in His kindness, but because thou livest in this abode of sorrow thou of thy folly hast taken the road of flight. Thou art as a shell for the pearl of the belief in the Unity; thou art a successor of the newly-created Adam;[4] if thou lose that pearl of thy belief, in being dispossessed of it thou wilt be parted from thy substance; but if thou guard that pearl, thou shalt raise thy head beyond the seven and the four;[5] thou shalt reach eternal happiness, and no created thing shall harm thee; thou shalt be exalted in the present time, and upon the plain of eternity thou shalt be as a hawk; thy alighting-place shall be the hand of kings, thy feet shall be freed from the depths of the mire.

Of Him who feeds me and gives me Drink.[6]

When they capture the hawk in the wilds, they secure it neck and feet; they quickly cover up both its eyes and proceed to teach it to hunt. The hawk becomes accustomed and habituated to the strangers,
81 and shuts its eyes upon its old associates; it is content with little food and thinks no more of what it used to eat. The falconer then becomes its attendant, and allows it to look out of one corner of an eye, so that

---

1 How then, asks L, explain the passages of the Qur'ān where God is spoken of as hating? They refer to the just punishment of man, not the rage of animal strength, which is reprobated.

2 *i.e.*, of sin, etc.

3 "By kindness, which appears as a noose; that is, by kindness in the dress of anger," L.

4 *i.e.*, Adam as he was when first created, a perfect man.

5 The seven planets, and the four elements; *i.e.*, shalt enter another region than that of matter and planetary influences.

6 A continuation of the former chapter, in connection with the mention of the hawk in the last lines of it.

it may only see himself, and come to prefer him before all others. From him it takes all its food and drink, and sleeps not for a moment apart from him. Then he opens one of its eyes completely, and it looks contentedly, not angrily, upon him ; it abandons its former habits and disposition, and cares not to associate with any other. And now it is fit for the assembly and the hand of kings, and with it they grace the chase. Had it not suffered hardship it would still have been intractable, and would have flown out at everyone it saw.

Others are heedless,—do thou be wise, and on this path keep thy tongue silent. The condition laid on such an one is that he should receive all food and drink from the Causer, not from the causes.[1] Go, suffer hardship, if thou wouldst be cherished ; and if not, be content with the road to Hell. None ever attained his object without enduring hardship ; till thou burn them, what difference canst thou see between the willow and aloes wood ?[2]

Of the Multitude ; they are like Cattle—nay, they are more erring.[3]

On the colt that is full three years old the breaker puts the saddle and bridle ; he gives him a training in manners, and takes his restiveness out of him ; he makes him obedient to the rein,—what is called a handy horse. Then he is fit for kings to ride, and they deck him with gold and jewels.

If that colt had not experienced these necessary hardships, he would have been of less use than an ass, only fit to carry millstones ; and would have been perpetually in pain from his loads, bearing now the Jew's baggage, now the Christian's, in pain and sorrow and tribulation.

The man who has never undergone hardship has not, so think the wise, received a full measure of blessing ; he is Hell's food, is in terror ; even in Hell he is no more than a stone ;[4] his is the place of fear **82**

---

[1] *i.e.*, recognise all blessings as coming from the Causer of causes, the First Cause, God ; not from any of His secondary manifestations.

[2] Aloes wood when burnt giving out a fragrant smell.

[3] A reference to Qur. 7 : 178 and 25 : 46, where these words occur. The following passage on the training of the colt is a continuation of the same line of thought as the above on the training of the hawk.

[4] *i.e.*, an idol ; v. note on next line.

and dread; it is read in His incontrovertible book,[1] '*Whose fuel is men.*'[2]

Though thou canst neither purpose nor compass aught withou Him, yet religion's task is not to be accomplished without thee, any more than without Him;[3] religion's task is not an easy business, God's religion is always a thing of heaviness.[4] God's religion is a man's crown and diadem; does a crown befit a worthless man? Guard thy religion, so mayest thou attain thy kingdom;[5] otherwise, know that without religion thou art a man of naught. Tread the path of religion, for if thou do so, thou shalt not tremble like a branch in nakedness. Sweet is religion's path and God's decree! leave the black mire, lift thy feet out of it.

On the Desire for God.[6]

Thereafter the desire for God,[7] existing in his heart and soul and reason and discernment,[8] becomes his horse;[9] when this creation has

---

[1] در مصحفش *i.e.*, the Qur'ān.

[2] Qur. 2: 22. "*Then fear the fire whose fuel is men and stones* (*i.e.*, idols) *prepared for misbelievers.*" There next follows a line in all the texts which runs "For him exist unbelief and faith, evil and good, who sees in religion its outward form, in the ass only its skin." The idea has been met with before, but it does not fit in here.

[3] "Thou canst not fully perform the task of thy religion without exerting thyself, nor canst thou attempt or find strength for the task without His command and permission." B.

[4] بازاری a substantive, from زار 'groaning, lamentation,' through بازار used as an adjective; not as B. 'a fresh brilliance, and active trading' رونق تره و گرمي بازار.

[5] "Thy religion,—the religion of the Knowers; thy Kingdom,—the kingdom of everlasting life." B.

[6] This chapter occurs in different places in different copies: the present is certainly an unsatisfactory place for it, since the first word 'thereafter' can hardly refer to the preceding chapter, and there is a sudden change from the use of the second person to that of the third.

[7] Here, as also in the title and subsequently, the word is simply شوق. 'desire.'

[8] ذوق *lit.*, tasting, trying, probing'; also 'the distinction of truth and falsehood by the light of divine grace.'

[9] براق, the animal on which Muḥammad took his night-journey to heaven; *lit.*, 'the bright one.' "After passing the various steps and stages of the journey

become a prison to him, his soul seeks freedom ; a fire is kindled within him, which burns up soul and reason and religion.[1]

So long as he seeks for love with self in view, there waits for him the crucible of renunciation ; whoso has newly undertaken the way of love, his renunciation is the key of the gate. Desire, when it is joined to its mistress, is gladness, but he who seeks mistress is far from God. The legion of thy pleasures will cast thee into the fire; the following out of thy desire for God will keep thee safe as a virgin of Paradise.

Then when the soul sets forth from the gate, the old heart becomes
new thereat ; his form escapes from the bonds of nature, the heart
gives back its charge to the spirit.[2] From earth to God's throne comes
forth a mighty shout by reason of his soul's progress ; the dust raised
by the wind of his desire and pain turns woman into man if it but pass
by her.[3] All that would cause him trouble in his way quits the path
before him; before him the mountains in fear become coloured wool
for his socks ; the fire in him destroys the glory of the sea for the sake
of his upward ascent. When he is roused to leave himself[4] they throw 83
down the stars before him; when his eye sees the brightness of the Path,

---

desire (for God) becomes the horse by whose help it is possible to reach the sought for goal ; but not by a corporeal Burāq, but by heart and soul and understanding and discernment,'' L. Omitting, with HIB, the و between عقل and ذوق in the second hemistich, the meaning would be '' his joy (ذوق) is of the heart and soul and understanding,'' *i.e.*, not sensual joys ; ذوق thus would have the same meaning as in l. 15 *inf.*

1 '' The natural soul (جان طبعي), worldly reason, and the religion of externals ; so that nothing remains of the soul's grief or gladness, of reason's right conduct or wrong, of religion's rule or bond.'' B.

2 صورت از بند طبع باز رهد دل ودیعت بروح باز دهد ; what صورت exactly means I do not know ; B, referring to the traveller or to the soul, says that '' it escapes from this unreal form (صورت خيالي) and these tyrannical mandates (مرسومات عرفيه), the necessities of human nature ; and comes forth from its bodily habitation.'' The heart's charge I suppose to be life, or the faculty or capacity or capability of life on earth, the Spirit to be the Spirit of God, روح الله ; though B continuing the note in a very unenlightening manner, speaks of 'the day of *alastu birabbikum* ', the day of the original covenant between God and man ; v. Qur. 7 : 172.

3 *i.e.*, as B explains, an imper ect being into a perfect.

4 '' When he is separated from his own existence.'' B.

the sun seems dark to him by its side. There is no evil or good in that world, no earth or sun or stars; but whoso walks not in love's street, nor in his heart seeks love, for him is made a different heaven, him they seat upon a different earth.

Because of the labour of his search Gabriel unceasingly bathes his face in the water of life. Understanding is bewildered by his soul's shout; devils become firewood for the lightning of his horse's hoofs; to pursue the path his pained heart [1] would burn mankind with fire of sighs. None of the contented [2] can know the secret of his sigh, none pious with earthly piety [3] can ever find his footprints. When his horse's hoof scatters the dust, Gabriel makes of it a life-giving fragrance; [4] as he makes towards the world of annihilation the wind cries 'Halt a moment'; [5] Mustafā [6] standing by his path in benevolence calls out 'O Lord, keep him safe!' Because of his high dignity God suspends the scales of justice from his heart; [7] the friend of God [8] sprinkles water in his path; Gabriel's self cracks the whip.[9]

On His Decree and Ordinance [10] and His Creative Power. [11]

All that comes forth in the world is by decree, and what the prophet

---

1 مالک درد او, "the owner of his pain," which B explains as his heart.

2 *i.e.*, none who is not eager, anxious.

3 غیور *lit.*, 'jealous, high-minded'; also in Persian 'a holy man.' I accept B's explanation غیور ظاهر, *i.e.*, 'one holy according to the religion of externals.'

4 حنوط being sweet smelling herbs laid on the dead. Here apparently the herbs are to have the power of restoring life.

5 *i.e.*, the wind is unable to come up with him in his rapid transit.

6 A name of Muhammad, *lit.*, 'the chosen.'

7 *i.e.*, as I take it, his position is so elevated that God uses his heart as a point from which to suspend the scales of His justice.

8 A title of Abraham.

9 To spur him on as he runs; or مقرعه may be 'a drumstick,' and so 'Gabriel beats the drum.' The ending of the chapter is very abrupt, another indication that it is misplaced here, and is probably continued elsewhere; though where, I have not discovered.

10 قضا و قدر, "the decree existing in the Divine mind from All eternity, and the execution and declaration of the decree at the appointed time," Stein.

11 The first line of the chapter in the texts should evidently go elsewhere; but where, I have, as in other such cases, not been able to determine. It runs,

speaks is also by decree;[1] infidelity and faith, good and evil, old and new,—all is referable to Him; whatso exists, is under the command of the Almighty; all things work in accordance with the decree. All are in subjection,—His Omnipotence the subduer; His creative Power appears high above all. All is subject to His Omnipotence, dependent 20
on His mercy; all were preceded in time by His eternal Omniscience. The man of the people, or he of the philosophers, he who is under command, or who is of the learned,—all must return to His Presence; whoso possesses power, it is of His favour. His causes have displaced **84**
Reason from her position;[2] His methods of deriving one thing from another[3] have cut off the soul's feet.

"Through the instrumentality of thy reason He has given to thy petitioning both the commands of religion and the understanding that belongs to this present life; عقل دنيي being the equivalent of عقل مكتبي. Or عقل in the first hemistich not having the izāfat, and the address being to God, not to man, 'Thou hast given to our petitioning, through the instrumentality of the Universal Reason (عقل = عقل كل) both the commands...." L.

[1] "امر, 'God's decree,' may be interpreted as equivalent to عالم امر 'the world of command,' *i.e.*, the world of incorporeal beings, the angel world, the world of meanings (عالم معاني). So 'whatso springs up in this world of mankind, originates in the world of meanings; and what the prophet utters, also originates there,'" L. As to the various worlds, or planes of existence, I may refer to Gibb, *op. cit.*, pp. 55-56. As he says, the accounts we have of them are confused, and differ more or less in the different authorities. Here, in L's note, the world of fixed prototypes (world of meanings,—the true meanings which underlie names and the outward show of things), the world of might, and the angel world (world of similitudes), are treated as one,—the '*Ālam-i-malakūt*, opposed to the '*Ālam-i-mulk*; the five worlds being reduced, as often, to two. The idea of the text is that which Gibb expresses thus (p. 56):—"The world of similitudes is so called because in it exist, ready to be materialized, the forms which are to be actualized on the Physical Plane. The number of these which are so actualized at any given time is in proportion to the whole 'as a little ring in the midst of a vast desert.'"

[2] "In the world of causes, the Causer of causes has so set causes in action that Reason has been removed from her place. Or 'His causes have made an old rag (نقل) of Reason,' *i.e.*, Reason is, as an old rag, powerless to comprehend them" B.

[3] انسابش, *lit.* used of tracing an individual's descent; the meaning of the sentence is that the soul is unable to follow His methods of working.

The soul's relation to the world of life [1] is like a blind man and a pearl of 'Ummān.[2] One showed a pearl to a blind man; the greedy fool asked him, 'How much wilt thou give for this pearl?'[3] He said, 'A round cake and two fishes; for no one can discern ruby or pearl,—why be angry?—except by the pearl of the eye. So, since God has not given me this pearl,[4] do thou take away that other pearl, and talk no more folly. If thou dost not wish to be laughed at by the ass, take thy pearl to one who is skilled in pearls; as soon as he puts the sole of his foot upon the oyster, his art knows well its value.'[5] Understanding is a tent before His gate, the soul a soldier in His army;[6] the soul from fear of being rejected by Him sweeps not the dust of His Court except by permission; all in place and time are His property, from the '*Be*' of His decree to the wicket of '*It was.*'[7] His decree has commanded the service of His Court to all intelligences in the words '*Obey God*'; from the vegetative to the reasonable soul [8] all like slaves are seeking Him.

---

1 *i.e.*, the world of eternal Truth, B. The present section is omitted by CH. and perhaps does not belong here. It may, however, be considered as a parenthesis exemplifying the preceding lines,—that the soul is incapable of understanding heavenly matters.

2 *i.e.*, he is unable to comprehend the value of it. 'Ummān (the same as 'Umān previously), the sea of Oman, famous for its pearl fisheries.

3 B takes زبن as equivalent to زهی and hence the hemistich as spoken in ironical praise,—'Well done, thou dissolute libertine'; also میخواهی as 'how much dost thou want' for the pearl, which would be the natural interpretation. I cannot, however, bring out the sense of the story otherwise than by supposing میخواهی داد = میخوهي,—'how much wilt thou give?'

4 *i.e.*, of the eye.

5 *i.e.*, in diving, when he lights on one at the bottom of the sea, he immediately knows its value, B.

6 عقل, the Primal Intelligence, pure thought, the first emanation of the First Cause; and جان, the First or Universal Soul, an emanation from the psychic aspect of the foregoing; v. Gibb, *op. cit.* p. 42. سایه بان, a tent, also an umbrella; B prefers 'an umbrella-holder,' *i.e.*, "not one who possesses the secrets of the Truth; so the soul, a soldier, is not a familiar companion of His glory."

7 *i.e.*, His decree and all intermediate causes, down to the material objects of this present creation.

8 روبنده in the text is the equivalent of the philosophical نباتیه, as گوینده of ناطقه. Cf. Gibb, *op. cit.* p. 48. "There are three degrees of soul: the 'Soul Vegetable' (Nefs-i-Nebátive), the Soul Sensible, *lit.*, 'Soul Animal'—

Well thou knowest that on the plain of eternity without beginning works the hand of the creative power of God, the Great and Glorious. God's decree has caused power in every sphere to become pregnant with act ;[1] so that when the way of the membranes is opened, there comes forth that wherewith they were pregnant.[2] How shall Existence rebel against Him, to whom non-Existence is obedient ? One word of command awakened the Universe ;[3] all things came together into the circle.[4]

The soul that obeys the command, and commands ; the intelligence that understands the Qur'ān and gives us our faith ; wisdom, and life, and abstract form,[5]—know that all proceed from the decree, and the decree from God. When the sun's light falls upon the water, the quiet water is stirred into activity ;[6] the sun's reflection from the water falls upon the wall and paints the ceiling with beauty ; know that that too, that second reflection, of the water on the wall, is a reflection of the sun.[7]

(Nefs-i-Haywániya), and the 'Soul Reasonable' (Nefs-i-Nátiqa). The first, which corresponds to what we should call the vital principle is shared in common by plants, brutes and man ; its functions are growth, nourishment and reproduction. The second, which represents the principle of sensation or perception, is confined to brutes and man ; its functions are sensation and voluntary movement. The third, the principle of reason, belongs to man alone.''

[1] Power, قوت, *i.e.*, the latent possibility of action ; it is by God's decree that matter possessing the latent possibility, shows forth its proper activity.

[2] The metaphor of the embryo and the fœtal membranes enclosing it.

[3] *i.e.*, the word '*kun*.' 'Be' spoken by God at the creation.

[4] The circle of contingent existences which the omnipotence of His knowledge circumscribed in eternity without beginning around the whole Universe, B.

[5] Abstract or absolute form corresponds to 'corporeal form,' صورت جسمیه, v. n. on p. 85 l. 14. The first two of the expressions in the text I take to refer to the human soul, which only by obedience is fitted for rank and command in the spiritual world, and the human reason respectively ; 'wisdom' and 'life' may refer, as L appears to think, to the Universal Reason and Universal Soul.

[6] The reflecting of the sun's light being conceived of as due to the active operation of the water.

[7] آنهم از عکس آفتاب شمار - آن دوم عکس آب بر دیوار. L, considering that آنهم and آن دوم may refer to different things, would relate آنهم to حق three lines previously, which being one of the names of God is a manifestation of His Essence ; آفتاب would then be the sun of Truth, of Real Existence (آفتاب)

He has caused all things to return to Himself; for none can escape from Him. All things are, yet all are far from All; thou hast read in the Qur'ān "*All things return.*"[1] From Him are evil and good, power and might;[2] '*the sentence is not changed*' is His decree.[3] His decree changes not; man can only stand in wonder before it.[4]

(حقیقی), and آن دوم would be امر, the decree, the origin of understanding and soul and life and abstract form. The meaning would then be, "Know that 'the Truth' as a name of God is a reflection of the sun of True Being, and the decree is the reflection of the water on the wall." But the comparison seems to be between God, the decree, and all created things, on the one hand, and the sun, the reflection in the water, and the light on the wall on the other.

1 Qur. 42 : 53. "*Shall not all things return unto God?*" 'All' in the first hemistich of this line is alternately 'all created things,' and 'God,' who is all. "All creation, though it possesses contingent existence, is far from God, and must return to Him; or, all things are contingencies of true Existence, and only externally have an (independent) existence; but from the All, all, *i.e.*, multiplicity and plurality, is far distant; for all springs from Unity, and to Unity must return, as is said in the second hemistich." L.

2 "If نیک be read without the iẓāfat, the meaning is that the bringing into being of bad and good, which is here credited to God, is (by) His power and might, i.e., His power and might are the origin (مصدر) of both good and bad deeds, not that the bad and good which are referable to His servants, are of Him, but that He gives the strength and power to perform them. This is in accordance with the beliefs of the Mu'tazila. If we read نیک with the iẓāfat ('from Him are the evil and the good wrought by strength and power'), then it means that the bad and good we do, is of God; for our power and strength is of him"; L, who thus appears, somewhat ineffectually, to distinguish between the being 'of God' (ازو), and the having an ultimate source (مصدر) in God. For the sect of the Mu'tazila v. Sale, Prel. Disc. Sect. VIII; Hughes, Dict. of Islam. s.v.; and especially Browne's Literary History of Persia, vol. i, pp. 281—289. The tenets held by them which more particularly bear on the present subject are that God is not the author of evil, but of good only, and that man is a free agent.

3 Qur. 50: 28. "*The sentence is not changed with me, nor am I unjust to my servants.*"

4 On this L remarks:—"The first statement requires explanation; for in appearance many changes take place, such as the abrogation of various religions, the change of qibla, etc. The explanation is that His decree, which is fixed in His eternal Omniscience and of which these changes are the result, is not susceptible of change; or we may say that every change which happens is again according to His decree, and the changes in His commands take place by the decree of none other than Himself. Which explanation is very fitting, for (Qur. 2: 100) '*Whatever verses we cancel or cause thee to forget, we bring a better, or*

He is all-powerful to do whatso He shall desire ; whatso He wills, He does, for His is the dominion. He who, invested with His authority, is in His secrets, and he whom He compels to be His slave,—all are subjected or exalted according to His decree. Mankind heed not the good or evil ; as to whatso has been, and whatso shall be, that only can they do which He commands. All that the Master has written and set forth, the boy in school cannot but read ; if from His records He has written out a certain alphabet, he cannot turn his head away from it. Whether thou existest or not is naught to the workings of God in the path of His might and power ; all is God's work,—happy is he who knows it.

Reason became the pen,[1] the soul the paper ; matter received form, and body was transformed into individual shapes.[2] To Love He said, 'Fear none but me' ; to Reason, 'Know thyself.' Reason is

---

its like ' ; so that in truth there has been no change except in mercy something better was given in exchange ; and so mankind can but wonder at the absence of change in the decree of the Essential and at the changes in the phenomenal (عدم تغير امر حقيقي و تغيرات مجازي)."

[1] The author's text has suffered very severely in this portion, and the preceding chapters (from the one I have called 'Of His mercy'), have needed a very large amount of rearrangement in order to exhibit even as much consecutiveness of thought as is displayed in the above translation. There remains over the present passage, which does not seem to me to fall into place in any of these. The passage which follows this was similarly left over from an earlier chapter ('On Laud and Praise').

[2] 'Reason' is the Universal Reason ; 'soul' is the reasonable soul, نفس ناطقة. B. "Reason is the active agent, the soul the passive object; Reason causes the effect, the soul is what it acts on. Matter it makes susceptible of receiving bodily form ; and body (جسم) which is compounded of matter and form it makes susceptible of receiving various outlines," L. Cf. Gibb, *op. cit.*, p. 45. "Within the hollow of the Sphere of the Moon lies the elemental world. The basis of this is no longer ether, but 'Matter' (Heyúla) [in the text '*māya*'], and immanent in 'Matter' is 'Form' (Súrat), without which its actualized existence is impossible. Form is in two degrees ; 'Corporeal Form' (Súret-i Jismíye) and 'Specific Form' (Súret-i Nev'íye). Matter, in combination with the first of these, produces 'Body in the Abstract' (Jism-i Mutlaq) ; and this, in combination with the second, produces the 'Individual Body.'"

ever Love's vassal; Love's point of honour lies in scorning life.[1] To Love He said, 'Do thou rule as king'; to human nature[2] He said, 'Live thou in thy household; in sorrow make the elements thy food, and afterwards take in thy hand the water of life.' So that when the reasonable soul[3] has made of it[4] her riches, and expends it in the path of the Holy Spirit, that Holy Spirit rejoices in the soul, and the soul becomes pure as the Primal Reason.[5] This is the soul's progress from life's beginning to its end.[6]

---

1 That is, perhaps, in acting in contradiction to Reason.

2 طبع, *i.e.*, نفس, apparently used as the equivalent of the preceding عقل H writes عقل.

3 نطق, *i.e.*, نفس ناطقة.

4 *i.e.*, the water of life.

5 عقل, *i.e.*, عقل كلّ. The passage is the occasion of a long commentary by L and, following him, B. "After the acquisition of eternal life and the characters of perfection, and the employment (در باختن, expending) of these in the path of the Holy Spirit (either Gabriel, or, more literally, the Spirit of God, روح الله), the Holy Spirit dilates (باز شود), *i.e.*, becomes expanded and rejoiced, because of the soul which has come to possess the characters of perfection. Or by the 'holy spirit' (روح قدس) may be meant that partial (جزئی) soul which is in relation to the human body; then the interpretation will be that when this sanctified spirit returns (باز شود, the same words, in a different sense, as those previously translated 'rejoices') to the Soul, *i.e.*, in this explanation, the Universal Soul, then the reasonable soul (*i.e.*, that sanctified spirit) becomes pure and stainless and free from taint like Reason (عقل or عقل كلّ the Universal Reason). Another reading is

روح قدسي بنفس يار شود نفس چون عقل بر كنار شود

'the Holy Spirit becomes the soul's friend; soul and reason alike have then reached the end.'"

6 "From its beginning as the partial soul to its end in the Universal Reason (B paraphrases L as usual, but here substitutes 'Universal Soul'), the road and path is thus, *i.e.*, as has been related in the preceding verses. Or 'life's beginning' may be the material reason (عقل هيولاني), which is a property of the reasonable soul (از احوال نفس ناطقه است), and life's end the Real Truth, which is above acquired understanding (وبالا تر از عقل المستفاد ست)." L.

In view of thy religion to fly from poetry is better,—to shatter 86
thy verse as thou wouldst an idol ;[1] for religion and poetry, though at present they are on an equality, are utterly foreign to each other.[2] The things that are permitted to us, are forbidden to one who is ignorant of both of these ;[3] he appreciates the difference between prohibition and permission who looks on ease in the light of a wound.[4]

---

1 The words 'religion' and 'poetry' occurring in this and the next few lines, differ only in the order of their letters (*shar'*, *shi'r*) ; so also the words for 'verse' and 'idol' resemble each other (*bait*, *but*).

2 "In reality they are utterly foreign ; for religion is extolled and poetry, according to "*The poets—those follow them who go astray*" (Qur. 26: 224), is condemned ; although in this age they are on an equality, *i.e.*, the foundations of religion are destroyed by the corruption of the times, and religion, like poetry, has lost its basis and support. If, however, when he says they are now on the same level, he is referring to his own poetry, full of truth and the knowledge of God, then the idea is one of praise, not blame," L. B adds the saying, "*Poets are the disciples of the Merciful.*"

3 *i.e.*, religion and poetry. "Whatso is permitted to us, *i.e.*, to the people who have only an exoteric knowledge of religion (اهل ظاهر شرع), is unlawful for one who is far removed from this and that, *i.e.*, worldly concerns. For "*The good deeds of the pious are the evil deeds of those who are brought near to God* ;" and true it is that those things which the people of externals regard as right for themselves are forbidden to the perfected," L. I give this note because of L's authority ; I think, however, that 'us' refers to the adepts, and that consequently the meaning is the exact opposite of this ; v. note on next line.

4 *i.e.*, "counts worldly gain and ease as an injury and a wound ; those who are at peace in the path of religion and truth, what have they to do with these things ?" L. The idea of this line is what the author appears to have been leading up to,—that only the man who regards earthly things as an encumbrance can judge of what is allowable or improper ; introducing the idea by reminding us that poetry is condemned by a strict religion, he follows up the idea further in the succeeding line ; then he asserts that he himself, being above these restrictions, may write poetry, while others on a lower plane are debarred therefrom, and ends with the general assertion of the present line.

The passage concludes with a line, "Kindness towards thine enemy is wisdom ; for heaven lays up for thee thy good or evil fame ;" which, occurring in this place, will serve again to illustrate the extraordinary confusion into which the text has fallen.

To Remember the Words of the All-knowing Lord renders easy the Accomplishment of the Aim. God Most High has said, Say, if Men and Jinns conspired to bring the like of this Qur'ān, they could not bring its like, not though they helped each other.[1] And said the Prophet (on whom be Mercy and Peace), The Qur'ān is Riches; there is no Poverty if it be given, and there is no Riches beside it. And he said (Peace be upon him), The Qur'ān is a medicine for every Disease except Death.[2]

By reason of its beauty and its pleasantness the discourse of the Qur'ān has no concern with clang of voice or travail of the letter; how shall phenomenal existence weigh its true nature,[3] or written characters contain its discourse? Thought is bewildered before its outward shape,[4] understanding stupefied before the secret of its sūras; full of meaning and beautiful are its words and sūras, ravishing and enchanting is its outward form. From it earth's produce[5] and the sons of the angel-world have ever drawn their strength and nurture; in the loosing of perplexities its hidden meaning is souls' repose and hearts' ease. The Qur'ān is balm for the wounded heart, and medicine for the pain of the sore at heart.[6] Do thou, if thou art not a parrot nor a donkey nor an ass, surely hold the word of God to be the root of the faith,

---

1 This is quoted from Qur. 17 : 90.

2 It must remain doubtful how much, if any, of the above long title is original. The remainder of the book is concerned with the Qur'ān.

3 For صفت in this sense cf. p. 2, l. 12, p. 45, l. 9. For حدوث cf. حدث with the same meaning of 'phenomenal existence' in p. 4, l. 2, p. 58, l. 5.

4 *i.e.*, the words in which it is clothed. "It is the task of thought (وهم) to comprehend the partial meanings connected with things perceived by the senses. The author asserts that notwithstanding the outward forms in which the Qur'ān is presented are sensible things, thought is unable to comprehend even the partial truths thus manifested." L.

5 دادهٔ مُلک, Adam and Adam's children, B.

6 Referring to Qur. 10; 58. "*O ye folk! there has come to you a warning from your Lord, and a balm for what is in your breasts, and a guidance and a mercy to believers*;" and Qur. 17 : 84. "*And we will send down of the Qur'ān that which is a healing and a mercy to the believers.*"

and the cornerstone of piety, a mine of rubies, a treasure of spiritual meaning. It is the canon of the wisdom of the wise, the standard of the practice of the learned ; to praise it is joy to the soul, to look on 87
it is solace to the mind. Its verses are healing to the soul of the pious, its banner [1] is pain and grief to the evil-doer ; it has thrown the Universal Reason into affliction, has made the Universal Soul sit down in widowhood.[2] Reason and Soul but hold men back from its true essence ;[3] the eloquent are impotent to rival its manner.[4]

On the Glory of the Qur'ān. 5

Glorious it is, though concealing its glory ; and a guide, though under the veil of coquetry.[5] Its discourse is bright and strong ; its argument clear and apt ; its words are a casket for the pearl of life,

---

1 " Its threatening and terrors and comminations," B.

2 " The Primal Reason, which comprehends everything in its completeness, is thrown into perplexity at the difficulty of finding out the secrets of the Qur'ān, and since Reason is the active and effective agent, and Soul the thing acted on, the latter has hence the feminine character, and it is very fitting that she should be supposed to be sitting in grief, by reason of the affliction that has befallen Reason, who is thus as if dead." L.

3 " Since Reason and Soul cannot themselves arrive at its true essence, they hold others back too ;" so L, who is however doubtful as to the explanation, adding " *And God knows best if this is right.*"

4 The Qur'ān has always, by orthodox Muslims, been held to be inimitable in style; and many passages of the Qur'ān itself, such as the one incorporated in the title of the present section, are adduced in support of this view. Cf. also Qur. 11 : 16, where Muḥammad challenges his opponents to bring ten sūras, and 2 : 21 and 10 : 39, where he challenges them to bring one sūra like it. Cf. also on this subject Hughes, Dict. of Islam, s.v. Quran, sects. IX and XI ; Sale, Prelim. Disc., sect. III, Palmer's Introd., p. lxxvi ; and especially Nöldeke, Gesch. d. Qorans, pp. 43, 44.

5 " Notwithstanding that by the various letters and characters which adorn the outward aspect of God's word its majesty is withdrawn behind a veil, it is still in spite of this concealment, glorious, and mighty, and venerable ; and notwithstanding that it has drawn over its beautiful countenance a hundred screens, of verses and chapters, and hidden its world-illuming splendour beneath the veil of coquetry, still with all this cloaking it is a guide on our path unapproached by any other." B.

its precepts a tower over the water-wheel of the faith;[1] to the Knowers it is love's garden, to the soul the highest heaven.

O thou to whom, by reason of thy heedlessness and sin, in reading the Qur'ān there comes upon thy tongue no sweetness from its words, into thy heart no yearning from their comprehension,—by its exceeding majesty and authority the Qur'ān, with argument and proof, is in its inner meaning the light of the high road of Islām, in its outward significance the guardian of the tenets of the multitude; life's sweetness to the wise, to the heedless but a recitation on the tongue,—phrases upon their tongue whose sweetness they cannot taste, while careless of their spirit and design.

There is an eye which sees the spirit of the Qur'ān, and an eye which sees the letter;[2]—for this the bodily eye, for that the eye of the soul; the body, through the ear, carries away the melody of its words; the soul, by its perceptive power, feeds on the delights of its spirit. For strangers the curtains of majesty are drawn together in darkness before its loveliness;[3] the curtain and the chamberlain know not aught of the king;—he knows who is possessed of sight,[4] but how can the curtain know aught of him?

The revolutions of the azure vault have brought no weakening of its power, no dimming of its lustre; its syntax and form, pronunciation and nunation, prevail from earth to Pleiades.

88 Now hast thou in thy daily provision tasted the nut's first husk; the first skin is rough and harsh, the second is like the moon's

---

1 "The words of the Qur'ān vivify and preserve the soul of the believer, and similarly its precepts, both positive and negative, are an ornament to the wheel of the faith; for unless a wheel have a tower, its results and workings and act and effect are not evidenced in the world in the way designed · and so it is with the precepts of the Qur'ān, without which the faith possesses not the necessary appliances for success." B.

2 Not our usual antithesis of 'spirit' and 'letter'; the letter is the actual letter of the written page.

3 مشک, 'musk,' is also 'blackness' and 'ink'; hence, as B says, "In the blackness of the ink of its lines the Qur'ān has drawn before its countenance the curtains of majesty and power; but the secret of that majesty exists like a lovely mistress beneath the veil."

4 "The eye of whose mind passes on without check till it reaches the exalted level of the Throne." B.

slough,[1] the third is silk, pale and fine, and fourth is the succulent cool kernel; the fifth degree is thy abode, where the prophets' law becomes thy threshold. Seeing then thou mayest delight thy soul with the fifth, why halt at the first? Thou hast seen of the Qur'ān but its veil,—hast seen its letters, which do but hide it; it does not reveal its countenance to the unworthy,—him only the letters confront. If it had seen thee to be worthy, it would have rent this subtle veil and shown its face to thee, and there thy soul might have found rest; for it heals the wounded heart, and medicines the disappointed soul;[2] the body tastes the flavour of the dregs that it may live; the soul knows the taste of the oil.[3]

What can sense see, but that the outward form is good? What there is within, wisdom knows. Thou recitest the form of its sūras, and its true nature thou knowest not; but know, that to him who truly reads the Qur'ān, the feast it gives comes not short of the guest-house of Paradise. It has made the letter its veil, because it is to be concealed from alien eyes; material existence knows naught of its inmost soul,—know, its body is one thing, its soul a thing apart; from its outward form thou seest but so much as do the common men from the appearance of a king.[4]

Why deemest thou that the words are the Qur'ān? What crude discourse is thine concerning it? Though the letter is its bed-fellow, it knows it not, no more than the figures on the bath;[5] nor do

---

[1] سلخ —, چون ز ماه سلخ being 'a serpent's slough'; and also 'the last day of the moon', the thin crescent being like the slough a serpent leaves behind.

[2] Cf. Qur. 10 : 58. "*O ye folk! there has come to you....a balm for what is in your breasts*;" and 17 : 84, "*And we will send down of the Qur'ān that which is a healing and a mercy to the believers.*"

[3] Possibly the first hemistich refers to the use of charms, etc., as *e.g.*, by writing a verse of the Qur'ān on paper, and then washing off the ink with water, which is used as a medicinal draught. This however is merely the employment of the dregs; the superjacent pure oil is food for the soul alone.

[4] اهل صورت = اهل ظاهر (opp. to اهل باطن), ordinary people, who live by sense. 'The appearance of a king' is "his bodily form, which holds a cloak over his true nature," B.

[5] *i.e.*, no more than the carved or painted figures on the warm bath (گرمابه) know anything of the bather inside.

the sleepers and the cut-purses[1] see, like those who watch,[2] the spirit of the Qur'ān.

Of the Recital of the Secret of the Qur'ān.

Tongue cannot tell the secret of the Qur'ān, for His intimates[3]
89 keep it concealed; the Qur'ān indeed knows its own secret,—hear it from itself, for itself knows it. Except by the soul's eye none knows the measurer of words from the true reader of the Qur'ān;—I will not take upon myself to say that thou truly knowest the Qur'ān though thou be 'Uthmān.[4]

The world is like the summer's heat, its people like drunkards therein, all wandering in the desert of indifference; death the shepherd, men his flock; and in this waste of desire[5] and wretchedness the hot sand shows as running water.[6] The Qur'ān is as the cool water of Euphrates, whilst thou art like a thirsty sinner on the plain of the Judgment. The letter and Qur'ān[7] hold thou as cup and water; drink the water, gaze not on the vessel.[8] Because it is summer, thy home seems to thee a mine of enmity; because the water is cold, the vessel of turquoise, thou usest not to fast.[9] To the pure heart suffering will tell in a cry of anguish the secret of the pure Qur'ān; how can Reason discover its interpretation? But a delight in it finds out its inmost secret.

---

1 *i.e.*, "the people of the world, lost in lust and desire," B.

2 *i.e.*, "the saintly and pure prophets and those who know God," B.

3 Or (B) محرمان = Muḥammad, God's confidant or intimate friend (plural of respect).

4 The third caliph, who caused the second and final recension of the Qur'ān to be made.

5 "The inclination of the soul towards the pursuits of the world," B.

6 *i.e.*, their sufferings are increased by the deceit of the mirage.

7 *i.e.*, the spirit of the Qur'ān.

8 "Explore the secret of the Qur'ān; be not in bondage to the letter, but turn thy soul's eye to the discovery of the secret," B.

9 Referring to the lettering and illumination of the Qur'ān, B. (On the various colours of ink used in the punctuation of MSS. of the Qur'ān, the use of gold for illumination, etc., v. Nöldeke. Gesch. d. Qorans, pp. 307, 310-13, 319-22, etc.)

Though the written characters are not of the word, the scent of Yūsuf is in his garment; the fair Yūsuf was cast away in Egypt, but the scent reached Ya'qūb in Canaan. The letter of the Qur'ān is to its sense as thy clothes to thy life; the letter may be uttered by the tongue, its soul can be read but by the soul. The letter is as the shell, the true Qur'ān the pearl; the heart of the free-born desires not the shell. Though its words are fair and finely traced, though the mountain becomes as carded wool before them,[1] make music of them in thy heart like Moses, not outwardly like the treble of the pipes. When the soul recites the Qur'ān it enjoys a luscious morsel; whoso hears it, mends his ragged robe.[2] The words, the voice, the letters of the verses, are as three stalks [3] in bowls of vegetables. Though the husk is not fair nor sweet, still it guards the kernel; but through thy impurity the mystery becomes a song, the word of God a tune through thy folly.

Whilst thou art in this tomb appointed for us, this residence contrived for us, in this world full of objects of pursuit, this abode of deceit, look with thy earthly sight upon the willow, and with thy soul upon the ṭūbā-tree;[4] read with thy tongue the letter, and the sense with thy soul.

Sacrifice, to honour the Qur'ān, thy reason before its discourse;[5] reason is no guide to its mysteries; reason is impotent here. Thou art now shameless, deceitful; thou art not worthy to have the curtain of the mystery drawn aside; thou knowest naught of its secret, hast

---

1 Referring to Qur. 59 : 21. "*Had we sent down this Qur'ān upon a mountain, thou wouldst have seen it humbling itself, splitting asunder from the fear of God!*" B.

2 لقمه چرب کند, *lit.*, 'smears the mouthful with oil.' "When the Qur'ān is read from the heart, the soul is strengthened: and whoso listens to it with his soul, puts a patch on his beggar's robe," B.

3 چوبک *i.e.*, comparatively innutritious morsels.

4 A tree of Paradise. "Though with thy bodily sight thou lookest on the willow, with thy seeing eye make for the ṭūbā-tree; the willow is plain to be seen, like the letter of the Qur'ān; the ṭuba is inwards, like its soul and sense." B.

5 نطق *lit.*, pronunciation; *i.e.*, "its import, which comes to light in reading and chanting it," B.

not yet arrived at 'Arafāt.[1] So long as thou desirest pleasure and cherishest desire, play as a child,—thou art not man enough for this.

But when wisdom has conquered the world of desire, pure goodness succeeds to evil ; the devil of passion flies to Hell, and Sulaimān regains his ring ;[2] the Qur'ān's secret routs the demon ;—what wonder if he flies in terror from the Qur'ān ?

Wait, for when the day of true religion dawns, the night of thought and fancy[3] and sense flies away. When the veiled ones of the unseen world see that thou art stainless, they will lead thee into the invisible abode and reveal to thee their faces ; and disclosing to thee the secret of the Qur'ān, they will withdraw the veil of letters. The earthy will have a reward of earth, the pure shall see purity. An understanding of the Qur'ān dwells not in the brain where pride starts up ; the ass is dumb as a mere stone, and lends not his ear to the secret of God's word,—turns away from hearing the Qur'ān and pays no heed to the sūra's secret ; but if the mind be disciplined of God it shall discover in the sūra the secret of the Qur'ān.

In the Recital of the Miracle wrought by the Qur'ān.

91 O thou, who hast got into thy palm but the ocean's foam, and of thy possessions hast made the semblance of an array ; thou hast not laid hold of the pearl's true substance, for that thou art occupied only concerning the shell; withhold thy hand from these lack-lustre shells, and bring up the bright pearl from the ocean depths. The pearl without its shell is cherished in the heart, the shell without its pearl is clay

---

[1] موقف *lit.* "place of standing," = Mt. 'Arafāt, which is "the place where the pilgrims stay on the ninth day of the pilgrimage and recite the midday and afternoon prayers and hear the khutbah or sermon" (Hughes, Dict. of Islam).

[2] Referring to the story of the demon Ṣakhr, who stole Solomon's seal-ring; he flew away and threw the ring into the sea, where it was swallowed by a fish, which was afterwards caught and brought to Solomon, the ring being found inside it.

[3] وهم و خيال, the operation of the mind, which is fallible, opposed to true knowledge.

to be thrown aside ;[1] the pearl's value comes not from the shell,—the arrow's value comes from its hitting the mark.[2]

He who knows of his own sight the pebbles of the sea-bottom[3] will not mistake sheep's dung for pearls of the sea ;[4] while he who stands aside on this stream's shore[5] can lay no claim to its shining pearls.

The lines of the Qur'ān are like unto faith's shore,[6] for it gives ease to heart and soul ; its bounty and its might are as the encircling sea[7] around the soul's world ; its depths are full of pearls and jewels, its shores abound in aloes-wood and ambergris ; knowledge of first and last is scattered from it for benefit of soul and body both.

Be pure, that the hidden meanings may appear to thee from out the cage of the letters, for till a man come forth from his impurity how can the Qur'ān come forth from its letters ? As long as thou art veiled inside thy Self,[8] what difference, to thee or to thy understanding,

---

1 So B :— قرارگاه او دل باشد ای عزیز و محفوظ امّا صدف بي گهر برون گل اي براي انداختن گل است مراد خوار وبي قدر

2 The 'mark' is complete attainment of the secrets of the Qur'ān, and the 'arrow' the desire of the rightly inclined mind towards the essence of those secrets. B.

3 *i.e.*, as I take it, the diver who has seen the pebbles at the bottom of the sea. In B the words فهر and قعر are marked by overlining, as if the meaning were, "He who can distinguish at sight فهر from قعر"; the words having some resemblance in form.

4 Both being small round bodies ; the implication being the converse statement, that the mysteries of the Qur'ān are not to be discriminated by the inexperienced.

5 The stream being the Qur'ān.

6 If thou wishest to travel on the sea without help from coast or shore, thou canst not ; so till thou reverencest the written lines of the Qur'ān thou wilt not obtain the jewel of true religion, B. This however does not explain the connection of the second hemistich ; and I think ایمان is to be taken in a less restricted sense, as 'trust', 'confidence' ; the written words of the Qur'ān are as the shores by which one approaches a feeling of trustfulness and security, or the Qur'ān itself gives ease to heart and soul.

7 v. note on p. 79, l. 6.

8 Or, reading with ALB نقش for نفس, "inside thine outward form" = نقش انانیت, 'the form of self,' B. One who is enveloped in a veil has no power of distinguishing objects.

is there between evil and good ? In the letter of the Qur'ān is no healing for thy soul,—the goat grows not fat on the goatherd's call; nor soon nor late the water of his dream satisfies the thirsty one in his helplessness. Thou, who art in thraldom to pen and ink,[1] canst not distinguish between face and veil; in the world of the Word at least,[2] the word's outward characters[3] are not esteemed to be its life.

When thou settest foot in that country[4] He will teach thee the alphabet of sincerity, and when thou shalt recite the alphabet of the faith thou shalt know sun and Pleiades for thy father and ancestors;[5] such is the way of the loyal followers, and such too is the alphabet of the lovers.

Dark is the veil on the face of day; the verse of its conceits is
92 very subtle.[6] If thou wouldst have a treasure for thy soul and heart, recite with heart and soul a verse from it; that in it thou mayest find the jewel of the truth, the essential basis of thy faith;[7] that thou mayest find the casket of the incomparable pearl, and know the pure gold from the silver;[8] that glorious as the sun and moon there may appear to thee from behind the dark screen its own beautiful face, like a bride who comes forth lovely and joyous from out her gauzy veil.

---

1 Plural, 'inks,' in the text; perhaps with reference to the various colours of inks used for the orthographical marks, etc., v. note *ant.* p. 89, l. 10.

2 جهان سخن cf. *ant.* p. 24, l. 14, p. 25, l. 12.

3 *lit.* 'colour and smell.'

4 *i.e.* the world of the Word, just alluded to.

5 *i.e.*, thou art of such lofty descent. Also a play on words (اب و جد — ابجد).

6 The 'veil on the face of day' is night, which brings forth day,—day being the inner meanings of the Qur'ān, and night the ink-written letters. The 'verse' is the words of the Qur'ān and their arrangement and style; by means of which it conceals so many quips and conceits (بذله و نکته), and in virtue of which it is so subtle, demanding such keenness of understanding, B.

7 "Essential basis," کیمیا, cf. p. 62, l. 3.

8 All the texts here insert a line "What are the caskets ? the divine secrets. What is in them ? the spiritual mystery;" which I think is a gloss, since it interrupts the sequence of lines beginning with تا, speaks of 'caskets' in the plural, and practically identifies the casket and the pearl it contains.

Of the Guidance of the Qur'ān.

It is the guide, and the lovers the travellers ; it is a rope, and the heedless sit in the pit. Thy soul has its home at the pit's bottom ; the Qur'ān's light is a rope let down to it ; rise and seize the rope, so thou mayest haply find salvation ; else thou art lost in the pit's depth,— flood and storm [1] will destroy thee. Like Yūsuf thou art brought by Satan into the pit ; be thy wisdom the glad tidings,[2] thy rope the Qur'ān ; if thou desirest to be as Yūsuf, and to enjoy high place, take hold of it and come forth from the well.

The wise use the rope to obtain the water of life, but thou makest ready thy rope to dance on it for daily bread.[3] No one learns two letters of the Qur'ān in a thousand centuries with such an eye as thine ; the understanding's arm turns about as does a wheel ; body and soul are captives of thy passions.[4] If thou desirest throne and crown and honour, why sittest thou for ever at the well's bottom? Thy Yūsuf[5] is helpless in the well, thy heart reciting the sūra '*safah*' ;[6] make of sorrow a rope, of thy sighs a bucket, and draw up thy Yūsuf from the well.

On the Greatness of the Qur'ān,—verily it consists not in its division into 'Tens' and 'Fives.'[7]

To attract a handful of boys thou hast made its honour to consist in the 'tens,' and 'fives' ;[8] thou hast abrogated the authority of every

---

1 "Thy lusts and passions," B.

2 بشرى, "a word used in the traditions for the publication of Islām" (Hughes, Dict. s.v.).

3 *i.e.* reading and intoning it in public.

4 دل = نفس اماره, B.

5 "Thy heart, dead within the curtain of heedlessness," B.

6 *Lit.* 'foolishness.' The reference is to Qur. 2: 12. "*And when it is said to them 'Believe as other men believe,' they say 'Shall we believe as fools believe?' Are they not themselves the fools? and yet they do not know.*"

7 The title varies in the various MSS ; none is particularly applicable ; the one here given was perhaps a gloss suggested by the first line.

8 *i.e.*, sets of ten, or of five verses. Such divisions were made, according to B, for two purposes ; embellishment, and for convenience of instruction, to mark the end of a lesson. On the manner of marking these, cf. Nöldeke, Gesch.

verse which abrogates another,[1] art still unlearned in its doctrines ;
93 the intricate passages seem to thee plain, while in its plain teachings thou hast no faith ;[2] thou hast abandoned the light of the Qur'ān, and for the sake of the multitude hast made its outward form the tool of thy hypocrisy for a measure of barley and two plates of chaff. Now thou intonest its cadences, now recitest its stories ; sometimes thou makest of it a weapon for strife ; sometimes in thy irreverence throwest it into disorder,[3] sometimes esteemest it a prodigy ; now thou interpretest it according to thine own conjecture, and again determinest to the contrary of that ; now in thy fancy thou takest the conclusion of its passages for the beginning, now absurdly turnest its meaning inside out ; again thou expoundest it by thine own opinion, and explainest it according to thine own knowledge ; amongst the thirty caskets of the Qur'ān [4] thou wanderest not except with railing.

Sometimes thou sayest to a foolish friend, perhaps a lazy cloth-weaver, "If I write thee a charm, keep it clean, O youth, and soil it not ; but there must be a sacrifice in the morning,—the blood of a black bird is required." All this deceit for a diram or two, a supper or a breakfast for thy belly !

Thou hast wasted thy life in folly ; what can I say ? begone, and shame to thee ! Thou creepest into some mosque or other in thy appetite,[5] thy throat full of wind, like a pipe or a bell ; shame on thy

---

d. Qorans, p. 324 ; who remarks (not. ad. loc.) that it is to be regretted that the later Muslims have again abandoned this method of verse-enumeration, which so greatly facilitates the quotation and identification of passages.

1 On the doctrine of abrogation see, for example, Hughes, Dict. s.v. Qur'ān, sect. viii. "Some passages of the Qur'ān are contradictory, and are often made the subject of attack ; but it is part of the theological belief of the Muslim doctors that certain passages of the Qur'ān are *mansūkh*, or abrogated by verses revealed afterwards entitled *nāsikh*. This was the doctrine taught by Muḥammad in the *Sūratu'l-Baqarah* (ii), 105. "*Whatsoever verses we* (i.e., God) *cancel or cause thee to forget, we bring a better or its like.*" A list of abrogated and abrogating verses follows, acknowledged by all commentators to be such.

2 معوّل, in the sense of the infinitive, L ; *i.e.*, = اعتماد.

3 "In disputing over it as it lies in thy hands thou often seizest it violently, and idiotically opening and shutting it thou continually dishonourest it," B.

4 *Sīpāra*, one of the thirty parts into which the Qur'ān is divided.

5 To gain a few coins by reading the Qur'ān, B.

religion and thy faith for this appetite! May either wisdom be thy portion, or death! Shame on thee for such a nature, such accomplishments and science,—they bring thee no esteem!

On the Allegations brought forward by the Word of God.

Wait till the Qur'ān shall make complaint of thee before God on the judgment day, and shall say, How much falsehood has this deceitful one, whom Thou trustedst,[1] drawn forth from Thy truth!—shall say, O God, thou knowest both the manifest and the hidden; night and day he recited me loudly, and rendered not justice to a single word of me. Neither in grammar, nor meaning, nor pure pronunciation did 94
I ever receive in the miḥrāb[2] my due from him with honesty. He has a good voice when he intones, and his robe of mourning is a pretty blue; but however he boasted his claims in respect of me, he knew not the depth of my meaning, for beyond talk and clamour this crowd are unable to utter a word. He never pushed forwards his horse towards my private grounds,[3]—could not distinguish my face from my veil; when he entered my street he showed in his discussions[4] no worth but only worthlessness. He surrendered not his mind and soul to my words, but forced me in the direction of his own decision and desire; now he wounded me with the sword of his lusts, and again he fettered me in the snare of his passions; now he brought me to his drinking-parties, and again sang me as a song; sometimes he would recite me by way of profanity, making a noise like an ass in his shamelessness; now he would break through the frigidity of my words with his amorousness, as a gimlet through wood;[5] now like a professional story-teller with his cadences he would scatter my words abroad to the stroke

---

1 B points مصدَّق, but nevertheless explains as بظاهر تصديق گوي امّا بباطن حيلت جوي.

2 The niche in the wall of the mosque, where the imām stands to lead the service.

3 "The knowledge of the mysteries and hidden secrets of the Qur'ān," B.

4 زشت و نكو cannot be referred to the Qur'ān itself; it is equivalent to 'conjectural explanations and contested interpretations made according to private judgment,' B.

5 I suppose by reading sensual meanings into the words.

of his plectrum.[1] O deviser of schemes ![2] I ask for a just decision on the day of judgment against such an affliction !

For the sake of blandishment in this transitory abode,—sometimes in the crowded street and sometimes at time of prayer, sometimes by thy words and sometimes by thy voice,—thou shinest but to attract admiration. The words that have been polluted by thee, though they be wise, yet are they folly; for though the breeze is pleasant and delightful, yet if it pass over ordure it is not so. Has not God by His command plainly denied His Qur'ān to the impure ?

On the Sweetness of the Qur'ān.

How shalt thou taste the flavour and delight of the Qur'ān, since thou chantest it without comprehension ?[3] Come forth through the door of the body into the landscape of the soul ; come and view the garden of the Qur'ān, that all things may appear before thy soul,—what has been, what is, and what shall be, the world's dry and moist,[4] within and without, whatsoever has been created by ' *Be, and it was*,' the decrees ordained by Him,—all will be made plain to thee through it. God's attributes shall obey thee, and shall truly recount their narrations before thee.

When the hearer hears God's word, the utterance of it causes him to tremble.[5] Till thou see with the eye of purity, how canst thou recite the sūra *Ikhlās*?[6]—a sūra like a cypress of Ghātfar,[7] its rhythm like the violets of Ṭabaristān.[8] The Qur'ān's loftiness and sublimity, if thou

---

1 زخمه چوبکی باشد که سازندها بدان ساز نوازند B.Q.

2 Addressed to the person the Qur'ān has been arraigning.

3 جان نبردن بمعني نرسيدن , B.

4 B refers to Qur. 6: 59. " *And there falls not a leaf save that He knows it ; nor a grain in the darkness of the earth, nor aught that is moist, nor aught that is dry, save that is in this perspicuous book.*"

5 *Lit.*, ' the utterance of it seizes the hair on his body ' ; موي بر اندام گرفتن لرزه افتادن و عاجز شدن درکار , B.

6 *Lit.* ' clearing oneself,' *i.e.* of belief in any but one God (Palmer). It is Sūra 112, one of the shortest in the Qur'ān, and one which is held in high esteem :—" *Say, ' He is God alone ! God the Eternal ! He begets not and is not begotten ! Nor is there like unto Him anyone !* ' "

7 A town in Māwarā' n-nahr (Turkestan) ; also a quarter of Samarqand.

8 The region on the south shore of the Caspian Sea.

ask thy preceptor, are as the throne and seat of God ;[1] its letters are the wings of the Spirit, the curtain of the Light ; its diacritical points black moles on the cheeks of the virgins of Paradise. Regard thou in this wise its outward form, that so thou mayest understand the secret of its sūras ; that it may place an *alif* in thy mind, and put *bā* and *tā* underneath thy feet ;[2] and, for the sake of life and wisdom, may dispose of thy fair Yūsuf [3] for eighteen worthless pieces,[4]—for in the street of the love of Unity and true wisdom beauty[5] is valued no higher than this.

The crucible of desire shall try him,[6] and afterwards he shall be made like gold of the mine ; yet again is the crucible prepared, that in it all fraud and deceit may be melted out ; then when the pure metal becomes soft, it is polished and made an ornament for its possessor's crown. The diadem and crown of every lord of rectitude and faith are such as this.[7]

On the Hearing of the Qur'ān.

When the pious reader[8] has set the book with reverence upon his lap, and has recited '*Let no one touch it*'[9] over both his hands, for a

---

1 A line occurs here which is apparently corrupt ; it contains grammatical allusions and puns. Similarly the words 'loftiness' and 'sublimity' in the preceding line are capable of a double interpretation ; نصب being the use of the vowel *fatḥa* in grammatical inflections, and رفع the use of *ḍamma*.

2 *Alif* being the symbol of the Unity, *bā* and *tā*, the next two letters of the alphabet, together giving *but*, 'an idol.'

3 "What thou lovest of the fragrance and charm of this transitory world," L. But cf. p. 92, l. 18, where the meaning is 'thy worldly self,' which here also seems more suitable.

4 Qur. 12 : 20. "*And they sold him for a mean price,—drachmæ counted out,—and they parted with him cheaply.*" "According to the commentators for 20 or 22 dirhems, and those not of full weight neither" (Sale *ad loc.*).

5 According to the Qur'ān and Muslim tradition Joseph was very beautiful.

6 *i.e.* thy Yūsuf.

7 The annotations of L and B are not helpful. A double trial in the furnace is apparently pictured ; the first, to ascertain if there is any gold in man's nature, does not complete the purification ; the second removes all the dross (fraud and deceit), and leaves only the pure gold.

8 The professional reader of the Qur'ān.

9 Referring to Qur. 56 : 78. "*Let none touch it but the purified.*" Since the Qur'ān and the 'preserved tablet' have both been mentioned in the verse

single copper he gives forth a lusty cry, like a turtledove for a grain of corn.[1] Hear God's word from God Himself, for the labour of the reader is only a veil. The Knower hears the word from the
96 Truth ;[2] the force of his desire denies him sleep. The feelings may be captive to the professional reciter, but Love has its songster in the heart itself. Set a mole in thy inmost heart, and not upon thy cheek ;[3] for it is thy thoughts are the true index of thy state. The Qur'ān tells its secret to the discerning thought; turn and twist and pause[4] are only matters of the voice, and whatso are matters of voice and written character and sound, reside outside the gate.

If there were any meaning in its song, a nightingale would not be sold for two coppers ; seek for the essence of the matter in the meaning, not in the written words,—thou wilt find no scent in a picture of ambergris. The time of waiting[5] in this transitory world deem but colour to the eye, and sound to the ear ; but the session of the Soul is a place where hearing is not, and song is silence there. How shall Love deem worthy notice a sweet that can be tasted ? Make not thy soul glad with song, for song brings no memories but of heaviness.

The friend who becomes thy friend at the bridge, take him not away from the water with thee ;[6] either drown him in thy hatred, or put him under ground, and then rest happy ; but in Love, to bear the burden of its commands, whether good or whether evil, is wisdom.[7] Give to the flames the gifts of the material world,—in thy smiling

---

immediately preceding, interpretations differ according as to which of these 'it' is supposed to refer to. If to the 'preserved tablet,' then none are to know what is in it except the pure beings, the angels ; if to the Qur'ān, none are to touch it except those technically in a state of purification.

1 دانگ may be pronounced *dānak*, or *dāng*,—a small grain of corn, or a small copper coin one-sixth of a diram.

2 *i.e.*, God.

3 *i.e.*, be beautiful of soul rather than in body.

4 Subtleties and intricacies in the ways of reading the Qur'ān (رموز و نکات وجوه قراي), B.

5 عدّت, the time a divorced or widowed woman must wait before re-marriage to see if she is pregnant by her former husband.

6 از اب دور داشتن خلاصي بخشيدن, B.

7 The difference between the earthly and the heavenly friendship.

heart place instead of smiles a cry of lamentation; and when one of smiling heart gives forth a plaint, seize him by the foot and drag him off to Hell.[1]

Knowest thou not, thou monster, that all those devils of thy lower nature, by using a hundred tricks and frauds and deceits, will break forth within thee, till thy reason and sense desert thee? O thou, who in this desert of injustice readest 'prosperity' for 'a whirlpool,' shame on thee![2] The path of religion consists not in works and words, not in syntax and accidence and metaphor; these kinds of things are far from God's word,—the contents of the Qur'ān are like scattered pearls. O Musalmāns, it may be the Qur'ān will one day depart again skywards; for though now its name is with us, its laws and commands are obeyed among us no longer.

The wise man listens to the Qur'ān with his soul, and abandons 97
the letter and the outward elegance; his soul takes its delight in it, and sets to work afresh on all its duties.[3] Know that to the eager disciple music and beating time are like poverty to a lover;[4] the state of ecstasy that comes of skill and fraud[5] is like the drowning cry of Pharaoh; his cry was useless to him as he drowned,—the fire of his reconciliation[6] gave forth no smoke.

On the path, the condition of pursuing which is the devotion of one's life, foolish shouting is asinine and shameless;[7] whoso gives forth three shouts in the assembly, know that he does it in his anxiety for two coppers; but the sigh of the disciple who has gained Love is like a serpent sleeping upon a treasure;[8] if the serpent raises himself upon

---

1 *i.e.*, as being an impostor, since those who rejoice in the world and its delights cannot belong to the spiritually minded.

2 *i.e.*, "canst thou not see the true desolation of the land?"

3 B interprets of the occupations of its former state, interrupted by its descent into this world, and now renewed.

4 *i.e.*, a hindrance to the accomplishment of his object.

5 *i.e.*, the state which some are able to attain almost at will by the help of music and beating time.

6 *i.e.*, attempted reconciliation. Cf. the story in Qur. 10 : 90 sqq. Pharaoh cried, "*I believe that there is no God but He in whom the children of Israel believed, and I am of those who are resigned.*"

7 ترّي from تر in the sense of 'polluted, impudent, obscene.'

8 *i.e.*, is the guardian of his spiritual experiences; the treasure being "the treasure of spiritual secrets, kept in the heart," B.

the treasure, the pearl in his mouth darts forth fire.[1] What is the darwish's laughter ?—folly; and what the crackling of a lamp?—water.[2] When water is mixed with the oil, the light, depending on the purity of the oil, is affected; when the oil begins to burn, the foreign moisture announces itself. Thy sighing is mere self-adornment, thy proper path is to observe God's law;—thy path is a polished mirror, but thy sighs veil it over.[3]

THE COMPARISON OF THE CREATION OF ADAM AND OF JESUS SON OF MARY (ON BOTH OF WHOM BE PEACE!).[4]

Adam's father in this world was the same breath which begot the son of Mary;[5] that which became his body was of the nature of humanity, and that which became his soul was of the fragrance of that breath. Whoso has in him that breath, is an Adam; and whoso has it not, is an effigy belonging to this world only. When Adam received that breath from the power of God his soul became conscious, and hastening towards the Universal Soul he asked, "What canst thou tell me of this breath?" Soul replied, "My cup and robe are empty; my robe and cup hold naught of it,—this precious gift has been given freely."

Wheresoever thou wilt incline, let it be in accordance with this
98 breath; incline not towards thyself in opposition to it; and soar above the snares of earth, gaining the abode of Godhead, viewing the confines of the spirit-land, like Jesus, with the eye of thy divinity.

Claim no distinction for thyself in thy village, for thou art only distinguished in that to be naught is better than such distinction.

---

1 Comparison intended with a sigh.

2 As the crackling noise made by a lamp denotes watered oil, so by the noise of laughter a falsely professing spiritual man is exposed.

3 Contrasting the sighs of the falsely professing with those of the true Lover; the former only serve to obscure the path, as breathing on glass obscures its brightness.

4 Cf. Qur. 3 : 52. "*Verily the likeness of Jesus with God is as the likeness of Adam. He created him from earth, then He said to him* BE, *and he was.*"

5 The commentators refer to Qur. 4 : 168. "*The Messiah, Jesus the son of Mary, is but the apostle of God and His Word, which He cast into Mary, and a spirit from Him; believe then in God and His apostles, and say not 'Three.' Have done! it were better for you. God is only one God, celebrated be His praise that He should beget a Son!*"

Like a dot on the die used as a tool of the game, thou thinkest thyself to be something, but that something is naught ; thou art indeed a unit, but like the dots on the dice hast a name merely for purposes of counting.

Fortunate is he who has effaced himself from the world ;[1] none seeks him, nor seeks he anyone. Whoso is caught in the bonds of this world, is a gainer if he escape from its forces; for this world is the source of pain and sorrow, and the wise man calls it 'the house of lodging.' Since in the light of reason and clear sight two flights at the proper time are as good as three victories,[2] so thou, O full of excellencies, art a fool,[3] if at this river thou stayest on the bridge or in the cave.[4]

Let the guide of thy bodily and of thy spiritual life be for this world wisdom, for the other thy faith ; fortunate is he whose guide is wisdom, for both worlds are his submissive servants. When the fruition of desire is attained, the go-between's talk becomes a heaviness ; though she sets the business going, yet when the closet is reached she is only a bore to thee.[5]

To commemorate the Prophets is better than speaking of Fools.[6] 15

The prophets were the upright ones of the faith, who showed to the people the path of rectitude ; the self-opinionated were bewildered

---

1 *Lit.*, "washed off, or erased, the picture of himself (*i.e.*, from the tablet of existence, L)."

2 L quotes, "A timely flight, the head on the shoulders, is better than to be a hero with head laid low."

3 Bulghār is Bulgaria, and Bulghārī a Bulgarian. The name is explained to mean 'a place abounding in caves,' (*bū'l-ghār*) ; hence the reference to the cave in the next hemistich.

4 *i.e.*, 'if thou stayest in such a place of danger.' That is, it is better to abandon the world than to struggle with it.

5 That is to say, all guides are dispensed with when the goal is reached.

6 The title differs in the various copies. B continues, "*And concerning the days of the intermission in the time of ignorance* (*i.e.*, between Jesus and Muhammad, when no prophets appeared), *and the raising up of prophets and apostles, the mercy of God be upon them all ; they are intercessors for us, peace be upon them.*" Perhaps the original title was simply "*In commemoration of the prophets.*"

when they disappeared in the sunset of annihilation.[1] The darkness of the night of polytheism drew close its curtains; infidelity placed kisses on the lips of idolatry; one bore a cross in his hand as it were a rose-branch, another like a waterlily worshipped the sun;[2] one worshipped idols continually, and another had no aims whatever; this one in his senseless folly deeming evil from the devil, good from God;[3] some strewers of dust, eaters of fire,—others beaters of the
99 water, calmers of the wind; here one scouring all sense out of his brain, as it were done by wine,—there another dashing the turban from his head, as if it were carried off by the gale; this one calling an image his god, and that one like the priest of an idol-temple wrecking all religion; one practising magic, another astrology,—one living in hope, another in fear; all were leading unlovely lives, all were blind of understanding.

The masses were suppliants to an impostor in the faith,—the magnates occupying the high places of religion; the religion of the Truth concealed its face, and everyone published a false faith; false doctrine and polytheism began to fly abroad, and every kind of heresy reared its head. Here one in bondage to the teachings of folly, there another satisfied with an empty deception; their ears listening to the devil's promptings of desire, their ravings displaying the devil's guidance. Folly and slander and idle chatter appeared wisdom alike to the crowd and to the wise; the great were the slaves of their lusts and pleasures, the populace of their jests and follies; the knowledge of God's religion was blotted out, all alike triflers, babbling folly; under pretence of knowledge each sought his own glory, and under cover of such knowledge each hid his reason. From fear of imposture and magic the virtues hid themselves, like the *alif* in *bism*;[4] when the great withdrew to their houses, the people returned to their impieties. One followed the path of Moses, Jesus the leader of another; the faith of Zoroaster proclaimed itself, the veil of mercy was torn to pieces.

---

1 Because men had no longer any guide.

2 Christians and Magians.

3 The Zoroastrians.

4 *Bism* (*illāh*) 'in the name of God.' *Alif*, the first letter of اسم *ism*, drops out, being the '*alif* of conjunction', when another word, such as the preposition ب precedes

The land of Tūrān[1] and kingdom of Īrān were each laid waste by
the other's violence ; the Ethiopians advanced towards Yat̲h̲rib, the 20
elephant and Abraha were routed by the birds.[2] The house of the Ka'ba, seized by the stranger, became an idol-temple ;[3] the world was full of stupidity and fraud, the man of wisdom found the path of religion difficult. In this world of the lost ones dog and ass raised their voices every morning ; it was a world full of the vile and worthless,—
'Utba and S̲h̲aiba and the cursed Bū Jahl ;[4] a world full of devil-like 100
beasts of prey,[5]—a hundred thousand paths with pits in the way, and all men blind ; ghouls on either hand, in front a monster,—the guide blind, his companion lame ; disabled by their ignorance, in the heaviness of sleep, the scorpion of their folly wards off from them the knowlcdgo of their danger.[6]

---

[1] The lands to the north of Persia, inhabited by people of non-Persian or Mongolian origin, the hereditary foes of the Iranian or Persian people in the mythical age.

[2] The reference is to the expedition led by Abraha, the Christian viceroy of Yaman, against Mecca (not Yat̲h̲rib, the later Medina) in the year of Muḥammad's birth, with the object of destroying the Ka'ba. Abraha rode on an elephant, an animal rarely seen in Arabia, from which the expedition afterwards took its name. The Meccans, unable to oppose Abraha's army, at its approach retired to the neighbouring mountains ; but the elephant refused to advance against the town ; and at the same time a large flock of birds flew over the host, each carrying three small stones, one in its bill and one in each of its claws, which they allowed to fall on the heads of the army. This occasioned the rout of the army. Cf. Qur. 105 and the commentators thereupon. "*Hast thou not seen what thy Lord did with the fellows of the elephant ; Did He not make their stratagem lead them astray, and send down on them birds in flocks, to throw down on them stones of baked clay, and make them like blades of herbage eaten down ?*" Cf. also Muir's Life of Mahomet, pp. *c—cii.*

[3] Referring perhaps to its use by the Meccans themselves ; at Muḥammad's conquest of Mecca there were said to be 360 idols ranged round the Ka'ba; these Muḥammad destroyed.

[4] 'Utba and S̲h̲aiba were the two sons of Rabī'a, notable men of the Qurais̲h̲ and Muḥammad's enemies. Abū Jahl, 'father of folly', was a nickname given to one of Muḥammad's opponents in Mecca.

[5] M alone seems to have preserved the correct reading, دیو دستور ; the change to the alternative و دیو و ستور being rendered easy by the immediately preceding ستور 'wild beasts,' and its affinity with سباع 'beasts of burden.'

[6] The meaning is not clear ; readings and interpretations vary, but none seems satisfactory. *D̲h̲abb* is 'to repel, ward off' ; *d̲h̲abbāb*, 'one who repels

5 Since somewhat has been said of the Unity, I will now speak of the glory of the prophets; especially the praise of the last of the apostles, the best and choicest of God's messengers.[1]

---

with violence: *dhabbābī* may be the action of a *dhabbāb*, and *dhabbābī kardan* again 'to ward off, repel.' I have added as object 'the knowledge of their danger.'

1 *i.e.*, Muḥammad, whose advent put an end to the horrors just recounted: referring to the subject-matter of the second Book.

List of Variants.

1. 2. M پروری I پرور و — 3. M transp. مکان و مکین and زمان و زمین — **4.** H از همه در صنع (در add. m. r.) C از امور — 5. H om., add. m. r. in marg. (H ins. later) H آب و باد C om. و before خاک H قدرتش — 6. CM با فرش — 9. C om. و before ملک C یکست صد M یکی ز صد L یکیست B یکی — 10. IAL ازان محجوب — 11. M محرم نامهای — 13. For the next three pp. the order of the couplets varies in the different MSS., I and A however agreeing together. I have not adopted the order of any single MS., but though I cannot suppose that the following exactly represents the original arrangement, which is perhaps irrecoverable, it seems more logical than that of any MS. I have examined. 14. C om. و before قیوم and before قادر C غافر و قاهر — 16. H و هش — 18. H om. هردو , add. m. r. C رای for زان —

2. 1. H عقل و وهم I عقل و حس و وهم B om. و before قیاس — 3. HM هرزه داند — 5. C رباب for اسباب — 10. M جان عقل -- 11. (α) H حسم عقل (حسم in ras.) B دل و عقل (β) H دل جان [دل in ras., the orig. readings probably having been (α) دل عقل and (β) حسم جان (for چشم)] B چشم و جان C عقل جان MIA عقل و جان. I have adopted what was probably H's orig. reading, of which B's is a corruption.— 12. M om. از CH transp. 12 and 13.— 14. C پي for پر H مفرش in ras.— 15. C مرکبش — 20. C از در — 21. H عشق را corr. ex عقل را CH داد CH کرد —

3. 1. C انک M آن for زان — 6. CMIBL بتوخت HA نتوخت (A apparently corr. ex بتوخت) CIAL بتاخت MB نتاخت H نباخت CIAL شناخت شناخت H شناخت بتاحت MB شناخت شتافت — 7. H اشناسد — 8. B بدلیل — 10. C خیز و جون — 12. For از نهاد B در نهاد CMAL از شناخت — 13. B تو که در علم — 14. For سر H تو سر CMALB سزا H (in β) شناختش کني — 16 (α) C خلق for عقل (β) B عقل for خلق C transp. غیرت and حیرت H has the couplet thus مایهٔ خلق سوی او حیرت * غایت خلق در رهش غیرت — 17. B ز for از I اند in marg. I میزنند corr. m. r. ex میزند — 18. H حدیث بی خردان in ras. m. r. H β ends as in text, but in ras. m. r. C transp. سر کردان and ها حیران ......— 19. M. om. و after مراد — 20. CHM ما for تا CHM پای پستي M has this line again in another place, where it has عقل ما از برای and (in β) عقلها زیر رای — 22. B ره I تن for دل AL چاک M om. this line.—

4. 1. H عقل بیکنه — 2. C بجستش H به نعشش M بجستش I به جستش erasures visible in C and M — 3. M فهم for وهم MIALB read (for هیچ جنبندهٔ) جز خدای ایچ کس (I آنچه for ایچ)— 4. M جو روی — 5. I نهد کسی — 9. HMIALB put و after عزت C بسیست — 12. C عدد for صمد — 14. L دو دوئي — 15. CH از درون I om. و — 16. (α) C دیو باریقین بجراکاه M بچراکاه دیو بزر یقین (but rec. in marg. as in text) (β) AL also M rec. in marg. جسم و for چه و C بین for هین H as in text but corr. in ras. perhaps from چون ببین B چون رچنین — 17. HB ز for از — 18. C هست از بهر طالب HIAL چرا چه و که کو M جی — 19. C کفت I از پي بعث طالب B چه و کي و کو و چه کي و کو — 20. C وحه for و وجه HMLB حکمش — 22. C نفسها علم و قدرت —

5. 2. H پرپر in ras. L یکه — 3. H غلامیست — 4. C om. M از ازل in α — After 5. H ins. **5.** 20. M ins. the foll. line شرع مقلوب را مکان کوئي عرش مقلوب را کجا جوئي — 6. M کو for کر H خرد سمان in ras. — 7. CM om. this and 13 ll. foll. H om. this and 12 ll. foll. IA om. this l. only. — 9. A marg. فرشي as alternative to نقشي B ins. after this l. that which M has after l. 5. — 11. α. AL ins. و after بود — β. I om. و after بود — 14. beg. β. B وز — 19. B زان — 21. CH ins. و after ببود H و for او — 22. C ins. و after رو —

6. 1. C قایم C پای with gloss لا — 2. V. note to translation.— 3. C نه ...... نه for نی ...... نی CMILB را for او both hemist. A و corr, ex را m. r. L gives او as an alternative reading.— 4. HIALB از نهاد — 5. C وان in β. L بی بر — 6. CM بجز او نیست so H also corr. m. r. ex جز او نیست and A corr. ex جز او او نیست — 8. C has a similar line subsequently, as follows:— زانکه هویتش HM فعل و دانش برون ز آلت دان سوی کنه هودش نیست بیان L که پس — 9. CHM om. L in α پیش in β بیش — 10. C بامر صنع H ساخته corr. m. r. ex ساخت — 11. CH om.— 12. CH om. I in α نیرنک — 13. M ني — 14. M نکاشتست — 15. CH بتو فلک H رنک و زرد — 17. C از پي رنک CH نیرنک — 18. MALB آفریدت — 19. H خالق — 20. H کرد C چو در rest بدر — 21. CH om. H in another place کیسهٔ پر — 22. M جمله با —

7. 1. C زامر H نیرنگ M نیرنگ در یکرنگ کرده — 2. C جار اختر H نیرنگ — 3. M زشت ز — 4. A هم before پیکر add. m. r.— 5. CHI صایهٔ — 6. C غایت تباهي — 7. V. note to translation — 8. C سوت را شود M سوی او سفرت نبود HILB سفرت (which will not scan) A سفرت بای corr. in سفر A پی corr. in پای — 9. H شاه را C نفس H اصل و om. و before بس — 10. C om. 10 and 11 IALB رنگ و زنگ نفاق — 11. IAL شما ...... شما IALB خالص for محض — 12. C کشی for صفت شکی — 13. MAB توی for بوی — 15. CH اینه صورت از HB صورت از M آینه و صورت از IALB سفر for سفر — 17. M همچو مثلش — 18. M اوست ضعف چشم وبینش — 19. CH om.— 20. M سطح وخط —

8. 1. C om. H دیدار سرزند H om. و — 2. CIALB آبکینه M از بس میغ — 3. M رویت — 4. C om. this and 3 foll. ll. — 5. H زنگ for ازان که — 8. B ازوی rest روی — 9. M نه جو ز امت A زهمّت — 11. M شهر — 12. CHM دران B om. و CH در دشت — 13. H transp. the two hemistichs.— 15. M نزد پیل H چون as in text, rest ازان CMI غوران — 16. CHM هیئت for صورت MIALB پا زنان — 17. CH om. M می سودند so prob. I originally, corr. m. r. in بیسودند — 18. HL هر عضوی B از عضوی — 21. CH om. M om. و — 22. CHM صورت for هیئت A هیئت in ras. corr. ead. m. ex شکل ? —

9. 1. M دیکر — 2. CM پهن صعب H و عظیم CM صعب و پهن — 7. HMLB همکنان B دید B فقاد — 8. HM نه ...... نه IALB هیچ دل را — 9. C همچو مانند M مانندهٔ — 10. M خدا هیچ خلق so also H in marg.— 11. V. note to translation — 12. CHM و before دیگر CM کفت وجل H کفته رجل — 13. HM وان یکي M برای حلول — 14. IAL وان دکر M استوای— and om. و A و erased CH تقریر — 15. B وان یکی C خری و H وان بکفته زجهل قعد M وان یکی کفته اش — 16. C تطلبک M مطبک B نطابک — 17. HM کفته M om. قیام و — 19. CHM في for طی — 21. H سخوان M از M پرهیز — 22. β. CH نیز for جمله —

10. 2. HM جاهل for غافل — 3. CHB نام بیش — 4. M نه مر — 5. B مرورا — 6. M چند ریش — 7. B transp. 7 and 8. — 8. IB دست پای را خواند I آنکه — 9. M عاجز اندرین B ز for از — 10. CI برین — 12. C om. M (in α) میبافند — 13. Adopting M's title.— 15. M بیهودهٔ — 18. C نوم M om. و — 21. C om. — 22. M جمع کرد وجان — CIALB یکدکر پایه all read در دوم B از برای این پایه

11. 1. CH om. — 2. M om. و — 4. B رة) C كرخه — 6. CHALB om. M كافري M رفت كار ز — 8. C حلقت M خلّقت — 9. H طالع; all introduce l. 19. here, after which I leaves a space for a title, but none is written.— 10. C om. rest of chap. after this l. C چو HM شصت — 11. M بيكار و شب بآساني M كي رسي B نه رسي — 12. H om.—13. H om. و B و دون — H here ins. 6. 21.— 14. H باش شكوه H ناتوات — 15. All have و زنبور — 16. M بی صوم ازان I صوم شفاء بيمار I here ins. a var. of **10.** 22. جمع كردي بر اولين بايه خرد و جان وصورت و مايه *cf.* M's reading *ad. loc.*— 17. B بپر — 18. H om. M اندر M پر آب M و آب (end l.)— 19. M برد for كند — 21. B بود ...... بود — 22. C om. M end l. كويد —

12. 1. C om.— 3. C om.— 4. C om. I دانک M درصاندده هرکه اين 7. HI خايد مردمی HM كندمی زان ميان — 8. B بود I چراد H orig. چراغ for جراد و مرغ but corr. as in text.— 9. H for first hemistich has عمروا از فتن بچندين هاى M دو پاى M خدا بخداى — 10. H بيخط H ازوى كرده — 11. C om. 11, 12, 13.— 12. H om. M بدين — پند چون قند من پذير بكوش M نكويم I منت كويم بدان بعقل 13. M H به بندي — 14. H بر خداى نصير — 16. Title varies.— 17. M كريم — 18. MI عدل H in marg. هزل — 19. M نصيبهٔ من كو M خرينه — 20. IAL باو دادم — 21. (a) B om. و — 22. M با تو B ز —

13. 1. M چون دری بر تو بست — 2. M's title.— 3. IALB كه for به 6. M جونكه بر I برتو چست C به add. m. r. B om. به C دو در ديكوت — 8. M دورا — 11. IALB بسته كرد برتو C بر حاست MB برخاست — 13. H همي — 16. CHIALB درخلد برتو HI بكشايد HI آيد B تو پيش به غلمان — 18. M از — 21. C كر HM او B حق for كو M also H in marg. هست for بود M (repeating the line in another place) چونكه او هست —

14. 1. C بدان M او دارد C استوار بدار CH om. next four ll., also A, but there written by the same hand in marg.— 2. I جو — 4. M بد او I om. از — 5. M آرای A, and B in marg. آری B in text آيا — 6. CH نی بد — 7. C زنی ز درش HMIAL رمی ز درش M (in β) يار مار CHMIAL روی ببرش — 8. CH والا L بالا H جامهٔ om. و M جامهٔ و M بده for بذه — 9. C repeating the line in another place has هستي حق به L زايد end l.— 10. CH om. this and two foll. ll. M از for در — 12. IA الخالقيت — 13. CI om. و after خيز M نفس دور كردن (? for كرد و) — 15. HMB كدية خويش — 16. M ins.

و after هدیه C ارادی — 17. C om. first و I و فرض و شرع و درة M اینمان I ایل L زاهل I از اهل C 20. —.M om 19. — فرض حق و corr. m. r. ex ? دینمان B دین تان I بیذان B بین تان — 21. C دین for بین — 22. B و I را ز بهر in ras. C زتیغ پیغمبر H پیغامبر —

15. 1. C امیر — 2. C برور H in marg. بدود M و که ش آورد M او نیامد — 3. M حق for او CB زان — 5. C نیست HMIAL مست CH رة — 6. C om. a long passage here.— 7. M نة first word.— 8. M کشته شد — 10. M پوستیها L points غم — 12. HAL عمل — 13. H طیور مور — 14. MB رای — 16. M کلدم کلدم — 18. B کردة — 19. B اهل M, and marg. of B پای او تاج فرق سینا — 20. H زو B زد ML زود for زد و —

16. 1. MALB بخوردیش B دل چو اورا — 3. H انکه (for اکمه) HM عایه عرش — 4. L او چون HM بذام جوید ننک — 5. M پشک for سنک H کردة ز — 6. M transp. the hemistichs.— 7. IA چو — 8. H پراز — 10. M شدش for از شد HIALB transp. ll. 10 and 11.— 11. I داری — 14. M را روی CHM در کدام M او آمد — 15. M خسی for کسی in β— 16. M میان معدود — 18. M خیز ازین — 19. CHB بدانی — 20. H که for کی H om. و — 21. C سنک نار M و کان B زیان for زبان I نیازبان C 22. — عقل وجان M بو فضول C بو الفضولی C om. و —

17. 1. H om. و in α H کیف وز M از ما و کیف وز A از این و کیف وز ما وز هل C ras. after برتر از with این in marg.— 2. HM عدل و حکمتست جلي H مکر و عزتست خفي M مکر او قهر و عزتست خفي B om. و both.— 3. M om. و in β. H marg. دور for کور — 5. M چون پدید H نیک for پیک — 7. M علم و نیرو B کوش MLB آید — 8. C حط سطح HMI بعد شش — 9. Texts درون — 10. H عیب for غیب — 11. M نور — 12. H چون but corr. in marg. نفود و I چز — 13. IALB om. 13—15 C زودش H طبع for نصب and in marg. صبر M بصر است نة — 14. C عملش texts دان و نة texts شذاش و نة — 16. CH om.; all but I have لیک — 17. H marg. M وصف او زیر عقل نیکو نیست *cf.* l. 7 *sup.*— 18. H نو آفریدة B نة آفریدة IAL بر کزیدة in β.— 19. C وانک اثبات هست (?) originally, altered to زانک اثبات رنک آور نست M وانکه اثبات هست — 21. H at beginning و * * * روزار and in ras. خاطر؟ C واز — 22. CHB ذوقش دو که M ذوقش او —

18. 1. H بکوي in α H او نکو که (او که written in ras.) I نکوي in β— 2. H کر نکوي in α— 3. M رود او in α MI بود او in β.— 4. CH

یاوه پویان C m. r. in marg. عابه حون سوی حصرتش H عامه چون نزد حضرتش M آنکه آنک I اینک ایتک — 6. C خواله first word.— 7. M بدانجه in α B کرد کند M بدانچه in β.— 9. CH بر کریمي A has ll. 9—12. in marg. (the same hand).— 10. C داد H آلت C پي نفع خیر so H prob. orig., corr. into جلب نفع and thence into جر نفع — 11. M از جهان B رفت آنچه — 12. I تو مکن — 14. C کمر ره M کمر جهد بند CHIAL راه — 15. CH om. 15. 16. A has 15. 16. in marg. (ead. man.) — 16. M برخر — 17. M سخن for عمل B نه نپسندد — 18. M هرانرا CH om. next 3 ll.— 20. M مراد for شکار — 21. B کهٔ داني — 22. B om. و after تلبیس C نه خرند C نه دکرند —

19. 1. CH عقل را — 2. I آب و CH om. 2.—3 is in HMI only, 4—10 in HM only; H راه دور از دل دورنکي تست کفر و دین از پی درنکي تست M as H exc. دلي, and has دورنکي twice; I as H exc. that both hemistichs end دل دورنکي تست — 4. H را H بدوي twice.— 5. H مجازي کن H دریا و بي نیازي کن — 8. H مفیات — 11. I adds کرچه نمرود آتشی بفروخت نه جو اتش علف نیافت بسوخت (perh. for همچو آتش علف نیافت نسوخت) — 12. M زهر M in α هیمش — 13. IALB که خستهٔ کون است CH om. 11, 12, 13. A has them (same hand) in marg.— 14. C خود و رخسار روز و شب M خود ز رخسار صبح و پشت HALB تست صبح و شفق I تست صبح — 15. I in α om. که after بود — 17. H دلي — 18. I adds شدي ایمن جو نام در طریقت قدم بیفشردي آن بردي — 19. A مرورا M خق for خود — 20. I لطف او سایه افکند — 21. حق so M, rest دل —

20. 3. B بیش B بحسن — 4. M om. و HB بباد و آب M بخاک و آب — 6. L پیش M کرکر — 7. M بر for در — 8. H transp. 8. 9. H سر for نکته — 11. This line is only in H and M; M راه او — 12. Occurs twice in IALB, with variations او خاموش and و هوش — 14. H in β اندیش — 15. B om. و M بهره — 18. CH هر for هو CHM بحر for حرف in β C هو rec. in marg.— 20. I om. و after سک M برون HM وحقه HMIL تهي —

21. 1. M خزینه both.— 2. M سیم ناب IA وارون I لعل شاه — 3. CH om. this passage B به for با — 7. C زاندرون M درون تو HI آینه تو ز پیش تو بر داشت, so M exc. پیش دل — 9. H دادهٔ بهرج — 10. C om. HM عقلش IAL عرش for عشق — 11. CH om. A om. in text, add. ead. m. in marg.— 15. C کرثي من H کژ من IALB

کجي من CH بنقش for بعيب H marg. بنقص — 16. C از for کز H orig. کز کژي راست چون کمان corr. as text.— 17. L ميان —

22. 1. CM آمد H marg. نايد کرت texts چفتي or چفتي — Texts insert here هرچه او کرد عيب او مکنيد با بد و نيک جز نکو مکنيد (H transp. the hemistichs, ending with نکو نکنيد ...... او نکند, which do not rhyme) perhaps compounded of two glosses, هرچه او کرد عيب او مکنيد and با بد و نيک جز نکو نکند — 2. Texts transpose the hemistichs H دست بر ابر از سخا به نيرو شد so also M but ابر for بر C بها — 3. M om. و CH om. 3—6 A om. 3—6 in text, add. ead. m. in marg.— 6. I ماري A prob. orig. ماري corr. in مار gloss يعني نفس — 8. B پسري H in marg. has β rewritten with سخنها for حديث تو — 10. MI از for ار — 11. AIL بس I آن جفت بيند طاق — 12. C احولي جو — 13. L om. که ILB کرده — 16 C را بابت M om. 11 ll.— 17. H کهي H طيب — 18. C خواهد for کاهد — 19. Texts نمودهٔ تو C رودهٔ H دودهٔ IAL بودهٔ — 20. CH om. 20, 21. A om. 20, 21 in text, add. ead. m. in marg.— 21. I om. چو —

23. 1. H بدر for بران M بدران — 2. C om. add. man. rec. H شبش MI شپش A شُپش I بر خ ت — 3. H corr. m. r. منکوه C om. و C باکوه — 4. C om. add. m. r. HM نشان داري — 5. H از for ار — 6. M چرخ — 7. M بهر for کشت CIAL om. و — 8. H orig. معده (?) corr. in لعل (?) MI اکحل for معده HM کرد — 9. C دهند — 10. CHA om. 10. 11 add. man. rec. in marg. in C, ead. man. in A; A بر عالم A ظلم in ras. I زبر و تحت — 11. M کرده A صايه ex پايه and بخش ex بخشش — 12. M راه لطف L خانرا M جان دارد M روان دارد — 13. I برون و درون C حان ز ذالملک ملکوت و تن ردي H om. و in β.— 14. is in CHB only C اندر ابناي خصم صنع لطيف B تشريف — 15. only in CHB also, B کانکه B خبرت — 16. M om. 16. 17. C عين عطا H آنچه — 17. C بد آر حون — 18. is in CHB only — 19. C in place of β زشت و نکو همه نکو باشد — 22. C خوردي —

24. 1. ALB بنهد ببرش — 5. M نزد او CM کم سايه — 6. C همي راند H که ميراند M شرط او همچنان هميراند — 8. H. خرمان — 10, 11, 12, om. IALB.—14. om IALB, CM نيست for بتست — 15. M شر for بد — 18. is in M only.— 19. Texts زايند perh. from confusion with preceding.— 20. M در شب — 22. M در درون —

25. 1. H با for تا HMB اوست .... اوست — 2. M از بر M کوره H سيمي B سمين — 3. CH om. A om. in text, add. ead. m.

in marg. M کرده — 5. M صورت both M ساده — 6. M ره به بیدادي
7. H که for کی — 8. H باد آب و HM om. و after خاک M برترش -
9. is only in HM.— 10. H بی رنگ و خانه M بیرنگ و خانه HIAL om. و
after نعمت M کذار end l.— 12. B کرد MI بفعل — 13. HAB آمد
HI سایش in *α* M زایش as given, rest رایش — 16. H سیاه الیج —
17. H انکز — 18. M تپش آن آتشي corr. ex پیش آتشي (?) rest
تپش آتشي (or تبش) — 19. M با سیه — 20. M مشک روئي HM
transp. 20. 21.— 21. So M rest وکفش — 22. So M rest om.
در —

26. 1. IB om. و— 3. H بکرد H کارها بسر نبرد M این اوزو دگر نپزد —
4. H اندرین راه — 5. M سنک for رنک — 6. H om. M وانکه —
7. M بکرارند I بکدازند — 8. I هرچه باطین M نه طریق M و دین — 9.
M باک تا — 10. HM transp. 10. 11. H om. که in *α* M زمانه بنوشتي
M هشت بکذشتي — 12. H puts 14 before 12.— 13. B نه کریم
M از بلکه — 14. B نه بکذري — 15. Texts جز پی H راد M برزاد
I روز لا — 16. M زعقل — 18. H و تو M بی نیازیست — 19. H́
بی زبانیش M om. و in *α* H *β* چه شک چه یقین بی نیازش را M as H
but بی زبانیش — 20. M حکمت دو سرای — 21. HB کو ...... جو M
نی نیاز و نیاز M پامدار و سپاس — 22. B خرد بزرک B یوسف کرک—

27. 1. HM چه ضایعي و چه I چه بالغي — 2. M ترا رنکست H
زین او — 3. M transp. 1. 2. H om. ز in *α* add. m. r. M transp.
عقل and نفس — 5. M om. و in *α* HB آسیایست M آسیابست B om.
و in *β* — 6. B عقل و — 7. H با supra بي scr. al. m. M با سکون
زمین H حوت M حور I صور و — 8. H حوت M حور — 9. M وار بر
MI پرکار — 11. M بود تست M شورای — 13. A marg. L marg. B
بفعل M باید که — 14. H om. M برخود — 16. M وزور M جوزر نبود —
17. B om. و M فلک for هوا — 18. M وانکه H از for کز H om. و
in *β* H کر (= کز) for از in *β* — 19. MB دعوی ز زور M چسم را —
20. HIB روی زر (I corr. ex رری وزر) MB جوي صلح — 21. M
ره فرد — 22. H ازدام (وام ?) M ارقام I دوختن H کین نیازي M بی نیازي —

28. 1. H tr. 1. 2. I بین corr. ex مبین; all but H have آزاد کن —
2. M بنوش H وربخود in *β* M بدور و بدر — 3. MIAL transp. 3. 4.
H تو بهانه مساز وباوه — 5. H om. M نکو کرده M تات چون کره بپرورد است
7. H om. و in *β* — 8. B افتی — 9. HM چون کرد A شوم corr.
ex شود — 10. M om. کند HM فرا وبه HB ز فر — 11. M ترو خشک —
13. H همکنان — 14. M بعلت درو — 15. HM مهر و کین H نیامد
B نقابد H خود بر آمد ز فرخود شد دین — 16. M اورا چه — 18. H بود

MB om. و — 19. H سعي — 20. H چه ازان M in *a* آلا شد M زیفت و قربت H دار ...... دار M آوه 21. HMI — آوه HMI یار خلیل وقربت و یقیندش — 22. HI آوه M اوه HMB مانده —

29. 1. H یادکار ازوي H نمودکار ازوي — 2. H om. 2. 3.— 4. M روز خود — M شود HM باید M صبح 5. M — وکر نباشي چه M بد نیازي 8. A om. in text, add. m. r. in marg. M و جان I ras. between نور رویش M طرقوي I طرقوي مشت M طرقوا ز 9. B — معض and جان H خویشس — 11. B بنشاند نه M جان این — 13. IB معذور so also AL marg. AL رنجور — 14. M بیمت از — 15. M عقل نرم و I کرد 18. AI — چوقي 17. H — شناس IALB خود تو M عقل و نرم و HM یکیک — 19. M بنمودي — 20. H وراي حرض M حفظ و ادب H پردهٔ ادب — 21. H بوسم طرب —

30. 3. M جفت عدل — 5. HM تو عدل پدشه خویش H بود و منزل — 6. H om.— 7. M عهد جمله — 8. M انچنا شو زغیرت دادش M bis — که همه یاد M bis بحیوت آبادش IALB سوز عبرت و دادش H زحیرت و دادش 10. M om. و — 11. M با حلم H یادست — 12. H om. از B است twice for اوست H وان که for دل گه — 14. H چو گل کند M دهان — 15. H کردهٔ H کردهٔ — 16. I om. و — 18. HM as title حکایت — 19. HM نوري — 21. H کتاب — 22. H بدروزي و ALB شبدا روزي —

31. 2. M بدتر از تو — 3. M وکني یادش M for *β* has نشکرد صرترا سبکبادش IL جرم — 14. HM غایب H آن زمان AL آنزمان پزمان both with alternative in marg. از زمان بزمان — 5. M om. in text, add. in marg. I یاد آر — 6. M الصّلوات — 9. M om. ll. 9-16 here, and inserts subsequently — 10. M اول corr. ex اصل — 11. H اندرون L اردرون — 12. I کوئي کو in *a* H ins. l. 17 after 12 — 13. *a*. H آمال MB ملال *β*. M بهرهٔ HM منال — 14. *β*. IAL شوق — 15. H وانکه — 17. H دربر من M بوي (for شوي) M ins. **32.** 2. after 17.— 18. M عالم for خطّهٔ — 19. H خط MB خطوهٔ برفت — 20. H بنده شد M مغران — M نفس زندکي M مرد که خلق زندکي و نیست بآتش دود — 22. H که بدین —

32. 3. H زندکیت — 4. M om — 5. M adds this l. and next to last chap — 7. H om. 7, M om. 7. 8. 9, and begins fresh chap. at 10 with title في نقد دار الفنا و دار البقا — 8. H از پی — 9. M دور in ras.— 10. M سنّجي H سرنامهٔ I مهر نامه AL نامهٔ B نامه with gloss فکّ اضافت — 11. B دینیت — 14. M (for کار) جاي — 15.

B هست — 16. M جان رسد — 17. MI زاغ H مرغ اواز — 18. M om.— 19. A in marg. خبر as altern. to خرد — 20. H om. و H موت — 21. M خفته for همه in β.— 22. M حياتى AL پيش —

33. 2. HIB A marg. ماتّ M شدن از براي كم زدن — 4. M عادورا H om. و in β.— 5. M يكى آن M ركاب M واندكر in ras. M نهاب — 6. M قدمِ قدَم كرده in β.— 7. HMB سزاي — 8. H بيم و HMIB نيكوان — 10. M سرسر in α M با دين سرسر داري in β.— 11. M om. 11—16 here, 11, 12 and 16 ins. later; H بنده M كرد نهاد corr. ex كرد و نهاد — 12. M واي — 13. C resumes here C خوبري — 14. CH هدج — 16. H آستين in α.— 17. C حان و دل در ره خدا M جان و تن — 18. M om. to **34.** 5, but ins. later, fresh chap. beginning here with title في الذكر — 19. M om. و — 20. CH om. M بلندي هست كردي پست — 21. L آزار M كرده corr. ex كرد B om. و — 22. C از بنده CM مركب و تخت H و بخت I تخت ex بخت C از حلقه C and A marg. حلقةُ تخت H حلقه و بخت M حله و بخت I حلقه بخت B حلّةُ تخت —

34. 1. M پلاسيت — 2. H معمل M transp. مفصل and مجمل — 3. H بانوائي را L om. و M زيركى — 4. B om. و in α H از و دينش H رضاي تمكينش B رضاي و — 6. H ins. 6 after 2.— 7. IAL دست را H با كمر CM زني — 8. M اكر را — 9. C om. 9. 10 M رسيد in β.— 10. H كز عالم هوا — 11. M في العدم والوجود — 12. C در كنج — 14. M خواندهٔ ex خواند M انكاه ex انكار (?) — 15. So C; H بكويند M آن نكوتر IALB او نكوتر — 16. C om. M as text, others داند رفت — 19. CM كيرم ار مويها — so also H originally but corr. m. r. in كيرم آنى (?) H كردد ...... كردد IALB for β have هر يكى صد هزار جان كردد and كردد also in α.— 20. H حق for او — 21. H شكر و M پس همه سوي شكر او — 22. CI شكر in α M سكر ex شكر —

35. 1. B از جوان از پير C om. 1. 2.— 3. C om.— 4. A orig. had the و after لطف, but it has been erased C شكر قهر و عزتش H عزلتش M عزتش — 5. H يابي M نايد for بايد H order of the next 8 lines differs.— 6. CH دويست H وشهوت — 7. CHM قهر و لطفش بجاي H شكر و شكرش M سكر و شكرش I سكر و سكرش — 9. M om. را in α.— 10. CM om., add. C m. r. in marg., M also has the line elsewhere CHM لطف او چون جمال — 11. H كوه را H بكذارد — 12. So with M, rest قهر و لطف exc. B قهر لطف — 14. M om. 14. 15 AB چو آمد — 17. M بلطف in α.— 18. After this line H leaves a space as if for a title, but nothing written.— 19. C زهي — 20. C مهرش C زبشهٔ H زپشهٔ — 21. M طعمهٔ کرم H چين را ملخ — 22. C om. this l. and next, H in α زرّين I in α زرين in β رزين —

36. 1. H putting this l. after 7 reads در عطا از بلا همي کريند M با عطا در بلا همي خنديد M در بلا با عطا — 2. H منکر ديد — 3. M آر در — M this line ends chap., tit. follows در آيد از درکار H چو B في لطفه و قهره CH بر در غار M ins after 3 اولياي ورا امين کردد در خور مدح و آفرين کردد 4. C سخره M سحَرَه B سَحر C hiat. after لا L آن M تا for با M کفت for کرد — 5. CAL خدا CH انج M هج — 6. C ناکسا C om. 6 β and 7 α.— 8. H فراغت L فراغنه B فراعِن — 9. HM غول پرورده — 10. M مستت with ras. above س IAL زان يکي دو نا B ins. از پيء لطف وغايت کرمش کرده بر اوج آيت کرمش — 11. Texts ins. 14 before this l.— 12. CH om. M اکرچه — 13. H in α از اسهالش M از امهالش B ز for از in α CM زاهمالش in β.— 16. CH پيدا بهر CH transp. 16, 17.— 17. M om. C از بي — 18. IALB transp. 18, 19. IALB عجب for نکو ALB غضب H 19. — ز باردانش کناه CHML تائب ذنب IB خوده — 20. CM om. HB و روحور H در و پرده — 22. CHM و جاهل —

37. 3. M کرد عالم و H علم C .5 — فضل را H .4 — صبر و شکري M ذُو for مرد MB کوئي — 6. CHM بر صحرا H بز C شوی — M از زبان بدان 7. CH transp. 7, 8. H عيب ما M خلق دانسته — 8. CHM غيب او B نکفته — 9. MB و جهول H وصل حق C om. this l. H ins. after 12 A om. in text, add. ead. man. in marg. M ins. after 9 the foll. پشت و پاي هميزند بدو دست * عقل و هشيار را چو مردم مست — 10. H خواب کار — 11. CH نکوتر M نکه کن از بی B بس H transp. غيب and عيب I غيب both — 12. H زدي M ازو M شد M مشت — 13. H شکر H پذيرد — 16. B ما جفا ALB باما in α CH زما in β ALB زما باما — 17. HMB باخاک — 18. MB and A marg. هرکه افتد — 19. CIALB نه پسندد H بپذيرد — 20. H داند in α B adds لطف او غمکسار مسکيذان قهر او جانکداز بيدينان — 22. I سير يکيک M دادن —

38. 1. C om. 1—3.- 2. M om. و B transp. 2, 3.— 4. M transp. 4, 5 M بخش خلق — 5. M خاطر آيد او I دادند — 6. C آراى H غمکسار I غمکداز LB غمکزار — 8. H از روان و جذان MB آرزوش — 9. C om. B کماهئي M ديدن — 10. I در نعيم کرد all but CH read يوم for ناز M ins. later a similar line, * جايقو در نعيم کشت معد تا تو با يار جفت کردي عد — 11. B om. و in both α and β.— 12. C om.— 13. (α) CH نيست هست M orig. had نيست نيست

IALB از نیست هست (β) all but M have هست را نیست — 14. C نظم غیب M عیب in α HI 15. C om. — برحم for رحم C و I om. و نظام صورت رنگ جون HM in β عیب — 16. CH محال کرد بهرزه M ins. here عالم غیب درون بداند او * عیب نداند درو عاقل هیچ — 19. C om. 19—12— 20. H om. B کو for اکر M ذرّهٔ کرم آن — 21. H و صوت —

39. 1. H او بصر M جافي بصير M عقلي H تعريفت — 2. HB om. و — 3. H نکرداني M تو پذرود — 5. HM حلم او — 6. C جمال افروز M in β خلق را — 9. C و for کر HIAL بداند ...... نداني CH (H ابلهي) — حس C بس HB و .H in α om کر نداني 10. C — مي کني ايذت ابله 12. C ذرهٔ علمش H نزره علمش M زتو داند آن علمش همي نه — 13. HM بروز بازارت — 15. Title varies.— 16. M om. به — 17. M روح for روز — 18. C om. 18, 19 — 20. H جاي حاجت — 22. H يوحيد M om. نان add. m. r. in marg. B and A marg. را چو نان همي بدهد —

40. 1. M خزينه C اوست in α M نداني CH او اوست بكفتهٔ M بكفته ورنه آرد M باترا I .3 — 2, 3 .C om .2 — بكفته او دوست ex اورا دوست HM بتو و تو — 4. CHM السّر — 5. M چون for جان — 6. H آورده — 7. C om. HI کردنان — 9. M in β مدخورد — 10. M om. CH آتش has دیک for 11. M زمان آن M زتو M نرسید — 12. H for دیک has آتش (? آتش) — 13. C by ras. نخو+د C چون سیر شود H سیرو — 14. M om. و — 15. HM om. و in α IALB وکیل for وزیر H om. و in β. — 16. CH از قوت مرد C دست و پاي M ذاي حلق — 17. M A in marg. L in marg. حکمت for نعمت — 21. Title varies.— 22. M کشتهٔ C ديدش کفت H om. و M ديد چه کفت —

41. 1. C هم از نو و هم از ان M خدای نو و خدای IAL همان ... همان — 2. M نه و ابرؤ C نه نه خنده — 3. C رازق M رازقت HM چنین دانم CH از تو ...... از تو B زود ...... زود 5. H — اندک او 4. C — نانم و جانم (om. و) — 6. C om. 6—12.— 7. Title in MB only.— 9. H سخان پیشهٔ M خرد پیشه — 10. HMB کرچه دانه — 11. H کبر کفت H نبکزیندد M آخرین H بینند — 14. C ار نخدای M بخدا کزز — 15. C دل درو 15 C add. after دل خود درفضول C و رستی M بعقل H بعقل فضول 17. —(سپنج for سنج) بند و رستي از غم و رنج دل منه هيچ درسراي سنج M و خدا بقای تا ALB شماست بقای تا L الَف B الف — 18. HM om. و H آب at end— 19. CH تو موسی زدرد بی نصیبي M درد موسی — 21. M قدم but د in ras. ? ex قلم H چو لنک مي پويش M کلک مي پويش —

42. 1. M در آنجا C نخست C بچست بباید — 2. M begins new chap. with title حکایت H به نپرسید C om. 2, 3, 4.— 3. M تا شب —

5. MB تپش CH راه for راز C به ز for به که — 6. H هر کرا ذرّهٔ C om. ز HMB تپش — 7. M om. CH با first word C با تو به مانده نیز — 10. C حو شوق H جو سوی براق او M براق I دل رکابش — 12. M corr. in نو اوست C آنچ اوست H آنچه اوست — 13. CH om. to **43.** 1.— 15 M داده— 20. M صحبت تلقین M نیک باشد صحب — 21. M که همی — 22. M وصال حضرت M فصال طلعت —

43. 2. C بدو سه حار ودنج M بدو و so probably A also orig. but corr. as given in text, L بدو و سه چهار — 3. H با و تا both hemist. M با الف هست بی و تی — 4. M ز هردو مکوی — 5. M om. رهي add. m. 2 in marg.— 6. M حدیث M پا ز سر — 8. H دست باز ست B دست باز C قابل M قالب C حایل — 9. CH کدم آدم — 11. C متابع — 12. HM order of lines varies considerably M و اورا — 13. H دیدن — 14. CL حدیثیست چه CH این حدیث توی — 16. M om. و before پس CHM تو و او — 17. M بندکي باشد آنکه — 18. C transp. جز and او H همه دم M همدم — 19. H بذوش M بذوق شمار دکی نوش و نیشش — 20. HI هستي پر A shows ز erased after برای — 21. M کلام CH مرد —

44. 1. M transp. یکسان and در جان — 2. IALB رحمان IALB لعن — 3. HM از قضای A بچنک corr. ex بچنک IALB بد خواست H باد یابي بدست و M بر در صبر LB آنکه نیست B om. 4. CH om. — دو یکونک باد پذیر LB end line باد و به ابر — 5. CH om tit.— 6. CH بدایت توحید M هدایت توحید end line.— 7. CH نیاید M نباشد in *α*.— 8. CH om. M om. و — 10. CH om. 10, 11, 12, MI in *α* om. و M in *β* داد L باد بر داده I و آب — 11. M بر for برش — 12. MI ترید — 13. CH transp. 13, 14.— 15. CHM نخواهد MI پند B خورسند — 16. C درتن M سازدت — 17. CH om. و CHM با سکان — 22. M که ز —

45. 1. HM جمعه و — 2. C بست کن M تا دلت — 3. C طاعت — 4. CH put this l. after 8. CH کر for ور M با تو — 5. CH om. MI برآفات — 6. M om. 6, 7.— 8. M انداز خواجه کربه ز کش CH تو ز کش — 9. I جنیها — 10. Title varies.— 11. C و جسم — 12. C om. ll. 12–15.— 13. M آنکه دستور عقل و — 14. M این نشان — 15. H پی مبهم M نه مبهم — 16. B رو بسوی H مي کردن — 17. M om.— 18. M دادن روان — 19. C om. M in *α* عاقل — 22. C آنک and tr. 21, 22, A انکه with erasure above ک prob. a fatḥa deleted.—

46. 1. C حو کشتی H transp. 1, 2.— 3. H om.— 4. M om.— 6. M om. و — 7. M آن زباني M بود حلّاج کو انا — 8. C om. 8—12,

H puts 13 before 8 M داد خود H راست نبشت ML راست جلاد B نه پشت دار B om. و — 9. H چو حق HM كفتن — 11. M صليب دار H in β دار M in β نار I بار — 14. CH ز تو — 15. H خطهٔ لاهوت — 16. H كه بود I راست كفت انكه كفت از سر حال M adds after 16 (cf. 13) تو ز من C تا ز ه خيز و دع نفسك خطير و تعال — 17. H بآشيان — 18. C om. 18, 19, H has 18, 19, between 20 and 21. M در آيد M in β تفريد — 19. HM نازد I بكدازد — 20. (α) H در مستي C مستي (β) IB زر and so also, doubtfully CH; M ins. after 20 همه را كرده مست و سوداپز جنبش سايهٔ قباله رز — 21. HIA مستي H خورده — 22. I دراد راز —

47. 1. H تو مدان از تو بارسي ناسي I چست — بدان — 2. (α) C خورديش M بخوردنش H نخورديش C چونكه (β) M ناسي HM چه داني B طعام CHI نشناسي M نشناسي — 3. C om.— 4. H بر آمد راز — 5. چونكه خوردي M چون CH انده حلال CI ش HI om. مدانش هيچ M — 6. C om. 7. C om. 7, 8, 9. H om. 7, 8 M جمله — 8. Most copies could be read as زر — 11. CHM شوى M جانت H transp. پايت and جانت — 12. M om.— 13. C om. HM بر درش هستند — بستة را دهند چو مور H همت و زور C عشق پدش و همت زور H كر ازل C **14.** زينجهان — 15. H بكوئى او يازد M ز كو برون نايد C روى جانت بكوي — 16. M C اربوى — 17. C om. 17, 18. M آنكسانى — 19. Title varies.— I كليد آن MI در B كر 21. CM — بهر رازهاى M پر حق شيخ H 20. نعب —

48. 1. C ساز و M ins. 3, 4 before 1.— 2. C om. 2, 3 HM اندرين سوال و جواب CHM هموكند — 4. CHM تو درين بوستان — 3. H وعنا — I اكر ايدون كه نبودم M كفت اكر 7. CH — 5. Title varies, or is omitted. B بدهم — 8. H ميدهم من ورا — 9. M اليوم — 10. M om. 10, 11 and ins. عد ملكتي C جان جانش ز ذكر يافت غدى * سمع قلبش ز تو شنيدندي — H و سودا را 12. CH — دهد آن را C سر بزد H تو بهر H تو قهر 11. C و حربا را — 13. H خوران H بيايد — 14. M تو نداني — 15. C om. 15—18. B روز شب — 18. H از هيچ I orig. از corr. ار M نائي اندر HM برين — 19. M has this line as the second of next chap., and CH add the second line of that chap. after 19; CH آن om. و — 20. CH om.— 21. C حانت —

49. 1. CH با تن — 2. CHM انكار نفس را در نار — 4. I نيك — 5. (α) I مست را (β) I پست را CHM ins. after 5 the line (C نفك) نزد آنكس كه ديد جوهر خود * چه قبول و چه رد چه نيك و چه بد — 6. M نزد آنكس CHM عقل for عشق M ins. و after دين — 7. M هستي اوست —

8. Title varies or wanting.— 9. H transp. 9, 10 CH for α have شاه دارد کرده بی نور (H ره) راه M in β بُرند — 10. M om. CH بدوست H اوست برفتن — 11. H پدید M پذیر B پذره — 13. C حور for خوار — 14. Title varies.— 16. M om. و — 17. CH om. 17—21. M substitutes for 17 بود آنجا زنی ز نیک زنان * حال او بشنو آنکه دادی نان —18 B نفقتی — 19. I مرد را I بوده نابود — 22. HM مردمان —

50. 1. C om. و — 2. CH om. H add. m. r. in marg. A om. in text, add. ead. m. in marg. I پی پند و نصیحت — 3. So H and marg. of IALB; texts (exc. H) ای زعفات — 4. CHM زخدای — 6. CH جمله کرد — 8. C رزق روح — 9. M خاربن — 10. CMI om. ت in β.— 11. H گفت ای B پر خیرہ — 12. C قلیل و کثیر (!)— 13. C کرحکم M خواستست حکم آنراست — 14. C دس دسازد M اوخواهد — 16. M هین بیاموز CH راه را — 17. C ز زن — 18. C دست نفس بدار HML انجای تو و C نفس دست بکذار I تو بیمار H — 19. C انجای تو و H توئی انجای ما M که او و تو ماند — 20. H om. M in α جو او C نرسید both ; CM and marg. of A درو in β. 21. C یکست - بهرهٔ این و آن ز بهر... نه بهر H یکیست H ... عقل یکیست - بهرهٔ این و آن یقین و شکیست M شکست شکیست —

51. 1. M عقل for عشق — 2. M کذي از بی خروش — 3. B points رُو نیست I شد بفرسنگ بیست M روي بپوش M ورنه بنهد B نه بنهد — 4. HM چار M چهار — 5. CH om.— 7. CH om. 7, 8. M نفاو و ریا I وکبرمرا — 8. M همه کونها — 9. CH put 9 after 11. C برای M خرد سخن زو کو CIAB om. و C این لا اله الا هو — 10. H om. AL marg. سخن as altern. for کلمه MB آید ... آید — 11. CH حرف جان B بهرجان CH transp. برج and درج CH حرف دین — 12. CH om. 12—14 —13. B نی ...... نی — 17. M om. H جواب — 18. CH آدمي در CH اسپابست C زان شان به بیند H as C, but ... سال و ماه ... — 19. M همه سال مانده در خواست CH از پی بینش ثواب M انچه M orig. آیدت, ت deleta— 20. M چشمهٔ آفتاب H نور آب — 21. IALB مایهٔ C بنده کي —

52. 2. C om. 2—6 M چون بود B om. و before زلال — 5. B گرم یا که سرد — 8. C om.— 10. B وخراب — 13. H میوهٔ M om. نه CHALB که اندر گاه I and alternative reading in margins of A and B که دیرانگاه — 16. CHM سیاه I بود — 17. MI دختران — CM وراست — 18. IB نسبت — 19. CH صدر — 22. C تو بید —

53. 2. H مبرز M جمله بر — 3. I زان for زن H وشتاب M — و می در C همی خورد — 4. CHM غلبه — 5. MA بیشلي شتاب — 6. H وآن — 7. CHM نوع for جنس in β. M سخت for صعنت C

را بزگالند — 8. HLB گر first word MIA از — 9. CMI om. first و
H بد بود نه نکو ز من — 10. M بیم و CB رشتی A alt. reading in marg.
دشتی — 11. CH در حبس و بند M در حبس بند — 12. H باشد for
بیند ML باشد for یابد — 14. B اندهٔ — 15. M زن CH کودکی —
16. HB گر حورد HB زو for رو A in marg. زود IAL تو زو طمع بردار —
17. CIAB و شراب — 19. H کنج و مال M کنج مال H جامهٔ نیکو —
20. Title varies. — 22. C همکفت H هم کفت —

54. 3. HB آلا معذنت — 6. M om. و M همه کذرست — 8. H
بکاه بستن — 9. CH put as first line of next chap. — 12. H مرد
غریب — 14. M om. و before نعلی C حرار H داند — 15. M وز زرکر —
16. H transp. 16, 17. C زادی M شادکانی — 17. I خود for چون
B om. و after بیطار — 18. CH مکر دان تو بر M حیلت و مرصاد —
19. CH همچو آن — 20. M سه تن را — 21. C om. فی H لرویا
M بهام — 22. M جاهل H تنبل —

55. 1. I باشد زن M om. و — 2. CH نبودش — 3. CH شتر I
آمد MA سفری CH و پر — 4. H کاوٴ H یا بر I بر با بادشا A بَکَر B بادشاه —
5. M om. title CH السبع — 6. CHM خصمی CH om. و I معاملة —
7. H شاهست M سهمناک از H همه کس CH شاهی شناس با M از صولت —
8. M مال غنیمت بود کوسفندت M om. ز — 9. HI کسانی M کسی کو دنی
H سرسر بکارها M بکار در پر — 10. H کبک M طریق معید — 11. M
بدانش داردت M میر — 12. CHM مکار — 13. HM اندرون چنین —
14. CHM دیدار او نیابی — 15. M transp. کرک and یوز CH کرک را رویا
I for یا C با یکی زخدا H بخدا — 16. C حیله ور — 17. M مار همچون
IAB کر H مارکان هم for ور — 18. CH باشد ز جملهٔ افات M هست هریک
ز جملهٔ — 19. CM لیک بی خواب پاسبان — 20. H فصل فی H adds
الخمسة M adds السيارة الخمسة — 21. C اندر خواب M بادشا M درهر —
22. C دیکری I راه زن —

56. 1. CM باز حل IALB معذنت اند — 2. M بود .... بود —
3. M اصل عیش و مراد و آرامش — 4. C برادر کان کاه بعیر رشان — 6. M
بدو پدر مادر — 7. CH om. 7, 8. M دیده M چیره — 9. H پس CH
فال و زجر HB وز M از فال درخور M تقریر — 10. C فصل فی — 11.
HMIB ماند نه — 12. CH ای دو در عمر M bis دو در زعم CH مرید و مزید
C عدّ در عقل H میر در عقل (for پیر ?) پر M bis در عقل دان نه در CH
در توحید — 13. CH om. — 14. C یکی ای M یکی است I یکی یکی یکیست
M bis در یکی را M bis om. و in β — 15. CH om. I صفاء صاحت —

16. M تاکه B نه بنهی — 18. I as text, ex سر آن L سرِ آن B زمان —
20. CH om. M بردن جان M در for ورا — 21. H گردور — 22. M
چونکه MLB نقل for نفس —

57. 1. M قلم شمع و چراغ چون بزنش — 3. H سبب است in α B
کل کُله — 4. CH om. M آرد دل را مرد — 5. CH تباه بود in β —
6. H کلافش داری — 8. CH نبیندی تاج — 9. CH om. 9, 10. M
ره جوید — 11. M او for آن H دژن آسیر C یسیر — 12. HM وربداری
چوشمع دار از نار — 13. M ورهمی بایدت کله ناچار CH ازش for از آتش —
15. H بازکونه CHMIL بال for باش A پال and so B in marg. CH
حو ماه — 16. C جمال in α — 17. H نفس in β — 18. M om.
H om. و — 19. CIA دل for دین C اوتو دل — 20. M نقش CM
om. و H علم و نفس و علم معرفت IALB نفس و علم و نفس — 21. M وصف عین
M این ...... آن ...... این — 22. C صفات بودهٔ C عین و سنک صفت H
ذات تو M شد عین و —

58. 1. C حو ای H چو این C اندراب CM bis وین دو I همچو —
2. M درین CH لعبتی — 3. M وین ز صورت I چنانچه in α — 4. M
om. C بی for تن — 5. C زانک M ثقلست وان دکر این صاف زانکه H
ازو ثقل B ثقل I نقل — 8. C تا زمی M زمین و کل H برجا — 9. M
om.— 10. C تا ازین H نرسد آن — 11. CH om. 11, 12, 13.— 12. M
bis نام بد مرد ازو بپرهیزد A مرورا — 14. C او تو و مرترا — 15. Titles
differ. — 16. M بکرد عالم تا نکردی — 17. M بحقیقت — 18. C
کوزکی M بکرده در بازی — 19. H پس C نازبار C خدای — 20. C
کو بری جنت H کبری جنت — 21. C توی داند — 22. CHM برتو عرضه
H زنیتّش —

59. 1. A بودن corr. m. 2 ex بود H کم از هریک M کم از هریک I
کم از یک یک — 2. H سبک زوی M ز تو ورا بپذیر — 3. C بتلتف —
4. M راضی او — 5. H سخت بمال M ور نخواهد IALB نیک بمال — 6.
M تا شود رَه رشد تهمیدش — 8. C نیاند بود — 9. C ها for هان H هین —
10. CH و برزخ — 11. M و دین ستم — 12. M اوح M β وز ضلال
و محال جان برهان — 13. M β حضرت آشنا کردی واندرین — 14. H
جون جهالت مدان بجان اندر * هیچ آفت درین جهان اندر M بذر ضرر — 15. C
که مردشی HM که مرد باشی مرد کر نیابی BH زاب M نبود — 16. CH H
ins. after 16 and M ins. after 17 —

تا بداند (بدانی M) حق از هوا و هوس * کین همه هیچ نیست ای تو و بس

عدمست چون وجود یکسانست * هرچه تو خواستی همه آنست

19. CHM آب و خاک M بر هوا — 21. CH transp. ملک and فلک HM بازگونه —

60. 1. C ایما in α M برکار HMIL ایمان in β M امید و بیم آر ست A altern. in marg. هر که ز ایمان نه پاک مردارست M here ins. ایمان نماز بیم آر نشناسي که — 2. H سرا for سر H ندانی M دل ز تیمار جهل بیمار ست — 3. CH om. 3, 4. M om. و — 4. M حق ز دل شده منصور IALB مقصور in α M مقصود IALB و قصور β — 5. Titles differ.— 6. I براه CHM هل الی — M bis او for حق — 7. CHIAL بهتر از — 8. M سر افراز H پیش سید آن بازار — 9. IAL زان سه B آن سه CH پیش مهتران بازار M بازار 10. C om. M title differs.— 11. CHM ذي IB (and M originally) پیش — 12. IALB قدر آنکه H سوي for بکرد نزول M ذالّذي — 13. از حال — 15. M وانچه IALB زانکه M هیچ ازو نه H om. M زر و سیم و — 16. CM om. و — 17. I حاضر M سیدش — 18. M نیستي تو نه ز حال بیگانه — 19. H کفتش M وانچه M orig. بدست من ار corr. as text.— 20. M om. و C جست — و درخانه — 21. M ازخانه H دمل M دُقلِ خشک B دقل او خُرد و خشک و H om. و M تا زیبا I and B in marg. مارا حال — 22. C تا بنوا —

61. 3. C اي — آوردی — 4. C متاع M چه میکنی — 5. CH کشت سخت خجل — 6. MB om. و CH سبک M حزین for قیس خوار و — 8. M بندہ را IA مرورا C آنچه — 9. H یکومون M انکاه — بغم — 10. CH transp. the two hemistichs A مرورا CM مرد در انتظار — 11. CIAL add است after زلزله C جاي فراق — 13. H وای CH کن ز دست قیس M کن ز قیس زود — 14. For 14, 15 C has

که بذرد من این متاع قلیل * هست مقبول نیست مرد بخیل
من پذیرفتم این دقل بعیان * هست بهتر ز گوهر دگران

H as C, but puts the wrong hemistichs together, has مقبول و مرد نیست and دقل with in marg. اقل; M has the first of C's two lines above, follows with 14 of text, then 15 α of text, completing the line with زانکه جز اینش نیست مال جلیل — 16. B جُهد — 17. M وان قیس را شد مراد دل حاصل * کرد حق M ins. after 17 بد کردار M بفعل و C — 18. M کشت کار MB زان H ازو بجمال — کید دشمنش باطل — 19. B transp. پیش and بیش HMB بد انسان — 20. H om. B خدا M فعل بد — 22. CHMM bis درمی C هزاران —

62. 1. C om. 1—5.— 2. H om. 2—5 IM توان — 4. M om. 1 یک الله in β.— 5. I عینهم B و عنهم with gloss اشباع over و M

عینک — 6. CH فصل فی الاتحاد — 7. CH جنس — 8. C باطل —
9. M ins. after 9 غیب کو کرد سرخ یزدانست * زرد دوئی کشوري زانست
10. C om. و in α — 11. C زدست — 12. L عقاب — 13. CHM
کفت رو نفس را بکن M ساز از دو H زود — 14. C مشکال — 15. C
عیش بر تو کشت H برتو عیش کشت M کشت برتو عیش — 19. C نا رسنده —
20. CH transp. 20, 21— 21. CH ماه و H واز B دیوی زادمی —
22. M ز فعل —

63. 1. M تا تو در شاهراه M خود اندرو H ودر خود و بدُو IALB نرسی
at beginning of β IAL برسی at end line.— 2. H الفی کرد H
ای صافی — 3. CH عشق در C لا یجوز هنوز — 4. CH om. 4—10.—
10. A تاج دارند — 11. M یکرنگ پوش — 13. CH همهٔ خود M همهٔ
خویش را ز خود M انکه C از دم — 15. H از هوا M om. و A بپسیچ —
16. Titles differ.— 17. C حو او ex حون او — 18. CH نفس خویش —
19. H خورم — 20. MI om. و — 21. M om.—

64. 1. C خواهی رفت H om. تا — 2. C من آن دم بس H زدن زدن
من آدم بس — 3. CHM آنرا که — 4. Titles differ. H om. this
chap.— 7. C کار ساز for پارسا M آن نکو پارسای — 8. C ویحیک
B ویچک I بدین M مقام مسکن — 10. C ست در دنیي شد M شد ست —
11. C om. 11, 12. M om. 11.— 12. A om., add. ead. m. in
marg.— 13. C خطر for نظر — 14. AL پر for بر CHMIAL قسطاط —
15. Titles differ.— 16. M شهر عظیم — 17. HM شهر for شهره
CHMIA قسطاط I ساختش H دیماط — 18. CHM اندرو CHM نبود CM
هوا ورا H هوا ور — 19. M اندران C om. در M هم دران ساعتش —
20. HMIA قسطاط C خانه زبون — 21. CHM آوریدم من بدست —
22. M حال تو چیست —

65. 1. H اندرون سکن — 2. CHM زاهدان B in marg. مبیچ
I ins. تو after زاهدی — 3. C ری H درف و M و بوویم فروخته —
5. M om. آن M نفس om. ت — 6. M نساخته corr. ex ساخته
(without dot)— 7. H شب ترا — 8. M مرا که — 9. C قصد for
قصد — 10. CM مصعد L قصد — 11. H مُسهي I بیالایم — 12. I
شو در حسد — 13. CHM transp. 13, 14. M خو بجمله باز — 15. C
من کنم B با قلا M با قلا و دانه — 16. CHM نفس جون شود در CHM
C رکعت — 18. I جو بی او M کشت نفس — 19. CHB برتن CH
ز وجد آن بدرید — 22. C از آرایش —

66. 1. CH om. M دم کز اندوه و آه و وه ALB واه — 2. HM پاک
زیرا بروی و موی و پیشانی M موی و ابروی و روی و پیشانی H بهر مهمانی —
3. CH om. ML عقد M بسته عقل را — 4. C از for کز — 5. M

و پرهدانست — 6. CHM کعبهٔ شد حو دل M bis خزینه H چکونه —
7. C تجّری — 8. CB بلهوسی HM نشود علم I بشنو و — 9. CH
om. M سوي برد و زیره — 10. CHM om. 10, 11. — 12. C قاصر —
13. CH خلقت بود و خلق H حلق نصیحت M نبوّی H خلق end line.—
14. HMIB om. و in β.— 15. HM نیاز H بیابی — 16. CHM om.
16, 17. — 18. CH حال هدج — 19. CH هرچه — 20. M چون دو دم
CH om. 20, 21.—

67. 2. M بقیامت — 4. CHM چیزی first word. — 5. MB
om. و — 9. CH add است حدیث جه * دوی عشق جهان بر نکیرد
(H نوی) توی حدیث ابن — 10. Titles vary.— 11. H عر نقاب — 13. C
اکر for کی in α M بام بفرق نه بر پای M ز بادهٔ تا کشي C فلک in β. —
14. H transp. 14, 15. B تا for یا H بطبع M بفضل — 15. C om.
M تا تو — 16. CH om. M بر آسمان — 17. M تا شود نامک از سمک
بسماک — 18. CH om. A om. add. ead. m. in marg. I نمازی M
مشت — 19. M فرض for پی HI و خدمت H نان last word.— 20.
AL و باز H بآب CIALB برای for باه — 21. M هرچه پاکی نفس و بابت
M جمله در — 22. CM خالق CHIAL در کیرد —

68. 1. H برون M باشد جون قبول را طاعت — 3. M تا حسد از دلی
M ننهی ستون دین ز را دل دار H نرهی وا — 4. H om. A om. add. ead.
m. in marg.— 5. M از نماز — 6. C om. و after غسل CM دای C
معطل I مفصل L علت (for معضل)— 7. M نرسی در — 8. CH om.
M تا تو در زیر چار — 9. M om. و HM ازو — 10. CH om. 10, 11.—
11. M فرض نماز — 14. CH om. 14—17 I بی نمازت M بپذیرد — 16
M کو (for اکو) — 17. M om. AB هرکه در — 18. M از درون —
20. C هشده I عالم جان — 21. M هرکه این — 22. CHL بدان for
مگو AB مدان M حدیث for حساب —

69. 1. M به بیند I به بیني M بکند — 2. CH om.— 3. M نزد حق
M جواز نماز M ز نکرده CHIAL بنماز end line.— 5. M چونکه کشتي —
7. CHM آن for کان M bis از حضور CM و تری A ترئي — 8. H om.
M نهادت — 9. CH om. M خاک جون تن کرفت و جانت فلک I om. و —
10. Titles differ.— 11. HM زخم— 13. M تا درون H مرد را — 14. M
دید جراحت آن جرّاح جونکه I مردی IL کلید بساخت را زخم بستهٔ for β.—
15. IALB آن زخم را قفل — 16. M چونکه طاقت I یا دم — 17. M
مبارک for لطیف; all texts have اندامش without از — 18. IAL تیغ
first word B تیر CH او شده I وا شده corr. ex واو M ز ضربت درد — 19. C

ان خدا خوانده مر اورا بولي H آنکه حق and thence as C, M آن ولی خدا
وصی نبی I خواند و ولی — 21. M دوده حسین C شد — 22. M

که جو تو در نماز رفته بدي * نزد ایـزد براز رفته بدي

70. 1. M برون ز تو — 2. M اکبر M زان — 4. H om. و in β.— 5. B همه با کام — 6. M بس جو بی M نه بوی پخته — 7. M سلامت B سلام H آزرد both hemistichs M آرد both, corr. in marg. ارزد — 8. HM آن M ins.

نکنـد کردکار مقبـولش * نبـود دار و جار مبذولش
هرکه باشد ز جفت معني فرد * جون زن بد ز مرد نیک بدرد

9. C تن H نماز قر پذیرد (?) M نماز نپذیرد H جنبان — 10. CH جون بجوید M جهل راه M بو جهلی در طریق فضوح — 11. CH اندرین HM جنبانی — 12. C را .... for حق .... را M حق یاد دار انابت حق — 13. CHM om., A om. add in marg. ead. m.— 14. M با دعا M نماز for بغفله — 15. M بخدا ربدو دهدت جواز — 16. CHM خدای CM for second hemistich جامهٔ کبریا کشان در پای (H has this version in marg.) H دعای — 18. CH کز روان M آن سوال — 19. C ز نزد نماز M ز صدق و نیاز C و از تو — 20. H حرام M که احتشام شود M به تکبیر بر علام شود — 21. I باز H نهد IAB همی نهی M دوستدار محکم پی I تو و — 22. M پیشه for رسم —

71. 2. IAL است .... است H آنکه او — 3. M

به جنین طاعت کم از عصـیان * خواجه خوان خویش را غلام مخوان

4. M باشد M نباشی AL altern. reading in marg. بفعل MIALB از for با — 5. CH om.— 8. M جمله را این غرور علت هست MI در for بهر — 9. M سر سر پنهان end α, and for β نکند هر کسی عیان بزبان H نهفت — 10. Titles vary.— 11. M ابی M که ازو بود خلق و حق خشنود — 12. M transp. 12, 13. M دادہ از زهد حق ورا بهری — 13. M شهر و B رحمت H om. و CHM انبوه — 14. C زنت بوم H زنت بود M for α از صلاح و سداد آن سره مرد and for β what in text is α. — 15. M از پی خدمت عیال — 16. H om. A om. in text, add. ead. m. in marg.— 17. H روانت بیسندم — 18. CH آن زن H عفیف HB یافت I transp. 18, 19. M

بود آن صالحه زن زیبا * جوهره نام دیسـم چون دیبا

19. CH om. A om., add. ead. m. in marg.— 20 MIB om. و M حکم مالک زن و مرد — 21. M جست و بوریا بر چید -- 22. M پس ورا -

72. 2. M این عبارت من از تو C اشنیدم — 3. CH حجاب آن M ins. after 3.

آنکه نبود حجاب طالب جود * جز تراب آنچ جز وقت سجود

4. M غیر for عین C در میانه بود — 7. C کشت و معذور بود وی معذور M کشت الحق دران بداو معذور — 8. HI قاعده — 9. I نهاد at end.— 10. M

بود کم — 14. H برنهمی C end line نزنعمی (?) — 16. CHM آن for
این — 19. M وجود او — 20. M نباشد H درسر — 21. C جشر —

73. 2. H om. و AL دیوبر — 3. CH om. 3-8 A om. 3-8, add. ead. m. in marg.— 5. B موزت B جه B كُله in β.— 6. M وعده A عدّه L غده — 9. M چونتو با لحن خوش بكوه H لحن for بانگ — 10. C om. H صوت بپای — 11. H برایت M برویت A in marg. از ثنای تو M که کرده‌انست M هم بر تو — 12. CH فصل فی — 13. M دعا بر پای H کرده در شه ره بو باشد — 14. M om. و in β. — 15. CH om.; A om. add. ead. m. in marg. M ذلت I بخس (?) A نحس ex بحس — 16. C om. L ثُرا M بندکانرا تو روز H جو روز H جویان in a چویان in β.— 17. CH om. 17-20; A om. 17-20, add. ead. m. in marg.— 18. B om. و in β.— 20. I کزبر — 21. IA در اکرچه — 22. CH نیست کس را H كه آن چرا این M for this line has

دست حکم ترا بکن فیکون * دریکی دم هزار اثر افزون

74. 1. CH فصل في — 2. CML نعمت — 3. H بغاز for نیاز — 4. H ins رایشي کان بودت کوناکون تکیه بر آب روی حون فرعون
C also, but a لونا لون (hiatus) آتشی کان — 7. CH om. 7—10.— 8. M زلف دوست — 9. M غم نیاز L غم و نیاز — 11. CH om. 11, 12.— 14. C متوحد (*i.e.*, متوجه) M transp. متفرد and متوحد C و جبروت — 15. H آیت عقل — 16. Titles vary.— 18. CHM تو ای زمن — 19. CH om., A om. add. ead. m. in marg. M نیست پدید both, and so A originally also. — 21. M از آب لطف خود خوش M نسبت باد و خاکم H یاد و خاکم آبش C باد C om. و — 22. H لحشیدن —

75. 1. CHIAL om. M بیفتاده ام — 2. M من بجرم و گناه مستورم C پای در پایم از خجالت ربّ * دست بر دست چون زنم ز طرب M ins. پرده بر شیب
3. I خواتمت — 5. C ذلکم راه C خیانت روي L جوی in β.— 6. C om.— 7. C كه نباشد in a M كه نپرسد in a IL بکارسازی A alternative reading in marg. نسازد بکارسازی — 8. C همه in a HM ای همه همه تو — 9. CH بکار خانت — 10. CH om. A om. add. ead. m. in marg. A نخواهد MIL نکاهد — 11. CHMI رفتند M خفتند in β.— 12. M جون کنم CH مرد — 13. H رحمت for نعمت M زحمت تونی دوئی ? corr. ex رحمت — 14. CH با تو تفّ و دود M جونتو بودي C و بود — 15. CH om. A om. add. in marg. ead. m. M یاد beginning.— 16. C این for آن— 17. M با تو آن — 19. I in a آنکه M هرچه M نخوردم M بکن — 20. C یک for شش — 21. M از غم مرک so A altern. in marg. C writes نمي دم — 22. H om. و —

76. 1. C زشت و حوب M مشت — 3. CH om.— 4. C بود که — 5. C یان بودی - 6. C که نه او به بود ر مستی ما M ماونه که HMIAL و هستی - 7. C om. A om. add. ead. m. in marg. I بخود یمان H for حکم تو کر M از خرد H حونان خرد 8. C — چه بود پدش پاک مشتی خاک β بکرفتی 9. M n β نیک ما کشت بد CH نیک اکر نبدرفتی MIALB خرد — —11. H om. M وز تو — 13. I و علم — 14. C اندر کرکسی کرد مالی — 15. CH om. M فضل و MIL بهر آنجا ز — 16. B آنچه in β.— 17. Titles vary.— 18. C om. M ذات تو — 19. M و بر تو in α C و بی تو in β.— 20. C تو دس تو دسوی — 21. M بهر دین دیده first words.— 22. CH om. —

77. 1. M به مان به است که H به end line.— 2. C ای in β.— 3. C om. A om. add. ead. m. in marg. H کمان ما — 4. M جامهٔ و جان و نان پر...... پر C 6. — تشنه را ز M om. CH 5. — وتست β I in بنعمت جز سوی تو تو ام CH نه از هنری M نز...... نز for تر......تر B بر...... بر H M وکیل کوی — 8. C هرکه C مرا بو پدیر — 9. M نواش — 10. CH om. B صدره — 11. M باز درمانده — 13. H om. B om. و after ونگ — 14. M نخوی هستی — 16. C همه کس را C همه دس بهای — 17. CH om. 17—19 M before 17 inserts همه را کام و کارو بار از تو * تارک عقل تاج دار از تو — 18. M جز خاک حضرتش پوید — 20. Titles differ.— 21. C om. M جهان آرای —

78. 2. CH om. 2—8 I کر first word.— 3. M از تپش جون جکر I مسجد از قهر تو کنشت شود M for β از لطف تو M in α 4. — جون کند جکر I جو خشت — 5. I کر بجندند — 6. A om. add. ead. m. in marg.— 7. I از درویش — 9. H کام و کار و بازار تو M as H but بار از B کار بار — 10. CHMI تاء من C شدم both — 11. I تلخی نیارم — 12. CH کو beginning β.— 14. M in α که یارد بود M in β طاعت بار یار ندارد — 15. M نبد از مکر تو بکاه کناه — 16. Titles vary.— 17. IAL روبه first word CH علم for رای M با مکر یار و با فن جفت — 18. C تو صد HM من for ما — 20. CH om. A om. add. in marg. ead. m. — 21. C ای منی M قضای عدل M نزد عقول — 22. M این عزازیل C ودن دکر —

79. 1. Titles vary.— 3. C از تو — 4. C جاه زر — 6. H تیری CHM om. — و 7. H ins. نیک درمانده ام درم تو کشای ره چه کم کرده ام رهم تو نمای — 8. B نشود........نشود — 10. H از بوت — 12. M راه ازین — 14. CHM in α — 15. CH om. M به قیروان — 16. H کرد بازار H چون کردی شدی کل کل حه C پل به بین — 17. L پارسا رو CH هیچ کس — 20. C om.— 21. B دنیی M قعر آب — 22. C om. M بحر دمان M کشته باز —

80. 2. C om. I قلزم — 3. C نُغُل H بغل C و درون بل H بیرون ومحیط
B ومحیط — 4. Titles given to this section are inapplicable, v. note
to trans.— 6. M حقد آلت خلق اند M در خور حق نه بابت خلق اند M
then ins. صاحب خشم و حقد مجبور است * واین دو از ذات پاک حق دور است
7. M غضب و حقد و خشم وصلح و حسد IAL غضب و عقد و جلک و بخل و حسد
B حرص for صلح C فرد و احد M قدس احد — 8. H بخالق — 9. C
و کمند — 10. M چو خواندت بر خویش L براندت B بخاندت CMLB
آدم خاک M توحید پاکرا صدفی 12. M in α بر کرفته — 11. M بهشت —
بر همه کام تو سرفراز 16. M از قرب و لطف سعد بعید — 13. M خلق را خلقي —
C قضای M خدای باز — 17. C تن for بن L همه for بن — 18. Titles
vary.— 20. CH فرا — 21. M دیده از دیکران —

81. 1. M نآورد یاد طعمه — 2. I باز دارد — 4. B بی او یک زمان —
5. H برو for درو — 6. M بخو نیامیزد — 9. H و تو هشیار H اندرین —
10. CHM شرح C مسیّب — 11. M تو for رو M نار for راه — 12. M
om. و — 13. Titles vary.— 14. CB ساله CM زخم for زین CH om.
و H بزم for بزین C لغام — 15. C ببرهنجد M in β برون هنجد —
16. M چون اورا بر C لغام both.— 19. M آسیاب بود M در عذاب بود —
20. M in α om. و M بلا و رنج و عنا — 21. M نزد دانا — 22. M در عذاب —

82. 1. M خوانده هم M خواند H باشدش جای خوف و بیم و هراس در نُبی
C در نصّ هم — 2. C نیرو قصد اوست H نیروئی M نیرو بیست CB بی تو نه
H بی توئي و بی اوئی M بی تو هست و بی او نیست — 4. I وحق H وافر —
6. H خوردی دین end α CH بنوی — 7. M دار for امر —` 8. Titles
vary.— 9. M جان و حال و ذوق HIB عقل دوق — 10. CH om. 10 to
end section.— 11. M آتشی I آتشش M جان و دل که درو عقل و — 12. M
تا که خود یار عشق و — 13. M کرا عشق کوی او — 14. M بی یار M in β
جو B یار خود — 15. MI in β شوق شوقت — 18. B جان بنداره — 19.
M مرد شود M کز راه شوق درد رود — 20. M همش —

83. 1. M چونکه اورا — 3. M om. 3, 4.— 4. B om. L ز هر beginning A ببود .... ببود -- 5. MA آسمانی AL زمینی M ins.

هر دمش رنگ کفر دین کردد * هر نفس آسمان زمین کردد

9. M آنچ ندارد M in β آنچ — 11. M بیست — 12. M در ره M از بی
لطف — 15. Titles vary.— 16. M آید H om. از in α L انچه in β.—
17. M زشت و خوب C مرجع H ترجع M ذی او — 18. M زیر نقش پرکارند
C وقف — 19. M om.— 20. CM محبوس for مسبوق M حکمت و علمش —
21. CH om. 21—8 next p.— 22. I هر کرا منتهی است —

84. 1. M عقد كرده — 2. MAB نسب — 3. M زین هنر پروري قوی نفسی — 5. M چشم in α M کوهر کان مکر -- 6. L ندارد بجای IAL این کهر — 7. M بس for نزد — 8. M ins.

تا دل و چشم مردم ابله * که نباشد ز قدر درّ آکه

10. C نروید — 11. M در for کن CHM جان — 12. CIAL درکه M جمله چون — 13. H بکویند M transp. کوینده and رونده M کاطیعوا — 14. L قضای M ید for دست — 15. MB بفعل — 16. M هرجه H حاملان -- 17. C آن اورا C بود for برد M طغیان last word.— 18. C و ایمان — 19. C اندر کار — M end line همکنان HM at end α داداد H دوار 20. CH om. 20—21.— 21. M آمد both M وآب A om. 21—22, add. ead. m. in marg.— 22. H om.—

85. 1. CH از همه CH آن دکر M reads

پس دو عکس آفتابّ و آب شمار * و آن سیوم عکس زآب بر دیوار

2. M om. 2—6 CH خود end α CH نیاید — 3. C وآن همه A تَسیرُ CB — با یبدّل الدولست C نیک و قوت CB از بد H .4 —.without article امور 6. HB om. و C om. کز — 7. H om. M بند — 8. M for β has بقضای ودست نفع و ضرر H ins.

کی بسازد بحکم مطلق تو * باد با بادبان زورق تو

11. H om. M کزان — 12. M امر for جبر — 14. H عشق شد C بدید H پذیر جسم و صور — 15. H خویش M را خویش — 17. CM first word زنده تر کن لسان H زندهٔ کن بسان حیوان را C .18 — عقل را H in β نفس — در یازد C و مایه C تا خرد نطق M .19 — کن تو for آر M حیوان را 20. I, and A altern. in marg. یار شود in α, بر کذار شود in β. — 21. M in α از در نفس تا بدایه CH تا رعایت CH in β تا بدایت M last word کان—

86. 1. B شعر ز — 3. CIL مباح و C محصور C کسی کین و آن برو دور شرع از کون شعر بس دوو M شرع و شعر از سرای تن دور است H for β has ست — 4. CI خط M همچو راحت — 5. Titles vary.— 12. C نه B in β صرف — 13. IALB in α در حدوث کي کنجد in β را حروف کی سنجد — 14. HB شکل و — 15. CHM دلپذیر — 16. M first word زان HM transp. داده and زاده — 17. C روح او انس — 18. H جان پر درد را دوا — 19. C om. 19-2 next p.— 21. M صفوت for عادت —

87. 1. IALB جانها in α — 2. H رایت — 4. C om. M in α او for آن M از معارضش عاجز — 7. I رایق for واثق — 8. IA حروف آن CH

جانرا for دین را — 10. CH om. 10–12 A om. 10—12, add. in marg. ead. m.— 12. M کمال و — 13. MIB حارس — 15. M om. I طرف و C om. و — 16. CH دیدهٔ روح و حرف so I orig., corr. in حروف m. 2 C حشم حشم ادن و حسم حسم I جسم جان — 17. CILB نعمت in α C اس آن C حشم corr. ex جسم I آن بدرده چشم M این بردهٔ چشم H بدرده حشم نغمت in β I نخورده — 18. HM به for ز M in β دلال — 19. I om. و CHM ز کار او آگاه — 20. M بی خبر باشد M که با بصر باشد — 22. CH نقش هست for ست L از نبی C تلقین C نقش حرف و قرأتش بیقین M ونحو —

33. 1. CH پوست اوّل — 2. C om. 2—5 H اولین H رُفت — 3. M از for آن — 5. M ins.

که نبودی دل تو در پـــرده   جانت در بند آز و کین برده
او ترا روی خویش بنمـــودي (cf. 9)   تا دل و جان بدو بیاسودی

6. C has β same as 8 β. — 10. H جان نا محرم آشنا — 11. C نقلش CHM جان شناسد M بجز که — 12. M ثفلش for روغن M طعم از پی نیست — خوان تو قرآن M خوآن — 14. H صفت و H صورتی — 13. I آنرا مغز — 15. C از قران — 18. CH سورت — 17. H in α زانک نا محرم تو —زبان چه داند M به .M om چون نباشد — 22. CMAL کی به بیند — 20. M

89. 1. ILB قرآن خدا نکو — 3. C om. 3—10 HMB اگرچه I دکر چه — نشسته — 7. H اندرین — 6. M دنیا مثال — 4. HMI نکو همیدانی M M کانکه این زان — 9. H تو طرف را مذکر H حرف قرآن تو طرف آب 8. HM نماندت نهاد نی — 10. H و .B om. in β کان و کین B کاب کین I کاه کین M کی for کو — 12. C بصورت C در دل — 11. M om. CH کاسه — L ز کنعان H بو for شم M ماند — 14. M هم از — 13. CH ذوق سر سرّ او نکو — 19. C .18. H om — و .17. HM om — در یعقوب H رسید CHB 21. C — دل که — 20. M شو I نز برون همچو زیر M تو برون شو حو M و .22. M om — سه جویند و کاسهای M آواز حرف H لفظ او از حروف — پوسقت پرده

90. 1. H از بهر خبث CH آمد CAB برون — 2. CH om. M بردن مرکبی in β. — 3. CM in β برین H in β بدین — 4. C بصیوت ببین پر از طوبی — بجان معنی M بر زبان H و .7. ML om — 9. C first word با HM — فرقان C رمید از M زمان C چون ز ظل عمر رمد — 12. M تو first word — حس for کین M خیال حس C آنکهی بو که صبح M باش ناکه صبح 13. C

14. C نه بیند — 18 CI کبر دیو M بوی کبر CHM دمد M سرّ قرآن CHM رمد — 19. IALB om. H و خموش C بسوی C نتازد — 20. M بنازد in α تازد in β, but the several hemistichs of this and the preceding

line show much confusion and many variations in the several MSS.— 21. C. om. —

91. 2. H مغزرا — 4. H first word کوهر — 5. C om. 5—8.—
6. M پدید HM قهر — 7. H انکه M ان برشط و شطر — 8. M سرقران
وشطر — 10. M پرجوهر CH ساحتش M پرعبیرو CM پرعنبر — 12 IB
پرده for پنجره — 14. M تا نباشي ALB نقش H عقل تا بود B om. last
و — 16. M و دیری دوری خیره نشود H بشده — 17. HM انفاسی -- 18.
M نشود — 19. CH om. 19—22.— 20. I آب —

92. 1. C دلت باشد M for β فَسِرُّ القرآن شو بدریای — 3. Texts ins.

درجها چیست سرّ ربّانـي   در میان چیست رمز روحاني

with variants C in α درمیان M in α در قرآن III در جهان M in β در بیان
C سحر روحاني H بحر روحاني — 4. H جه مهر و چه C و ماه — 5. CHB
لطیف روح و سبک M om. و — 6. Titles differ.— 7. M in β om. او —
8. H بسوی او M بسویتو — 9. M in β om. و HIALB خویش for بوک و—
10. M گردی — 13. M زاد for آب — 14. H بدان همی — 15. H
ور ترا تاج M .17 —.16—18 CH om. 16. — دو معنی C نه بیند دو حرفی
و تخت باید و کاه — 18. M سوی ره — 19. C درد for دلو — 20. Titles
differ.— 21. H اعشاره — 22. M تا شده —

93. 1. I ماول — 3. C om.— 4. C سلح — 5. C در نغمش بی H ز
in α for به — 6. C حکم آن برین H خود برین M را برین — 7. M پایان
بسر C برون کني — 8. M in α کند تقصیر C بعلمش کني بخود M in β کند
H تقدیر — 9. C om. 9—15 H کرده — 11. M دارش چو جان HMIB
پلید — 13. B تا for یا — 14. H om.— 15. H خری L خلق M
پر بانک H جرس بانک B om. و — 16. C om. و — 17. C om. و H
فضل و خوی M فعل for حو I جود و I ست ... ست at end of hemistichs
for ت ... ت — 18. Titles vary.— 19. C om. second hemistich and
onwards to second hemistich of next section exc. **94**, 16, 17, 18; H
پاش تا M روز حشر IAL با for بر H از جان کله — 20. H حامل M
جاهل — 21. M تو خدا کردکار —

94. 1. H بخود — 3. H transp. the two hemistichs HM که بسی
لاف M کس for پس H قدر و — 4. B گفت گوی AL in β گوشی forگوئی
H نصیبش از رمهٔ M نصیب زمزمه — 5. IB بقاخت — 7. M بحکم من M
رای هوای — 10. H حجاز — 11. HM in α شکنه H in β شک نه M
in β سکنه — 13. HM خود for تو — 14. H om. L بازار و گاه -- 15. M
مرا for براه B برای M بایجازی — 17. M آمد H بگذارد CB نیاید —

18. HB پس M کرد مهجور دور قرآنش -- 19. Titles differ.— 20. M نچشی C نودی و نبودی M ins.

گاه درس و تلاوت قرآن * از کمال حلاوت قرآن
ای بدست هوا شده ز نیاز * پای بست هوان بچاه مجاز

21. M بتماشا بباغ — 22. MI و آنچه آید —

95. 1. C و جهان and so also H originally; M in β هرچه — 2. M جمله — 3. M شده for گشته — 4. H گرددش M نطق — سوی — 5. C om. 5-10. M سوره اخلاص — 7. I عرش چون M مخبر حق چوز و خبر H از امر 8. H hiatus after سیر M و سرّ سیر قلم L altern. in marg. سرّ نون قلم B altern. in marg. سرّ نون و قلم — 9. H, and ALB altern. in marg. پاک for بال H om. و L نور in β. — 10. M چون بخوانی تو — 11. H om. CM بی و تی I in β آورد — 12. M بفروشد برای CB را خویش H نیک for خوب B بهرهٔ — 13. CM و وحدت M ندارد for نیارد — 14. M وحدت C end both hemistichs کن M پاک و صافی چو زرّ H بکانش — 15. HB بار ML درد H غش ز خشم M غش جسم — 16. M تاج سلطان بدو بیارآید — 17. M هرکرا ملک عدل C in α om. و M افسر شاه او — 18. Titles vary.— 19. C om. HM لایمه I دوستش — 20. CB مغز —

96. 1. CH اندرون — 2. CH om. M in β کز — 3. M for β has وقف C بحقیقت نه از طریق مجاز M ins. a line with first hemistich هست کذب و ریا نه صدق و نیاز and second as text 3 β except و رقه for و وفقه — 4. B in α om. first و MI om. second و C اوازست C دروازست— 8. H in α توشیست C om. و — 9. C شنیدنی — 10. M om. C از غذا C ندارد — 11. C om. 11--16 M آید H آرد بار — 12. H یا بالش MIB یا بآتش — 13. H بد آنچه AL خریدن — 14. H بآبش H در دلش M ده for نه — 15. HM om. و — 16. M خبرت نیست ای خرنساس M و وسواس — 17. M آن نفس دیو M هوش و دین برهد — 18. CH تو first word CMI غمزرا H غمز H را in ras. MH مغز for عمر — 19. M علم حق صنعت M اسارت H in β om. و M ins.

راه دین را و علم حق را زاد * هست صدق و صلاح و علم و سداد

20. MI منشور — 21. I بيني for باشد H سوی آسمان شود — 22. B مانده است C om. و —

97. 1. C طرفش IB, and A altern. in marg. صوتش — 3. C سرود شفق H, and B altern. in marg. شغف AL altern. in marg. شعف I سبق M صفق C in β om. و H دف ALB all give altern. in marg. دف—

4. C om. 4–8 HM محال — 5. M وقت for حال M از آستینش سود H
آلا آن ای مخنث ملعون * بهر میویز باد دادی کون M ins. آستینش
so also I, but الآن and برمویزی بباد — 10. C first word شفق H شغف
H فقیه — 11. M صف — 14. M زآلا — 15. Titles differ.— 16. HM
هست آن دم H مادر for زاده — 17. H رنگ عالم C in β سنگ آدم —
18. CHM in β هرکرا C نفس — 19. CH om. 19—22 M بشقاب I شقافت —
20. M جای for جام — 21. M جای for جام — 22. H برو و سوی —

98. 1. C beginning در H خریده — 3. C نه last word.— 4. C
سوی for بهر M بشوی C آن سو for آن یک — 5. M ز نقش — 6. C
نفس M نقش نفس بشست — 7. M هرکه H بر بند H ناویخت M for β
has خون دل وآبروی عقل بریخت M ins.

وانکه از پای دام کار کشاد * بر سر عقل تاج شرع نهاد

8. CHM این M نیست جهان I است جهان CH خواند — 9. H om
9—10.— 10. M om. و M ins.

بر کناری بر از میان هستي جون بدیـدار یار پدوستی
هرکه دل در عرور دهر نبست سود کرد از زیان وحالي رست

11. I سوی for بهر C corruptly این جهان جهان بهر آن جهان ایمان —
12. M for β has نفس در کار دین مسخر اوست — 14. H وقت for گاه M
عجب for ترا — 15. Titles differ.— 17. M بغرت — 21. M بجهل —
22. CH om. B و آتش B و باد M باد همایان —

99. 3. M in β وین — 6. I خود for بد — 7. C ضد for پر —
8. M هرزه اندر بند — 9. IALB end α ریو M هنر for هدی — 10. CHM
in α om. و M خدعه و حماقت بند H at end چند — 11. HM خاصه M
در دام C in α om. و — 12. HMB همکنان CH یافه for هرزه — 14. M
شد LB دین زردشت — 17. CHM وین — 16. M بر سر — 15. M در اسم —
both.— 20. C om. I ویرانه end line.— 21. CHM ضلالت — 22. CHM
اسپ و سگ —

100. 2. I عالم all but M سباع و دیو و ستور M for β has صد هزاران
HA رُبّانی C خوانی — 4. C راه پُر C غول پیش — 3. M چه و رهبر کور
دبّابی; all but C insert here

ای سنائی چو بر گرفتی کلک در معنی کشیدی اندر سلک
(— زاول HM) چون بگفتی ثنای حق اول پس بگو نعت احمد مرسل

6. C پیغامبران H مهین; all except CH add

احمد مرسل آن چراغ جهان رحمت عالم آشکار و نهان

بسم الله الرحمن الرحيم

ای درون پرور برون آرای   وی خرد بخش بیخرد بخشای
خالق و رازق زمین و زمان   حافظ و ناصر مکین و مکان
همه از صنع تو مکان و مکین   همه در امر تو زمان و زمین
آتش و باد و آب و خاک سکون   همه در امر قدرتت بیچون
عرش تا فرش جزو مبدع تست   عقل با روح پیک مسرع تست
در دهان هر زبان که گردانست   از ثناي تو اندرو جانست
نامهای بزرگ محترمت   رهبر جود و نعمت و کرمت
هریک افزون ز عرش و فرش و ملک   زان هزار و یکست و صد کم یک
هر یکی زان بحاجتی منسوب   لیک نامحرمان ازو محجوب
یا رب از فضل و رحمت این دل و جان   محرم دید نام خود گردان
کفر و دین هر دو در رهت پویان   وحده لا شریک له گویان
صانع و مکرم و توانا اوست   واحد و کامران نه چون ما اوست
حي و قیوم و عالم و قادر   رازق خلق و قاهر و غافر
فاعل جنبش است و تسکین است   وحده لا شریک له اینست
هرچه را هست گفتي از بن و بار   گفتي او را شریک هش میدار
عجز ما حجت تمامي اوست   قدرتش نائب اسامي اوست
لا و هو هر دو زان سرای بهي   باز گشتند جیب و کیسه تهي

برتر از وهم و عقل و حس و قیاس   چیست جز خاطر خدای شناس
هر کجا عارفیست در همه فرش   هست چون فرش زیر نعلش عرش
هرزه بیند روان بیننده   آفرین جز بر آفریننده
آنکه داند ز خاک تن کردن   باد را دفتر سخن کردن
واهب عقل و ملهم الباب   منشي نفس و مبدع اسباب
همه از صنع اوست کون و فساد   خلق را جمله مبدا است و معاد
همه ازو و باز گشت بدو   خیر و شر جمله سرگذشت بدو
اختیار آفرین نیک و بد اوست   باعث نفس و مبدع خرد اوست
او ز ناچیز چیز کرد ترا   خوار بودي عزیز کرد ترا
هیچ دل را بکنه او ره نیست   عقل و جان از کمالش آگه نیست
دل عقل از جلال او خیره   چشم جان با کمال او تیره
عقل اول نتیجه از صفتش   راه داده ورا بمعرفتش
سست جولان ز عز ذاتش وهم   تنگ میدان ز کنه وصفش فهم
عقل را پر بسوخت آتش او   از پی رشک کرد مفرش او
نفس در موکبش کمر دوزیست   عقل در مکتبش نو آموزیست
چیست عقل اندر این سپنج سرای   جز مزور نویس خط خدای
چند ازین عقل ترّهات انگیز   چند ازین چرخ و طبع رنگ آمیز
عقل را خود بخود چو راه نمود   پس بشایستگي ورا بستود
کاول آفریدها عقل است   برتر از برگزیدها عقل است
عقل کلّ یک سخن ز دفتر او   نفس کلّ یک پیاده بر در او
عشق را داده هم بعشق کمال   عقل را کرده هم بعقل عقال
عقل مانند ماست سرگردان   در ره کنه او چو ما حیران

عقل عقلست و جان جانست او — آنچه زان برترست آنست او
بتقاضای عقل و نفس و حواس — کی توان بود کردگار شناس
گر نه ایزد ورا نمودی راه — از خدائی کجا شدی آگاه

فی المعرفة

بخودش کس شناخت نتوانست — ذات او هم بدو توان دانست
عقل حقش بتوخت نیک نتاخت — عجز در راه او شتافت شناخت
کرمش گفت مر مرا بشناس — ورنه که شناسدی بعقل و حواس
بدلیلی حواس کی شاید — کوز بر پشت قبه کی پاید
عقل رهبر ولیک تا در او — فضل او مر ترا برد بر او
بدلیلی عقل ره نبری — خیره چون دیگران مکن تو خری
فضل او در طریق رهبر ماست — صنع او سوی او دلیل و گواست
ای شده از نهاد خود عاجز — کی شناسی خدای را هرگز
چون تو در علم خود زبون باشی — عارف کردگار چون باشی
چون ندانی سر شناختنش — چون توهم کنی بساختنش
هست در وصف او بوقت دلیل — نطق تشبیه و خامشی تعطیل
غایت عقل در رهش حیرت — مایهٔ خلق سوی او غیرت
وهمها قاصرست از اوصافش — فهمها هرزه میزند لافش
انبیا زین حدیثها حیران — اولیا زین صفات سرگردان
عقل و جانرا مراد و مالک اوست — منتهای مرید و سالک اوست
عقل تا رهنمای هستی اوست — هستها زیر پای هستی اوست
فعل او خارج از درون و برون — ذات او برتر از چگونه و چون
ذات اورا نبرده راه ادراک — عقل را جان و دل درین ره خاک

عقل بی کحل آشنائی او بیخبر بوده از خدائی او
چه کنی وهم را ببحثش حث کی بود با قدم حدیث حدث
نیست از راه عقل و وهم و حواس هیچ جنبندهٔ خدای شناس
عز وصفش که روی بنماید عقل را جان و عقل برباید
عقل را خود کسی نهد تمکین در مقامی که جبرئیل امین
کم ز کنجشکی آید از هیبت جبرئیلی بدان همه صولت
عقل کانجا رسید سر بنهد مرغ کانجا پرید پر بنهد
جز بحس رکیک و نفس خبیث نکند در قدم حدیث حدیث
در رهٔ قهر و عزت صفتش کنه تو بس بود بمعرفتش

فی التوحید

احدست و شمار ازو معزول صمدست و نیاز ازو مخذول
آن احد نی که عقل داند و فهم وان صمد نی که حس شناسد و وهم
نه فراوان نه اندکی باشد یکی اندر یکی یکی باشد
در دوئی جز بد و سقط نبود هرگز اندر یکی غلط نبود
تا ترا در درون شمار و شکیست چه یکی خوان چه دو که هردو یکیست
تو چراگاه دیو دان بیقین چه و چند و چرا و چون را هین
نه بزرگیش هست از افزونی ذات او بر ز چندی و چونی
نیست از بهر طالب عاجز هل و من گفتن اندرو جائز
کس نگفته صفات مبدع هو چند و چون و چرا چه و که و کو
ید او قدرتست و وجه بقاش آمدن حکمت و نزول عطاش
قدمینش جلال قهر و خطر اصبعینش نفاذ حکم و قدر
هستها تحت قدرت اویند همه با او و او همی جویند

جنبش نور سوی نور بود — نور کی ز آفتاب دور بود
با وجودش ازل پریر آمد — پگه آمد و لیک دیر آمد
در ازل بسته کی بود عملش — یک غلامست خانه زاد ازلش
از ابد دور دار وهم و گمان — که ابد از ازل گرفت نشان
کی مکان باشدش ز بیش و ز کم — که مکان خود مکان ندارد هم
با مکان آفرین مکان چه کند — آسمان گر خود آسمان چه کند
نه مکان پی برد بدو نه زمان — نه بیان زو خبر دهد نه عیان
نه بارکان ثبات اوقاتش — نه مکان جای هستي ذاتش
ای که در بند صورت و نقشي — بستهٔ استوی علی العرشي
صورت از محدثات خالي نیست — در خور عز لایزالي نیست
زانکه نقاش بود نقش نبود — استوی بود و عرش و فرش نبود
استوی از میان جان میخوان — ذات او بستهٔ جهات مدان
کاستوی آیتی ز قرآنست — گفتن لا مکان ز ایمانست
عرش چون حلقه از برون درست — از صفات خدای بیخبرست
در صحیفه کلام مسطورست — نقش و آواز و شکل ازو دورست
ینزل الله هست در اخبار — آمد و شد تو اعتقاد مدار
رقم عرش بهر تشریف است — نسبت کعبه بهر تعریف است
لا مکان گوی حاصل دین است — سر بجنبان که جای تحسین است
دشمني حسین ازان جست ست — که علی لفظ لا مکان گفت ست
خلق را زین صفات جهانی ساخت — تا ز بهر تو آشیانی ساخت
آسمان دی نبود امروزست — باز فردا نباشد او نوزست
در نوردد ز پیش ستردخان — یوم نطوی السماء رو برخوان

عارفان چون دم از قدیم زنند ‌ ‌ ها و هو را میان دو نیم زنند

فی القدم

دهر نی قالب قدیمی او ‌ ‌ طبع نی باعث کریمی او
نشود دهر و طبع بی قولش ‌ ‌ همچو جان در نهاد بی طولش
این و آن هر دو ناقص و ابتر ‌ ‌ آن و این هر دو ابله و بی پر
مادهٔ او ز کهنه و نو نیست ‌ ‌ اوست کز هستها جز او او نیست
بنهایت نه ملک او معروف ‌ ‌ ببدایت نه ذات او موصوف
فعل و ذاتش برون ز آلت و سوست ‌ ‌ بس که هویتش بر از کُن و هوست
جمع کرد از پی تو بیش از تو ‌ ‌ آنچه اسباب تست پیش از تو
زیر گردون ز امر و صنع خدای ‌ ‌ ساخته چار طبع بر یکجای
جمع ایشان دلیل قدرت اوست ‌ ‌ قدرتش نقشبند حکمت اوست
آنکه بی خامه زد ترا بیرنگ ‌ ‌ هم تواند گزاردن بی رنگ
از درونت نگاشت صنع اله ‌ ‌ نه ز زرد و سپید و سرخ و سیاه
وز برونت نگاشته افلاک ‌ ‌ از چه از باد و آب و آتش و خاک
نگذارد فلک بتو جاوید ‌ ‌ رنگ زرد و سیاه و سرخ و سپید
دادهٔ خود سپهر بستاند ‌ ‌ نقش الله جاودان ماند
آنکه بی رنگ زد ترا بیرنگ ‌ ‌ باز نستاند از تو هرگز رنگ
آوریدت ز صنع در تکلیف ‌ ‌ کرد فضلش ترا بخود تعریف
گفت گنجی بُدم نهانی من ‌ ‌ خُلِقَ الخَلْقُ تا بدانی من
کرده از کاف و نون چو درّ ثمین ‌ ‌ دیده را یک دهان پر از یاسین
کیسهٔ را مدوز و پرده مدر ‌ ‌ کاسهٔ را ملیس و عشوه مخر
همه اضداد و لیک ز امر اله ‌ ‌ همه با یکدگر شده همراه

همه را تا ابد بامر قدم　　زده بیرنگ در سرای عدم
چار گوهر بسعی هفت اختر　　شده بیرنگ را گزار شکر
نیست گوی جهان زشت و نکو　　جز ازو و بدو و بلکه خود او
همه زو یافته نگار و صور　　هم هیولانی اصل و هم پیکر
عنصر و ماده هیولانی　　طبع و الوان چار ارکانی
همه را غایت و تناهی دان　　نردبان پایهٔ الهی دان

فی الصفا والاخلاص

پس چو مطلوب نبود اندر جای　　سوی او کی بود سرت از پای
سوی حق شاهراه نفس و نفس　　آینه دل زدودن آمد و بس
آینه دل ز زنگ کفر و نفاق　　نشود روشن از خلاف و شقاق
صیقل آینه یقین شماست　　چیست محض صفای دین شماست
پیش آن کش بدل شکی نبود　　صورت و آینه یکی نبود
گرچه در آینه بشکل بوی　　آنکه در آینه بود نه توی
دیگری تو چو آینه دگرست　　آینه از صورت تو بیخبرست
آینه از صورتت سفر دورست　　کان پذیرای صورت از نورست
نور خود ز آفتاب نبرید ست　　عیب در آینه ست و در دید ست
هرکه اندر حجاب جاوید ست　　مثل او چو بوم و خورشید ست
گر ز خورشید بوم بی نیروست　　از پی ضعف خود نه از پی اوست
نور خورشید در جهان فاش ست　　آفت از ضعف چشم خفاش ست
تو نه بینی جز از خیال و حواس　　چون نهٔ خط و سطح و نقطه شناس
تو درین راه معرفت غلطی　　سال و مه مانده در حدیث بطی
گوید آنکس درین مقام فضول　　که تجلی نداند او ز حلول

گرت باید که بر دهد دیدار   آینه کژ مدار و روشن دار
کافتابی که نیست نور دریغ   آبگینت نماید اندر میغ
یوسفی از فرشته نیکو تر   دیو روئی نماید از خنجر
حق ز باطل معاینه نکند   خنجرت کار آینه نکند
صورت خود در آینهٔ دل خویش   به توان دید ازان که در گلِ خویش
بگسل از سلسله که پیوستی   که ز گل دور چون شدي رستي
زانکه گل مظلمست و دل روشن   گل تو گلخن است و دل گلشن
هرچه از وی دلت مصفا تر   زو تجلي ترا مهيا تر
چون ز امت فزونش بود اخلاص   گشت بوبکر در تجلي خاص

فی جماعة العمیان و احوال الفیل

بود شهری بزرگ در حد غور   واندران شهر مردمان همه کور
بادشاهی بران مکان بگذشت   لشکر آورد و خیمه زد بر دشت
داشت پیلی بزرگ با هیبت   از پی جاه و حشمت و صولت
مردمان را ز بهر دیدن پیل   آرزو خاست ز انچنان تهویل
چند کور از میان آن کوران   برِ پیل آمدند چون عوران
تا بدانند شکل و صورت پیل   هر یکی تازیان دران تعجیل
آمدند و بدست بپسودند   زانکه از چشم بی بصر بودند
هر یکی را بلمس بر عضوی   اطلاع اوفتاد بر جزوی
هر یکی صورت محالی بست   دل و جان در پی خیالی بست
چون برِ اهل شهر باز شدند   بر شان دیگران فراز شدند
آرزو کرد هر یکی ز ایشان   آنچنان گمرهان و بدکیشان
هیئت و شکل پیل پرسیدند   وانچه گفتند جمله بشنیدند

آنکه دستش بسوی گوش رسید — دیگری حال پیل ازو پرسید
گفت شکلیست سهمناک عظیم — پهن و صعب و فراخ همچو گلیم
وانکه دستش رسید زی خرطوم — گفت گشتست مر مرا معلوم
راست چون ناودان میانه تهیست — سهمناکست و مایهٔ تبهیست
وانکه را بُد ز پیل ملموسش — دست و پای سطبر پر بوسش
گفت شکلش چنانکه مضبوطست — راست همچون عمود مخروطست
هر یکی دیده جزوی از اجزا — همگان را نظر فتاده خطا
هیچ را دل ز کلّی آگه نی — علم با هیچ کور همره نی
جملگی را خیالهای محال — کرده مانند غتفره بجوال
از خدائی خلائق آگه نیست — عقلا را درین سخن ره نیست

فی التمثیل

آن یکی رجل گفته دیگر ید — بیهده گفتها ببرده ز حد
وان دگر اصبعین و نقل و نزول — گفته و آمده براه حلول
وان یکی استوا و عرش و سریر — کرده در علم خویشتن تقدیر
وان بگفت از خوی قعد و جلس — بسته بر گردن از خیال جرس
وجه گفته یکی دگر قدمین — کس نگفته ورا که مَطْلَبُک اَیْن
زین همه گفت قال و قیل آمد — حال کوران و حال پیل آمد
جل ذکره منزه از چه و چون — انبیا را شده جگرها خون
عقل را زین حدیث پی کردند — علما را علوم طی کردند
همه بر عجز خود شدند مُقرّ — وای آنکو بجهل گشت مُصرّ
متشابه بخوان درو مآویز — وز خیالات بیهده بگریز
آنچه نص است جمله آمنّا — وانچه اخبار جمله سلّمنا

في اصحاب الغفلة

راد مردی ز غافلی پرسید   چون ورا سخت جلف و غافل دید
گفت هرگز تو زعفران دیدی   یا جز از نام ایچ نشنیدی
گفت با ماست خورده ام بسیار   صد ره و بیشتر نه خود یکبار
تا ورا گفت راد مرد حکیم   اینت بیچاره اینت قلب سلیم
تو بصل نیز هم نمیدانی   بیهده ریش چند جنبانی
آنکه او نفس خویش نشناسد   نفس دیگر کسی چه پرماسد
وانکه او دست و پای را داند   او چگونه خدای را داند
انبیا عاجزند ازین معنی   تو چرا هرزه میکنی دعوی
چون نمودی بدین سخن برهان   پس بدانی مجرد ایمان
ورنه او از کجا و تو ز کجا   خامشی به ترا تو ژاژ مخا
علما جمله هرزه میلافند   دین نه برپای هر کسی بافند

فی الدرجات

جانت را دوزخ آشیانه مکن   خاطرت را محال خانه مکن
گرد بیهوده و محال مگرد   بر در خانه خیال مگرد
از خیال محال دست بدار   تا بدان بارگه بیابی بار
کان سرای بقا برای تو است   وین سرای فنا نه جای تو است
آن سرای بقا تراست معد   یوم بگذار و جان کن از پی غد
در جهان زشت و نیکو و چپ و راست   ناخلف زادگان آدم راست
پایه بسیار سوی بام بلند   تو بیک پایه چون شوی خرسند
پایهٔ اول اندرو حلمست   کو بتحقیق خواجهٔ علمست
شده در دُم بدیگری پایه   خرد جان و صورت و مایه

تو حقیقت بدان که در عالم   از برای نتیجهٔ آدم
نیست از بهر آسمان ازل   نردبان پایه به ز علم و عمل
بهر بالا و شیب منزل را   حکمت جان قوی کند دل را
اندرین راه اگرچه آن نکنی   دست و پائی بزن زیان نکنی
هرکه او تخم کاهلی کارد   کاهلی کافریش بار آرد
هرکه با جهل و کاهلی پیوست   پایش از کار رفت و کار از دست
بتر از کاهلی ندانم چیز   کاهلی کرد رستمانرا حیز
از پی کارت آفریدستند   جامهٔ خلعتت بریدستند
تو بخلقان چرا شوی قانع   چون نگردی بدان حلل طامع
مِلک و مُلک از کجا بدست آری   چون مهی شست روز بیکاری
روز بیکاری و شب آسانی   بد رسی بر سریر ساسانی
تاج و تخت ملوک بی نم میغ   دستهٔ گرز دان و قبضهٔ تیغ
از پی سیم و طعمهٔ گردون   پیش مشتی خسیس ناکس دون
علم داری بحلم باش چو کوه   مشو از نایبات چرخ ستوه
علم بی حلم شمع بی نورست   هر دو باهم چو شهد زنبورست
شهد بی موم رمز احرارست   موم بی شهد بابت نارست
برگذر زین سرای کون و فساد   ببُر از معدن و برو بمعاد
کاندرین خاک تودهٔ بی آب   آتش آب پیکرست سراب
در دو عالم یکی کند صادق   سه سه منزل یکی کند عاشق

فی الحفظ و المراقبة

هرکرا عون حق حصار شود   عنکبوتیش پرده دار شود
سوسماری ثنای او گوید   اژدهائی رضای او جوید

نعل او فرق عرش را ساید   لعل او زیب فرش را شاید
زهر در کام او شکر گردد   سنگ در دست او گهر گردد
هرکه او سر برین ستانه نهد   پای بر تارک زمانه نهد
عقل داننده اندرین درماند   زانکه درماند هرکه زین درماند
ترسم از جاهلي و نادانی   ناگهان بر صراط درماني
جاهلي مر ترا بنار دهد   تا ترا کوک و کوکنار دهد
لقمه دیدي که مرد میخاید   زان میان گندمي برون آید
بوده پیش جراد و مرغ و ستور   دیده تاب خراس و تف تنور
داشته زیر آسیای تو پای   که نگهداشتش خدای خدای
از پی حفظ مال و نفس و نفس   او ترا بس تو کردهٔ زو بس
سگ و زنجیر چون بدست آري   آهوی دشت را شکست آري
پس برین اعتقاد و این اخلاص   از برای معاش و کسب خلاص
من بگویم ترا بعقل و بهوش   که نه بندي ز پند من در گوش
اعتماد تو بر سگ و زنجیر   بیش بینم که بر سمیع و بصیر
نور ایمانت را درین بنیاد   آهنی و سگی بغارت داد

التمثیل في قوم یوتون الزکوة

راد مردی حکیم پیش پسر   داد چندین هزار بدرهٔ زر
پسرش چون بدید بذل پدر   تر زبان شد بعیب و عذل پدر
گفت بابا نصیب من زین کو   گفت ای پور در خزانهٔ هو
قسم تو بی وصي و بی انباز   من بحق دادم او دهد بتو باز
اوست خود کارساز و مولی ما   او نه بس دین ما و دنیي ما
او بجز کارساز جانها نیست   نکند بر تو ظلم از آنها نیست

هر یکی را عوض دهد هفتاد   گر دری بست بر تو ده بگشاد

في سبب الرزق

آن نه بیني که پیشتر ز وجود   چون ترا کرد در رحم موجود
روزیت داد نُه مه از خونی   کردگار حکیم بیچونی
در شکم مادرت همي پرورد   بعد نه ماه در وجود آورد
آن در رزق چست بر تو ببست   دو در بهترت بداد بدست
بعد ازان الف داد با پستان   روز و شب پیش تو دو چشمه روان
گفت کین هر دوان همي آشام   کُل هنیأً که نیست بر تو حرام
چون نمودت فطام بعد دو سال   شد دگرگون ترا همه احوال
داد رزق تو از دو دست و دو پای   زین بگیر و ازان برو هر جای
گر دو در بر تو بسته کرد رواست   عوض دو چهار در بر جاست
زین ستان زان برو به پیروزي   گرد عالم همي طلب روزي
چون اجل ناگهان فراز آید   کار دنیا همه مجاز آید
باز ماند دو دست و پای از کار   بدل چار بدهدت ناچار
در لحد هر چهار بسته شود   هشت جنت ترا خجسته شود
هشت در بر تو باز بکشایند   حور و غلمان ترا به پیش آیند
تا به هر در چنانکه خواهي شاد   میروي ناوري ز دنیا یاد
ای جوانمرد نکتهٔ بشنو   وز عطای خدا نمید مشو
چون ترا داد معرفت یزدان   در درون دلت نهاد ایمان
خلعتی کان تراست همچو جهیز   نستاند بروز رستاخیز
گر ترا دانش و درم نبود   کو ترا بود هیچ کم نبود
او بفخر آردت نبیني عار   او عزیزت کند نگردي خوار

آنچه داري تو دل بدو مسپار آنچه او داد استوار آن در
تو خزینه نهي نه بیني باز چون بدو دادی او دهد بتو باز
زر بآتش دهي خبث سوزد زر صافي ترا بیفروزد
بد که او سوخت نیک داد بتو دولت از چرخ سر نهاد بتو
نفع آتش اگر مقیم ترست آتش آرا ازو کریم ترست
تو نداني نه نیک و نه بد را خازن او به ترا که تو خود را
یار مارست چون روي به درش مار یارست چون رمي ز برش
ای صدف جوی جوهر الّا جامه و جان بنه بساحل لا
هست حق جز به نیست نگراید زاد این راه نیستي باید
تا تو در نیستي کله ننهي روی را در بقا بره ننهي
چون شوي نیست سوی حق پوئي تا بوی هست راه دق جوئي
گرت هست زمانه پست کند احسن الخالقینت هست کند
خیز و بگذار قصه‌های محال از سر نفس شوم دع و تعال

فی الهدایة

هر هدایت که داري ای درویش هدیهٔ حق شمر نه کردهٔ خویش
سبب هدیهٔ ایادي او نفس را مهتدي و هادي او
در ره فرض و شرع و سنت خویش مِنّت حق شمر نه مُنّت خویش
نور بخش یقین و تلقین اوست هم جهانبان و هم جهانبین اوست
مهربانتر ز مادر و پدرست مر ترا او بخلد راهبرست
از پس کفر اهل دین مان کرد بسیاهي سپید بین مان کرد
منت کردگار هادي بین کادمي را ز جمله کرد گزین
حضرتش را برای ماده و نر بینیازی ز پیر و پیغمبر

کرده از بهر رهبری شش میر　گربهٔ را نبی سگی را پیر
هرکه آمد بدو و گوش آورد　خود نیامد که لطف اوش آورد
رهبرت لطف او تمام بود　چرخ ازان پس ترا غلام بود
هم ازو دان که جان سجود کند　کابر هم ز آفتاب جود کند

گرت باید که شسته گردد زه　اولا پوستین بگازر ده
پوستین باز کن که تا در شاه　پوستین در بسیست اندر راه
بنخستین قدم که زد آدم　پوستینش درید گرگ ستم
نه چو قابیل تشنه شد بجفا　داد هابیل پوستین بفنا
نه چو ادریس پوستین بفگند　در فردوس را ندید بند
چون خلیل از ستاره و مه و خور　پوستینها درید بی غم خور
شب او همچو روز روشن شد　نار نمرود باغ و گلشن شد
بسلیمان نگر که از سر داد　پوستین امل بگازر داد
جن و انس و طیور و مور و ملخ　در بن آب قلزم و سر شخ
روی او را همه رفیع شدند　امر او را همه مطیع شدند
ز آتش دل چو سوخت آب نهاد　خاک بر دوش باد چرخ نهاد
چون کلیم کریم غم پرورد　رخ بمدین نهاد با غم و درد
پوستین را ز روی مزدوری　بر کشید از نهاد رنجوری
کرد ده سال چاکری شعیب　تا کشادند بر دلش در غیب
دست او همچو چشم بینا شد　تاج بر فرق آل سینا شد
روح چون دم ز بحر روحانی　زد و پذرفت لطف ربانی
پوستین را باولین منزل　بفرستاد سوی گازر دل

دل او را فر الهی داد   هم بخردیش پادشاهی داد
گشت بی او بقدرت ازلی   از ثنای خفی و لطف جلی
تن ابرص ازو چو سایهٔ فرش   چشم اکمه ازو چو پایهٔ عرش
هرکه چون او نه نام جوید و ننگ   از یکی خم بر آورد ده رنگ
سنگ با او چو مشک شد بویا   زنده کردار مردگان گویا
گل دل را ز لطف جان سر کرد   دل گل را ز دست جانور کرد
چون دکانها بمهر کرد قضا   دست تقدیر در نشیب فنا
ماند عالم پر از هوا و هوس   گشته بازار پر عوان و عسس
شحنهٔ را ز بهر دفع ستم   بفرستاد اندر این عالم
چون شد از آسمان دل ظاهر   هم بجان مست و هم بتن طاهر
پوستین خود نداشت در ره دین   پس چه دادی بگازران زمین
از فنا چون سوی بقا آمد   زینت و زیب این فنا آمد

فی التقدیس

خلق را ذات چون نماید او   بکدام آینه در آید او
بار توحید هر کسی نکشد   طعم توحید هر کسی نچشد
هست در هر مکان خدا معبود   نیست معبود در مکان محدود
مرد جسمی ز راه گمراه ست   کفر و تشبیه هر دو همراه ست
در ره صدق نفس را بگذار   خیز و زین نفس شوم دست بدار
چون برون آمدی ز جان و ز جای   پس به بینی خدایرا بخدای
چون پرستد تن گران اورا   کی شناسد روان و جان اورا
سنگ پاره ست لعل کان آنجا   بوالفضولست فضل جان آنجا
بی زبانی ثنا زبان تو بس   هرزه گوئی غم و زیان تو بس

ذات او سوی عارف و عالم برتر از کیف و ما و از هل و لم
صنع او عدل حکمت ست و جلي قهر او مکر عزت ست و خفي
پیکر آب و گل ز شوقش عور لعبت چشم و دل ز کنهش کور
عقل آلوده از پی دیدار اَرِنی گوی گشته موسی وار
چون برون آمد از تجلي پیگ گفت در گوش او که تُبتُ الیک

صفت ذات او بعلم بدان نام پاکش هزار و یک برخوان
وصف او زیر علم نیکو نیست هرچه در گوشت آمد آن او نیست
نقطه و خط و سطح بر صفتش هست چون جسم و بعد و شش جهتش
مبدع آن سه از ورای مکان خالق این سه از برون زمان
هیچ عاقل درو نداند عیب او بداند درون عالم غیب

مطّلع بر ضمائر و اسرار نوز نا کرده بر دل تو گذار
کاف و نون نیست جز نبشتهٔ ما چیست کن سرعت نفوذ قضا
نه ز عجز ست دیري و زودیش نه ز نصب ست خشم و خشنودیش
علتش را نه کفر داند و دین صفتش را نه آن شناسد و این
پاک ازانها که غافلان گفتند پاکتر زانکه عاقلان گفتند

عقل باشد بخلط وهم محیط هر دو آن لنگ بر بساط بسیط
وهم و خاطر دلیل نیکو نیست هرکجا وهم و خاطرست او نیست
وهم و خاطر ز آفریدهٔ اوست آدم و عقل نو رسیدهٔ اوست
زانکه اثبات رنگ او برنیست همچو اثبات مادر اعمیست
داند اعمی که مادري دارد لیک چوني بوهم در نارد

وهم او فارغ ست از چونی زشت و نیکو درون و بیرونی
در چنین عالمی که رویش دو زشت باشد تو او بوی او تو

گر نگوئي بد و نکو نبود   ور بگوئي تو باشي او نبود
گر ندانی ز دین تهي باشي   ور بگوئي مشبّهي باشي
چون برون از کجا و کی بود او   گوشهٔ خاطر تو کی شود او
راه جویان چو سوی او پویند   آنک آنک بهرزه میگویند
باز مردان چو فاختـه در کوی   طوق در گردنند کوکو گوی
خواهي امید گبر و خواهي بیم   هیچ برهرزه نافرید حکیم
عالمست او بهرچه کرد و کند   تو ندانی بدانت درد کند
به ز تسلیم نیست در علمش   تا بدانی حکیمي و حلمش
خلق را داده از حکیمي خویش   هر کرا بیش حاجت آلت بیش
همه را داده آلتی در خور   از پی جرّ نفع و دفع ضرر
در جهان آنچه رفت وانچ آید   وانچه هست آنچنان همي باید
تو مگو در میانه هیچ فضول   راندهٔ او بدیده کن تو قبول

فی المجاهدة

چون تو از بود خویش گشتي نیست   کمر دل ببند و در ره ایست
چون کمر بسته ایستادي تو   تاج بر فرق دل نهادي تو
تاج اقبال بر سر دل نِه   پای ادبار بر خور گل نِه
گرچه غافل برین عمل خندد   لیک عاقل جزین به نپسندد
تو مر آنرا که رخ بحق نارد   بت شمر هرچه داند و دارد
روی برتافته ز حضرت حق   من نگویم که مردم است الحق
سگ به از ناکسی که روی بتافت   زانکه ناجسته سگ شکار نیافت
سگ کهدانی ارچه فربه شد   نه ز تازی بکارها به شد
رزق و تلبیس و مخرقه نخرد   سوی توحید و صدق بنگرد

دیدهٔ عقل بین گزیند حق　　دیدهٔ رنگ بین نبیند حق
باطلست آنچه دیده آراید　　حق در اوهام آب و گل ناید
کفر و دین از دل دو رنگي تست　　راه دور از پی درنگي تست
ورنه یک خطوتست راه بدو　　بنده باشي شوي تو شاه بدو
لقب رنگها مجازي دان　　خور ز دریای بینیازي دان
گفت بگذار و گرد گرد برای　　بندهای گران ز خود بکشای
ذوق ایمان مگر چشیده نهٔ　　روی تحقیق و صدق دیده نهٔ
تا ترا رمز واضحات آمد　　واضحاتت مغیبات آمد
در تو رشدی همي نمي بینم　　ورنه من صبح صادق دینم
راه دین بر تو کردمی پیدا　　گر نبودی تو اهوج و شیدا

مرد باید که چون خلیل بود　　تا ز حق ظل او ظلیل بود
زهره دارد زمانه کز بیمش　　یک نفس بر زند به تعلیمش
موسیٔ را که حق ورا عونست　　فرّعونش هلاک فرعونست
خود ز رخسار اوست صبح شفق　　در ره عشق پیش رهرو حق
روز که بود که پرده در باشد　　شب که باشد که پرده گر باشد
دلش از بند ملک بربایند　　ملکوت جهانش بنمایند
عرش چون فرش زیر پای آرد　　چغد باشد ولی همای آرد
خواجهٔ این و آن سرای شود　　بندهٔ مخلص خدای شود
مرد را عقل روی بنماید　　تنش از نور خود بیاراید
لطف حق سایه اش افگند بر دل　　پس بگوید که کیف مدّ الظل
چون ز حق جان او بیابد لمس　　روی بنمایدش جعلنا الشمس

از درونش چو بوی جان یابند   بی‌زبانان همه زبان یابند
در رهش خوانده عاشقان برجان   آیهٔ کُلُّ من علیها فان
پیش بنمایدش بحسّ زبون   فلک و طبع و رنگ بوقلمون
هرکرا توبه زین شراب دهند   بوی و رنگش همه بآب دهند
تا ازان نعره‌ها بگوش نوی   وحده لا شریک له شنوی
بیش سودای رنگها نپزی   گر کند عیسی تو رنگرزی
هرچه خواهی ز رنگ برداری   در یکی خم زنی برون آری
بحقیقت شنو نه از سر جهل   نیست این نکته بابت نا اهل
کین همه رنگهای پر نیرنگ   خم وحدت کند همه یکرنگ
پس چو یکرنگ شد همه او شد   رشته باریک شد چو یکتو شد

راه دین صنعت و عبارت نیست   جز خرابی درو عمارت نیست
هرکه گشت از برای راه خموش   سخن او حیات باشد و نوش
گر بگوید ز جاهلی نبود   ور نگوید ز کاهلی نبود
در خموشی نه بوده لهو اندیش   گاه گفتن نه بوده لغو پریش
آن سفیهان که دزد و طرارند   عقل را بهر ره زدن دارند
دیدی ای خواجهٔ سخن فربه   که ترا در دل از سخن فربه
چون تو گشتی خموش منطیقی   ور بگوئی بسان بطریقی
کن دو حرفست بی نوا هر دو   هو دو حرفست بی هوا هر دو
تو درین گفت من مدار شکی   باز کن دیده بر گمار یکی

سگ و سنگست گلخنی و رهی   تو چو لعل از درون حقه بهی

سیم بهر هزینه دارد شاه   لعل بهر خزینه دارد شاه
سیم بد از نهاد وازون ست   لعل شاد از درون پر خون ست

آل برمک ز جود کس گشتند   با سخاوت چو همنفس گشتند
نام ایشان چو روح باقي ماند   ورچه گردون فنای ایشان خواند
قوم این روزگار گرچه خوشند   چون مگس شوخ چشم و دیده کشند
بسخن چون شکر همه نوشند   بسخا دلدرند و جانجوشند

چون ترا از درون دل بنگاشت   آینه نور پیش تو برداشت
تا ترا کبر تیز خشم نکرد   تا ترا چشم تو بچشم نکرد

روز و شب را بمسطر انصاف   تسویت داده نه بهرج و گزاف

تا کند عقل از پی رازي   گرد میدان عشق پردازي

دل و جانش نهفته شد حق جوی   شد زبانش بحق انا الحق گوی

التمثیل في اصحاب الغفلة

ابلهی دید اشتری بچرا   گفت نقشت همه کژست چرا
گفت اشتر که اندرین پیکار   عیب نقاش میکني هش دار
در کژی ام مکن بعیب نگاه   تو ز من راه راست رفتن خواه
نقشم از مصلحت چنان آمد   کز کژي راستي کمان آمد
تو فضول از میانه بیرون بر   گوش خر در خورست با سر خر

هست شایسته گرچت آید خشم طاق ابرو برای جفتهٔ چشم
چشم خورشید بین ز ابرو شد چهره ساز از بهار نیرو شد
زشت و نیکو بنزد اهل خرد سخت نیک ست ازو نیاید بد
آن نکوتر که هرچه زو بینی گرچه زشت آن همه نکو بینی
جسم را قسم راحت آمد و رنج روح را راحت ست همچو گنج
لیک مارشکنج بر سر اوست دست و پای خرد برابر اوست

التمثیل بعین الاحول

پسر احول از پدر پرسید کای حدیث تو بسته را چو کلید
گفتی احول یکی دو بیند چون من نه بینم از آنچه هست فزون
احول ار هیچ کژ شمارستی بر فلک مه که دوست چارستی
پس خطا گفت آنکه این گفتست کاحول ار طاق بنگرد جفتست
ترسم اندر طریق شارع دین همچنانی که احول کژ بین
یا چو ابله که با شتر پیکار کرد بیهوده از پی کردار
قبلهٔ عقل صنع بی خللش کعبهٔ شوق ذات بی بدلش
روح را از خرد شرف او داد عفو را از گنه علف او داد
نیک داند خدای انابت را حکمتش مانعست اجابت را
گرچه باشد که سوال مجیب ندهد گِل بگِل خورنده طبیب
گُل عمر کسی که گِل کاهد کی دهد گِلش اگرچه دل خواهد
کی شود بی سبب نمودهٔ او بودهٔ حق چو عقل بودهٔ تو
سخت بسیار کس بود که خورد قدح زهر صرف و زان نمرد
بلکه اورا غذای جان باشد که ز بحران چو خیزران باشد
همه را از طریق حکمت و داد آنچه بایست بیش ازان همه داد

پیل را پشّه گر بدرّد پوست   گو بران گوش پشه ران با اوست
سپش ار هست ناخفت هم هست   کیک را گوش مال چون برجست
کوه اگر پر ز مار شد مشکوه   سنگ و تریاک هست هم در کوه
ور ز کژدم بدل گمان داري   کفش و نعل از برای آن داري
درد در عالم ار فراوان ست   هر یکی را هزار درمان ست
درهم آویخت از پی تصویر   کرهٔ زمهریر و گوی اثیر
معتدل گشت جنبش گل را   سردی مغز و گرمي دل را
جگر و دل ز معده و شریان   سوی تن آب و باد کرده روان
تا جسد را بواسطهٔ دم و خون   جان دهد این بجنبش آن بسکون
ملکوتست و ملک در عالم   زبر تخت نور و تحت ظلم
کرد بخش این دو مایه را در صنع   چون بگسترد سایه را بر صنع
ملک از بهر لطف جانرا داد   ملکوت از شرف روان را داد
تا درون و برون پذیرد قوت   تن ز ذی الملک وجان ز ذی الملکوت
هست حق را ز بهر جان شریف   اندر اثنای صنع لطف لطیف
داند آنکس که خورده دان باشد   کانچه او کرد خیرت آن باشد
سوی تو نام زشت و نام نکوست   ورنه محض عطاست هرچه ازوست
بد ازو در وجود خود ناید   بغدائی بد از کجا شاید
بد بجز جلف و بیخرد نکند   خود نکوکار هیچ بد نکند
نوش دان هرچه زهر او باشد   لطف دان هرچه قهر او باشد
باشد از مادران ما برما   هم حجامت نکو و هم خرما

ایضاً التمثیل في اصحاب الغفلة

آن نه بیني که طفل را دایه   گاه خردي باولین پایه

گاه بندد ورا به گهواره   گاه بو بر نهدش همواره
گه زند صعب و گاه بنوازد   گاه دورش کند بیندازد
گاه بوسد بمهر رخسارش   گاه بنوازد و کشد بارش
مرد بیگانه چون نگاه کند   خشم گیرد ز دایه آه کند
گویدش نیست مهربان دایه   بر او هست طفل کم مایه

تو چه داني که دایه به داند   شرط کار آنچنان همي ماند
بنده را نیز کردگار بشرط   میگذارد بجمله کار بشرط
آنچه باید همي دهد روزي   گاه حرمان و گاه پیروزي
گاه برسر نهد ز گوهر تاج   گه بدانگی ورا کند محتاج
تو بحکم خدای راضي شو   ورنه بخروش و پیش قاضي شو

تا ترا از قضاش برهاند   ابله آنکس که اینچنین داند
هرچه هست از بلا و عافیتی   خیر محض است و شر عاریتی
آنکه آرد جهان بکن فیکون   چون کند بد بخلق عالم چون
خیر و شر نیست درجهان سخن   لقب خیر و شر بتست و بمن
آنزمان کایزد آفرید آفاق   هیچ بد نافرید بر اطلاق

مرگ اینرا هلاک و آنرا برگ   زهر اینرا غذا و آنرا مرگ
آینه همچو پشت روی سیاه   گر بدي کس نکرد ایچ نگاه
ز آینه روی را هنر باشد   گرچه پشتش پر از گهر باشد
آینه روی به بود خورشید   پشت خواهي سیاه و خواه سفید
پای طاوس اگرچه پر بودی   بشب و روز جلوه گر بودی

في صفة قدرته

نقشبند برون گِلها اوست   نقش دان درون دلها اوست

مبدع هست وانچه نا هست او صانع دست وانچه در دست او
ساخت دولابي از زبرجد ناب كوزهٔ سيمين ببست بر دولاب
كرد در راه نا جوانمردان در هوا شمع و شمعدان گردان
صنع اورا مقدّم است عدم ذات او را مسلّم است قِدم
عقل را كرده قائل سَورت مايه را كرده قابل صورت
عقل را داده راه بيداري تو همي عقل را چه پنداري
كی تواند نگاشت در آدم نقشبند قلم نگار قدم
آتش و باد و آب و خاك و فلك زبرش عقل و جان ميانه ملك
خرد و جان و صورت مطلق همه از امر دان و امر از حق
اوست نيرنگ و مايهٔ پركار نعمت و شكر و شكر گوی نگار
كرده در شه ره معاش و معاد فعل و قوت قرين كون و فساد
قدرتش كرده در جهان سخن قوتی را بفعلی آبستن
هرچه آيد بفعل جايش را هرچه در قوت ست زايش را

فی الامثال والمواعظ والفقر سواد الوجه ذكر الامثال خير المقال والدنيا دار الزوال وتغير الامور والانتقال

با سيه باش چونت نگزيرد كه سيه هيچ رنگ نپذيرد
با سيه روی خوشدلي بهم ست طرب انگيز سرخ روی كم ست
پيش آن آتشی كه دلجويست طالب سوخته سيه رويست
زنگي زشت با بلا جوي خوشدلي يافت از سيه روي
طرب او نه از نكوئي اوست خوشدلي او از مشكبوي اوست
هست روشنتر از ضياى هلال كشف حال هلال كفش بلال
راز دل گر همي نخواهي فاش با سيه روی در دو عالم باش

زانکه آنرا که آرزو طلب ست   پرده در روز و پرده دار شب ست
زین هوسهای هرزه دست بدار   آرزو زهر دان و معده چو مار
افعی آرزو گرت بگزد   با تو این رنگها بسی نپزد
که بدین راه در بدی نیکیست   آب حیوان درون تاریکیست
دل ز رنگ سیه چه غم دارد   زانکه شب روز در شکم دارد
زانکه مردان درین کهن خانه   نو گرفتند بی دم و دانه
چون به باغ خدای بگرازند   هرچه تلقین بود بیندازند
هرچه جز حق هرانچه با طین ست   جز طریق حقیقت دین ست
بیخودی منتهای راز همه ست   مرجع روح پاک با کلمه ست
ای که فرش زمان نوشتستی   وی که از چار و نه گذشتستی
بگذر از جان و عقل یکباری   تا بفرمان حق رسی باری
می نبینی ازانکه شبکوری   روز چون عقل ابلهان عوری
من بگویم ترا سخن نه بغمز   لیکن از راه حق بنکته و رمز
تا ز باطل به نگذری حق نیست   که ازین نیمه حق مطلق نیست
از پی زاد راه عالم حی   زور لا خیر دان و زر لا شی
هست لا خیر زور زرداران   همچو لا شی عقل میخواران

فی الفقر الی الله و الاستغنا عمن سواه

از من و از تو کارسازی را   بی زیانیست بی نیازی را
بی نیازیش را چه کفر و چه دین   بی زیانیش را چه آن و چه این
بحقیقت بدان که هست خدای   از پی حکم و حکمت بسزای
بی نیازی نیاز جوی از تو   پاسداری سپاس گوی از تو
گرگ و یوسف به تست خرد و بزرگ   ورنه زی او یکیست یوسف و گرگ

لطف اورا چه مانعی و چه عون / قهر اورا چه موسی و فرعون
طاعت و معصیت ترا ننگست / ورنه زی او برنگ یکرنگست
چه عزیزی ز عقل و برخ اورا / چه بزرگی ز نفس و چرخ اورا
نفس و افلاک آفریدهٔ اوست / خنک آنکس که برگزیدهٔ اوست
چرخ و آنکس که چرخ گردان ست / آسیا هست و آسیابان ست

حکم فرمان و عقل فرمان گیر / نفس نقاش و طبع نقش پذیر
جنبش چرخ بی سکون و زمین / هست چون مور در دم تنّین
مور را اژدها فرو نبرد / گردش چرخ بیخبر گذرد
بیخبروار در مشیمهٔ لا / کرده برکار آسیای بلا
عمر تو دانه دار در دم او / سور او همنشین ماتم او

نزد تست آنکه از پی شو و آی / کاسهٔ تو چهار دارد پای
جز بفضلش براه او نرسی / ورچه در طاعتش قوی نفسی
کی بعقل و بدست و پای رسد / بنده خواهد که در خدای رسد
آنکه در خود بدست و پای رسد / کی تواند که در خدای رسد

فی التضرع والخشوع

از تو زاری نکوست زور بدست / عور زنبور خانه شور بدست
زور بگذار و گِرد زاری گرد / تا ز فرق هوا برآری گرد
زانکه داند خدای کز سر حق / از تو زور است زُور و زاری صدق
چون تو دعوی زور و زر داری / دیده را کور و گوش کر داری
روی و زر سرخ و جامه رنگارنگ / نام تو ننگ جوی و صلح تو جنگ

بر در حق بگرد زور مگرد / که بزاری شوی درین ره مرد
این نه از نام توختن باشد / که نیازی فروختن باشد

قدرتش را بچشم عجز مبین　　خواجه آزار کن مباش چنین
تا بخود قائمي بپوش و بخور　　ور بدو قائمي مدوز و مدر
هرچه هست ای عزیز هست از وی　　بود تو چون بهانه یاره مگوی
بی توگل مسجد ست و با تو کنشت　　با تو دل دوزخ ست و بی تو بهشت
بی تو خود کارها همه کرده است　　با تو چون کُرّهٔ نه پرورده است
تو توی مهر و کین ازان آمد　　تو توی کفر و دین ازان آمد
بندهٔ باش بی نصیبه و چیر　　که فرشته نه گرسنه است و نه سیر
از تو بیم و اُمید دولت راند　　چون تو رفتي امید و بیم نماند
بوم کو گرد کاخ شه گردد　　شوم و بد روز و پر گنه گردد
چون قناعت کند بویران جای　　پر او به بود که فرّ همای
زاب و آتش زیان پذیرد مشک　　نافهٔ مشک را چه تر و چه خشک
چه مسلمان چه گبر بر درِ او　　چه کنشت و چه صومعه برِ او
گبر و ترسا و نیکو و معیوب　　همگان طالبند و او مطلوب
نیست علت پذیر ذات خدای　　تو بعلت کنون چه جوئي جای
مهر دین بر نیاید از تلقین　　مه فرو شد چو تافت نور یقین
پارسا گر به است او را به　　پادشا گر بد است ما را چه
تو نکوکار باش تا برهي　　با قضا و قدر چرا ستهي
اندر این منزلی که یک هفته است　　بوده نا بوده وامده رفته است
لفظ یسعی بخوان که اندر نشر　　طرقوا گوی مومن است بحشر
مصطفی گفت خه ازان مه شد　　دست موسی خلیل آوّه شد
واو اوّه وفای دینش داد　　رتبت و زینت یقینش داد
پس چو واو از میان اوّه رفت　　ماند آه مجرد اینت شگفت

آه ماندست یادگاري ازو　　ملت او نمودکاري ازو
پیش تا صور در دهد آواز　　خویشتن را بکش به تیغ نیاز
گر پذیرند گشتي آسوده　　ورنه انکار بوده نابوده
بر در بی نیازي از که و مه　　گر تو باشي و گر نه اورا چه
روز بهر خروس کی پاید　　چون بود وقت خود برون آید
چه وجودت بنزد او چه عدم　　مثل تو بر درش نیاید کم
چون برون تاخت چشمهٔ روشن　　حاجتی نایدش به مقرعه زن
این همه طمطراق آب و گل ست　　ورنه آنجا که محض جان و دل ست
چه کند طرقواء مشتي خس　　طرقوا گوی نور خویشتن بس
آن چراغ ترا به تست امید　　خود بر آید بتافتن خورشید
صرصر این شمع را به نفشاند　　جان او نیم عطسه بستاند
پس درین کوچه نیست راه شما　　راه اگر هست هست آه شما
همه از راه بندگي دورید　　چون خران سال و ماه مغرورید
چون تو گه نیک باشي و گه بد　　ترست از خود بود امید بخود
پس چو شد روی عقل و شرم سپید　　رو تو یکسان شمار بیم و امید

فی عدل الامیر و امن الرعایا

کرد روزی عمر به رهگذری　　سوی جوقی ز کودکان نظری
همه مشغول گشته در بازي　　کرده هر یک همي سرافرازي
هر یکی از پی مصارعتی　　مینمودی ز خود مسارعتي
بر کشیده برای خط ادب　　جامه از سر برون برسم عرب
چون عمر سوی کودکان نگرید　　حشمتش پردهٔ طرب بدرید
کودکان زو گریختند بتفت　　جز که عبد اللّه زبیر نرفت

گفت عمر ز پیش من بچه فن   تو بنگریختي بگفتا من
چه گریزم ز پیشت ای مکرم   نه تو بیدادگر نه من مجرم
میر چون جفت دین و داد بود   خلق را دل ز عدل شاد بود
ور بود رای او سوی بیداد   ملک خود داد سر بسر برباد
چون گرفتي ز عدل توشهٔ خویش   مرکب تو بود دو منزل بیش
نزد آنکس که دید جوهر خود   چه قبول و چه رد چه نیک و چه بد
نیک باشي ز درد سر رستي   ور بدي جمله عهد بشکستي
آنچنان شو ز حیرت دادش   که دگر یاد ناید از یادش

فی التسبیح و التهلیل

ذکر بر دوستان و کم سخنان   چه شماري بسان پیر زنان
جور با حکم او همه داد ست   عمر بی یاد او همه باد ست
آنکه گریان ازوست خندان اوست   دل که بی یاد اوست سندان اوست
شدي ایمن چو نام او بردي   در طریقت قدم بیفشردي
تو بیادش چو گل زبان کن تر   تا دهانت کند چو گل پر زر
سیر جان کرد جان بخورد را   تشنه دل کرد عاشق خود را
یک زمان از درش مشو غائب   تا بود عزم و رای تو صائب
کار نادان کوته اندیش ست   یاد کرد کسی که در پیش ست

فی المرید الرشید و الشیخ العمید

ثَوری از بایزید بسطامي   از پی طاعت و نکونامي
کرد نیکو سوالی و بگریست   گفت پیرا بگو که ظالم کیست
پیر وی مر ورا جواب بداد   شربت وی هم از کتاب بداد
گفت ظالم کسی ست بد روزی   که یکی لحظه در شبانروزی

کند از غافلي فراموشش　　نبود بنده حلقه در گوشش
گر فراموش کردیش نفسی　　ظالمی نیست خیره چونتو کسی
رو بوی حاضر و بري نامش　　نیست گردی ز جزم احکامش
آنچنان یاد کن که از دل و جان　　نشوي غافل از زمان بزمان
یاد دار این سخن ازان بیدار　　مرد این راه حیدر کرّار
فاعبد الرّب في الصّلوة تراه　　ور نباشي چنین تو وا غوثاه
آنچنانش پرست در کونین　　که همي بینیش برای العین
گرچه چشمت ورا نمیبیند　　خالق تو ترا همي بیند
ذکر جز در ره مجاهده نیست　　ذکر در مجلس مشاهده نیست
رهبرت اول ارچه یاد بود　　رسد آنجا که یاد باد بود
زانکه غواص از درون بحار　　آب جوید کشد هم آبش زار
فاخته غائب ست گوید کو　　تو اگر حاضري چه گوئي هو
حاضران را ز هیبت ست منال　　گر ترا حصه غیبت ست بنال
نالهٔ شوق فاخته بشنو　　حالت ذوق ساخته بدو جو
کانکه خوشنودی احد جوید　　نور توحید در لحد جوید
لحدش روضهٔ بهشت شود　　در دو چشمش بهشت زشت شود
حاضر آنگه شوي که در مامن　　حاضر دل بوی نه حاضر تن
تا درین خطهٔ تگاپوئي　　یا همه پشت یا همه روئي
چون ازین خطه یکدو خطوت رفت　　جان طالب عنان عشق گرفت
مردگي کفر و زندگي دین ست　　هرچه گفتند مغز آن این ست
هرکه شد لحظهٔ ز خود خشنود　　سالها بند شد بدوزخ و دود
کی بدین اصل و منصب ارزانیست　　جز کسی کش سر مسلمانیست

عشق و آهنگ آنجهان کردن   شرط نبود حدیث جان کردن
آنکسانی که مرد این راه اند   از غم جان و دل نه آگاه اند
چون گذشتی ز عالم تگ‌وپوی   چشمهٔ زندگانی آنجا جوی

في دار الغرور

اجل آمد کلید خانهٔ راز   در دین بی اجل نگردد باز
تا بود این جهان نباشد آن   تا تو باشي نباشدت یزدان
حقهٔ سربمهر دان جانت   مهرهٔ مهر نور ایمانت
سابقت نامهٔ بمهر آورد   وز پی تو بخاتمت بسپرد
تا ز دور زمانه خواهي زیست   تو نداني که اندر آن جا چیست
سحي نامه خدای عز و جل   بر نگیرد مگر که دست اجل
تا دم آدمي ز تو نرمد   صبح دینت ز شرق جان ندمد
سرد و گرم زمانه نا خورده   نرسي بر در سراپرده
تو نداري خبر ز عالم غیب   باز نشناسي از هنرها عیب
حال آنجای صورتی نبود   چون دگر کار عادتی نبود
جان بحضرت رسد بیاساید   وانچه کژّ است راست بنماید
چون رسیدی بحضرت فرمان   پس از آنجا روانه گردد جان
رخش دین آشنای راغ شود   مرغوار از قفص بباغ شود
با حیات تو دین برون ناید   شب مرگ تو روز دین زاید
گفت مرد خرد درین معنی   که سخنهای اوست چون فتوی
خفته اند آدمي ز حرص و غلو   مرگ چون رخ نمود فانتبهوا
خلق عالم همه بخواب درند   همه در عالم خراب درند
آن هوائی که بیش ازین باشد   رسم و عادت بود نه دین باشد

ورنه دینی کزین حیات بود　　دین نباشد که ترّهات بود
دین و دولت در عدم زدنست　　کم زدن از برای کم شدنست
آنکه کم زد وجود عالم را　　گو ببین مصطفی و آدم را
وانکه او طالب ست افزون را　　گو ببین عاد را و قارون را
این یکی پای در رکیب بماند　　وان دگر خستهٔ نهیب بماند
پای آنرا قدم عدم کرده　　دست اینرا ندم قلم کرده
باد هیبت بعاد مقرون ست　　خاک لعنت سرای قارون ست
چه زیان دارد ار ز بیم گزند　　نیکوئی را فدی شوی چو سپند
پیش مردان راه رخ مفروز　　خویشتن را تو چون سپند بسوز
خرد و دین سرسری داری　　گر تو با حق سرسری داری
مرد گرد نهاد خود نه تند　　شیر صندوق خویش خود شکند
ای ز خود سیر گشته جوع آنست　　وی دوتا از ندم رکوع آنست
کز تن و جان خود بری گردی　　گرد تنهای و سری گردی
ایچ منمای روی شهر افروز　　چون نمودی برو سپند بسوز
آن جمال تو چیست مستی تو　　وان سپند تو چیست هستی تو
لب چو بر آستان دین باشد　　عیسی مریم آستین باشد
خویشتن را درین طلب بگداز　　در ره صدق جان و دل در باز
جهد کن تا ز نیست هست شوی　　وز شراب خدای مست شوی
باشد آنرا که دین کند هستش　　گوی و چوگان دهر در دستش
چون ازین جرعه گشت جان تو مست　　بر بلندی ز نیست گردی هست
هرکه آزاد کرد آنجای است　　حلقه در گوش و بند بر پای است
لیکن آن بند به که مرکب بخت　　لیکن آن حلقه به که حُلّه و تخت

بنده کو برنهد تو تاج شمر   ور پلاست دهد دواج شمر
زانکه هم محسن ست و هم مجمل   زانکه هم مکرم ست و هم مفضل
چه کنی بهر بینوای را   شادي و زیرک بهای را
شاد ازو باش و زیرک از دینش   تا بیابي رضا و تمکینش
زیرک آنست کوش بردارد   شادي آنست کوش نگذارد
نیکبخت آنکسی که بندۀ اوست   در همه کارها پسندۀ اوست
چون ازین شاخها شدي بی برگ   دستها در کمر زدي با مرگ
نشوي مرگ را دگر منکر   یابي از عالم حیات خبر
دست تو چون بشاخ مرگ رسید   پای تو گرد کاخ برگ دوید
پای کز طارم هدی دور ست   نیست پای آن دماغ مخمور ست

فی الشّکر

موضع کفر نیست جز درِ رنج   مرجع شکر نیست جز سر گنج
شکر گوی از پی زیادت را   عالم الغیب و الشهادت را
چون شدي بر قضای وی صابر   خواند آنگاه مر ترا شاکر
آدمي سوی حق همي پوید   او نگوید که شکر حق گوید
شکّر شکر او که بپذیرفت   گوهر ذکر او که داند سفت
او ببخشد هم او ثواب دهد   او بگوید هم او جواب دهد
هرچه بستد ز نعمت و نازت   به ازان یا همان دهد بازت
گر همه مویها زبان گردند   بر در شکر ترجمان گردند
تا بدان شکر او فزون گویند   شکر توفیق شکر چون گویند
پس سوی شکر نعمتش پویند   گر بگویند هم بدو گویند
تن و جان از پی قضا در شکر   دل ترنم کنان که یا رب شکر

ورنه در راه دانش و تدبیر   از زن و مرد وز جوان وز پیر
کور چشمان عالم هوس اند   عور جسمان چو مور و چون مگس اند

فی القهر و اللطف

شاکر لطف و رحمتش دیندار   شاکي قهر و غیرتش کفّار
بیني آنگه که گیرد ایزد خشم   آنچه در چشمه باید اندر چشم
قهر و لطفش که در جهان نویست   تهمت گبر و شبهت ثنویست
لطف و قهرش نشان منبر و دار   شکر و شکرش مقام مفخر و عار
لطف او راحت است جانها را   قهر او آتشی روانها را
لطف او بنده را سرور دهد   قهر او مرد را غرور دهد
لام لطفش چو روی بنماید   دال دولت دوال بربايد
قاف قهرش اگر برون تازد   قاف را همچو سیم بگدازد
عالم از قهر و مکر او ترسان   صالح و طالح از فزع یکسان
لطف او چون مفرح آمیزد   کفش صوفي بکشف برخیزد
باز قهرش چو آید اندر کار   کشْف سر درکشد کَشَف کردار
قهر او نازنین گدازنده   لطف او بینوا نوازنده
کفر و دین پرور روان تو اوست   اختیار آفرین جان تو اوست
جان جانت ز لطف او زنده است   که روانت بلطف پاینده است
آرد از قهر و لطف سازنده   زنده از مرده مرده از زنده
دانش او رهی رعایت کن   بخشش او مهم کفایت کن
کشت قهرش چو آمد اندر جنگ   باشهٔ ملک را به پشهٔ لنگ
باز چون اسپ لطف را زین کرد   لقمهٔ کرم را ملخ چین کرد
خود از او نزد عقل و رای رزین   کرم سیمین بود ملخ زرّین

در عطا چون بلای مُبلی دید	با بلا در عطا همی خندید
قهر او چون بگستراند دام	سگی آرد ز صورت بلعام
لطف او چون در آمد اندر کار	سگ اصحاب کهف برد بغار
سحره از لطف گفت اَنْ لاَّ ضَیْرَ	با عزازیل قهر کرد انا خیر
با خدا ایچ نیک و بد بس نیست	با که گویم که در جهان کس نیست
چه سوی ناکسان چه سوی کسان	قهر و لطفش به هرکه هست رسان
خسروان در رهش کله بازان	گُردنان بر درش سر اندازان
پادشاهان چو خاک بر در او	برمیده فراغنه از بر او
بیکی ترک غول نو بَرده	صد هزاران علم نگون کرده
فرش مشتی گرسنه بنوشته	چاکرش از یکی دوتا گشته
گر بگوید به مردهٔ که بر آی	مرده آید کفن کشان در پای
ور بگوید به زندهٔ که بمیر	مُرد در حال ورچه باشد میر
خلق مغرور نفس از افضالش	هیچ ترسان نبوده ز امهالش
هرکه در ملک او منی کرده	از ره راست توسنی کرده
گردنان را طعام زهرش بس	سرکشان را لگام قهرش بس
گردن گردنان شکسته به قهر	ضعفا را ز لطف داده دو بهر
سرعت عفوش از ره گفتار	برگرفتست رسم استغفار
تائب الذنب را بداده پناه	پاک کرده صحائفش ز گناه
عفو او بر گنه سبق برده	سَبَقَتْ رَحْمَتِیْ عجب خورده
روح بخشش ست روحور نه چو ما	پرده‌دارست پرده‌در نه چو ما
او ترا راعی و تو گرگ پسند	او ترا داعی و تو حاجتمند
او ترا حافظ و تو خود غافل	اینت بی عقل ظالم جاهل

خوی ما او نکو کند در ما　　مهربانتر ز ماست او بر ما
آنچنان مهر کو کند پیوند　　مادران را کجاست بر فرزند
ناکسان را بلطف خود کس کرد　　شکر و صبری ز بندگان بس کرد
فضل او پیش چشم دانش و داد　　در حس بست و راه جان بکشاد
چون ترا کرد حلم او ساکن　　از ربایندگان شدي ایمن
رسته باشد همیشه در صحرا　　مرد کوهي ز نکبت نکبا
غیب او عیبها بدانسته　　عفو او شستنش توانسته
علم او عیب ما بپوشیده　　تو نگفته سِر او نیوشیده
آدمي زادهٔ ظلوم جهول　　فضل حق را همي زند بفضول
خوب کار او و زشت کار شما　　غیبدان او و عیبدار شما
این عنایت نگر تو از پس ریب　　عالِم غیب را به عالَم عیب
گر نبودی ز وی عنایت پاک　　کی شدی تاجدار مشتی خاک
منزل عفو او بدشت گناه　　لشکر لطف او پذیرهٔ آه
آه عارف چو پرده برگیرد　　دوزخ از بیم او سپر گیرد
عفو او را قبول بهر خطاست　　کرمش را نزول بهر عطاست
تو جفا کرده او وفا با تو　　او وفادارتر ز تو با تو
فضل او آوریدت اندر کار　　ورنه بر خاک کی بُد این بازار
هر که شد نیست باشد او را هست　　هر که آمد ز پای گیرد دست
دستگیرست بیکسان را او　　بپسندد چو ما خسان را او
زانکه پاک است پاک را خواهد　　عالم الغیب خاک را خواهد

في علمه و اطلاعه في ضماير العباد

شِرب یکیک ز خلق دانسته　　داده و ضدّ آن توانسته

اوست مر فطرت ترا فاطر   دانش او منزه از خاطر
او ز تو داند آنچه در دل تست   زانکه او خالق دل و گل تست
چون تو داني که او همیداند   خبر طبع تو در گلت ماند
مصلحت بین خلق پیش از آز   مطلع بر ضمیر پیش از راز
آنچه در خاطر تو او داند   لفظ نا گفته کار میراند
شادي آرست و غمگذار خدای   رازدانست و رازدار خدای
بی زباني برش زباندانیست   قوّت جانت ز خوان بی نانیست
آنچه از بهر آدمي آراست   آرزو آنچنان نداند خواست
او کما بیش خلق دانسته   دیده و دادنش توانسته
جای تو کرد در نعیم مُعَد   تا تو با ناز جفت گردي غد
قائل او بس تو گنگ باش و مگوی   طالب او بس تو لنگ باش و مپوی
هست با قهر و علم یزداني   ناتواني نکو و ناداني
هرکه او هست نیست داند کرد   نیست را هست هم تواند کرد
کرد قائم برای نظم و قِوام   متقاضی برحم در ارحام
غیب خود زانکه صورت تو نگاشت   تو نداني که غیب نتوان داشت
او ترا بهتر از تو داند حال   تو چه گردي بگرد هزل و محال
تو مگو درد دل که او گوید   تو مجو مر ورا که او جوید
گردد از حس پای مور آگاه   مور و سنگ و شب و زمانه سیاه
سنگ در قعر آب اگر جنبید   در شب داج علمش آنرا دید
در دل سنگ اگر بود کرمی   دارد آن کم ز ذرهٔ جرمی
صوت تسبیح و راز پنهانش   مي بداند بعلم یزدانش
بنموده ترا ره آموزي   داده در سنگ کرم را روزي

هیچ جانی بصبر ازو نشکیفت   هیچ عقلش بزیرکی نفریفت
مطلع بر ضمائر ست مدام   تو بر اندیش و کار گشت تمام
روی از آئین بد بگردانی   رای تو پرورد مسلمانی
چون بعلمش غرور خواهی داشت   نار در دل نه نور خواهی داشت
چون بعلمش نگه نخواهی کرد   طمع حلم ازو مدار ای مرد
علم او عقل را چراغ افروز   حلم او طبع را گناه آموز
گرنه حلمش بُدی همیشه پناه   بنده کی زهره داشتی بگناه
گر گناهی همی کنی اکنون   آن گناه از دو حال نیست برون
گر ندانی که می نداند حق   گویمت اینت کافر مطلق
ور بدانی که می بداند و پس   میکنی اینت شوخ دیده و خس
خود گرفتم کسیت محرم نیست   حق بداند حق از کسی کم نیست
عفو او گیرم ار بپوشاند   نه ز تو علمش آن همی داند
توبه کن زین شنیع کردارت   ورنه بینی بروز دیدارت
نفس خود را میان حالت خویش   غرقه در قلزم خجالت خویش

فِي كَرَمِهِ وَ اَنَّهُ رَازِقُ الْاَرْزَاقِ

جانور را چو خوان به پیش نهاد   خوردنی از خورنده بیش نهاد
همه را روح و روز و روزی ازوست   نیکبختی و نیکروزی ازوست
روزی هر یکی پدید آورد   در انبار خانه مُهر نکرد
کافر و مومن و شقی و سعید   همه را روزی و حیات جدید
حاء حاجت هنوز شان در حلق   جیم جودش بداده روزی خلق
جز بنان نیست پرورش ما را   جز شره نیست نانخورش ما را
او ز توجیه بندگان نجهد   نانخورش داد نان همو بدهد

نان و جان تو در خزانهٔ هوست | تو نداري بگفته او را اوست
روزي تو اگر بچین باشد | اسپ کسب تو زیر زین باشد
تا ترا نزد او برد بشتاب | ورنه او را بر تو تو در خواب
نه ترا گفت رازق تو منم | عالم سِرّ و عالم علنم
جان بدادم وجوه نان بدهم | هرچه خواهي تو در زمان بدهم
کار روزي چو روزدان به درست | کِه ره آورد روز روزي تست
با تو زانجا که لطف یزدانست | گِرَوِ نان بدست تو جانست
غم جان خور که آن جان خورده است | تا لب گور گرده بو گرده است
این گرو سخت دار و نان میخور | چون گرو رفت قوت جان میخور
جان بی نان بکس نداد خدای | زانکه از نان بماند جان بر جای
آن زمانی که جان ز تن برمید | بیقین دان که روزیت برسید
سفله دارد ز بهر روزي بیم | نخورد دیگ گرم کرده کریم
نخورد شیر صید خود تنها | چون شود سیر مانده کرد رها
مر زنان راست کهنه تو بر تو | مرد را روز نو و روزي نو
روزي تست بر علیم و قدیر | تو ز میر و وزیر خشم مگیر
روزیت از در خدای بود | نه ز دندان و حلق و نای بود
کدخدائي خدائي است برنج | خاصه آنرا که نیست نعمت و گنج
کدخدائي همه غم و هوس است | کد رها کن ترا خدای بس است
اعتماد تو در همه احوال | بر خدا به که بر خراس و جوال
ابر اگر نم نداد یک سالت | سخت شوریده بینم احوالت

حکایت

زالکی کرد سر برون ز نهفت | کشتک خویش خشک دید و بگفت

کای هم آنِ نو و هم آن کهن　　رزق بر تست هرچه خواهي کن
علت رزق تو بخوب و بزشت　　گريهٔ ابر نی و خندهٔ کشت
بی سبب رازقي يقين دانم　　همه از تست جانم و نانم
از هزاران هزار بِه يکِ تو　　زانکه اندک نباشد اندک تو
شعلهٔ زو و صد هزار اختر　　قطرهٔ زو و صد هزار اخضر
مرد نبود کسی که در غم خور　　در يقين باشد از زنی کمتر

حکايت

آن به نشنيدهٔ که بی نم ابر　　مرغ روزي بيافت از در گبر
گبر را گفت بس مسلمانی　　زين هنر پيشهٔ سخندانی
کز تو اين مکرمت به نپذيرند　　مرغکان دانه ارچه برگيرند
گفت گبر ار مرا به نگزينند　　آخر اين رنج من همي بينند
زانکه او مکرم ست و با احسان　　نکند بخل با کرم يکسان
دست درباخت در رهش جعفر　　داد ايزد بجای دستش پر
کار تو جز خدای نکشايد　　بخدا گر ز خلق هيچ آيد
دل بفعل و فضول خلق مبند　　دل در او بند رستي از غم و بند
تا تواني جز او بيار مگير　　خلق را هيچ در شمار مگير
با بقای خدای نان شما ست　　اِلْف آلای او و جان شما ست
هر دو را در جهان عشق و طلب　　پارسي آب دان و تازي اب

تا جدائي ز نور موسیِ تو　　روز کوري چو مرغ عيسیِ تو
چون نداري خبر ز راه نياز　　در حجابي بسان مغز پياز
اول از بهر عشق دلجويش　　سر قدم کن چو کلک و ميجويش

تا بدانجا رسي بجست درست که بداني که مي نبايد جست
نه بپرسید کاهلی ز علي چون شنید از زبان دل کسلي
که بگو ای امیر جان افروز که شب تیره به بود یا روز
مرتضی گفت بشنو ای سائل سوی ادبار خود مشو مائل
عاشقان را درین ره جانسوز تبش راز به که تابش روز
هرکه دارد ز ره تبش در دل در نماند پیاده در منزل
در جهانی که عشق گوید راز نه تو ماني نه نیز عقل تو باز

فی المحبّة و التجرید

عاشقان سوی حضرتش سرمست عقل در آستین و جان بر دست
تا چو سویش براق دل رانند در رکابش همه برافشانند
جان و دل در رهش نثار کنند خویشتن را ازان شمار کنند
پیش توحید او نه کهنه نه نوست همه هیچند هیچ اوست که اوست
عقل و جانرا بنزد او چه خطر دل و دین هم گذر کنند گذر
پردهٔ عاشقان رقیق ترست نقش این پردهها دقیق ترست
غالب عشق هست مغلوبش خود ترا شرح داد مقلوبش
ابر چون زافتاب دور شود عالم عشق پر ز نور شود
ابر چون گبر مظلم ست و کدر آب در جمله نافع ست و مضر
اندک او حیات انسان ست باز بسیارش آفت جان ست
پس موحد محب حضرت اوست که محبت حجاب عزت اوست
بد نباشد محدّث تلقین بد چه باشد محب محدث بین
در محبت نگر به تعلیفش که همان محدث ست تصحیفش
ای محب جمال حضرت غیب تا نجوئي وصال طلعت غیب

نکشي شربت ملاقاتش نچشي لذت مناجاتش
چون یکی داني و یکی گوئي بدو سه و چهار چون پوئي
با الف بی و تی بود همراه بی و تی بت شمر الف اللّٰه
دست و پائی همي زن اندر جوی چون بدریا رسي ز جوی مگوی
چون رهی کرد فخر و عار ترا ای حدث با قِدم چه کار ترا
تو حدیثي نفس مزن ز قدم ای ندانسته باز سر ز قدم
صد هزارت حجاب در راه است همتت قاصرست و کوتاه است
دستبازیست قالت تو هنوز پای دامیست حالت تو هنوز
شو بدریای داد و دین یکدم تن برهنه چو گندم و آدم
تا کند توبهٔ تو جمله قبول تا نگردي دگر بگرد فضول
تو هنوز از متابعی شیطان توبه نا کرده کی بوی انسان
چون ترا بار داد بر درگاه آرزو زو مخواه اورا خواه
چون خدایت بدوستي بگزید چشم شوخ تو دیدني همه دید
بر نگیرد جهان عشق دوي چه حدیث ست این مني و توي
توئي تو چو رخت برگیرد رخت و تخت تو بخت برگیرد
نیست در شرط اتحاد نکو دعوئ دوستي و پس من و تو
بنده کی گردد آنچه باشد حُر کی توان کرد ظرف پُر را پُر
همه شو بر درش که در عالم هرکه او جز همه بود همه کم
چون رسیدي ببوس و غمزهٔ یار نیش نوشش شمار و خیري خار
از پئ زنگ آینه دل حُر لاست ناخن برای هستي بُر
مي نخواهي تو از کتاب خدای نیست اموات مرده بل احیای
مشو از راه نا توانستن همچو کشتي بهر دم آبستن

نیک و بد خوب و زشت یکسان گیر   هرچه دادت خدای در جان گیر
نه عزازیل چون ز یزدان دید   رحمت و لعنه هر دو یکسان دید
آنچه آوردش از خدای بچنگ   نیک و بد داشت هر دو را یکرنگ
صورت آنکه هست بر در میر   بادبانی بدست بی تدبیر

فی التجرّد و المجاهدة

هرکه خواهد ولایت تجرید   وانکه جوید رعایت تفرید
از درونش نبایدْ آسایش   وز برونش نشاید آرایش
آن ستایش که از نمایش اوست   ترک آرایش و ستایش اوست
بر در شه گدای نان خواهد   باز عاشق غذای جان خواهد
در طریقت مجرد و چالاک   دادهٔ برباد آب و آتش و خاک
زانکه در عرصهٔ معالم عصر   چه برش جاهلان چه عالم عصر
ای برادر بر آذر تجرید   جگر خود کباب دان نه ثرید
سگ دون همت استخوان جوید   بچهٔ شیر مغز جان جوید
عاشقان جان و دل فدی کردند   ذکر او روز و شب غذی کردند
مرد عالي همم نجوید بند   سگ بود سگ بلقمهٔ خرسند
کشف اگر بند گرددت بر تن   کشف را کفش ساز و بر سر زن
فُضله کم گوی و عاجزي پیش آر   استخوان را تو بر سگان بگذار
تو بگوهر گرفتهٔ رفعت   پس چرائي چو سگ تو دون همت
هرکرا عالیست همتِ او   هر دو عالم شدست نعمت او
وانکه دون همت ست همچون سگ   هست چون سگ ز بهر نان در تگ
گر همي روح خواهي از تن فرد   لا چو دار ست گرد او بر گرد
کی ز لاهوت خود بیابي بار   تات ناسوت بر نشد بر دار

زانکه عیسیت را سوی لاهوت　　هست در راه جمعهٔ صلبوت
نیست کن هرچه راه و رای بود　　تات دل خانهٔ خدای بود
تا ترا بود با تو در ذات ست　　کعبه با طاعتت خرابات ست
ور ز ذات تو بود تو دور ست　　بتکده از تو بیت معمور ست
ای خرابات جوی پر آفات　　پسر خر توئي و خر آبات
با تو و بود تو خرد تیره است　　چشم عقلت از آن جهان خیره است
نفس تست آنکه کفر و دین آورد　　لاجرم چشم رنگ بین آورد
بی توخوش باتوهست بس ناخوش　　بدر انداز گربه را از کش
در قِدم کفرها و دینها نیست　　در صفای صفت چنینها نیست

في سلوك طريق الآخرة

این همه علم جسم مختصر ست　　علم رفتن براه حق دگر ست
علم آن کش نظر ادق باشد　　علم رفتن براه حق باشد
سوی آنکس که عقل و دین دارد　　نان و گفتار گندمین دارد
چیست این راه را نشان و دلیل　　آن نشان از کلیم پرس و خلیل
ور ز من پرسي ای برادر هم　　باز گویم صریح نی مبهم
روی سوی جهان حي کردن　　عقبهٔ جاه زیر پی کردن
جاه و حرمت ز دل رها کردن　　پشت در خدمتش دوتا کردن
تنقیت کردن نفوس از بد　　تقویت کردن روان بخرد
چیست زاد چنین ره ای غافل　　حق بدیدن بریدن از باطل
رفتن از منزل سخنکوشان　　برنشستن بصدر خاموشان
رفتن از فعل حق سوی صفتش　　وز صفت زي مقام معرفتش
آنگه از معرفت بعالم راز　　پس رسیدن بآستان نیاز

با نیاز آنگهی که گشتی یار   دل برآرد ز نفس تیره دمار
در درون تو نفس دل گردد   زان همه کردها خجل گردد
خان و مانش همه براندازد   در ره امتحانش بگدازد
در تن تو چو نفس تو بگداخت   دل بتدریج کار خویش بساخت
پس ازو حق نیاز بستاند   چون نیازش نماند حق ماند
نه ز بیهوده گفت و نادانی   بایزید ار بگفت سبحانی
پس زبانی که راز مطلق گفت   راست جنبید کو انا الحق گفت
راز خود چون ز روی داد به پشت   راز جلاد گشت و اورا کشت
روز رازش چو شب نمای آمد   نطق او گفتهٔ خدای آمد
راز چون کرد ناگهانی فاش   بی اجازت میانهٔ اوباش
صورت او نصیب دار آمد   سیرت او نصیب یار آمد
جان جانش چو شد تهی ز آواز   خون دل گشت بر نهان غماز
راست گفت آنکه گفت از سر حال   گفت دع نفسک ای پسر و تعال
از تو تا دوست نیست ره بسیار   ره توئی پس بزیر پای در آر
تا ببینی بدیدهٔ لاهوت   خط ذی الملک و خطهٔ ملکوت
کی بود ما ز ما جدا مانده   من و تو رفته و خدا مانده
دل شده تا بآستان خدای   روح گفته من اینکم تو در آی
چون درآمد به طارم توحید   دل و روح از ستانهٔ تجرید
روح با حور همبری سازد   دل به دیدار دوست بگرازد
ای ندیده ز آب رز هستی   تا کی آخر ز نقش رز مستی
چه کنی لاف مستیی بدروغ   تات گویند خورد مردک دوغ
تو اگر می خوری مده آواز   دوغ خواره نگاه دارد راز

چه کني جست و جوی چون جان تو   تو مدان نوش کن چو ایمان تو
تو نداني بپارسي ماسي   چون بخوردي تو طعم بشناسي
من بیاموزمت که جام شراب   چون کني نوش در سرای خراب
بر مدار از مقام مستي پی   سر همانجا بنه که خوردي می
تا نخوردي مدارش ایچ حلال   چون بخوردي کلموخ بر لب مال
چون بخوردي دو دُرد با صد درد   گویم احسنت اینت مردی مرد
بیشتر زین خران بی افسار   همه میخوارگان دل مردار
می همي عقل و جان شان بخورد   رز همي این و آن شان ببرد
اندرین مجمع جوانمردان   از سر بد دلي چو نامردان
گر نگوئي تو صادقی باشي   ور بگوئي منافقی باشي
پیشتر چون روي که جایت نیست   باز پس چون جهي که پایت نیست
آنکه را جای نیست غمخوار ست   وانکه را پای نیست بیچار ست
نیستانی که بر در هست اند   نه کمر بر درش کنون بستند
کز ازل پیش عشق بی زر و زور   خود کمر بسته زاده اند چو مور
جهد کن تا چو مرگ بشتابد   بوی جانت ز کوی او یابد
در گذر زین سرای پر اوباش   گر بوی ورنه بر در او باش
کان کسانیکه بنده اند اورا   بخدائي بسنده اند اورا
کمر بندگي به بستهٔ مدام   خواجهٔ هفت بام همچو غلام

فی العالم و الجاهل

به پسر شیخ گورگانی گفت   که ترا بهر کارهای نهفت
اندرین کوچه خانهٔ باید   ور کلیدان بچپ بود شاید

ساز پیرایه در ره تجرید   هم سَر از شرع و هم سِر از توحید
واندرین منزل عنا و ضرر   چون مسافر درآی و زود گذر
بر در بوستان الّا اللّه   برکش و نیست کن قبا و کلاه
نیست شو تا هم او دهد بصواب   لمن الملک را بشرط جواب

حکایت

در مناجات پیر شبلي گفت   چون برون آمد از حدیث نهفت
که اگر زانکه نبودم دوری   بدهدم در حدیث دستوری
لمن الملک گوید او بصواب   من دهم مرورا بصدق جواب
گویم امروز مملکت آنراست   که ز دي و پریر مي آراست
یوم و غد مملکت ای بما برچیر   هست آنرا که بود دی و پریر
تیغ قهر تو سرفرازانرا   سر برد پس بسر دهد جانرا
نوش دان بهر سود سودا را   حَربهٔ آفتاب حِربا را

هرچه جز حق چو زان گرفتي خشم   جبرئیلت نیاید اندر چشم
زانکه از حرف لا همي بالّه   کس نداند که چند باشد راه
راه تا با خودي هزاران سال   بروي روز و شب یمین و شمال
پس بآخر چو چشم باز کني   کار بر خویشتن دراز کني
خویشتن بیني از نهاد و قیاس   گِرد خود گشته همچو گاو خراس
بیخود ار هیچ آئي اندر کار   یابي اندر دو دم بدین در بار
زین مسافت دو دست عقل تهیست   وان مسافت خدای داند چیست
ای سکندر درین ره آفات   همچو خضر نبي درین ظلمات
زیر پای آر گوهر کانت   تا بدست آید آب حیوانت

با دل و جان نباشدت یزدان   هردو نبود ترا همین و همان
نفس را سال و ماه کوفته دار   مرده انگارش و بجا بگذار
چون تو فارغ شدی ز نفس لئیم   برسیدی بخلد و ناز و نعیم
بیم و امید را بجای بمان   چه کنی ننگ مالک و رضوان
نیست را مسجد و کنشت یکیست   سایه را دوزخ و بهشت یکیست
پیش آنکس که عشق رهبر اوست   کفر و دین هردو پردهٔ در اوست
هستی دوست پیش دیدهٔ دوست   پردهٔ بارگاه اوئی اوست

فی التوکّل

پی منه با نفاق بر درگاه   بتوکل روند مردان راه
گر توکل ترا بروست همی   چون نداری برزقش اوست همی
پس بکوی توکل آور رخت   بعد ازانت پذیره آید بخت
در توکل یکی سخن بشنو   تا نمانی بدست دیو گرو
اندر آموز شرط ره ز زنی   که ازو گشت خوار لاف زنی

فی توکّل العجائز

حاتم آنکه که کرد عزم حرم   آنکه خوانی ورا همی باصم
کرد عزم حجاز و بیت حرام   سوی قبر نبی علیه سلام
مانده بر جای یک کُره ز عیال   بی قلیل و کثیر و بی اموال
زن به تنها به خانه دربگذاشت   نفقت هیچ نی و ره برداشت
مرورا فرد و ممتحن بگذاشت   بود و نابود او یکی پنداشت
بر توکل زنیش همره بود   که ز رزاق خویش آگه بود
در پس پرده داشت انبازی   که ورا بود با خدا رازی
جمع گشتند مردم برزن   شاد رفتند جمله تا برِ زن

حال او سر بسر بپرسیدند   چون ورا فرد و ممتحن دیدند
از ره پند و نصحت آموزی   جمله گفتند بهر دلسوزی
شهرت چون برفت زی عرفات   هیچ بگذاشت مر ترا نفقات
گفت بگذاشت راضیم بخدای   آنچه رزق منست ماند بجای
باز گفتند رزق تو چندست   که دلت قانع ست و خرسند ست
گفت چندانکه عمر ماندستم   رزق من کرد جمله در دستم
آن یکی گفت می ندانی تو   او چه داند ز زندگانی تو
گفت روزیدهم همی داند   تا بود روح رزق نستاند
باز گفتند بی سبب ندهد   هرگز از بید بن رطب ندهد
نیست دنیا ترا بهیچ سبیل   نفرستدت زاسمان زنبیل
گفت کای رای تان شده تیره   چند گوئید هرزه بر خیره
حاجت آنرا بود سوی زنبیل   کش نباشد زمین کثیر و قلیل
آسمان و زمین بجمله وراست   هرچه خود خواست کرد حکم اوراست
برساند چنانکه خود خواهد   گه بیفزاید و گهی کاهد
از توکل نفس تو چند زنی   مرد نامی و لیک کم ز زنی
چون نهٔ راهرو تو چون مردان   رو بیاموز رهروی ز زنان
کاهلی پیشه کردی ای تن زن   وای آن مرد کو کم ست از زن

دل نگه دار و نفس را بگذار   کین چو باز ست و آن چو بوتیمار
تا بدانجا که ما و تو دانند   چون همه سوخت او و او ماند
عقل کاندر جهان چنو نرسد   برسد در خود و بدو نرسد
گوش سر دوست گوش عشق یکی   بهر دین این و آن ز بهر شکی

بیشمار ارچه گوش سر شنود   گوش عشق از یکی خبر شنود

بر دو سوی سر آن دو گوش چو نیو   چه کنی بیش ازین خروش و غریو

کودکی رو ز دیو چشم بپوش   تا به نفهد سرت میان دو گوش

ربع مسکون چو از طریق شمار   هست فرسنگ بست و چار هزار

ساعت شب چو ضم کنی با روز   هم بود بست و چار آدم سوز

تو اگر واقفی به صرف و صروف   بدلش کن به بست و چار حروف

قاف قول شهادتین ترا   بی ریا و نفاق و کیف و مرا

از همه عالمت برون آرد   نه بآلت به کاف و نون آرد

از ورای خرد درین ره و کو   وردت این بس که لا هو الّا هو

کلمهٔ حق چو در شمار آمد   عدد حرف بست و چار آمد

نیمی از بحر جان دوازده درج   نیمی از چرخ دین دوازده برج

درجها پر ز دُرّ امیدست   برجها پر ز ماه و خورشید ست

دُر دریای این جهانی نه   ماه و خورشید آسمانی نه

دُر دریای عالم جبروت   ماه و خورشید آسمان سکوت

في تعبير الرّويا

او نهاد از پی اولو الالباب   بیم و امید در نمایش خواب

آدمی چون نهاد سر در خواب   خیمهٔ او شود گسسته طناب

خلق تا در جهان اسبابند   همه در کشتی اند و در خوابند

تا روان شان چه بیند اندر خواب   زانچه پیش آید از ثواب و عقاب

آتش تیز تاب خشم بود   چشمهٔ آب نور چشم بود

گریه در خواب مؤنث شادیست   بندگی از مذلت آزادیست

نردبازي به خواب یا شطرنج | سبب جنگ و غلبه باشد و رنج
آب در خواب روزیست حلال | گر بود پاک و عذب و صاف و زلال
ور بود تیره عیش نا خوش دان | گرچه آب ست عین آتش دان
خاک در خواب مایهٔ روزیست | برزگر را دلیل بهروزیست
باد اگر گرم نیست سرد بود | هر دو گنجور رنج و درد بود
باز اگر هست معتدل در پوست | اندہ دشمن ست و شادي دوست
چیز دادن به مرده اندر خواب | عدم مال باشد و اسباب
خنده اندوه باشد و اهوال | خامشي بستن دل اندر مال
شرب آب و زیادت عطشان | علم باشد که نیست سیري ازان
وانکه باشد برهنه اندر خواب | شد فضیحت بسان مست خراب
طبل در خواب راز گردد فاش | بوق در خواب مایهٔ پرخاش
بند و غُل توبهٔ نصوح بود | باغ دیدن غذای روح بود
میوه در خواب روزیست از شاه | لیک نه اندر زمان که در بیگاه
وقت ادراک چون فراز رسد | مرد بیننده زو بناز رسد
دست خود چون دراز بیند مرد | شود اندر سخا و رادی فرد
ور شود دستهای او کوتاه | کشد از بخل گِرد خویش سپاه
دست باشد برادر و خواهر | آن چپ دختر آن راست پسر
باشد انگشت همچو فرزندان | نسب مادر و پدر دندان
دخترانند سینه با پستان | چون شکم مال و نعمت پنهان
جگر و دل بخواب گنج بود | ساق و زانو عنا و رنج بود
مغز مال نهان و پهلو زن | پوست چون ستر در کشیده بتن
هست فرزند آلت تولید | نیک و بد زشت وخوش شقي وسعید

دست شستن ز کار نومیدیست   رقص کردن وقاحت و شیدیست
میزر و سطل و آلت تغسیل   همه بر خادمان کنند دلیل
وانکه بربط زند بخواب اندر   زن کند بیشک او بتاب اندر
با دگر کس مصارعت کردن   غلبت کردن ست و آزردن
وانکه دارو خورد همي در خواب   رسته گردد ز درد و رنج و عذاب
طیب باشد دو گونه اندر خواب   این یکی راحت آن دگر همه تاب
راحت آن نوع را که در مالند   محنت آن جنس را که بر کالند
کز دخان رنج بیشتر باشد   راحتش کمتر از ضرر باشد
مرد بیمار و طیب و جامهٔ نو   بد بود بد ز من نکو بشنو
رقص کردن بخواب در کشتي   بیم غرقست و مایهٔ زشتي
وانکه در بند حبس بسته بود   رقص کردن ورا خجسته بود
هرکه بیند ز تن روان شده خون   نعمتی یابد از حلال برون
چون نه بیند جراحت این باشد   ور جراحت بود جز این باشد
اندهی صعب یابد از کاری   بسته گردد بدست خونخواری
وان زنی کش ز فرج خون آید   کودک مرده زو برون آید
گوشت بیند بخواب در بیمار   که خورد رو امید ازو بردار
مستي و بیخودي ز شرب شراب   آنکه تازیست بد بود در خواب
وانکه او پارسیست روزي دان   سرفرازي و نیکروزي دان
شیر در خواب ربح مال بود   روزي نیکو و حلال بود

في روياء الاواني و الاثواب

جامهٔ کهنه رنج و اندوه است   جامهٔ نو ز دولت انبوه است
بهترین جامهٔ بود هنگفت   مر مرا اوستاد چونین گفت

مر زنان راست جامهٔ رنگین   اصل شادي و راحت و تزئین
جامهٔ سرخ مایهٔ شادیست   سال و مه بخت ازو بآزادیست
جامهٔ هیبت ست رنگ سیاه   ور بود زرد درد و محنت و آه
جامهای کبود اندوه است   رنج بر دل فزونتر از کوه است
طیلسان و ردا جمال بود   کیسه و صرّة اصل مال بود
نردبان اصل و مایهٔ سفر ست   لیک زان مرد را همه خطر ست
آسیا مردم امین باشد   آنکه در خانه به گُزین باشد
دام باشد بخواب بستن کار   آینه زن بود نکو هُش دار
بستگي آیدت ز قفل پدید   چون کشایش که آیدت ز کلید

في روياء الصّناعين

مرد طبّاخ نعمت بسیار   همچو قصّاب در تباهي کار
رنج و بیماریست مرد طبیب   خاصه آنرا که هست خوار و غریب
درزي آنکس که رنجها و بلا   همه بر دست او شود زیبا
مرد خفّاف و نعلي و خرّاز   از مواریث آنکه دارد راز
مرد بزّاز و زرگر و عطّار   خوبي کار و نعمت بسیار
مرد خمّار و مطرب و رادي   مایهٔ شادماني و شادي
مرد بیطار و رایض و کحّال   چون دلیل اند بر تباهي حال
هست در خواب دیدن صیّاد   مایهٔ مکر و حیله بر مرصاد
مرد شمشیرگر دلیل عناست   همچنین تیرگر که تیر آراست
مرد سقا و گلگر و حمّال   هر سه آنرا دلیل دان بر مال

في روياء البهائم

خر بود خادمي ولي کاهل   که بکار اندرون بود مُنبِل

اسپ زن باشد ای بدانش فرد   مرد را اسپ و زن بود درخورد
استر آنرا که زن بود حامل   بد بود بچه نایدش حاصل
اشتر آید ترا سفر در خواب   سفر سهمناک پرغم و تاب
گاو باشد دلیل سال فراخ   به بر پادشا شود گستاخ

في روياء السبّاع

شیر خصم مسلط و مغرور   که بود کارش از مجامله دور
پیل شاهیست لیک با هیبت   هرکسی ترسناک ازان صولت
گوسفند آیدت غنیمت و مال   اقتضا زان کند فراخي سال
بز کسان دني و بد گوهر   پرخروش و بکارها پرشر
لیک باشد بهر سبیل مفید   نیست برقول اوستاد مزید
آهو از خانهٔ زنان تعبیر   بیشتر دارد ای بدانش پیر
دشمن آمد پلنگ بد کردار   که بود در معاملت غدّار
ببر را هم به دشمن انگارند   بکتاب اندر اینچنین آرند
خرس خصمیست پرخیانت و دزد   که ز دیدنش کس نیابد مزد
یوز و کفتار و گرگ با روباه   دشمنانند هریکی بدخواه
ورچه روباه حیله گر باشد   مرده بیني ورا بتر باشد
مار هرگه عدوی کینه ورست   ور کند قصد تو ترا بترست
کژدم و غنده و دگر حشرات   همه هستند یک بیک آفات
سگ بخواب اندرون عوان باشد   گرچه بیدار پاسبان باشد

في روياء النيران و الكواكب

دیدن آفتاب را در خواب   بادشه گفته اند از هرباب
ماه مانند رای زن باشد   دگری گفت نی که زن باشد

جرم مریخ یا زحل در خواب   صاحب محنت ست و رنج و عذاب
تیر ماننده دبیر آمد   مشتري خازن و وزیر آمد
زهره خود هست مایهٔ رامش   مایهٔ عیش و کام و آرامش
وان دگر کوکبان برادر دان   گاه تعبیر شان برادر خوان
همچو یعقوب کین طریق نهاد   راز این علم بر پسر بکشاد
مهر و ماهش پدر بُد و مادر   کوکبان چون برادران درخور
کس چو ما دید خیره غمخواران   میگذاریم خواب بیداران
خفته بیدار کردن آسان ست   غافل و مرده هر دو یکسان ست
بس کن از زجر و فال و از تعبیر   درگذر زین که کردهٔ تقدیر

في تناقض الدّارين

علت روز و شب خورست و زمین   چون گذشتي نه آنت ماند و نه این
ای دو بر زعم تو مراد و مرید   دوئي از عقل دان نه از توحید
در چنین حضرت ار ز من شنوي   چون همه شد یکي مجوی دوئي
در دوئي دان مشقت و تمییز   در یکیئي یکیست رستم و حیز
در مصاف صفا و صاحت دل   بر فراز روان و تارک گل
تیغ تا نفگني سپر نشوي   تا به ننهي کلاه سر نشوي
تا دلت بندهٔ کلاه بود   فعل تو سال و مه گناه بود
چون شدي فارغ از کلاه و کمر   بر سرانِ زمانه گشتي سر
ترک ترکیب رخش توفیق ست   نفي ترتیب محض تحقیق ست
مردن دل هلاک جان باشد   مردن جان ورا امان باشد
اندرین ره بهیچ روی مایست   نیست گود و ز نیست گشتن نیست
چون تو بر خاستي ز نفس و ز عقل   اینجهانت بدانجهان شد نقل

هر سری کز تو رُست هم در دم   سر بزن چون چراغ و شمع و قلم
زانکه هر سر که دیدني باشد   در طریقت بریدني باشد
بی سري پیش گردنان ادبست   زانکه پیوسته سر کله طلبست
بی سري مر ترا سر آرد بار   درج پر دُر ز بیسریست انار
سر کَل را کله پناه بود   با چنین سر کله گناه بود
تو بزیر کلاه غش داري   لاجرم جسر نار نگذاري
آدمي را ز جاه بهتر چاه   کَل فضولي شود چو یافت کلاه
آن نکوتر که اندرین معراج   دست بر سر کني نیابي تاج
کز پی غیب مرد ره پوید   وز پی عیب کَل کله جوید
با کلاهت اگر زیان باشد   قلب او خود هلاک جان باشد
سر که آن بندهٔ کلاه بود   همچو بیژن اسیر چاه بود
در طریقت سر و کلاه مدار   ورنه داري چو شمع دل پر نار
ور کله بایدت همي ناچار   همچو شمع آن کلاه از آتش دار
کانکه در عشق شمع ره باشد   همچو شمع آتشین کله باشد
گر همي یوسفیت باید و جاه   پیش حق باشگونه باش چو چاه
چون سلیمان کمال ره را دار   همچو یوسف جمال چه را دار
تا نشد نقش صورتت چاهی   نشود نقش سِرّت اللّهي
خیز و بگذار دنیئی دون را   تا بیابي خدای بیچون را
از تن و جان و عقل و دین بگذر   در ره او دلی بدست آور
هرچه از نفس علم و معرفتست   دان که آن کفر عالم صفتست
صورت و وصف و عین در مانند   آن رحم این مشیمه آن فرزند
صورتت پردهٔ صفات بود   صفتت سدّ عین ذات بود

آن چو مصباح روشن اندر ذات   وان دو همچون زجاجه و مشکات
تا نگشتي دران گذرگه تنگ   با دو روحی و لعبت یکرنگ
ای ز صورت چنانکه جان از جسم   دل ز وحدت چنانکه مرد از اسم
کوشش از تن کشش ز جان خیزد   جستن از ترک این و آن خیزد
تا ابد با قدم حدث طفلست   وانکه صافي برون ازین ثفلست
تا بود نسل آدمي برجای   هست آراسته ورا دو سرای
این سرای از برای رنج و نیاز   وان سرای از برای نعمت و ناز
تا زمین جای آدمي زایست   خیمهٔ روزگار بر پایست
این زمین میهمان سرائی دان   آدمي را چو کدخدائی دان
تا درین خاکدان نه بیند رنج   نرسد زان سرای بر سر گنج
از تو پرسم که علم حکمت و شرع   وارث آئي همي باصل و بفرع
دین ز صورت همیشه بگریزد   تا ز بد مرد را بپرهیزد
یک جوابم بده ز روی صواب   گر نهٔ مرده یا نهٔ در خواب
چون ترا بر نهاد خود نفس ست   از تو او مر ترا عوض نه بس ست

التمثیل في صبیان المکتب

تو نداني ز حال عالم راز   از بلا عافیت نداني باز
تو حقیقت نه مرد این راهي   طفل راهي ز ره نه آگاهي
کودکي رو بگرد بازي گرد   ببر کبر و بی نیازي گرد
بس بود کبر و ناز یار ترا   با خدا ای پسر چه کار ترا
چه کني جنت و نعیم ابد   کرده عقبی ز بهر دنیا رد
او ز تو خسّت تو میداند   چون توي را بخود همي خواند
میکند عرضه بر تو حور و قصور   تو بدنیا و زینتش مغرور

از پی راه حق کم از کودک نتوان بودن ای کم از یک و یک
گر در آموختن کند تقصیر هرچه خواهد ز وی سبک بپذیر
بتلطف بدار و بنوازش خیره در انتظار مگدازش
در کنارش نه آن زمان کاکا تا شود راضي و مکنش جفا
ور نخواند بخواه زود دوال گوشهایش بگیر و صعب بمال
به معلم نمای تهدیدش تا بود گوشمال تاکیدش
بند و حبسش کند بخانهٔ موش میر موشان کند فشرده گلوش
در ره آخرت ز بهر شنود کمتر از کودکی نباید بود
خلد کاکای تست هین بشتاب بدو رکعت بهشت را دریاب
ورنه شد موشخانه دوزخ تو در ره آن سرای برزخ تو
رو بکُتّاب انبیا یکچند بر خود این جهل و این ستم مپسند
لوحی از شرع انبیا برخوان چون نداني برو بخوان و بدان
تا مگر یار انبیا گردي زین جهالت مگر جدا گردي
در جهان خراب پر ز ضرر از جهالت مدان تو هیچ بتر

گرت باید که دُر کشي ای مرد خشک بگذار و گرد دریا گرد
گرت ناید ز بحر دُر خوش آب هم تو داني که در نماني از آب
چنگ در راه حق زن ای سرهنگ گرت نبود مراد نبود ننگ
بارگي را بساز آلت و زین از پئ بارگاه علیین
مرد کز خاک و آب دارد عار بهوا برنشیند آتش وار
کلهٔ آسمان منه بر سر تا بیابي ز جبرئیل افسر
تاج گردد ترا کلاه ملک باشگونه شود کلاه فلک

مرد ایمان همیشه در کارست　　زانکه ایما نماز بیمار ست
تا نداري سرِ سرانداري　　تو چه داني که چيست جانبازي
چون سرانداز وصف جود شدي　　بر در رُوم در سجود شدي
کعبهٔ دل ز حق شده معمور　　همت سگ بر استخوان مقصور

فی الایثار و العطیه

هرچه داري براى حق بگذار　　كز گدايان ظريفتر ايثار
جان و دل بذل كن كز آب و ز گل　　بهترين جودها ست جهد مقل
سيّد و سرفراز آل عبا　　يافت تشريف سورهٔ هل اتى
از سه قرص جوين بيمقدار　　يافت در پيش حق چنين بازار

في قصة قيس بن عَاصِم

آن زمان كز خداى نزد رسول　　حكم من ذا الذي نمود نزول
هر كسى آن قدر كه دست رسيد　　پيش مهتر كشيد و سر نكشيد
گوهر و زر ستور و بنده و مال　　هرچه در وسع بود شان در حال
قيس عاصم ضعيف حالى بود　　كه نكردى طلب ز دنيا سود
رفت در خانه با عيال بگفت　　زانچه بشنيد هيچ يک نه نهفت
كاينچنين آيت آمد ست امروز　　خيز و مارا در انتظار مسوز
آنچه در خانه حاصل ست بيار　　تا كنم پيش سيّد آن ايثار
گفت زن چيز نيست در خانه　　تو نهٔ زين سراى بيگانه
گفت آخر بجوى آن مقدار　　هرچه يابي سبک بنزد من آر
رفت و خانه بجست بسيارى　　تا بر آيد ورا مگر كارى
يافت در خانه صاعى از خرما　　دقل و خشک گشته نا بنوا
پيش قيس آوريد زن در حال　　گفت زين بيش نيست مارا مال

قیس خرما بآستین در کرد   شادمانه بر رسول آورد
چون درون رفت قیس در مسجد   نز سر هزل بلکه از سر جد
گفت با وی منافقی که بیار   تا چه آوردهٔ سبک پیش آر
گوهرست این متاع یا زر و سیم   پیش مهتر همیکنی تسلیم
زان سخن قیس گشت زود خجل   بنگر تا چه آمدش حاصل
رفت و در گوشهٔ بغم بنشست   بر نهاده ز شرم دست بدست
آمد از سدره جبرئیل امین   گفت کای سیّد زمان و زمین
مرد را اندر انتظار مدار   وانچه آورده است خوار مدار
مصطفی را ز حال کرد آگاه   یَلْمِزُونَ الْمُطَّوِّعِيْن ناگاه
ملکوت آمده بنظارند   مرد را انتظار چون دارند
زلزله اوفتاده در ملکوت   نیست جای قرار و جای سکوت
حق تعالی چنین همي گوید   دل اورا بلطف میجوید
کای سرافراز وی گزیده رسول   اینقدر زود کن ز قیس قبول
که بنزد من این دقل بعیان   بهتر از زرّ و گوهر دگران
زو پذیرفتم این متاع قلیل   زانکه دستش رسید نیست نخیل
از همه چیزهای بگزیده   هست جَهْد المُقِل پسندیده
قیس را زان سبب برآمد کار   زان منافق بفعل بد گفتار
گشت رسوا منافق اندر حال   قیس را کار گشت ازان بکمال
تا بدانی که هرکه پیش آمد   هم بر آنسان که بود بیش آمد
با خدای آنکه او دو دل باشد   از همه فعل خود خجل باشد
راستي بهتر از همه کاری   خوانده باشي تو اینقدر باری
یک درم صدقه از کف درویش   از هزار توانگر آمد بیش

زانکه درویش را دل ریش ست   از دل ریش صدقه زان بیش ست
به توانگر تو آن نگر که دلش   هست تاریک و تیره همچو گلش
گل درویش صفوت ازلیست   دل او کیمیای لم یزلیست
بشنو تا چه گفت فضل اله   با که گویم که نیست یک همراه
با شهنشاه و خواجهٔ لولاک   گفت لا تعد عنهم عیناک

فی الاتحاد و المودة

در جهان یک زیان چو سود تو نیست   هیچ حبس ابد چو بود تو نیست
ظهر النور ذو المنن باشد   بطل الزور جان و تن باشد
غیب خواهی خودی ز ره بردار   عیب را با سرای غیب چه کار
تو پر از عیب و قصد عالم غیب   نتوان کرد خاصه با شک و ریب
بر نخیزد بدست بیخردیت   از دو پای نهاد بند خودیت
بود تو چون ترا حجاب آمد   عقل تو با تو در عتاب آمد
گفت بگذار و نفس کن پدرود   ورنه برساز زین دو چشم دو رود
روز و شب در فراق عقل بنال   بیش با عقل خود بدی مسگال
عقل را زین عقیله باز رهان   بعد ازان گشت بر تو کار آسان
بینی آنگه که یابی از دل قوت   ملک را از دریچهٔ ملکوت
چند گوئی رسیدگی چه بود   در ره دین گزیدگی چه بود
بند بر خود نهی گزیده شوی   پای بر سر نهی رسیده شوی
تا گزنده بوی گزیده نهٔ   تا رسنده بوی رسیده نهٔ
آدمی کی بود گزنده چو تو   دیو و دد کی بود درنده چو تو
غافلی سال و ماه مغروری   دد و دیوی و ز آدمی دوری
سال و مه کینه جوی همچو پلنگ   خلق عالم ز طبع تو دل تنگ

بر سر شاهراه هیچ کسی   برسي در خود و درو نرسي
آیتی کرد کوفي از صوفي   عشق و رای قریشي و کوفي
صوفي و عشق و در حدیث هنوز   سلب و ایجاب و لا یجوز و یجوز
صوفیان دستها برآورده   که بلی را بلا بدل کرده
خاک پاشان حجلهٔ انسش   ره نشینان حجرهٔ قدسش
همه بدر آیتان پردهٔ رشک   غرقه از پای تا بسر در اشک
همه ارزانیان حلم شده   همه زندانیان علم شده
خویشتن را فرو نِه از گردن   تا شوي نازنین هر برزن
دیدهٔ پاک پاک دین بیند   دیده چون پاک شد چنین بیند
خاکسارند بادسارانش   تاجدارند تاجدارانش
از سر این دلق هفت رنگ برآر   جامه یک رنگ دار عیسی وار
تا چو عیسی بر آب راه کني   همره از آفتاب و ماه کني
همگي خود ز خویشتن کم کن   وانگه آندم حدیث آدم کن
تا بود نفس ذرهٔ با تو   نرسي هیچگونه آنجا تو
نفس را آن هوا نسازد هیچ   خیز و بی نفس راه را بپیچ

مَنْ زَهِدَ فِی الدُّنْیَا وَجَدَ مُلْكًا لَا یَبْلَی

بود پیری به بصره در زاهد   که نبود آنزمان چنو عابد
گفت هر بامداد برخیزم   تا ازین نفس شوم بگریزم
نفس گوید مرا که هان ای پیر   چه خوري بامداد کن تدبیر
باز گو مر مرا که تا چه خورم   منش گویم که مرگ و در گذرم
گوید آنگاه نفس من با من   که چه پوشم بگویمش که کفن
بعد ازان مر مرا سوال کند   آرزوهای بس محال کند

که کجا رفت خواهي ای دل کور   منش گویم خموش تا لب گور
تا مگر بر خلاف نفس نفَس   بتوانم زدن ز بیم عسس
بخ بخ آنکس که نفس را دارد   خوار و در پیش خویش نگذارد

في زهد الزاهد

زاهدی از میان قوم بتاخت   بر سر کوه رفت و صومعه ساخت
روزی از اتفاق دانای   عالمی پر خرد توانای
برگذشت و بدید زاهد را   آنچنان پارسا و عابد را
گفت ویحک چرا برین بالای   ساختستي مقام و مسکن و جای
گفت زاهد که اهل دنیا پاک   در طلب کردنش شدند هلاک
باز دنیا فتاده در پرواز   در فگنده بهر دیار آواز
بزبان فصیح میگوید   درجهان صید خویش میجوید
هر زمان گوید اهل دنیا را   جفت بلوی و فرد مولا را
وای آنکو ز من حذر نکند   در طلب کردنم نظر نکند
تا نگردد چنانکه در فسطاط   اندکی مرغ و باز بر افراط

في حبّ الدنیا و صفة اهله

هست شهری بزرگ در حد روم   باز بسیار اندران بر و بوم
نام آن شهر شهره فسطاط ست   ساحتش تا بحد دمیاط ست
واندرو مرغ خانگي نپرد   زانکه باز از هوا همي شکرد
واندر آن شهر مرغ نگذارد   زانکه در ساعتش بیوبارد
همچو فسطاط شد زمانه کنون   علما همچو مرغ خوار و زبون
من نهان گشته ام بدین بالا   تا شوم ایمن از بدِ دنیا
گفت دانا که با تو اینجا کیست   بر سر کوه پایه حالت چیست

گفت زاهد که نفس من با من — هست روز و شب اندرین مسکن
گفت دانا که پس نکردی هیچ — بیهده راه زاهدی مبسیچ
گفت زاهد که نفس دوخته اند — در من و زی ویم فروخته اند
نتوانم ز وی جدا گشتن — چکنم چارهٔ رها گشتن
گفت با زاهد آن ستوده حکیم — نفست افعال بد کند تعلیم
گفت زاهد که من بساخته ام — زانکه من نفس را شناخته ام
هست بیمار نفس و من چو طبیب — میکنم روز و شب ورا ترتیب
بمداوای نفس مشغولم — زانکه گوید همی که معلولم
گه ورا قصد فصد فرمایم — اکحل از دیدگانش بکشایم
چون تصعد کند فرو بارد — فصد تسکینی اندرو آرد
گه ورا مسهلی بفرمایم — عِلَل از جسم او بپالایم
حب دنیا و بغض و حقد و حسد — غل و غشش برون شود ز جسد
از خورش خوی خویش باز کند — در شهوت بخود فراز کند
گاه نهیش کنم من از شهوات — تا مگر باز ماند از لذّات
قوتش از باقلی دو دانه کنم — خانه بر وی چو گور خانه کنم
ساعتی نفس را کنم در خواب — پس کنم یکدو رکعتی بشتاب
پیش ازان کو ز خواب بر خیزد — همچو بیمار در من آویزد
یکدو رکعت بی او چو بگذارم — بعد ازان گشت نفس بیدارم
مرد دانا چو این سخن بشنید — جامه بر خود یگان یگان بدرید
گفت لِلّه درّک ای زاهد — بارک اللّه عمرک ای عابد
این سخن جز ترا مسلم نیست — ملکت تو ز ملک جم کم نیست
هرچت امروز هست آرایش — وانکه فردات باشد آلایش

نیست آلوده کز گنه خیزد / آن کز اندوه آهِ وه خیزد
زن کند بهر میهمانی پاک / موی ابرو و موی رخ چالاک
در سه زندان غل و حقد و حسد / عقل را بستهٔ به بند جسد
پنج حس کز چهار ارکان اند / پنج غماز این سه زندان اند
دل بدینجا غریب و نادان ست / تا به بند چهار ارکان ست

دل که شد محرم خزانهٔ راز / چه کند ننگ منهي و غماز
خرد اینجا تهي کند جعبه / که تحري بدست در کعبه
پیش کعبه مگر که بو الهوسی / بشنود علم سمت قبله بسی
هرکه در کعبه با تحري مُرد / زیرهٔ تر بسوی کرمان برد
بیزبانان زبان او گویند / بینشانان نشان او جویند

هرچه جز دوست آتش اندر زن / آنگه از آب عشق سر بر زن
بنده را در ره معاش و معاد / نیست کس ناصر از صلاح و فساد
دل و همت مده بصحبت خلق / بُبر از خلق تا نبُرّد حلق
روزی آخر ز خلق سیر شوي / لیک دوري هنوز و دیر شوي
آنگه آگه شوي ز نرخ پیاز / که نیابي براه راست جواز

که نه یار اند و یار میبیني / همه زنهار خوار میبیني
گلبن باغ خویشتن بینان / شده چون دُلم دلم بد بنیان
نیک معلوم کن که در محشر / نشود هیچ حال خلق دگر
پیشش آید هرانچه بگزیند / آنچه زینجا برد همان بیند
چون دوم کرد امر یزدانت / چار تکبیر بر سه ارکانت

فوطه بافان عالم ازلت / بر تو خوانند نکته و غزلت
هرچه آن کدخدای دکّاندار / سوی خانه فرستد از بازار

آنکه باشد بخانه در خویشش　　در شبانگاه آورد پیشش
هرچه زینجا بری نگه دارند　　در قیامت همانت پیش آرند
نیست آنجا تغیّر و تبدیل　　نشود نیک بد بهیچ سبیل
هیچ آنجا بکس نخواهد داد　　دادنی داد و آن دگر همه باد
خیز و برخوان اگر نمیدانی　　شرح این از کلام ربّانی
لن تجد سنّتش ز تبدیلا　　لن تجد ملّتش ز تحویلا
نیست بر حکم قاطعش تبدیل　　نیست بر امر جامعش تحویل
خیز و تر دامنی ز خود کن دور　　ورنه نبوی درانجهان معذور
آتش اندر غم و زحیر زنی　　گر کنون نفس را بتیر زنی

فی المناجات والتضرع والخشوع

بنده تا از حدث برون ناید　　پردهٔ عزّ نماز نکشاید
چون کلید نماز پاکی تست　　قفل آن دان که عیبناکی تست
پای کی بر نهی بجام فلک　　باده کی در کشی ز جام ملک
کی ترا حق بلطف بر گیرد　　یا نمازت بطوع بپذیرد
تات چون خر درین سرای خراب　　شکم از نان پرست و پشت از آب
روی سلطان شرع کی بینی　　کون در آب و در آسمان بینی
لقمه و خرقه هر دو باید پاک　　ورنه گردی میان خاک هلاک
چونت نبود طعام و کسوت پاک　　چه نمازت بود چه مشتی خاک
از پی جاه خدمت یزدان　　دار پاکیزه جای و جامه و جان
سگ به دُم جای خود بروبد باز　　تو نروبی باه جای نماز
گرچه پاکست هرچه بابت تست　　همه در جنب حق جنابت تست
طالب اول ز غسل بر گیرد　　کز جُنب حق نماز نپذیرد

تا ترا غل و غش درون باشد　　غسل نا کردهٔ تو چون باشد
حسد و خشم و بخل و شهوت و آز　　بخدای ار گذاردت به نماز
تا حسد را ز دل برون ننهی　　از عملهای زشت او نرهی
غسل نا کرده از صفات ذمیم　　نپذیرد نماز رب عظیم
چون ترا از تو دل برانگیزد　　پس نماز از نیاز برخیزد
اصل و فرع نماز غسل و وضوست　　صحت داء معضل از داروست
تا به جاروب لا نروبی راه　　کی شوی در سرای الّا اللّه
تا بزیر چهار و پنج و ششی　　باده جز از خم هوس نچشی
هرچه جز حق بسوز و غارت کن　　هرچه جز دین ازان طهارت کن
قبلهٔ جان ستانهٔ صمد ست　　اُحد سینه کعبهٔ اَحد ست
در اُحد حمزه وار جان درباز　　تا بیابی مزه ز بانگ نماز
به رعونت سوی نماز میای　　شرم دار و بترس تو ز خدای
سوی خود هرکه نیست بار خدای　　دهدش در نماز بار خدای
با نیازت بلطف برگیرند　　بی نیازت نماز نپذیرند
بی نیاز ار غم نماز خوری　　از جگر قلیهٔ پیاز خوری
باز اگر با نماز هست نیاز　　بر گِرَد دست لطف پردهٔ راز
پس چو در بارگاه لطف شتافت　　دادنی داد و جستنی دریافت
ورنه ابلیس در درون نماز　　گوش گیرد برونت آرد باز
تو لئیم آمدی نماز کریم　　تو حدیث آمدی نماز قدیم
هفده رکعت نماز از دل و جان　　ملک هژده هزار عالم دان
هرکه او هفده رکعه بگذارد　　ملک هژده هزار او دارد
پس مگو کاین حساب باریکست　　زانکه هفده بهژده نزدیکست

چون نبیند ز دین غنیمت تو   نکند هم نماز قیمت تو
قیمت تو عنان چو بر تابد   والله ار جبرئیل دریابد
ندهد سوی حق نماز جواز   چون طهارت نکردهٔ بنیاز
زاري و بیخودي طهارت تست   کشتن نفس تو کفارت تست
چون بکشتي تو نفس را در راه   زوی بنمود زود فضل الله
با نیاز آی تا بیابي بار   ورنه یابي سبک طلاق سه بار
کان نمازی که در حضور بود   از تري آب روی دور بود
مرگ چون جان تو بر انگیزد   از نیازت نماز بر خیزد
تن چو در خاک رفت و جان بفلک   روح خود در نماز بین چو ملک

في حضور القلب فی الصلوٰة

در اُحد میر حیدر کرّار   یافت زخمی قوی دران پیکار
ماند پیکان تیر در پایش   اقتضا کرد آن زمان رایش
که برون آرد از قدم پیکان   که همان بود مرورا درمان
زود مرد جرایحی چو بدید   گفت باید به تیغ باز بُرید
تا که پیکان مگر پدید آید   بستهٔ زخم را کلید آید
هیچ طاقت نداشت با دم گاز   گفت بگذار تا بوقت نماز
چون شد اندر نماز حجامش   ببرید آن لطیف از اندامش
جمله پیکان ازو برون آورد   واُو شده بیخبر ز ناله و درد
چون برون آمد از نماز علي   آن مر اورا خدای خوانده ولي
گفت کمتر شد آن الم چونست   وز چه جای نماز پر خونست
گفت با او جمال عصر حسین   آن بر اولاد مصطفی شده زین
گفت چون در نماز رفتي تو   برِ ایزد فراز رفتي تو

کرد پیکان ز تو برون حجام   باز ناداده از نماز سلام
گفت حیدر بخالق الاکبر   که مرا زین الم نبود خبر
ای شده در نماز بس معروف   به عبادت بر کسان موصوف
اینچنین کن نماز و شرح بدان   ورنه بر خیز و خیره ریش ملان
چون تو با صدق در نماز آئي   با همه کام خویش باز آئي
ور تو بی صدق صد سلام کني   نیستي پخته کار خام کني
یک سلامی دو صد سلام ارزد   سجدهٔ صدق صد قیام ارزد
کان نمازی که عادتي باشد   خاک باشد که باد بر پاشد
جان گذارد نماز بار خدای   خشک خنبان بود همیشه گدای
گوید از روی جهل و نا اهلي   چون پذیرد طریق بو جهلي
کاندرین ره نماز روحاني   آن به آید که خشک خنباني
با دعا یا رب آر بابت حق   تا قبولت کند اجابت حق
گه گه آئي ز بهر فرض نماز   از حقیقت جدا قرین مجاز
بی دعا و تضرع و زاري   یک دو رکعت بغفله بگذاري
ظن چنان آیدت که هست نماز   بخدای ار دهندت ایچ جواز
با رعونت شوي بنزد خدا   از تو کی بشنود خدای دعا
بی تو باشد بپاک بر گیرد   کز تو آلوده گشت نپذیرد
نامهٔ کز زبان درد رود   آن رسول از جهان مرد رود
چون ز نزد نیاز باشد پیک   از تو یا رب بود و زو لبیک
همچو خواجه که در خرام شود   ببر بنده و غلام شود
بار منت نهي همي بروي   که منم دوست تو عزّ علي
دوست داني نه بنده مر خود را   این بود رسم مرد بخرد را

اینچنین طاعت ای پسر آن به　　که نیاری برش برو مسته
بی هدی آدمی کم از دده ایست　　هرکه او بی هدی ست بیهده ایست
توبه زین طاعت تو ای نادان　　خویشتن را دگر تو بنده مخوان
گر ترا در زمانه بودی عون　　کم نبودی بلفظ با فرعون
که وی از غایت پریشانی　　وز کمال غرور و نادانی
چو سر بندگی و عجز نداشت　　پرده از روی کار خود برداشت
گفت من برتر از خدایانم　　در جهان از بلند رایانم
همه را این غرور و نخوت هست　　لفظ فرعون بهر جبلت هست
لیکن از بیم سر نیارد گفت　　دارد آنرا ز خویشتن بنهفت

فی التقصیر فی الصلوٰة

بو شُعَیْب الاُبَی امامی بود　　که ورا هر کسی همی بستود
قائم اللیل و صائم الدهری　　یافت از زهد در زمان بهری
برده از شهر صومعه بر کوه　　جسته بیرون ز زحمت و اندوه
زنی از اتفاق رغبت کرد　　گفت شیخا بُوَدْت زن در خورد
گر بخواهی ترا حلال شوم　　بقناعت ترا عیال شوم
بقناعت زیم بکم راضی　　نکنم یاد نعمت ماضی
گفت بخ بخ رواست بپسندم　　گر قناعت کنی تو خرسندم
بود این زن عفیفه جوهره نام　　یافته از حسن و زیب بهره تمام
با عفاف و کفاف و خلق حسان　　غایت حسن و آیت احسان
شهر بگذاشت و عزم صومعه کرد　　قانع از حکم چرخ گرداگرد
بوریا پارهٔ فگنده بدید　　جوهره بوریا سبک برچید
مرورا بو شعیب زاهد گفت　　کای شده مرمرا گرامی جفت

از برای چه بر گرفتی فرش　　که بود خاک تیره موضع کفش
گفت بهر صلاح بر چیدم　　که من این معنی از تو بشنیدم
که بود بهترین هر طاعت　　که نباشد حجابش آن ساعت
جبهت بنده را ز عین تراب　　بوریا بود در میانه حجاب
بود هر شب دو قرص راتب او　　به وظیفه گهِ معاتب او
بدو قرص جوین گهِ افطار　　بود قانع همیشه آن دیندار
بو شعیب از قیام شب رنجور　　گشت رنجور و بود وی معذور
آن شب از ضعف روزه آن سره مرد　　فرض و سنت نماز قاعد کرد
زن یکی قرص پیش شیخ نهاد　　قطرهٔ سرکه داد و بیش نداد
شیخ گفت ای زن این وظیفهٔ من　　بیش ازین ست کم چرا شد زن
گفت زیرا نماز قاعد را　　مزد یک نیمه است عابد را
تو نماز ار نشسته کردستی　　نیمهٔ از وظیفه خوردستی
بیش یک نیمه از وظیفه مخواه　　از من ای شیخ کردمت آگاه
که نماز نشسته را نیمی　　مزد استاده است تقسیمی
چون تو نیمی عباده بگذاری　　جمله را مزد چشم چون داری
جمله بگذار و مزد جمله بخواه　　ورنه این طاعت ست عین گناه
ای تو در راه صدق کم ز زنی　　باز پستر ز همچو خویشتنی
مر ترا زین نمازِ نز سر دل　　نیست جان کندنی مگر حاصل
طاعتی کان ز دل ندارد روح　　کس ندارد وجود آن بفتوح
زانکه در اصل خود نیاید نغز　　بر سر کاسه استخوان بی مغز
هر نمازی که با خلل باشد　　دان که در حشر بی محل باشد
از خشوع دل ست مغز نماز　　ور نباشد خشوع نیست جواز

مرد باید که در نماز آید   خسته با درد و با نیاز آید
ور نباشد خشوع و دمسازی   دیو با سبلتش کند بازی
آنکه در بند روزه ماند و نماز   بر در جانش ماند قفل نیاز
زان درین عالم فریب و هوس   واندرین صد هزار ساله قفس
دست موزه ات کلاه جاه آمد   که سرت برتر از کلاه آمد
هر کرا در نماز عدّه نکوست   غار مغرب سزای سجدهٔ اوست
رو قضا کن نماز بی دم آز   که نمازت تبه شد از نم آز
شد ز ننگ نماز و روزهٔ تو   کفش پای تو دست موزهٔ تو
لحن خوش دار چون بکوه آئی   کوه را بانگ خرچه فرمائی
کردهٔ در ره دعا بر پای   صد هزاران عوان صوت ربای
لاجرم حرف آن ز کوه مجاز   چون صدا هم برمّت آید باز

فی الحمد والثنا

در دهان هر زبان که گویا شد   از ثنایت چو مشک بویا شد
دل و جان را ببعد و قربت تو   هست در امر و در مشیت تو
دولت سرمدی و نحس ردی   ملک بی هلک و عزت ابدی
بندگانت بروز و شب پویان   همه از تو ترا شده جویان
دولت و ملک و عز هر دو جهان   پیش عاقل به آشکار و نهان
هست معلوم بی هوا و هوس   کان همه هیچ نیست بی تو و بس
عدمت چون وجود آسان ست   هرچه تو خواستی همه آن ست
در ثنای تو هر که گربزتر   گرچه قادر تر است عاجزتر
که برین درگه ارچه پر شورست   زال زر همچو زال بی زورست
نیست در امر تو بکن فیکون   زهره کس را که این چه یا آن چون

فی الافتقار والتحیر

مستمع نغمت نیاز از دل　　مطلع بر طلوع راز از دل
چون درِ دل نیاز بکشاید　　آنچه خواهد به پیش باز آید
یا ربش را ز شه رهٔ اقبال　　کرده لبیک دوست استقبال
یا ربی از تو زو دو صد لبیک　　یک سلام از تو زو هزار علیک
از بد و نیک خلق پیوسته　　رحمت و نعمتش بنگسسته
درگهش را نیاز پیرایه　　تو نیاز آرِ سود و سرمایه
در پذیرد غم دراز ترا　　بی نیازي او نیاز ترا
دوست بودش بلال بر درگاه　　پوست بر تن چو زلف یار سیاه
جامهٔ ظاهرش ز بهر دلال　　گشت بر روی حور مشکین خال
ای صف آرای جمع درویشان　　وي نگهدار درد دلریشان
آنکه شد چون بهي بهش گردان　　وانکه شد چون کمان زهش گردان
نیک در مانده ام بدست نیاز　　کارم ای کارساز خلق بساز
متفرَّد به خطهٔ ملکوت　　متوحّد به عزت جبروت
آیت علم را بدایت نیست　　غایت شوق را نهایت نیست

فی الانبساط و التضرع الی الله تعالی

ای روان همه تنو مندان　　آرزو بخش آرزو مندان
تو کني فعل من نکو در من　　مهربانتر ز من تو‌ي بر من
رحمتت را کرانه پیدا نیست　　نعمتت را میانه پیدا نیست
آنچه بدهي به بنده دیني ده　　با رضای خودش قریني ده
دلم از یاد قدس دین خوش کن　　نسب خاک و بادم آتش کن
از تو بخشودن ست و بخیشدن　　وز من افتادن ست و شخشیدن

من نیم هوشیار مستم گیر من بلخشیده ام تو دستم گیر
از تو دانم یقین که مستورم پرده پوشیت کرده مغرورم
راندهٔ سابقت ندانم چیست خواندهٔ خاتمت ندانم کیست
عاجزم من ز خشم و خشنودیت نکند نیز لابه ام سودیت
دل گمراه گشت انابت جوی مردم دیده شد جنابت شوی
دل گمراه را رهی بنمای مردم دیده را دری بکشای
که ننازد ز کارسازی تو که نترسد ز بی نیازی تو
ای برحمت شبان این رمه تو چه حدیث ست اینهمه همه تو
ای یکی خدمت ستانت را گرگ و یوسف نگارخانت را
تو ببخشای بر گل و دل ما که بکاهد غم دل از گل ما
تو نوازم که دیگران زفت اند تو پذیرم که دیگران کفت اند
چه کنم با جز از تو همنفسی مرده ایشان مرا تو یار بسی
چه کنم نعمت توئی و دوئی چون یقین شد که من منم تو توئی
چه کنم با تف تو دود همه چون تو هستی مباد بود همه
باد نعمای تست بود جهان ای زیان تو به که سود جهان
من ندانم که آن چه کس باشد کز تو اورا بخیره بس باشد
کس بود زنده بی عنایت تو یا توان زیست بی رعایت تو
آنکه با تست سوز کی دارد وانکه بی تست روز کی دارد
آنچه گفتی مخور بخوردم من وانچه گفتی مکن بکردم من
با تو باشم درست شش دانگم بی تو باشم ز آسیا بانگم
از پی مرگ در زحیرم من جان من باش تا نمیرم من
چه فرستی حدیث و تیغ بمن من کیم از تو ای دریغ بمن

با قبول تو ای زعلت پاک   چه بود خوب و زشت مشتي خاک
خاک را خود محل آن باشد   کز ثنای تو اش زبان باشد
عز تو ذل خاک را برداشت   خاک را تا بعرش سر بفراشت
گر ندادي کلام دستوري   که برد نامت از سرِ دوري
خلق را هیچ زهره آن بودی   که ترا بر مجاز بستودی
چه کشاید زعقل و مستي ما   که نه ما و نبود هستي ما
بخودي مان کن از بدیها پاک   به نجاتی امان دهم ز هلاک
پیش حکمت خود ارخرد باشم   من که باشم که نیک و بد باشم
بد ما نیک شد چو پذرفتي   بد شود نیک ما چو نگرفتي
بد و نیکم همه توئي یارب   وز تو خود بد نیاید اینت عجب
آنکسی بد کند که بدکارست   از تو نیکي همه سزاوارست
نیک خواهي به بندگان یکسر   بندگان را خود از تو نیست خبر
اندرین پردهٔ هوا و هوس   جهل ما عذر خواه علم تو بس
گر سگي کردهایم اندر کار   تو نه شیري گرفتهٔ بگذار
بر در فضل حضرت خودت   بهر انجاز لطف موعودت
آنچه نسبت به تست توفیر ست   وانچه از فعل ماست تقصیر ست

في کرمه و فضله

ای خداوند قائم قدوس   ملک تو نا مماس و نا محسوس
از تو چیریم و بی تو چیر نه ایم   به تو سیریم و از تو سیر نه ایم
سوی ما گرچه هیچکس کس نیست   کرم تو نویدگر بس نیست
دین مان دادهٔ یقین مان ده   گرچه این هست بیش ازین مان ده
گرچه بر نطع نفس شهماتیم   تشنهٔ وادي سماواتیم

کسی از بد همی نداند به آنچه دانی که آن به است آن ده
ای مراد امل نگاران تو وی امید امیدواران تو
ای نهان دان آشکارا بین تو رسانی امید ما به یقین
همه امید من برحمت تست جان و روزی همه ز نعمت تست
جگر تشنه مان ز کوثر دین شربتی بخش پر ز نور یقین
نیست نز دانشی و نز هنری جز تو ام سوی تو وکیل دری
هرچه بر من قضای تو بنوشت همه نیکو بود نباشد زشت
هستم از هرچه هست جمله گُزیر نا گزیروم توئی مرا بپذیر
بلبل عشق را ز گلبن جست در ترنم نوای ای همه تست
باز ناز من از طریق نیاز بر سر سدره میکند پرواز
ملکها راند هرکه سوی تو راند باز در ماند هرکه زین در ماند
که رساند بمن سخن جز تو که رهاند مرا ز من جز تو
نه خری بوی و رنگ و دمدمه تو زین همه وا رهانم ای همه تو
عجز و بیچارگی و ضعف خری نخری سستی و خری و تری
رنج بر درگه تو آسانیست بیزبانی همه زباندانیست
همه را کش پس از برای همه بس قبول تو خونبهای همه
از تو بر تافتن عنان امل چیست جز آیه و نشان زلل
صورت قهر در دلش روید هرکه جز مهر حضرتت جوید
سیرت ما ز صورت اشرار وا رهان ای مهیمن اسرار

فی الانابة

ای جهان آفرین جان آرای وی خرد را بصدق راهنمای
در بهشت فلک همه خامان در بهشت تو دوزخ آشامان

بر درت خوب و زشت را چه کنم   چون تو هستی بهشت را هه کنم
که نماید در آینهٔ تزویر   غرض نکتهٔ علیم و قدیر
خون دل چون جگر کند سوراخ   چه جهنم چه جمرهٔ طباخ
دوزخ از بیم او بهشت شود   خاک بی کالبد چه خشت شود
خنده گریند عاشقان از تو   گریه خندند عارفان از تو
در جحیم تو جنت آرامان   بی تو راضی به حور عین عامان
گر بدوزخ فرستی از در خویش   میروم نی بپای بر سر خویش
وانکه امر ترا خلاف آرد   دل خود از غفلتش غلاف آرد
همه را گاه و کار و بار از تو   یار مارست و مار یار از تو
نه بلا یَأمَن از تو سیر شوم   نه بلا تَقْنَطُوا دلیر شوم
گر کفی زهر با روانم جفت   از شکر تلخ تر نیارم گفت
ایمن از مکر تو کسی باشد   که فرومایهٔ خسی باشد
امن و مکر تو هر دو یکسان ست   عاقل از مکر تو هراسان ست
ایمن از مکر تو نشاید بود   طاعت و معصیت ندارد سود
ایمن آنکس بود که وی آگاه   نبود از مکر تو بفعل گناه

مَنْ اَمَنَ بِطَاعَتِهِ فَقَدْ خَسِرَ خُسْرَانًا مُبِيْنًا

روبهی پیر روبهی را گفت   کای تو با عقل و رای و دانش جفت
چابکی کن دو صد درم بستان   نامهٔ ما بدین سگان برسان
گفت اجرت فزون ز درد سر ست   لیک کاری عظیم با خطر ست
زین زیان چونکه جان من فرسود   درمت آنگهم چه دارد سود
ایمنی از قضایت ای الله   هست نزدیک عقل عین گناه
ایمنی کرد هر دو را بدنام   آن عزازیل وآن دگر بلعام

فی الاخلاص

چون ز درگاه تست گو میمال   خواب را زیر پای خیل خیال
همچو شمع آنکه را نماند منی   در تو خندد چو گردنش بزنی
با تو با عقل و جاه و زر چه کنم   دین و دنیا توئی دگر چه کنم
تو مرا دل ده و دلیری بین   روبه خویش خوان و شیری بین
گر ز تیر تو پر کنم ترکش   کمر کوه قاف گیرم و کش
یار آنی که بی خرد نبود   وآنِ آنی که آنِ خود نبود
هیچ خود بین خدای بین نبود   مرد خود دیده مرد دین نبود
گر تو مرد شریعت و دینی   یک زمان دور شو ز خودبینی
ای خداوند کردگار غفور   بنده را از درت مگردان دور
بستهٔ خویش کن ببر خوابم   تشنهٔ خویش کن مده آبم
دل ازین و ازان چه باید جست   درد خود رهنمای مقصد تست
عمر ضائع همی کنی در کار   همچو خر پیش سبزه بی افسار
گرد هر شهر هرزه میگردی   خر دران ره طلب که گم کردی
خر اگر در عراق دزدیدند   پس ترا چون به یزد و ری دیدند
پل بود پیش تا نگردی کُل   چون شدی کل ترا چه بحر و چه پل
اندرین ره ز داد و دانش خویش   بار ساز و ز هیچ پل مندیش
قصد کشتی مکن که پر خطر ست   مرد کشتی ز بحر بیخبر ست
گرچه نوخیز و نو گرفت بود   بط کشتی طلب شگفت بود
بچهٔ بط اگرچه دینه بود   آب دریاش تا به سینه بود
تو چو بط باش و دینی آب روان   ایمن از قعر بحر بی پایان
بچهٔ بط میان بحر عمان   خربطی باز گشته کشتیبان

یا رب این خربطان عالم را　　گم کن از بهر عز آدم را
قدم ار در ره قدم داري　　قلزمی را ز دست نگذاري
قدمی را که با قدم بُقل است　　سطح بیروني محیط پل است

بغض و حقد از صفات او دورست　　غضب آنرا بود که مقدورست
در حق حق غضب روا نبود　　زانکه صاحب غضب خدا نبود
غضب و حقد هر دو مجبور اند　　وین صفت هر دو از خدا دور اند
غضب و خشم و صلح و حقد و حسد　　نیست اندر صفات فرد احد
همه رحمت بود ز خالق بار　　هست بر بندگان خود ستّار
میدهد مر ترا ز رحمت پند　　بخودت میکشد بلطف کمند
گر نیائي بخواندت سوی خویش　　بتلطف بهشتت آرد پیش
زانکه هستي بدین سرای دریغ　　تو گرفته ز جهل راه گریغ
دُرِّ توحید را توئي چو صدف　　آدم تازه را شدی تو خلف
گر کني ضائع آن در توحید　　شوی از مفلسي ز مایه فرید
ور تو آن دُرّ را نگهداري　　سر ز هفت و چهار بگذاري
به سرور ابد رسي پس ازان　　نرسد مر ترا ز خلق زیان
در زمانه تو سرفراز شوي　　در فضای ازل چو باز شوي
دست شاهان ترا شود منزل　　هر دو پایت بر آید از بن گل

في الَّذِي هُوَ يُطْعِمُنِي وَيَسْقِينِ

باز را چون ز بیشه صید کنند　　گردن و هر دو پاش قید کنند
هر دو چشمش سبک فرو دوزند　　صید کردن ورا بیاموزند
خو ز اغیار و عاده باز کند　　چشم ازان دیگران فراز کند

اندکی طعمه را شود راضی   یاد نارد ز طعمهٔ ماضی
بازدارش ز خود پیاده کند   گوشهٔ چشم او کشاده کند
تا همه بازدار را بینند   خلق بر بازدار نگزینند
زو ستانند همه طعام و شراب   نشود یک زمان بی او در خواب
بعد ازان بر کشایدش یک چشم   به رضا بنگرد درو نه بخشم
از سر رسم و عاده بر خیزد   با دگر کس بطبع نامیزد
بزم و دست ملوک را شاید   صیدگه را بدو بیاراید
چون ریاضت نیافت وحشی ماند   هرکه دیدش ز پیش خویش براند
دیگران غافل اند تو هش دار   واندرین ره زبانت خامش دار
شرط آن کو همه طعام و شراب   از مسبب ستد نه از اسباب
رو ریاضت کش ارت باید ناز   ورنه راه جحیم را میساز
بی ریاضت نیافت کس مقصود   تا نسوزی ترا چه بید و چه عود

فی اَلْعَوَامِ اُولَئِکَ کَالْأَنْعَامِ بَلْ هُمْ اَضَلّ

کرّهٔ را که شد سه سال تمام   رایضش در کشد بزین و لگام
مرورا در هنر بفرهنجد   توسنی از تنش بیاهنجد
کرّه را بر لگام رام کند   نام او اسپ خوش لگام کند
بار گیر ملوک را شاید   بزر و زیورش بیاراید
چون ندید این ریاضت درخور   باشد آن کرّه از خری کمتر
بابت بار آسیا باشد   دائم از بار درعنا باشد
گاه بار جهود و گه ترسا   میکشد در عنا و رنج و بلا
آدمی نیز کش ریاضت نیست   پیش دانا ورا افاضت نیست
علف دوزخ ست و ترسان ست   با حجر در جحیم یکسان ست

مرورا هست جای خوف و هراس   خوانده در محکمش وقود الناس
گرچه بی اوت قصد و نیرو نه   کار دین بی تو نی و بی او نه
کار دین خود نه سرسري کاریست   دین حق را همیشه بازاریست
دین حق تاج و افسر مردست   تاج نامرد را چه در خوردست
دین نگهدار تا به ملک رسي   ورنه بی دین بدان که هیچکسي
راه دین رو که راه دین چو روی   همچو شاخ از برهنگي نه نوی
ای خوشا راه دین و امر خدای   از گل تیره رو برآر دو پای

فی الشوق

از پس این براق شوق بود   به دل و جان و عقل و ذوق بود
آفرینش چو گشت زندانش   پس خلاصي طلب کند جانش
آتشیش از درون برافروزند   که ازو جان و عقل و دین سوزند
تا که جویای عشق خود بین ست   بوتهٔ توبه از پی این ست
هر کرا کوی عشق او تازه است   توبهٔ او کلید دروازه است
شوق با یار خود سرور بود   یار جوی از خدای دور بود
جوق ذوقت بآتش اندازد   سوق شوقت چو حور بنوازد
چون برون رفت جان ز دروازه   دل کهنه ازو شود تازه
صورت از بند طبع باز رهد   دل ودیعت بروح باز دهد
افتد از سیر جان بی اندازه   از زمین تا به عرش آوازه
گرد کز باد شوق و درد بود   بر زن ار بگذرد چو مرد بود
هرچه در راه فتنه انگیزد   همه اش از پیش راه برخیزد
از پی پایتابهٔ بشکوه   پشم رنگین شود به پیشش کوه
آتش او ز بهر بالا را   ببرد آبروی دریا را

چون مر اورا ازو بر انگیزند اختران پیش او فرو ریزند
دیدهٔ او چو نور ره بیند شمس در جذب او سیه بیند
بد و نیک اندر آن جهان نبود خاک و خورشید و اختران نبود
هر کرا عشق کوی او نبود در دلش جست و جوی او نبود
آسمان دگرش گردانند بر زمین دگرش بنشانند
هر زمان شوید از پی تگ و پوی جبرئیلش بآب حیوان روی
خرد از نعرهٔ دلش کالیو هیزم برق نعل اسپش دیو
آدمی سوز گشته از پی راه مالک درد او بآتش آه
سرّ آهش نداند ایچ صبور پی او در نیابد ایچ غیور
نعل اسپش چو گرد بندازد جبرئیلش حنوط جان سازد
او روان گشته سوی عالم نیست باد فریاد کن که یکدم بایست
مصطفی ایستاده بر ره اوی از ره لطف رَبِّ سَلِّم گوی
اندر آویزد از پی اشراف از درونش ترازوی انصاف
آب در راه او خلیل زند مقرعه‌اش جان جبرئیل زند

فی قضائه و قدره و صنعه

آنچه زاید ز عالم از امر ست وانچه گوید نبی هم از امرست
کفر و دین خوب و زشت و کهنه و نو یرجع الامر کله زی او
هرچه در زیر امر جبّار اند همه بر وفق امر بر کار اند
همه مقهور و قدرتش قاهر صنع او بر ظهور شان ظاهر
همه موقوف قدرت و حلمش همه مسبوق سابق علمش
آنکه عامی و آنکه از علماست آنکه محکوم و آنکه از حکما ست
همه را باز گشت حضرت اوست هر کوا مُنّتیست مِنّت اوست

عقل را نقل کرده اسبابش   نفس را پی بریده انسابش
نسبت نفس سوی عالم جان   همچو کورست و گوهر عمان
کور را گوهری نمود کسی   زین هوس پیشه مرد بوالهوسی
که ازین مهره چند میخواهي   گفت یک گرده و دو تا ماهي
نشناسد کسی چه داري خشم   لعل و گوهر مگر بگوهر چشم
پس چو این گوهرم نداد خدای   آن گهر را بهر تو ژاژ مخای
گر نخواهي که بر تو خندد خر   نزد گوهر شناس بر گوهر
دست گوهر شناس به داند   چون کف پای بر صدف راند
سایبانیست عقل بر در او   خیلتاشیست جان ز لشکر او
جان فروبد ز بیم مهجوري   خاک درگاه جز بدستوري
آن اوینند در مکان و زمان   از کن امر تا دریچهٔ کان
گفته از بهر خدمت درگاه   امر با عقلها اطیعوا الله
نفس روینده تا به گوینده   همه چو بنده اند جوینده
نیک داني که در فضای ازل   دست صنع خدای عز و جل
کرده امر خدای در هر فن   قوتی را بفعلی آبستن
تا چو راه مشیمه بکشایند   زانچه گشتند حامل آن زایند
آنکه اورا عدم برد فرمان   کی وجود آرد اندرو عصیان
کرده یک امر جمله را بیدار   همگان آمدند در پرکار
نفس فرمان پذیر فرمان ده   عقل قرآن شناس ایمان ده
خرد و جان و صورت مطلق   همه از امر دان و امر از حق
نور خورشید چون بر آب آید   آب از آرام در شتاب آید
عکس خور زاب بر جدار شود   سقف از نقش او نگار شود

انهم از عکس آفتاب شمار   آن دوم عکس آب بر دیوار
همه را باز خود رساند بخود   کایچ یک را ازو نیامد بُد
همه هستند و از همه همه دور   در نُبي خواندهٔ تَصِيرُ الأُمُورْ
زو بد و نیک قوت و حول ست   امر او مَا یُبَدَّلُ القَوْل ست
امر اورا تغیری نبود   خلق را جز تحیری نبود
اوست قادر بهرچه خواهد و خواست   هرچه خواهد کند که حکم اوراست
آنکه مختار زیر پردهٔ اوست   وانکه مجبور بندهٔ کردهٔ اوست
همه از امر اوست زیر و زبر   غافلند آدمي ز خیر و ز شر
هرچه بودست و هرچه خواهد بود   آن توانند کرد کو فرمود
هرچه استاد بر نبشت و براند   طفل در مکتب آن تواند خواند
گر نوشت ابجدي ز دفتر خویش   نتواند کزو کشد سر خویش
در ره جبر و اختیار خدای   بی تو و با تو نیست کار خدای
همه از کار کرد الله است   نیکبخت آنکسی که آگاه است

عقل شد خامه نفس شد دفتر   مایه صورت پذیر و جسم صور
عشق را گفت جز ز من مهراس   عقل را گفت خویشتن بشناس
عقل دائم رعیت عشق ست   جانسپاري حمیت عشق ست
عشق را گفت بادشاهي کن   طبع را گفت کدخدائي کن
از عنا طعمه ساز ارکان را   پس بکف کن تو آب حیوان را
تا چو زو نطق مایهٔ سازد   در ره روح قدس در بازد
روح قدسي بنفس باز شود   نفس چون عقل پاکباز شود
همچنین ست از بدایت جان   روش اوست تا نهایت جان

پیش شرعت ز شعر جستن به   بیت را همچو بت شکستن به
شرع از اشعار سخت بیگانه است   گرچه با او کنون هم از خانه است
هرچه مارا مباح محظور ست   بر کسی کو ازین و آن دور ست
فرق حظر و اباحت او داند   کانچه راحت جراحت او داند

ذِکْرُ کَلَامِ الْمَلِکِ الْعَلَّامِ یُسَهِّلُ الْمَرَامَ قَالَ اللّٰهُ تَعَالیٰ

قُلْ لَئِنِ اجْتَمَعَتِ الْاِنْسُ وَالْجِنُّ عَلیٰ اَنْ یَاتُوا بِمِثْلِ هٰذَا الْقُرْآنِ لَا یَاتُونَ بِمِثْلِهِ وَلَوْ کَانَ بَعْضُهُمْ لِبَعْضٍ ظَهِیرًا وَقَالَ النَّبِیُّ عَلَیْهِ الصَّلٰوةُ وَالسَّلَامُ اَلْقُرْآنُ غِنًی لَا فَقْرَ بَعْدَهُ وَلَا غِنًی دُونَهُ وَقَالَ عَلَیْهِ السَّلَامُ الْقُرْآنُ هُوَ الدَّوَاءُ مِنْ کُلِّ دَاءٍ اِلَّا الْمَوْتُ

سخنش را ز بس لطافت و ظرف   صدمت صوت نی و زحمت حرف
صفتش را حدوث کی سنجد   سخنش در حروف کی گنجد
وهم حیران ز شکل صورتهاش   عقل واله ز سرّ سورتهاش
مغز و نغزست حرف و سورت او   دلبر و دلفریب صورت او
زو گرفته مقیم قوت و قوت   دادهٔ ملک و زادهٔ ملکوت
سرّ او بهر حل مشکلها   رَوح جانها و راحت دلها
دل مجروح را شفا قرآن   درد دلسوز را دوا قرآن
تو کلام خدای را بیشک   گرنهٔ طوطی و حمار و اشک
اصل ایمان و رکن تقوی دان   کان یاقوت و گنج معنی دان
هست قانون حکمت حکما   هست معیار عادت علما

نزهت روحها مدایش اوست   سلوت عقلها نمایش اوست
آیت او شفای جان تقی   رایتش درد و اندهان شقی
عقل کل را فگنده در شدّت   نفس کل را نشانده در عدت
عقل و نفس از نهاد آن حاجز   فصحا از طریق آن عاجز

فی جلال القرآن

هم جلیل ست با حجاب جلال   هم دلیل ست با نقاب دلال
سخن اوست واضح و واثق   حجت اوست لایح و لائق
درّ جان را حروف او درج ست   چرخ دین را هدایتش برج ست
روضهٔ انس عارفان ست او   جنت الاعلی روان ست او
ای ترا از قراءت قرآن   از سر غفلت و ره عصیان
بر زبان از حروف ذوقی نه   در جنان از وقوف شوقی نه
از کمال جلالت و سلطان   هست قرآن به حجت و برهان
از درون شمع منهج اسلام   وز برون خازن عقیدهٔ عام
عاقلان را حلاوتی در جان   غافلان را تلاوتی بزبان
بر زبان طرف حرف و ذوقی نه   غافل از معنیش که از پی چه
دیده روح و حروف قرآن را   چشم جسم این و چشم جان آنرا
نغمت آن ببرده جسم ز گوش   نعمت این بخورده روح ز هوش
بهر نامحرمان ز پیش جمال   بسته از مشک پردهای جلال
پرده و پردهدار را از شاه   نبود دل بهیچ سان آگاه
داند آنکس که وی بصر دارد   پرده از شاه کی خبر دارد
نشد از دور طارم ازرق   عرق او سست و تازگیش خلق
نحو و نقش و قرأت و تدوین   از زمین هست تا سر پروین

تو هنوز از کفایت شب و روز قشر اوّل چشیدهٔ از کوز
کاولین پوست زفت و تلخ بود دومین چون ز ماه سلخ بود
سیومین آن حریر زرد تنک چارمین مغز آبدار خنک
پنجمین منزل ست خانهٔ تو سنت انبیا ستانهٔ تو
چون ز پنجم روان بیارائي پس باول چرا فرودآئي
تو ز قرآن نقاب او دیدي حرف اورا حجاب او دیدي
پیش نا اهل چهره نکشادست نقش او پیش او بر استادست
گر ترا هیچ اهل آن دیدی این نقاب رقیق بدریدی
مر ترا روی خویش بنمودی تا روانت بدو بیاسودی
دل مجروح را شفا ز ویست جان محروم را دوا ز ویست
تن چشد طعم ثفلش از پی زیست جان شناسد که طعم روغن چیست
حس چه بیند مگر که صورت نغز مغز داند که چیست اندر مغز
صورت سورتش همیخواني صفت سیرتش نمیداني
کم ز مهمان سرای عدن مدان خوان قرآن به پیش قرآن خوان
حرف را زان نقاب خود کرده است که ز نامحرمیت در پرده است
صورت از عین روح بیخبرست تن دگر دان که روح خود دگرست
تو همان دیدهٔ ز صورت آن کاهل صورت ز صورت سلطان
چه شماري حروف را قرآن چه حدیث حدث کفي با آن
حرف با او اگرچه همخوابه است بیخبر همچو نقش گرمابه است
که نه بینند همچو بیداران ذات او خفتگان و طراران

في ذكر سر القرآن

چونکه باشد ز محرمان به نهفت سر قرآن زبان ندانـد گفت

سر قرآن نکو داند — زو شنو زانکه خود همو داند
کس بنشناخت جز بدیدهٔ جان — حرف پیمای را ز قرآن خوان
من نگویم و گرچه عثمانی — که تو قرآن همی نکو دانی
هست دنیا بسان تابستان — خلق دروی بسان سرمستان
در بیابان غفلتند همه — مرگ همچون شبان و خلق رمه
واندرین بادیهٔ هوا و هوان — ریگ گرمست همچو آب روان
هست قرآن چو آب سرد فرات — تو چو عاصی تشنه در عرصات
حرف و قرآن تو ظرف و آب شمر — آب میخور بظرف در منگر
کان کین زان نمایدت اوطان — که تموزست و مهر در سرطان
زان بماندت نهاد بی روزه — کاب سردست و کوزه پیروزه
سر قرآن پاک با دل پاک — درد گوید بصوت اندهناک
عقل کی شرح و بسط او داند — ذوق او سرّ سرّ نکو داند
گرچه نقش سخن نه از سخنست — بوی یوسف درون پیرهنست
بود در مصر ماندهٔ یوسف خوب — بو بکنعان رسیده زی یعقوب
حرف قرآن ز معنی قرآن — همچنانست کز لباس تو جان
حرف را بر زبان توان راندن — جان قرآن بجان توان خواندن
صدف آمد حروف و قرآن دُر — نشود مائل صدف دل حر
حرف او گرچه خوب و منقوشست — کوه ازو همچو عهن منفوشست
از درون کن سماع موسی وار — نز برون سو چو زیر موسیقار
جان چو آن خواند لقمه چرب کند — هرکه بشنود خرقه ضرب کند
لفظ و آواز و حرف در آیات — چون سه چوبک ز کاسهای نبات
پوست ارچه نه خوب و نغز بود — پوست هم پردهٔ دار مغز بود

حکمت از خدمت تو سرود آید   نُبی از جهل تو فرود آید
تا درین تربتی که ترتیبست   تا درین مرکزی که ترکیبست
تا درین عالمی که پر صیدست   تا درین مرکزی که پر کیدست
ببصر بیند بین بدل طوبی   بزبان حرف خوان بدل معنی
بکن از بهر حرمت قرآن   عقل را پیش نطق او قربان
عقل نبود دلیل اسرارش   عقل عاجز شدست در کارش
تو کنون نا حفاظ و غمازی   نه سزاوار پردهٔ رازی
تو نگشتی بسرّ او واقف   نرسیدی هنوز در موقف
تا هوا خواهی و هوا داری   کودکی کن نه مرد این کاری
چون جهان هوا خرد بگرفت   نیکی محض جای بد بگرفت
دیو بگریخت هم بدوزخ آز   یافت انگشتری سلیمان باز
شد هزیمت ز سرّ او شیطان   چه عجب گر رمان شد از قرآن
باش کانگه که صبح دین بدمد   شب وهم و خیال و حس برمد
چون ببینند مر ترا بی عیب   روی پوشیدگان عالم غیب
مر ترا در سرای غیب آرند   پرده از پیش روی بر دارند
سرّ قرآن ترا چو بنمایند   پردهای حروف بکشایند
خاکی اجزای خاک را بیند   پاک باید که پاک را بیند
در دماغی که دیو کبر دمید   فهم قرآن ازان دماغ رمید
خر بود همچو سنگ خشک خموش   سوی سرّ نُبی نیارد گوش
زاستماع قرآن بتابد گوش   وز پی سرّ سوره نارد هوش
هوش اگر گوشمال حق یابد   سرّ قرآن ز سوره در یابد

فی ذکر اعجاز القرآن

ای ز دریا بکف کف آورده   وز مَلک صورتِ صف آورده
مغز دُر زان بدست ناوردی   که بگرد صدف همی گردی
زین صدفهای تیره دست بدار   دُر صافی ز قعر بحر برآر
گهر بی صدف درون دلست   صدف بی گهر برون گلست
قیمت دُر نه از صدف باشد   تیر را قیمت از هدف باشد
آنکه داند بدید فهر از قعر   بشناسد ز دُر دریا بعر
وانکه بر شطر شط این دریاست   نه سزاوار لولوِ لالاست
سطر قرآن چو شطر ایمانست   که ازو راحت دل و جانست
صفت لطف و عزت قرآن   هست بحر محیط عالم جان
قعر او پر ز دُر و پر ز گهر   ساحلش پر ز عود و از عنبر
زوست از بهر باطن و ظاهر   منشعب علم اول و آخر
پاک شو تا معانی مکنون   آید از پنجرهٔ حروف برون
تا برون ناید از حدث انسان   کی برون آید از حروف قرآن
تا تو باشی ز نفس خود محجوب   با تو و عقل تو چه زشت و چه خوب
نشود دل ز حرف قرآن به   نشود بُز به بچ بچی فربه
نکند خیره زودی و دیری   آب در خواب تشنه را سیری
تو که در بند کلک و انقاسی   چهره را از نقاب نشناسی
نبود خاصه در جهان سخن   رنگ و بوی سخن چو جان سخن
چون قدم در نهی دران اقلیم   کندت ابجد وفا تعلیم
چون بخوانی تو ابجد دین را   اب و جد دان تو شمس و پروین را
سیرت صادقان چنین باشد   ابجد عاشقان همین باشد
پردهٔ روی روز تاریکست   نظم این نکته سخت باریکست

گر همي گنج دلت باید و جان   آیتی زو بجان و دل برخوان
تا درو گوهر یقین یابي   تا درو کیمیای دین یابي
تا بیابي تو درج دُرِّ یتیم   تا بداني تو زرِّ ناب از سیم
تا نماید بتو چو مهر و چو ماه   روی خوب خود از نقاب سیاه
چون عروسي که از نقاب تنگ   بدر آید لطیف و روح سبک

في هداية القرآن

رهبرست او و عاشقان راهی   رسنست او و غافلان چاهی
در بن چاه جانت را وطنست   نور قرآن بسوی آن رسنست
خیز و خود را رسن بچنگ آور   تا بیابي نجات بوک و مگر
ورنه گشتي بقعر چاه هلاک   آب و بادت دهد بآتش و خاک
تو چو یوسف بچاهی از شیطان   خردت بشری و رسن قرآن
گر همي یوسفیت باید و جاه   چنگ در وی زن و برآی از چاه
راد مردان رسن بدان دارند   تا بدان آب جان بدست آرند
تو رسن را همي بدان سازي   تا کني بهر نان رسن بازي
کس نداند دو حرف از قرآن   با چنین دیده در هزار قِران
دست عقلت چو چرخ گردانست   پای بند دلت تن و جانست
گر ترا تخت و تاج باید و جاه   چه نشیني مقیم در بن چاه
یوسف تو بچاه در ماندست   دل تو سورهٔ سفه خواندست
رسن از درد ساز و دلو از آه   یوسف خویش را برآر از چاه

في عِزَّةِ القُرْآنِ اِنَّهَا لَيْسَتْ بِالاَعْشارِ و الاَخْمَاسِ

بهر یک مشت کودک از وسواس   نامش اعشار کردهٔ و اخماس
کرده منسوخ حکم هر ناسخ   نشده در علوم آن راسخ

متشابه ترا شده محکم   کرده بر محکمش معوّل کم
تو رها کرده نور قرآن را   وز پی عامه صورت آن را
ساخته دست موزهٔ سالوس   بهر یک من جو و دو کاسهٔ سبوس
گه سرودش کني و گاه مثل   گاه سازي ازو سلاح جدل
گه زني درهمش به بی ادبي   گه شمارش کني به بوالعجبي
گه کني بر قیاس خود تاویل   گه کني حکم را بران تحویل
گه ز پایانش سر بري بخیال   گه درونش کني برون بمحال
گه برای خودش کني تفسیر   گه بعلم خودش کني تقریر
مي نگردي مگر به پیغاره   گرد صندوقهای سیپاره
گاه گوئي رفیق جاهل را   یا نه کرباس باف کاهل را
که نویسم ترا یکی تعویذ   پاک دار ای جوان مدار پلیذ
لیک هدیه پگاه مي باید   خون مرغ سیاه مي باید
این همه حیله بهر یکدو درم   شام یا چاشتي ز بهر شکم
عمر بر دادهٔ بخیره بباد   من چه گویم برو که شرمت باد
در یکی مسجدی خزي بهوس   حلق پرباد همچو نای و جرس
زین هوس شرم شرع و دینت باد   یا خرد یا اجل قرینت باد
با چنین خو و فضل و فرهنگت   شرم بادت که نیست خود ننگت

في حجة الكلام

باش تا روز عرض بر یزدان   گلهٔ جان تو کند قرآن
گوید این ماحل مصدق تو   چند باطل کشید از حق تو
گوید ای کردگار میداني   آشکارا چنانکه پنهاني
شب و روزم بخواند با فریاد   داد یک حرف من بصدق نداد

حق نحو و معاني و اعراب   زو ندیدم بصدق در محراب
حنجره در سرود نیک آید   جامهٔ غم کبود نیک آید
چند کو لاف زد بدعوي ما   پس ندانست قدر معني ما
بجز از گفت و گوی و دمدمهٔ   نیست گوئي نصیب این رمهٔ
سوی میدان خاص اسپ نتاخت   روی ما از نقاب ما نشناخت
بر سر کوی ما بزشت و نکو   سگی آمد کسی نیامد ازو
عقل و جان را بقول من نسپرد   سوی رای و هوای خویشم برد
گه بتیغ هوا بخست مرا   گاه بر دام نفس بست مرا
گه بسوی شراب راند مرا   گه براه سرود خواند مرا
گه بخواندي مرا براه مجاز   خیره بکشاده چون خران آواز
گه شکستي چو چوب را سکنه   سرد روی حروفم از شکنه
گه چو قوال کرده از نغمه   متفرق حروفم از زخمه
ای مدبّر ز مدبري چنین   خواهم انصاف تو بیوم الدین
در سرای مجاز از سر ناز   گه به بازارگاه و گه بنماز
جلوه کردي براه اعجازي   گه بحرفي و گه بآوازي
سخنی کز تو گشت آلوده   گرچه نیکوست هست بیهوده
باد اگرچه خوش آید و دلکش   بر حدث بگذرد نباشد خوش
مر جنب را بامر یزدانش   بس نه مهجور کرد قرآنش

في حلاوة القرآن

کی چشي طعم و لذت قرآن   چون زبان بردی و نبردي جان
از در تن بمنظر جان آی   بتماشای باغ قرآن آی
تا بجان تو جمله بنماید   آنچه بود آنچه هست آنچه آید

تر و خشک جهان درون و برون | آنچه موجود شد بکن فیکون
حکمهای که گشت ازو محکوم | همه گردد ترا ازو معلوم
بشنواند ترا صفات خدای | گشته پیشت بصدق قصه سرای
مستمع چون کند سماع کلام | گیردش نطق موی بر اندام
تا ببینی بدیدهٔ اخلاص | چون بخوانی تو سورة الاخلاص
سورتی همچو سرو غاتفری | نظم او چون بنفشهٔ طبري
نصب و رفعش چو عرش و چون کرسي | گر تو از مرشدي خبر پرسي
جرّ و جزم وی از طریق قدم | لوح محفوظ و سیر سنّ قلم
حرفها بال روح و پردهٔ نور | نقطها خال مشک بر رخ حور
اینچنین در نگر بصورت او | تا بداني تو سرّ سورت او
تا الف را درون رای آرد | با و تا را بزیر پای آرد
تا فروشد بجای جان و خرد | یوسف خوب را بهزدهٔ بد
زانکه در کوی عشق وحدت و هنگ | بیش ازین قیمتی نیارد رنگ
بوتهٔ شهوت امتحانش کند | پس ازان همچو زرّ کانش کند
پس دگر باره بوتهٔ سازد | تا درو غل و غش بگدازد
پس چو نرمش کند فرو ساید | پس بدو تاج او بیاراید
هر ملک را که عدل و دین باشد | افسر و تاج او چنین باشد

في استماع القرآن

پس زانوی حیرتش بنشاند | لا یمسّه چو بر دو دستش خواند
مقري زاهد از پی یک دانگ | همچو قمري دو مغزه دارد بانگ
قول باری شنو هم از باري | که حجابست صنعت قاري
مرد عارف سخن ز حق شنود | لا جرم ز اشتیاق کم غنود

طبع قوّال را زبون باشد — عشق را مطرب از درون باشد
در دل نفس نِه نه بر رخ خال — که خیالت نشان دهد از حال
با خیال لطیف گوید راز — شکن و پیچ و وقفه در آواز
هرچه آواز و نقش و آوازه است — خانه شان از برون دروازه است
هیچ معنیستی اگر در بانگ — بلبلی بنده نیستی بدو دانگ
دل ز معنی طلب ز حرف مجوی — که نیابی ز نقش عنبر بوی
عدتی دان درین سرای مجاز — چشم را رنگ و گوش را آواز
مجلس روح جای بی گوشیست — واندر آنجا سماع خاموشیست
کی سوی عشق دیدنی باشد — لذتی کان چشیدنی باشد
طبع را از غنا مگردان شاد — که غنا جز عنا نیارد یاد
یار کو بر سر پل آمد یار — تو مر اورا ز آب دور مدار
یا بآبش فرو بر از هرکین — یا بخاکش سپار و خوش بنشین
هرچه درعشق نیک وهرچه بدست — بار حکمش کشیدن از خردست
هرچه صورت دهد بآتش ده — نالهٔ زار در دل خوش نه
چون برون ناله آید از دل خوش — پای او گیر و سوی دوزخ کش
می نداری خبر تو ای نسناس — که بصد بند و حیلت و ریواس
آن همه دیو نفس در تو دمد — تا ز تو عقل و هوش تو برمد
ای درین بادیهٔ پر از بیداد — غَمر را عُمر خوانده شرمت باد
راه دین صنعت و عبارت نیست — نحو و تصریف و استعارت نیست
این صفات از کلام حق دورست — ضمن قرآن چو درّ منثور ست
ناگهی باشد ای مسلمانان — که شود سوی آسمان قرآن
گرچه ماندست نزد ما نامش — نیست مانده شروع و احکامش

مرد دانا بجان سماع کند　　حرف و ظرفش همه وداع کند
جان ازو حظّ خویش بر گیرد　　کارها جملگی ز سر گیرد
با مرید جوان سرود و شفق　　همچنان دان که مرد عاشق و دق
حال کان از مجال و زرق بود　　همچو فرعون و بانگ غرق بود
بانگ او حال غرق سود نکرد　　آتش آشتیش دود نکرد
در طریقی که شرط جان سپریست　　نعرهٔ بیهده خري و تریست
هرکه در مجلسی سه بانگ کند　　دان کز اندیشهٔ دو دانگ کند
ورنه آه مرید عشق الفنج　　همچو ماریست خفته بر سر گنج
اژدها گر ز گنج بر خیزد　　مهرهٔ کامش آتش انگیزد
کفکف اندر فقیر چیست خري　　چک چک اندر چراغ چیست تري
آب و روغن چو درهم آمیزد　　نور در صفو روغن آویزد
تف چو روغن ز پیش برگیرد　　نم بیگانه بانگ در گیرد
آه رعنائي طبیعت تست　　راه بینائي شریعت تست
آینه روشنست راه شما　　پردهٔ آینه ست آه شما

التمثیل في خلقة آدم وعیسى بن مریم علیهما السلام

پدر آدم اندرین عالم　　هست ازان دم که زادهٔ مریم
تن که تن شد ز رنگ آدم شد　　جان که جان شد ز بوی آندم شد
هرکرا آن دمست آدم اوست　　وان کرا نیست نقش عالم اوست
آدم آندم که از قدر دریافت　　دل خبر یافت سوی جان بشتافت
که ازین دم خبر چگونه دهي　　گفت هستم ز جام و جامه تهي
جامه و جام ما تهي زانست　　کین گرانمایه سخت ارزانست
همه خواهي که باشي اورا باش　　بر او سوی خویش هیچ مباش

بر پریده ز دام ناسوتي — در خزیده بدار لاهوتي
دیده خطهای خطّهٔ ملکوت — همچو عیسی بدیدهٔ لاهوت
خویشتن را یکی مخوان در ده — کان یکیی که هیچ ازان یک به
همچو نقش زیاد بهر پسیچ — بسوی خود یکی و آن یک هیچ
تو یکیي و لیک هم ز اعداد — نام داري و بس چو نقش زیاد
خنک آنکس که نقش خویش بشست — نه کس اورا نه او کسی را جست
آنکه در بند این جهان آویخت — سود کرد ار ز لشکرش بگریخت
کاین جهانیست مایهٔ غم و رنج — خوانده عاقل ورا سرای سپنج
زانکه باشد ز روی عقل و نظر — در هزیمت بوقت خود سه ظفر
پس تو ای بو الفضول بلغاري — چون درین رود بر پل و غاري
رهبرت باد بهر صورت و جان — این جهان عقل و آنجهان ایمان
خنک آنکس که عقل رهبر اوست — هر دو عالم بطوع چاکر اوست
چون در آمد وصال را حاله — سرد شد گفت و گوی دلّاله
گرچه دلّاله مبنی کار ست — گاه خلوت ترا گرانبار ست

ذِكْرُ الأَنْبِيَاءِ خَيْرٌ مِنْ حَدِيثِ الْجُهَلَا

انبیا راستان دین بودند — خلق را راه راست بنمودند
چون بغرب فنا فرو رفتند — باز خود کامگان بر آشفتند
پردها بست ظلمت از شب شرک — بوسها داد کفر بر لب شرک
این چلیپا چو شاخ گل در دست — وان چو نیلوفر آفتاب پرست
این صنم کرده سال و مه معبود — وان جدا مانده از همه مقصود
این شمرده ز جهل بی برهان — بدي از دیو و نیکي از یزدان
خاک پاشانِ آتش آشامان — آب کوبانِ باد آرامان

این چو باده ز مغز عقل زدای   وان چو نکبا ز سر عمامه ربای
این وثن را خدای خود خوانده   وان ثمن وار دین بر افشانده
این یکی سحر و آن دگر تنجیم   این یکی در امید و آن در بیم
همه نا خوب سیرتان بودند   همه اعمی بصیرتان بودند
عام قانع شده بریمن دین   خاص مشغول در نشیمن دین

دین حق روی خود نهان کرده   هر یکی دین بد عیان کرده
بدعت و شرک پر بر آورده   زندقه جمله سر بر آورده
این به تلقین هرزهٔ دربند   وان بتخئیل بیهده خرسند
گوش سر شان هوس شنوده ز دیو   هذیان شان هدی نموده ز دیو
شده نزدیک عام و دانشمند   سفه و غیبت و فضولی پند

خاص در بند شهوت و لذات   عام در بند هزل و ترّهات
مندرس گشته علم دین خدای   همگان ژاژ خای و هرزه درای
عزّ خود جسته در بهانهٔ علم   عقل پوشیده در میانهٔ علم
راستیها ز بیم بند و طلسم   روی پوشیده چون الف در بسم
خاصگان چون بتخانه باز شدند   عامه هم با سر مجاز شدند

آن یکی رفته بر ره موسی   وان دگر مقتدای او عیسی
کیش زردشتی آشکارا شده   پردهٔ رحم پاره پاره شده
ملک توران و ملکت ایران   شده از جور یکدگر ویران
حبشه تاخته سوی یثرب   فیل با ابرهه ز مرغ هرب
خانهٔ کعبه گشته بتخانه   بگرفته بغصب بیگانه

پر جهالت جهان و پر نیرنگ   بر خردمند راه دین شده تنگ
بانگ برداشته سحرگاهان   سگ و خر در جهان گمراهان

عتبه و شیبه و لعین بو جهل   یک جهان پر ز ناکس و نا اهل
عالمی پر سباع دیو دستور   صد هزاران ره و چه و همه کور
بر چپ و راست غول و پیش نهنگ   راهبر گشته کور و همره لنگ
خستهٔ جهل را ز پر خوابی   کژدم حمق کرده ذبّابی
چون ز توحید گفته شد طرفی   گفت خواهم ز انبیا شرفی
خاصه نعت رسول بازپسین   آن ز پیغمبران بهین و گزین